PostgreSQL 11 Administration Cookbook

Over 175 recipes for database administrators to manage enterprise databases

Simon Riggs
Gianni Ciolli
Sudheer Kumar Meesala

BIRMINGHAM - MUMBAI

PostgreSQL 11 Administration Cookbook

Commissioning Editor: Pravin Dhandre
Acquisition Editor: Ali Abidi
Content Development Editor: Karan Thakkar
Technical Editor: Sagar Sawant
Copy Editor: Safis Editing
Project Coordinator: Hardik Bhinde
Proofreader: Safis Editing
Indexer: Priyanka Dhadke
Graphics: Jisha Chirayil
Production Coordinator: Shraddha Falebhai

First published: May 2019

Production reference: 1020519

Published by Packt Publishing Ltd.
Livery Place
35 Livery Street
Birmingham
B3 2PB, UK.

ISBN 978-1-78953-758-1

www.packtpub.com

`mapt.io`

Mapt is an online digital library that gives you full access to over 5,000 books and videos, as well as industry leading tools to help you plan your personal development and advance your career. For more information, please visit our website.

Why subscribe?

- Spend less time learning and more time coding with practical eBooks and Videos from over 4,000 industry professionals

- Improve your learning with Skill Plans built especially for you

- Get a free eBook or video every month

- Mapt is fully searchable

- Copy and paste, print, and bookmark content

Packt.com

Did you know that Packt offers eBook versions of every book published, with PDF and ePub files available? You can upgrade to the eBook version at `www.packt.com` and as a print book customer, you are entitled to a discount on the eBook copy. Get in touch with us at `customercare@packtpub.com` for more details.

At `www.packt.com`, you can also read a collection of free technical articles, sign up for a range of free newsletters, and receive exclusive discounts and offers on Packt books and eBooks.

Contributors

About the authors

Simon Riggs is the CTO of 2ndQuadrant, having contributed to PostgreSQL as a major developer and committer for 14 years. He has written and designed features for replication, performance, BI, management, and security. Under his guidance, 2ndQuadrant is now a leading developer of open source PostgreSQL, serving hundreds of clients in USA, Europe, and worldwide. Simon is a frequent speaker at many conferences on PostgreSQL Futures. He has worked as a database architect for 30 years.

Gianni Ciolli is the head of professional services at 2ndQuadrant and has been a PostgreSQL consultant, trainer, and speaker at many PostgreSQL conferences in Europe and abroad over the last 10 years. He has a PhD in Mathematics from the University of Florence. He has worked with free and open source software since the 1990s and is active in the community (the Prato Linux User Group and the Italian PostgreSQL Users Group). He lives in London with his son. His other interests include music, drama, poetry, and athletics.

Sudheer Kumar Meesala is a lead architect at Endurance International Group and has spent the last few years designing and building scalable and secure web applications within finance and internet industries. A large part of his job has included decomposing monolithic legacy applications into microservices. This has required a deep understanding of PostgreSQL, Cassandra, and other NoSQL databases. Other key areas of interest are container orchestration, DevOps, and more. He is also an accomplished speaker and trainer. He lives in Bangalore, India, and spends far too much time in traffic jams.

My contributions to this book would not have been possible without the support and understanding of my wife, Sarika, and my mother, Rama. My colleagues at Endurance International Group have inspired, challenged, and driven my technical growth.

About the reviewers

Sheldon Strauch is a twenty-year veteran of software consulting at companies such as IBM, Sears, Ernst & Young, and Kraft Foods. He has a Bachelor's degree in Business Administration and leverages his technical skills to improve businesses self-awareness. His interests include data gathering, management, and mining; maps and mapping; business intelligence; and the application of data analysis for continuous improvement. He is currently focused on the development of end-to-end data management and mining at Enova International, a financial services company located in Chicago. In his spare time, he enjoys the performing arts, particularly music, and traveling with his wife Marilyn.

Birju Shah is the principal architect for Endurance International Group and he is the co-author of *Advanced MySql 8*. He has the experience and expertise to build scalable products for hosting domains. He is passionate about the latest architectural patterns, tools, and technologies. He also helps organizations to follow best practices. He is passionate about technical training and technical sessions.

I would like to thank my family and my colleagues for their help and continuous support.

Packt is searching for authors like you

If you're interested in becoming an author for Packt, please visit `authors.packtpub.com` and apply today. We have worked with thousands of developers and tech professionals, just like you, to help them share their insight with the global tech community. You can make a general application, apply for a specific hot topic that we are recruiting an author for, or submit your own idea.

Table of Contents

Preface   1

Chapter 1: First Steps   9
  Introducing PostgreSQL 11   10
    What makes PostgreSQL different?   10
      Robustness   12
      Security   12
      Ease of use   13
      Extensibility   13
      Performance and concurrency   14
      Scalability   14
      SQL and NoSQL data models   14
      Popularity   15
      Commercial support   15
      Research and development funding   16
  Getting PostgreSQL   16
    How to do it...   16
    How it works...   17
    There's more...   17
  Connecting to the PostgreSQL server   18
    Getting ready   18
    How to do it...   18
    How it works...   20
    There's more...   21
    See also   21
  Enabling access for network/remote users   21
    How to do it...   22
    How it works...   22
    There's more...   24
    See also   24
  Using graphical administration tools   24
    How to do it...   24
    How it works...   28
  OmniDB   29
    How to do it...   29
    See also   34
  Using the psql query and scripting tool   34
    Getting ready   35
    How to do it...   35
    How it works...   37
    There's more...   38

See also	38
Changing your password securely	39
How to do it...	39
How it works...	39
Avoiding hardcoding your password	40
Getting ready	40
How to do it...	40
How it works...	41
There's more...	42
Using a connection service file	42
How to do it...	42
How it works...	43
Troubleshooting a failed connection	43
How to do it...	43
There's more...	45
Chapter 2: Exploring the Database	47
What type of server is this?	48
How to do it...	48
There's more...	49
What version is the server?	49
How to do it...	49
How it works...	50
There's more...	50
What is the server uptime?	51
How to do it...	51
How it works...	52
See also	52
Locating the database server files	52
Getting ready	52
How to do it...	53
How it works...	54
There's more...	55
Locating the database server's message log	56
Getting ready	56
How to do it...	57
How it works...	57
There's more...	58
See also	58
Locating the database's system identifier	59
Getting ready	59
How to do it...	59
How it works...	60
Listing databases on the database server	60
How to do it...	61

How it works...   61
There's more...   62
How many tables are there in a database?   64
How to do it...   64
How it works...   65
There's more...   66
How much disk space does a database use?   66
How to do it...   67
How it works...   67
How much disk space does a table use?   67
How to do it...   68
How it works...   68
There's more...   69
Which are my biggest tables?   69
How to do it...   69
How it works...   70
How many rows are there in a table?   70
How to do it...   70
How it works...   71
Quickly estimating the number of rows in a table   72
How to do it...   72
How it works...   73
There's more...   74
Listing extensions in this database   77
How to do it...   77
How it works...   78
There's more...   78
See also   79
Understanding object dependencies   79
Getting ready   79
How to do it...   80
How it works...   80
There's more...   80

Chapter 3: Configuration   83
Reading the fine manual   84
How to do it...   84
How it works...   85
There's more...   85
Planning a new database   85
Getting ready   85
How to do it...   86
How it works...   86
There's more...   87
Changing parameters in your programs   87

How to do it...	87
How it works...	88
There's more...	88
Finding the current configuration settings	**89**
How to do it...	89
How it works...	91
Which parameters are at non-default settings?	**91**
How to do it...	92
How it works...	93
There's more...	93
Updating the parameter file	**93**
Getting ready	94
How to do it...	94
How it works...	95
There's more...	95
Setting parameters for particular groups of users	**96**
How to do it...	96
How it works...	97
The basic server configuration checklist	**97**
Getting ready	97
How to do it...	98
There's more...	98
Adding an external module to PostgreSQL	**99**
Getting ready	100
How to do it...	101
Installing modules using a software installer	101
Installing modules from PGXN	102
Installing modules from source code	103
How it works...	104
Using an installed module	**104**
Getting ready	105
How to do it...	105
How it works...	105
Managing installed extensions	**105**
How to do it...	105
How it works...	108
There's more...	108
Chapter 4: Server Control	**111**
Introduction	**111**
Starting the database server manually	**112**
Getting ready	113
How to do it...	113
How it works...	115
Stopping the server safely and quickly	**116**

How to do it...	116
How it works...	117
See also	117
Stopping the server in an emergency	**118**
How to do it...	118
How it works...	118
Reloading the server configuration files	**119**
How to do it...	119
How it works...	120
There's more...	121
Restarting the server quickly	**121**
How to do it...	121
There's more...	123
Preventing new connections	**123**
How to do it...	123
How it works...	125
Restricting users to only one session each	**125**
How to do it...	125
How it works...	126
Pushing users off the system	**126**
How to do it...	127
How it works...	128
Deciding on a design for multitenancy	**129**
How to do it...	129
How it works...	130
Using multiple schemas	**130**
Getting ready	130
How to do it...	131
How it works...	132
Giving users their own private database	**133**
Getting ready	133
How to do it...	133
How it works...	134
There's more...	135
See also	135
Running multiple servers on one system	**135**
Getting ready	135
How to do it...	135
How it works...	137
Setting up a connection pool	**137**
Getting ready	137
How to do it...	138
How it works...	139
There's more...	140
Accessing multiple servers using the same host and port	**142**

Getting ready 142
How to do it... 142
There's more... 143

Chapter 5: Tables and Data 145
Choosing good names for database objects 145
Getting ready 146
How to do it... 146
There's more... 147
Handling objects with quoted names 148
Getting ready 148
How to do it... 149
How it works... 149
There's more... 150
Enforcing the same name and definition for columns 150
Getting ready 151
How to do it... 151
How it works... 153
There's more... 153
Identifying and removing duplicates 154
Getting ready 154
How to do it... 155
How it works... 157
There's more... 159
Preventing duplicate rows 159
Getting ready 159
How to do it... 160
How it works... 162
There's more... 163
Duplicate indexes 163
Uniqueness without indexes 163
Real-world example – IP address range allocation 164
Real-world example – range of time 165
Real-world example – prefix ranges 165
Finding a unique key for a set of data 166
Getting ready 166
How to do it... 166
How it works... 168
Generating test data 168
How to do it... 168
How it works... 171
There's more... 172
See also 172
Randomly sampling data 172
How to do it... 173
How it works... 174

Loading data from a spreadsheet   176
   Getting ready   176
   How to do it...   177
   How it works...   178
   There's more...   179
Loading data from flat files   179
   Getting ready   179
   How to do it...   179
   How it works...   181
   There's more...   182
Making bulk data changes using server-side procedures with transactions   183
   How to do it...   184
   There's more...   185

Chapter 6: Security   189
Introduction   190
   Typical user role   190
The PostgreSQL superuser   191
   How to do it...   191
   How it works...   191
   There's more...   192
     Other superuser-like attributes   192
     Attributes are never inherited   192
   See also   192
Revoking user access to a table   192
   Getting ready   192
   How to do it...   193
   How it works...   194
   There's more...   195
     Database creation scripts   195
     Default search path   195
     Securing views   196
Granting user access to a table   197
   Getting ready   197
   How to do it...   197
   How it works...   198
   There's more...   198
Granting user access to specific columns   198
   Getting ready   198
   How to do it...   199
   How it works...   199
   There's more...   200
Granting user access to specific rows   200
   Getting ready   201
   How to do it...   201

How it works…	203
There's more…	203
Creating a new user	**203**
Getting ready	203
How to do it…	204
How it works…	204
There's more…	204
Temporarily preventing a user from connecting	**205**
Getting ready	205
How to do it…	205
How it works…	206
There's more…	206
Limiting the number of concurrent connections by a user	206
Forcing NOLOGIN users to disconnect	206
Removing a user without dropping their data	**207**
Getting ready	207
How to do it…	207
How it works…	208
Checking whether all users have a secure password	**208**
How to do it…	209
How it works…	209
Giving limited superuser powers to specific users	**209**
Getting ready	210
How to do it…	210
How it works…	212
There's more…	212
Writing a debugging_info function for developers	212
Auditing database access	**213**
Getting ready	213
Auditing SQL	214
Auditing table access	215
Managing the audit log	216
Auditing data changes	217
Always knowing which user is logged in	**219**
Getting ready	219
How to do it…	220
How it works…	221
There's more…	221
Not inheriting user attributes	221
Integrating with LDAP	**221**
Getting ready	222
How to do it…	222
How it works…	222
There's more…	222
Setting up the client to use LDAP	222
Replacement for the User Name Map feature	223

See also	223
Connecting using SSL	223
Getting ready	223
How to do it...	224
How it works...	224
There's more...	224
Getting the SSL key and certificate	225
Setting up a client to use SSL	225
Checking server authenticity	226
Using SSL certificates to authenticate	226
Getting ready	226
How to do it...	227
How it works...	227
There's more...	228
Avoiding duplicate SSL connection attempts	228
Using multiple client certificates	228
Using the client certificate to select the database user	229
See also	229
Mapping external usernames to database roles	230
Getting ready	230
How to do it...	230
How it works...	231
There's more...	231
Encrypting sensitive data	231
Getting ready	232
How to do it...	233
How it works...	235
There's more...	235
For really sensitive data	235
For really, really, really sensitive data	236
See also	236
Chapter 7: Database Administration	237
Writing a script that either succeeds entirely or fails entirely	238
How to do it...	239
How it works...	239
There's more...	241
Writing a psql script that exits on the first error	243
Getting ready	243
How to do it...	243
How it works...	244
There's more...	244
Using psql variables	245
Getting ready	245
How to do it...	245
How it works...	245

There's more...	246
Placing query output into psql variables	246
Getting ready	246
How to do it...	247
How it works...	247
There's more...	248
Writing a conditional psql script	248
Getting ready	248
How to do it...	248
How it works...	249
There's more...	249
Investigating a psql error	249
Getting ready	250
How to do it...	251
There's more...	251
Using pgAdmin for DBA tasks	251
Getting ready	251
How to do it...	252
How it works...	256
There's more	256
Using OmniDB for DBA tasks	256
Getting ready	257
How to do it...	257
How it works	260
There's more...	261
Performing actions on many tables	261
Getting ready	262
How to do it...	262
How it works...	264
There's more...	266
Adding/removing columns on a table	268
How to do it...	268
How it works...	269
There's more...	270
Changing the data type of a column	271
Getting ready	271
How to do it...	272
How it works...	273
There's more...	273
Changing the definition of a data type	275
Getting ready	275
How to do it...	275
How it works...	276
There's more...	278
Adding/removing schemas	278

How to do it...   279
There's more...   280
    Using schema-level privileges   280
Moving objects between schemas   281
How to do it...   281
How it works...   281
There's more...   282
Adding/removing tablespaces   282
Getting ready   282
How to do it...   283
How it works...   285
There's more...   285
    Putting pg_wal on a separate device   286
    Tablespace-level tuning   286
Moving objects between tablespaces   287
Getting ready   287
How to do it...   287
How it works...   288
There's more...   289
Accessing objects in other PostgreSQL databases   290
Getting ready   290
How to do it...   291
How it works...   296
There's more...   297
Accessing objects in other foreign databases   300
Getting ready   301
How to do it...   301
How it works...   302
There's more...   303
Updatable views   303
Getting ready   303
How to do it...   305
How it works...   309
There's more...   310
Using materialized views   311
Getting ready   312
How to do it...   312
How it works...   313
There's more...   313

Chapter 8: Monitoring and Diagnosis   315
Introduction   315
Providing PostgreSQL information to monitoring tools   317
    Finding more information about generic monitoring tools   318
Real-time viewing using pgAdmin or OmniDB   319

Getting ready 319
How to do it... 319
    Using pgAdmin 319
    Using OmniDB 320
Checking whether a user is connected 321
Getting ready 322
How to do it... 322
How it works... 322
There's more... 322
Checking whether a computer is connected 322
How to do it... 323
There's more... 323
Repeatedly executing a query in psql 323
How to do it... 323
There's more... 324
Checking which queries are running 324
Getting ready 324
How to do it... 324
How it works... 325
There's more... 325
    Catching queries that only run for a few milliseconds 325
    Watching the longest queries 326
    Watching queries from ps 326
See also 327
Checking which queries are active or blocked 327
Getting ready 327
How to do it... 327
How it works... 328
There's more... 328
Knowing who is blocking a query 329
Getting ready 329
How to do it... 329
How it works... 330
Killing a specific session 330
How to do it... 330
How it works... 330
There's more... 331
    Try to cancel the query first 331
    What if the backend won't terminate? 331
    Using statement_timeout to clean up queries that take too long to run 332
    Killing idle in-transaction queries 332
    Killing the backend from the command line 333
Detecting an in-doubt prepared transaction 333
How to do it... 333
Knowing whether anybody is using a specific table 334
Getting ready 334

How to do it...   334
How it works...   335
There's more...   335
    The quick-and-dirty way   335
    Collecting daily usage statistics   335
Knowing when a table was last used   336
Getting ready   336
How to do it...   336
How it works...   338
There's more...   338
Usage of disk space by temporary data   338
Getting ready   338
How to do it...   339
How it works...   341
There's more...   341
    Finding out whether a temporary file is in use anymore   341
    Logging temporary file usage   341
Understanding why queries slow down   341
Getting ready   342
How to do it...   342
How it works...   343
There's more...   343
    Do queries return significantly more data than they did earlier?   343
    Do queries also run slowly when they run alone?   344
    Is the second run of the same query also slow?   344
    Table and index bloat   344
See also   345
Investigating and reporting a bug   345
Getting ready   346
How to do it...   346
How it works...   347
Producing a daily summary of log file errors   347
Getting ready   347
How to do it...   349
How it works...   350
There's more...   350
Analyzing the real-time performance of your queries   351
Getting ready   351
How to do it...   351
How it works...   352
There's more...   352

Chapter 9: Regular Maintenance   355
Controlling automatic database maintenance   356
Getting ready   356
How to do it...   357

How it works…	358
There's more…	361
See also	362
Avoiding auto-freezing and page corruptions	362
How to do it…	363
Removing issues that cause bloat	364
Getting ready	364
How to do it…	365
How it works…	365
There's more…	366
Removing old prepared transactions	366
Getting ready	366
How to do it…	367
How it works…	367
There's more…	368
Actions for heavy users of temporary tables	369
How to do it…	369
How it works…	370
Identifying and fixing bloated tables and indexes	371
Getting ready	371
How to do it…	372
How it works…	374
There's more…	376
Monitoring and tuning a vacuum	376
Getting ready	376
How to do it…	377
How it works…	377
There's more…	379
Maintaining indexes	379
Getting ready	380
How to do it…	381
How it works…	382
There's more…	382
Adding a constraint without checking existing rows	383
Getting ready	383
How to do it…	384
How it works…	385
Finding unused indexes	385
How to do it…	386
How it works…	386
Carefully removing unwanted indexes	387
Getting ready	387
How to do it…	388
How it works…	389
Planning maintenance	389

How to do it...	389
How it works...	390
There's more...	391
Chapter 10: Performance and Concurrency	**393**
Finding slow SQL statements	**394**
Getting ready	394
How to do it...	395
How it works...	396
There's more...	396
Finding out what makes SQL slow	**396**
Getting ready	396
How to do it...	397
There's more...	399
Not enough CPU power or disk I/O capacity for the current load	400
Locking problems	400
EXPLAIN options	400
See also	401
Collect regular statistics from pg_stat* views	**401**
Getting ready	401
How to do it...	402
How it works...	402
There's more...	402
Another statistics collection package	403
Reducing the number of rows returned	**403**
How to do it...	403
There's more...	404
Simplifying complex SQL queries	**406**
Getting ready	406
How to do it...	407
There's more...	411
Using materialized views (long-living temporary tables)	412
Using set-returning functions for some parts of queries	413
Speeding up queries without rewriting them	**414**
How to do it...	414
Increasing work_mem	414
More ideas with indexes	414
There's more...	416
Time series partitioning	416
Using a TABLESAMPLE view	416
In case of many updates, set fillfactor on the table	417
Rewriting the schema – a more radical approach	417
Discovering why a query is not using an index	**417**
Getting ready	418
How to do it...	418
How it works...	419
There's more...	419

Forcing a query to use an index 419
  Getting ready 420
  How to do it... 420
  There's more... 422
  There's more 422
Using parallel query 422
  How to do it... 423
  How it works... 423
  There's more... 425
Creating time series tables 425
  How to do it... 425
  How it works... 427
  There's more... 427
Using optimistic locking 428
  How to do it... 428
  How it works... 428
  There's more... 429
Reporting performance problems 430
  How to do it... 430
  There's more... 431

Chapter 11: Backup and Recovery 433
  Understanding and controlling crash recovery 434
    How to do it... 435
    How it works... 436
    There's more... 437
  Planning backups 437
    How to do it... 438
  Hot logical backups of one database 439
    How to do it... 440
    How it works... 440
    There's more... 442
    See also 442
  Hot logical backups of all databases 443
    How to do it... 443
    How it works... 443
    See also 444
  Backups of database object definitions 444
    How to do it... 444
    There's more... 445
  Standalone hot physical database backup 445
    Getting ready 446
    How to do it... 446
    How it works... 449
    There's more... 450

See also 451
Hot physical backup and continuous archiving 451
   Getting ready 452
   How to do it… 452
   How it works… 454
Recovery of all databases 455
   Getting ready 455
   How to do it… 455
      Logical – from custom dump taken with pg_dump -F c 455
      Logical – from the script dump created by pg_dump -F p 456
      Logical – from the script dump created by pg_dumpall 456
      Physical 456
   How it works… 458
   There's more… 459
   See also 459
Recovery to a point in time 459
   Getting ready 460
   How to do it… 460
   How it works… 460
   There's more… 462
   See also 462
Recovery of a dropped/damaged table 463
   How to do it… 463
      Logical – from custom dump taken with pg_dump -F c 463
      Logical – from the script dump 465
      Physical 465
   How it works… 466
   See also 466
Recovery of a dropped/damaged database 466
   How to do it… 467
      Logical – from the custom dump -F c 467
      Logical – from the script dump created by pg_dump 467
      Logical – from the script dump created by pg_dumpall 467
      Physical 468
Improving performance of backup/recovery 468
   Getting ready 468
   How to do it… 469
   How it works… 470
   There's more… 471
   See also 471
Incremental/differential backup and restore 471
   How to do it… 472
   How it works… 472
   There's more… 473
Hot physical backups with Barman 474
   Getting ready 475

How to do it...	476
How it works...	480
There's more...	481
Recovery with Barman	483
Getting ready	484
How to do it...	485
How it works...	486
There's more...	487
Validating backups	489
Getting ready	489
How to do it...	490
How it works...	491
There's more...	491
Chapter 12: Replication and Upgrades	493
Replication concepts	494
Topics	495
Basic concepts	495
History and scope	496
Practical aspects	497
Data loss	498
Single-master replication	499
Multinode architectures	499
Clustered or massively parallel databases	500
Multimaster replication	500
Scalability tools	501
Other approaches to replication	502
Replication best practices	502
Getting ready	502
How to do it...	502
There's more...	504
Setting up file-based replication – deprecated	504
Getting ready	505
How to do it...	505
How it works...	506
There's more...	508
See also	508
Setting up streaming replication	508
Getting ready	509
How to do it...	509
How it works...	512
There's more...	513
Setting up streaming replication security	514
Getting ready	515
How to do it...	515

How it works…	516
There's more…	516
Hot standby and read scalability	**517**
Getting ready	517
How to do it…	518
How it works…	521
Managing streaming replication	**521**
Getting ready	522
How to do it…	522
There's more…	523
See also	524
Using repmgr	**524**
Getting ready	525
How to do it…	525
How it works…	527
There's more…	527
Using replication slots	**527**
Getting ready	528
How to do it…	528
There's more…	529
See also	529
Monitoring replication	**530**
Getting ready	530
How to do it…	531
There's more…	533
Performance and synchronous replication	**534**
Getting ready	534
How to do it…	535
How it works…	537
There's more…	537
Delaying, pausing, and synchronizing replication	**538**
Getting ready	538
How to do it…	538
There's more…	539
See also	540
Logical replication	**540**
Getting ready	542
How to do it…	544
How it works…	545
There's more…	546
See also	546
Bidirectional replication	**547**
Getting ready	548
How to do it…	549
How it works…	549

There's more...   550
Archiving transaction log data   550
   Getting ready   551
   How to do it...   551
   There's more...   552
   See also   552
Upgrading minor releases   553
   Getting ready   553
   How to do it...   553
   How it works...   554
   There's more...   554
Major upgrades in-place   555
   Getting ready   555
   How to do it...   555
   How it works...   556
Major upgrades online   557
   How to do it...   557
   How it works...   558

Other Books You May Enjoy   559

Index   563

Preface

PostgreSQL is an advanced SQL database server; it is available on a wide range of platforms and is fast becoming one of the world's most popular server databases with an enviable reputation for performance, stability, and an enormous range of advanced features. PostgreSQL is one of the oldest open source projects; it is completely free to use and was developed by a diverse worldwide community. Most of all, it just works!

One of the clearest benefits of PostgreSQL is that it is open source, meaning that you have a permissive license to install, use, and distribute PostgreSQL without paying anyone any fees or royalties. Additionally, PostgreSQL is well known as a database that stays up for long periods, and requires little or no maintenance. Overall, PostgreSQL provides a very low total cost of ownership.

PostgreSQL 11 Administration Cookbook offers the information you need to manage your live production databases on PostgreSQL. The book contains direct insights into PostgreSQL replication and recovery features from the main author and the 2ndQuadrant team. This hands-on guide will assist developers who are working on live databases, and who are supporting web or enterprise software applications using Java, Python, Ruby, and .NET from any development framework. It's easy to manage your database when you've got *PostgreSQL 11 Administration Cookbook* at hand.

This practical guide gives you quick answers to common questions and problems, and builds on the author's experience as a trainer, user, and core developer of the PostgreSQL database server.

Each technical aspect is broken down into short recipes that demonstrate solutions with working code, and then explain how and why that works. The book is intended to be a desk reference for both new users and technical experts.

The book covers all the latest features available in PostgreSQL 11. Soon you will be running a smooth database with ease!

Who this book is for

This book is for system administrators, database administrators, architects, developers, and anyone with an interest in planning or running a live production database. This book is most suited to those who have some technical experience.

What this book covers

Chapter 1, *First Steps*, introduces you PostgreSQL 11; it explains how to download and install PostgreSQL 11, connect to a PostgreSQL server, enable server access to the network or remote users, use graphical administration tools, use PSQL query and scripting tools, change your password securely, avoid hardcoding your password, use a connection service file, and troubleshoot a failed connection.

Chapter 2, *Exploring the Database,* demonstrates how to identify the version of the database server you are using, as well as the server uptime. It helps you locate the database server files, the database server message log, and the database's system identifier. It explains how to list a database on the database server, and it contains recipes that let you know the number of tables in your database, how much disk space is used by the database and tables, what the the biggest tables are, how many rows a table has, how to estimate rows in a table, and how to understand object dependencies.

Chapter 3, *Configuration*, explains topics such as **Reading the Fine Manual** (**RTFM**), how to plan a new database, how to change the parameters in your programs, the current configuration settings, the parameters that are at non-default settings, how to update the parameter file, how to set parameters for particular groups of users, the basic server configuration checklist, how to add an external module into the PostgreSQL server, and how to run the server in power-saving mode.

Chapter 4, *Server Control*, provides information about starting the database server manually, stopping the server quickly and safely, stopping the server in an emergency, reloading the server configuration files, restarting the server quickly, preventing new connections, restricting users to just one session each, and pushing users off the system. It contains recipes that help you choose a design for multi-tenancy, as well as recipes that explain how to use multiple schemas, give users their own private database, run multiple database servers on one system, and set up a connection pool.

Chapter 5, *Tables and Data*, guides you through the process of choosing good names for database objects. Additionally, it explains how to handle objects with quoted names, enforce the same name, maintain the same definition for columns, identify and remove duplicate rows, prevent duplicate rows, find a unique key for a set of data, generate test data, randomly sample data, load data from a spreadsheet, and load data from flat files.

Chapter 6, *Security*, provides recipes on revoking user access to a table, granting user access to a table, creating a new user, temporarily preventing a user from connecting, removing a user without dropping their data, checking whether all users have a secure password, giving limited superuser powers to specific users, auditing DDL changes, auditing data changes, integrating with LDAP, connecting using SSL, and encrypting sensitive data.

Chapter 7, *Database Administration*, provides recipes on useful topics such as writing a script where all either succeed or fail, writing a PSQL script that exits on the first error, performing actions on many tables, adding and removing columns in tables, changing the data type of a column, adding and removing schemas, moving objects between schemas, adding and removing tablespaces, moving objects between tablespaces, accessing objects in other PostgreSQL databases, and enabling views to be updated.

Chapter 8, *Monitoring and Diagnosis*, provides recipes that answer questions such as whether the user is connected, what they are running, whether they are active or blocked, who they are being blocked by, whether anybody is using a specific table, when the table it was last used, how much disk space is being used by temporary data, and why your queries could be slowing down. It also demonstrates how to investigate and report a bug, produce a daily summary report of log file errors, kill a specific session, and resolve an in-doubt prepared transaction.

Chapter 9, *Regular Maintenance*, provides useful recipes on how to control automatic database maintenance, avoid auto-freezing and page corruptions, avoid transaction wraparound, remove old prepared transactions, offer solutions for heavy users of temporary tables, identify and fix bloated tables and indexes, maintain indexes, find unused indexes, carefully remove unwanted indexes, and plan maintenance.

Chapter 10, *Performance and Concurrency*, covers topics such as how to find slow SQL statements, collect regular statistics from `pg_stat*` views, discover what makes SQL slow, reduce the number of rows returned, simplify complex SQL, speed up queries without rewriting them, understand why some queries are not using an index, force a query to use an index, use optimistic locking, and report performance problems. And, of course, you'll learn about the new parallel query features.

`Chapter 11`, *Backup and Recovery*, explains that backups are essential, although this topic is only covered very briefly. So, this chapter provides useful information about the backup and recovery of your PostgreSQL database through recipes on how to understand and control crash recovery and how to plan backups. Additionally, you will learn about the hot logical backup of one database, the hot logical backup of all databases, the hot logical backup of all tables in a tablespace, the backup of database object definitions, the standalone hot physical database backup, the hot physical backup, and continuous archiving. It also includes topics such as the recovery of all databases, recovery to a point in time, the recovery of a dropped or damaged table, the recovery of a dropped or damaged database, the recovery of a dropped or damaged tablespace, how to improve the performance of backup/recovery, and incremental/differential backup and restore.

`Chapter 12`, *Replication and Upgrades*, explains that replication isn't magic, although it can be pretty cool. It's even cooler when it works, and that's what this chapter is all about. This chapter covers replication concepts, replication best practices, how to set up file-based log shipping replication, how to set up streaming log replication, how to manage log shipping replication, how to manage hot standby, synchronous replication, how to upgrade to a new minor release, in-place major upgrades, major upgrades online, and logical replication and Postgres-BDR.

To get the most out of this book

In order for this book to be useful, you need access to a PostgreSQL client that is allowed to execute queries on a server. Ideally, you'll also be the server administrator. Full client and server packages for PostgreSQL are available for most popular operating systems at `http://www.postgresql.org/download/`. All the examples here are executed at the Command Prompt, usually running the PSQL program. This makes them applicable to most platforms. It's straightforward to do most of these operations by using a GUI tool for PostgreSQL, such as pgAdmin or OmniDB:

- pgAdmin: `https://www.pgadmin.org/download/`
- OmniDB: `https://omnidb.org/en/downloads-en`

Download the color images

We also provide a PDF file that has color images of the screenshots/diagrams used in this book. You can download it here: `http://www.packtpub.com/sites/default/files/downloads/9781789537581_ColorImages.pdf`.

Conventions used

There are a number of text conventions used throughout this book.

`CodeInText`: Indicates code words in text, database table names, folder names, filenames, file extensions, pathnames, dummy URLs, user input, and Twitter handles. Here is an example: "Copy the data files (excluding the `pg_wal` directory)."

A block of code is set as follows:

```
CREATE USER repuser
        SUPERUSER
        LOGIN
        CONNECTION LIMIT 1
        ENCRYPTED PASSWORD 'changeme';
```

When we wish to draw your attention to a particular part of a code block, the relevant lines or items are set in bold:

```
SELECT *FROM mytable
  WHERE   (col1, col2, ... ,colN) IN
  (SELECT col1, col2, ... ,colN
  FROM mytable
  GROUP BY col1, col2, ... ,colN
  HAVING count(*) > 1);
```

Any command-line input or output is written as follows:

```
$ postgres --single -D /full/path/to/datadir postgres
```

Bold: Indicates a new term, an important word, or words that you see onscreen. For example, words in menus or dialog boxes appear in the text like this. Here is an example: "Select **System info** from the **Administration** panel."

Warnings or important notes appear like this.

Tips and tricks appear like this.

Sections

In this book, you will find several headings that appear frequently (*Getting ready, How to do it..., How it works..., There's more...,* and *See also*).

To give clear instructions on how to complete a recipe, use these sections as follows:

Getting ready

This section tells you what to expect in the recipe and describes how to set up any software or any preliminary settings required for the recipe.

How to do it...

This section contains the steps required to follow the recipe.

How it works...

This section usually consists of a detailed explanation of what happened in the previous section.

There's more...

This section consists of additional information about the recipe in order to make you more knowledgeable about the recipe.

See also

This section provides helpful links to other useful information for the recipe.

Get in touch

Feedback from our readers is always welcome.

General feedback: Email `feedback@packtpub.com` and mention the book title in the subject of your message. If you have questions about any aspect of this book, please email us at `questions@packtpub.com`.

Errata: Although we have taken every care to ensure the accuracy of our content, mistakes do happen. If you have found a mistake in this book, we would be grateful if you would report this to us. Please visit www.packtpub.com/submit-errata, selecting your book, clicking on the Errata Submission Form link, and entering the details.

Piracy: If you come across any illegal copies of our works in any form on the internet, we would be grateful if you would provide us with the location address or website name. Please contact us at copyright@packtpub.com with a link to the material.

If you are interested in becoming an author: If there is a topic that you have expertise in and you are interested in either writing or contributing to a book, please visit authors.packtpub.com.

Reviews

Please leave a review. Once you have read and used this book, why not leave a review on the site that you purchased it from? Potential readers can then see and use your unbiased opinion to make purchase decisions, we at Packt can understand what you think about our products, and our authors can see your feedback on their book. Thank you!

For more information about Packt, please visit packtpub.com.

1
First Steps

PostgreSQL is a feature-rich, general-purpose, database-management system. It's a complex piece of software, but every journey begins with the first step.

We'll start with your first connection. Many people fall at the first hurdle, so we'll try not to skip that too swiftly. We'll quickly move on to enabling remote users, and from there we will move on to getting access through GUI administration tools.

We will also introduce the `psql` query tool, which is the tool used to load our sample database, as well as many other examples in the book.

For additional help, we've included a few useful recipes that you may need for reference.

In this chapter, we will cover the following recipes:

- Getting PostgreSQL
- Connecting to the PostgreSQL server
- Enabling access for network/remote users
- Using graphical administration tools
- Using the psql query and scripting tool
- Changing your password securely
- Avoiding hardcoding your password
- Using a connection service file
- Troubleshooting a failed connection

Introducing PostgreSQL 11

PostgreSQL is an advanced SQL database server, available on a wide range of platforms. One of the clearest benefits of PostgreSQL is that it is open source, meaning that you have a very permissive license to install, use, and distribute PostgreSQL, without paying anyone any fees or royalties. On top of that, PostgreSQL is known as a database that stays up for long periods and requires little or no maintenance, in most cases. Overall, PostgreSQL provides a very low total cost of ownership.

PostgreSQL is also known for its huge range of advanced features, developed over the course of more than 30 years of continuous development and enhancement. Originally developed by the Database Research Group at the University of California, Berkeley, PostgreSQL is now developed and maintained by a huge army of developers and contributors. Many of these contributors have full-time jobs related to PostgreSQL, working as designers, developers, database administrators, and trainers. Some, but not many, of these contributors work for companies that specialize in support for PostgreSQL. No single company owns PostgreSQL, nor are you required (or even encouraged) to register your usage.

PostgreSQL has the following main features:

- Excellent SQL standards compliance, up to SQL: 2016
- Client-server architecture
- It has a highly concurrent design, where readers and writers don't block each other
- It is highly configurable and extensible for many types of applications
- It has excellent scalability and performance, with extensive tuning features
- It offers support for many kinds of data models, such as relational, post-relational (arrays, nested relations via record types), document (JSON and XML), and key/value

What makes PostgreSQL different?

The PostgreSQL project focuses on the following objectives:

- Robust, high-quality software with maintainable, well-commented code
- Low-maintenance administration for both embedded and enterprise use
- Standards-compliant SQL, interoperability, and compatibility
- Performance, security, and high availability

What surprises many people is that PostgreSQL's feature set is more similar to Oracle or SQL Server than it is to MySQL. The only connection between MySQL and PostgreSQL is that these two projects are open source; apart from that, the features and philosophies are almost totally different.

One of the key features of Oracle, since Oracle 7, has been snapshot isolation, where readers don't block writers and writers don't block readers. You may be surprised to learn that PostgreSQL was the first database to be designed with this feature, and it offers a complete implementation. In PostgreSQL, this feature is called **Multiversion Concurrency Control** (**MVCC**), and we will discuss this in more detail later in the book.

PostgreSQL is a general-purpose database management system. You define the database that you would like to manage with it. PostgreSQL offers you many ways in which to work. You can either use a normalized database model, augmented with features such as arrays and record subtypes, or use a fully dynamic schema with the help of JSONB and an extension named `hstore`. PostgreSQL also allows you to create your own server-side functions in any of a dozen different languages.

PostgreSQL is highly extensible, so you can add your own data types, operators, index types, and functional languages. You can even override different parts of the system, using plugins to alter the execution of commands, or add a new query optimizer.

All of these features offer a huge range of implementation options to software architects. There are many ways out of trouble when building applications and maintaining them over long periods of time. Regrettably, we simply don't have space in this book for all the cool features for developers; this book is about administration, maintenance, and backup.

In the early days, when PostgreSQL was still a research database, the focus was solely on the cool new features. Over the last 20 years, enormous amounts of code have been rewritten and improved, giving us one of the largest and most stable software servers available for operational use.

Who is using PostgreSQL? Prominent users include Apple, BASF, Genentech, Heroku, IMDB, Skype, McAfee, NTT, the UK Met Office, and the US National Weather Service. Early in 2010, PostgreSQL received well in excess of 1,000,000 downloads per year, according to data submitted to the European Commission, which concluded that *PostgreSQL is considered by many database users to be a credible alternative.*

We need to mention one last thing: when PostgreSQL was first developed, it was named **Postgres**, and therefore, many aspects of the project still refer to the word *Postgres*; for example, the default database is named `postgres`, and the software is frequently installed using the Postgres user ID. As a result, people shorten the name PostgreSQL to simply Postgres, and, in many cases, use the two names interchangeably.

PostgreSQL is pronounced as *post-grez-q-l*. Postgres is pronounced as *post-grez*.

Some people get confused and refer to it as *Postgre*, which is hard to say and likely to confuse people. Two names are enough, so don't use a third name!

The following sections explain the key areas in more detail.

Robustness

PostgreSQL is robust, high-quality software, supported by testing for both features and concurrency. By default, the database provides strong disk-write guarantees, and developers take the risk of data loss very seriously in everything they do. Options to trade robustness for performance exist, though they are not enabled by default.

All actions on the database are performed within transactions, protected by a transaction log that will perform automatic crash recovery in case of software failure.

Databases may optionally be created with data block checksums to help diagnose hardware faults. Multiple backup mechanisms exist, with full and detailed **Point-in-time recovery (PITR)**, in case you need a detailed recovery. A variety of diagnostic tools are available as well.

Database replication is supported natively. Synchronous replication can provide greater than *5 nines* (99.999%) availability and data protection, if properly configured and managed, or even higher with appropriate redundancy.

Security

Access to PostgreSQL is controllable via host-based access rules. Authentication is flexible and pluggable, allowing for easy integration with any external security architecture. The latest **Salted Challenge Response Authentication Mechanism (SCRAM)** provides full 256-bit protection.

Full SSL-encrypted access is supported natively for both user access and replication. A full-featured cryptographic function library is available for database users.

PostgreSQL provides role-based access privileges to access data, by command type. PostgreSQL also provides Row-Level Security for privacy, medical, and military-grade security.

Functions may execute with the permissions of the definer, while views may be defined with security barriers to ensure that security is enforced ahead of other processing.

All aspects of PostgreSQL are assessed by an active security team, while known exploits are categorized and reported at `http://www.postgresql.org/support/security/`.

Ease of use

Clear, full, and accurate documentation exists as a result of a development process where documentation changes are required. Hundreds of small changes occur with each release, which smooth off any rough edges of usage, supplied directly by knowledgeable users.

PostgreSQL works on small and large systems in the same way, and across operating systems.

Client access and drivers exist for every language and environment, so there is no restriction on what type of development environment is chosen now, or in the future.

The SQL standard is followed very closely; there is no weird behavior, such as silent truncation of data.

Text data is supported via a single data type that allows the storage of anything from 1 byte to 1 gigabyte. This storage is optimized in multiple ways, so 1 byte is stored efficiently, and much larger values are automatically managed and compressed.

PostgreSQL has the clear policy of minimizing the number of configuration parameters, and with each release, we work out ways to auto-tune the settings.

Extensibility

PostgreSQL is designed to be highly extensible. Database extensions can be easily loaded by using `CREATE EXTENSION`, which automates version checks, dependencies, and other aspects of configuration.

PostgreSQL supports user-defined data types, operators, indexes, functions, and languages.

Many extensions are available for PostgreSQL, including the PostGIS extension, which provides world-class **Geographical Information System** (**GIS**) features.

Performance and concurrency

PostgreSQL 11 can achieve significantly more than 1,000,000 reads per second on a 4-socket server, and it benchmarks at more than 30,000 write transactions per second with full durability, depending upon your hardware. With advanced hardware, even higher levels of performance are possible.

PostgreSQL has an advanced optimizer that considers a variety of join types, utilizing user data statistics to guide its choices. PostgreSQL provides the widest range of index types of any commonly available database server, fully supporting all data types.

PostgreSQL provides MVCC, which enables readers and writers to avoid blocking each other.

Taken together, the performance features of PostgreSQL allow a mixed workload of transactional systems and complex search and analytical tasks. This is important because it means we don't always need to unload our data from production systems and reload it into analytical data stores just to execute a few ad hoc queries. PostgreSQL's capabilities make it the database of choice for new systems, as well as the correct long-term choice in almost every case.

Scalability

PostgreSQL 11 scales well on a single node up to four CPU sockets. PostgreSQL efficiently runs up to hundreds of active sessions, and up to thousands of connected sessions when using a session pool. Further scalability is achieved in each annual release.

PostgreSQL provides multi-node read scalability using the **Hot Standby** feature. Multi-node write scalability is under active development. The starting point for this is *Bi-Directional Replication* (discussed in `Chapter 12`, *Replication and Upgrades*).

SQL and NoSQL data models

PostgreSQL follows the SQL standard very closely. SQL itself does not force any particular type of model to be used, so PostgreSQL can easily be used for many types of models at the same time, in the same database.

With PostgreSQL acting as a relational database, we can utilize any level of denormalization, from the full third normal form (3NF), to the more normalized star schema models. PostgreSQL extends the relational model to provide arrays, row types, and range types.

A document-centric database is also possible using PostgreSQL's text, XML, and binary JSON (JSONB) data types, supported by indexes optimized for documents and by full text search capabilities.

Key/value stores are supported using the `hstore` extension.

Popularity

When MySQL was taken over by a commercial database vendor some years back, it was agreed in the EU monopoly investigation that followed that PostgreSQL was a viable competitor. That's certainly been true, with the PostgreSQL user base expanding consistently for more than a decade.

Various polls have indicated that PostgreSQL is the favorite database for building new, enterprise-class applications. The PostgreSQL feature set attracts serious users who have serious applications. Financial services companies may be PostgreSQL's largest user group, though governments, telecommunication companies, and many other segments are strong users as well. This popularity extends across the world; Japan, Ecuador, Argentina, and Russia have very large user groups, as do the US, Europe, and Australasia.

Amazon Web Services' chief technology officer, Dr. Werner Vogels, described PostgreSQL as *An amazing database*, going on to say that *PostgreSQL has become the preferred open source relational database for many enterprise developers and start-ups, powering leading geospatial and mobile applications.* AWS have more recently revealed that PostgreSQL is their fastest growing service.

Commercial support

Many people have commented that strong commercial support is what enterprises need before they can invest in open source technology. Strong support is available worldwide from a number of companies.

The authors (Gianni and Simon) work for 2nd quadrant, which provides commercial support for open source PostgreSQL, offering 24/7 support in English and Spanish with bug-fix resolution times.

Many other companies provide strong and knowledgeable support to specific geographic regions, vertical markets, and specialized technology stacks.

PostgreSQL is also available as a hosted or cloud solution from a variety of companies, since it runs very well in cloud environments.

A full list of companies is kept up to date at
`http://www.postgresql.org/support/professional_support/`.

Research and development funding

PostgreSQL was originally developed as a research project at the University of California, Berkeley, in the late 1980s and early 1990s. Further work was carried out by volunteers until the late 1990s. Then, the first professional developer became involved. Over time, more and more companies and research groups became involved, supporting many professional contributors. Further funding for research and development was provided by the NSF. The project also received funding from the EU FP7 Programme, in the form of the 4CaaST project for cloud computing, and the AXLE project for scalable data analytics. AXLE deserves a special mention because it was a three-year project aimed at enhancing PostgreSQL's business-intelligence capabilities, specifically for very large databases. The project covered security, privacy, integration with data mining, and visualization tools and interfaces for new hardware.

Further details about the AXLE project are available at `http://www.axleproject.eu`. Other funding for PostgreSQL development comes from users who directly sponsor features and companies that sell products and services based around PostgreSQL.

Getting PostgreSQL

PostgreSQL is 100% open source software and is freely available to use, alter, or redistribute in any way you choose. Its license is an approved open source license, very similar to the **Berkeley Software Distribution** (**BSD**) license, though only just different enough that it is now known as **The PostgreSQL License** (TPL).

How to do it...

PostgreSQL is already being used by many different application packages, so you may find it already installed on your servers. Many Linux distributions include PostgreSQL as part of the basic installation, or include it with the installation disk.

One thing to be wary of is that the included version of PostgreSQL may not be the latest release. It would typically be the latest major release that was available when that operating system release was published. There is usually no good reason to stick to that level – there is no increased stability implied there—and later production versions are just as well supported by the various Linux distributions as the earlier versions.

If you don't have a copy yet, or you don't have the latest version, you can download the source code or binary packages for a wide variety of operating systems from `http://www.postgresql.org/download/`.

Installation details vary significantly from platform to platform, and there aren't any special tricks or recipes to mention. Just follow the installation guide, and away you go! We've consciously avoided describing the installation processes here to make sure we don't garble or override the information published to assist you.

If you would like to receive email updates of the latest news, you can subscribe to the PostgreSQL announce mailing list, which contains updates from all the vendors that support PostgreSQL. You'll get a few emails each month about new releases of core PostgreSQL, related software, conferences, and user group information. It's worth keeping in touch with these developments.

For more information about the PostgreSQL announcement mailing list, visit `http://archives.postgresql.org/pgsql-announce/`.

How it works...

Many people ask questions such as, *How can this be free?*, *Are you sure I don't have to pay someone?* or, *Who gives this stuff away for nothing?*

Open source applications such as PostgreSQL work on a community basis, where many contributors perform tasks that make the whole process work. For many of these people, their involvement is professional, rather a hobby, and they can do this because there is generally great value for both the contributors and their employers alike.

You might not believe it. You don't have to, because it just works!

There's more...

Remember that PostgreSQL is more than just the core software. There is a huge range of websites that offer add-ons, extensions, and tools for PostgreSQL. You'll also find an army of bloggers who describe useful tricks and discoveries that will help you in your work.

Besides these, a range of professional companies can offer you help when you need it.

Connecting to the PostgreSQL server

How do we access PostgreSQL?

Connecting to the database is the first experience of PostgreSQL for most people, so we want to make it a good one. Let's do it now, and fix any problems we have along the way. Remember that a connection needs to be made secure, so there may be some hoops for us to jump through to ensure that the data we wish to access is secure.

Before we can execute commands against the database, we need to connect to the database server, to give us a session.

Sessions are designed to be long-lived, so you connect once, perform many requests, and eventually disconnect. There is a small overhead during connection. It may become noticeable if you connect and disconnect repeatedly, so you may wish to investigate the use of connection pools. Connection pools allow pre-connected sessions to be quickly served to you when you wish to reconnect.

Getting ready

First, cache your database. If you don't know where it is, you'll probably have difficulty accessing it. There may be more than one database, and you'll need to know the right one to access, and also have the authority to connect to it.

How to do it...

You need to specify the following parameters to connect to PostgreSQL:

- Host or host address
- Port
- Database name
- User
- Password (or other means of authentication, if any)

To connect, there must be a PostgreSQL server running on `host`, listening to port number `port`. On that server, a database named `dbname` and a user named `user` must also exist. The host must explicitly allow connections from your client (explained in the *Enabling access for network/remote users* recipe), and you must also pass authentication using the method the server specifies; for example, specifying a password won't work if the server has requested a different form of authentication.

Almost all PostgreSQL interfaces use the `libpq` interface library. When using `libpq`, most of the connection parameter handling is identical, so we can discuss that just once.

If you don't specify the preceding parameters, PostgreSQL looks for values set through environment variables, which are as follows:

- `PGHOST` or `PGHOSTADDR`
- `PGPORT` (set this to `5432` if it is not set already)
- `PGDATABASE`
- `PGUSER`
- `PGPASSWORD` (this is definitely not recommended)

If you somehow specify the first four parameters, but not the password, PostgreSQL looks for a password file, discussed in the *Avoiding hardcoding your password* recipe.

Some PostgreSQL interfaces use the client-server protocol directly, so the ways in which the defaults are handled may differ. The information we need to supply won't vary significantly, so check the exact syntax for that interface.

Connection details can also be specified using a **Uniform Resource Identifier** (**URI**) format, as follows:

```
psql postgresql://myuser:mypasswd@myhost:5432/mydb
```

This specifies that we will connect the `psql` client application to the PostgreSQL server at the `myhost` host, on the `5432` port, with the `mydb` database name, `myuser` user, and `mypasswd` password.

> If you do not set `mypasswd` in the preceding URI, you will be prompted to enter the password.

How it works...

PostgreSQL is a client-server database. The system it runs on is known as the **host**. We can access the PostgreSQL server remotely, through the network. However, we must specify host, which is a hostname, or hostaddr, which is an IP address. We can specify a host as localhost if we wish to make a TCP/IP connection to the same system. It is often better to use a Unix socket connection, which is attempted if the host begins with a slash (/) and the name is presumed to be a directory name (the default is /tmp).

On any system, there can be more than one database server. Each database server listens to exactly one well-known network port, which cannot be shared between servers on the same system. The default port number for PostgreSQL is 5432, which has been registered with the **Internet Assigned Numbers Authority** (**IANA**) and is uniquely assigned to PostgreSQL (you can see it used in the /etc/services file on most *nix servers). The port number can be used to uniquely identify a specific database server, if many exist. IANA (http://www.iana.org) is the organization that coordinates the allocation of available numbers for various internet protocols.

A database server is also sometimes known as a **database cluster**, because the PostgreSQL server allows you to define one or more databases on each server. Each connection request must identify exactly one database, identified by its dbname. When you connect, you will only be able to see only the database objects created within that database.

A database user is used to identify the connection. By default, there is no limit on the number of connections for a particular user. In the *Enabling access for network/remote users* recipe, we will cover how to restrict that. In the more recent versions of PostgreSQL, users are referred to as login roles, though many clues remind us of the earlier nomenclature, and that still makes sense in many ways. A login role is a role that has been assigned the CONNECT privilege.

Each connection will typically be authenticated in some way. This is defined at the server level: client authentication will not be optional at connection time if the administrator has configured the server to require it.

Once you've connected, each connection can have one active transaction at a time and one fully active statement at any time.

The server will have a defined limit on the number of connections it can serve, so a connection request can be refused if the server is oversubscribed.

There's more...

If you are already connected to a database server with psql and you want to confirm that you've connected to the right place and in the right way, you can execute some, or all, of the following commands. Here is the command that shows the current_database:

```
SELECT current_database();
```

The following command shows the current_user ID:

```
SELECT current_user;
```

The next command shows the IP address and port of the current connection, unless you are using Unix sockets, in which case both values are NULL:

```
SELECT inet_server_addr(), inet_server_port();
```

A user's password is not accessible using general SQL, for obvious reasons.

You may also need the following:

```
SELECT version();
```

From PostgreSQL version 9.1 onward, you can also use the new psql meta-command, \conninfo. This displays most of the preceding information in a single line:

```
postgres=# \conninfo
You are connected to database postgres, as user postgres, via socket in
/var/run/postgresql, at port 5432.
```

See also

There are many other snippets of information required to understand connections. Some of them are mentioned in this chapter, and others are discussed in Chapter 6, *Security*. For further details, refer to the PostgreSQL server documentation.

Enabling access for network/remote users

PostgreSQL comes in a variety of distributions. In many of these, you will note that remote access is initially disabled as a security measure.

How to do it...

By default, PostgreSQL gives access to clients who connect using Unix sockets, provided that the database user is the same as the system's username. Here, we'll show you how to enable other connections.

 In this recipe, we mention configuration files, which can be located as shown in the *Finding the current configuration settings* recipe in Chapter 3, *Configuration*.

The steps are as follows:

1. Add or edit this line in your `postgresql.conf` file:

   ```
   listen_addresses = '*'
   ```

2. Add the following line as the first line of `pg_hba.conf` to allow access to all databases for all users with an encrypted password:

   ```
   # TYPE    DATABASE    USER       CIDR-ADDRESS    METHOD
   host      all         all        0.0.0.0/0        md5
   ```

3. After changing `listen_addresses`, we restart the PostgreSQL server, as explained in the *Updating the parameter file* recipe in Chapter 3, *Configuration*

 This recipe assumes that `postgresql.conf` does not include any other configuration files, which is the case in a default installation. If changing `listen_addresses` in `postgresql.conf` does not seem to work, perhaps that setting is overridden by another configuration file. Check out the *Updating the parameter file* recipe in Chapter 3, *Configuration*, for more details.

How it works...

The `listen_addresses` parameter specifies which IP addresses to listen to. This allows you to flexibly enable and disable listening on interfaces of multiple network cards (NICs) or virtual networks on the same system. In most cases, we want to accept connections on all NICs, so we use *, meaning all IP addresses.

The `pg_hba.conf` file contains a set of host-based authentication rules. Each rule is considered in sequence, until one rule fires or the attempt is specifically rejected with a `reject` method.

The preceding rule means that a remote connection that specifies any user or database on any IP address will be asked to authenticate using an MD5-encrypted password. The following are the parameters required for MD5-encrypted passwords:

- **Type**: For this, `host` means a remote connection.
- **Database**: For this, `all` means for all databases. Other names match exactly, except when prefixed with a plus (+) symbol, in which case we mean a group role rather than a single user. You can also specify a comma-separated list of users, or use the @ symbol to include a file with a list of users. You can even specify `sameuser`, so that the rule matches when you specify the same name for the user and database.
- **User**: For this, `all` means for all users. Other names match exactly, except when prefixed with a plus (+) symbol, in which case we mean a group role rather than a single user. You can also specify a comma-separated list of users, or use the @ symbol to include a file with a list of users.
- **CIDR-ADDRESS**: This consists of two parts: an IP address and a subnet mask. The subnet mask is specified as the number of leading bits of the IP address that make up the mask. Thus, `/0` means 0 bits of the IP address, so that all IP addresses will be matched. For example, `192.168.0.0/24` would mean matching of the first 24 bits, so any IP address of the form `192.168.0.x` would match. You can also use `samenet` or `samehost`.
- **Method**: For this, `md5` means that PostgreSQL will ask the client to provide a password encrypted with MD5. Another common setting is `trust`, which effectively means no authentication. Other authentication methods include GSSAPI, SSPI, LDAP, RADIUS, and PAM. PostgreSQL connections can also be made using SSL, in which case client SSL certificates provide authentication. See the *Using SSL certificates to authenticate the client* recipe in `Chapter 6`, *Security*, for more details.

Don't use the `password` setting, as this sends the password in plain text. This is not a real security issue if your connection is encrypted with SSL, and there are normally no downsides with MD5 anyway, and you have extra security for non-SSL connections.

There's more...

In earlier versions of PostgreSQL, access through the network was enabled by adding the –i command-line switch when you started the server. This is still a valid option, but now it means the following:

```
listen_addresses = '*'
```

So, if you're reading some notes about how to set things up and this is mentioned, be warned that those notes are probably long out of date. They are not necessarily wrong, but it's worth looking further to see whether anything else has changed.

See also

Look at installer and/or operating system-specific documentation to find the standard location of the files.

Using graphical administration tools

Graphical administration tools are often requested by system administrators. PostgreSQL has a range of tool options. In this book, we'll cover pgAdmin4 and OmniDB, which offers access to PostgreSQL and other databases.

Both of these tools are client applications that send and receive SQL to PostgreSQL, displaying the results for you. The admin client can access many databases servers, allowing you to manage a fleet of servers. Both tools work in standalone app mode and within web browsers.

How to do it...

pgAdmin 4 is usually named just pgAdmin. The 4 at the end has a long history, but isn't that important. It is not the release level; pgAdmin 4 replaces the earlier pgAdmin 3.

When you start pgAdmin, you will be prompted to register a new server.

Give your server a name on the **General** tab, and then click **Connection** and fill in the five basic connection parameters, as well as the other information. You should uncheck the **Save password?** box:

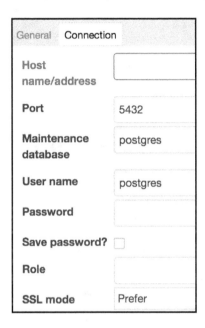

If you have many database servers, you can group them together. I suggest keeping any replicated servers together in the same server group. Give each server a sensible name.

Once you've added a server, you can connect to it and display information about it.

The default screen is the **Dashboard**, which presents a few interesting graphs based on the data it polls from the server. That's not very useful, so click on the **Statistics** tab.

You will then get access to the main browser screen, with the object tree view on the left and statistics on the right, as shown in the following screenshot:

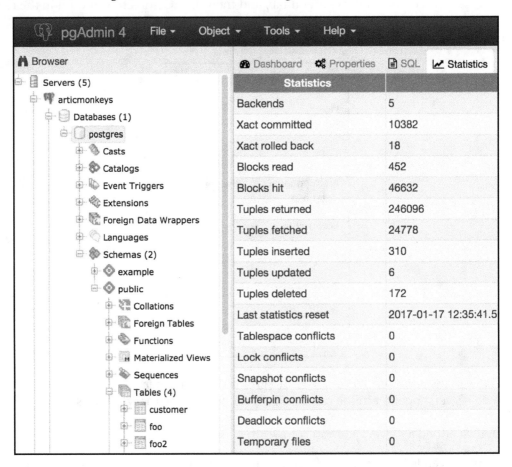

pgAdmin easily displays much of the data that is available from PostgreSQL. The information is context-sensitive, allowing you to navigate and see everything quickly and easily. The information is not dynamically updated; this will occur only when you click to refresh, so bear this in mind when using the application.

pgAdmin also provides **Grant Wizard**. This is useful for DBAs for review and immediate maintenance:

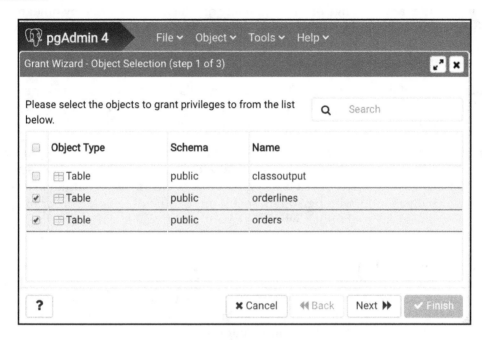

The pgAdmin query tool allows you to have multiple active sessions. The query tool has a good-looking visual **Explain** feature, which displays the EXPLAIN plan for your query:

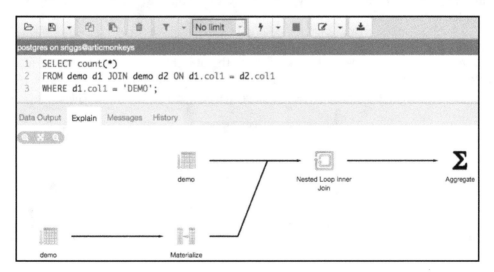

How it works...

pgAdmin provides a wide range of features, many of which are provided by other tools as well. This gives us the opportunity to choose which of those tools we want. For many reasons, it is best to use the right tool for the right job, and that is always a matter of expertise, experience, and personal taste.

pgAdmin submits SQL to the PostgreSQL server, and displays the results quickly and easily. As a browser, it is fantastic. For performing small DBA tasks, it is ideal. As you might've guessed from these comments, I don't recommend pgAdmin for every task.

Scripting is an important technique for DBAs. You keep a copy of the task executed, and you can edit and resubmit if problems occur. It's also easy to put all the tasks in a script into a single transaction, which isn't possible using the current GUI tools. pgAdmin provides pgScript, which only works with pgAdmin, so it is more difficult to port. For scripting, I strongly recommend the psql utility, which has many additional features that you'll increasingly appreciate over time.

Although I recommend psql as a scripting tool, many people find it convenient as a query tool. Some people may find this strange, and assume it is a choice for experts only. Two great features of psql are the online help for SQL and the tab completion feature, which allows you to build up SQL quickly without having to remember the syntax. See the *Using the psql query and scripting tool* recipe for more information.

pgAdmin also provides pgAgent, which is a task scheduler. Again, more portable schedulers are available, and you may wish to use those instead. Schedulers aren't covered in this book.

A quick warning! When you create an object in pgAdmin, the object will be created with a mixed case name if you use capitals anywhere in the object name. If I ask for a table named **MyTable**, the only way to access that table is by referring to it in double quotes as **MyTable**. See the *Handling objects with quoted names* recipe in Chapter 5, *Tables and Data*:

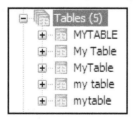

OmniDB

OmniDB is designed to access PostgreSQL, MySQL, MariaDB, and Oracle in one interface, though it makes sure it provides full features for the PostgreSQL database.

OmniDB is developing quickly, with monthly feature releases, so I recommend that you check out the latest information at `https://omnidb.org/`.

OmniDB provides a very responsive interface and is designed with full security in mind. It can be used as a desktop application and it can also be served using a web server, to be accessed by the web browser of your choice.

How to do it...

OmniDB has the standard tree-view browsing interface, with multi-tab access for each database server you access. It's easy to be connected to multiple PostgreSQL, MySQL, and Oracle database servers at the same time:

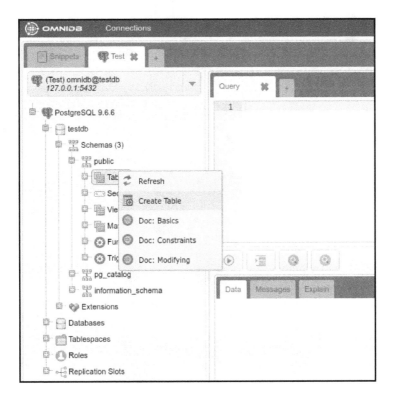

OmniDB has a SQL editor that has code completion and debugging. The EXPLAIN ANALYZE output is colored to highlight the areas of the plan that take the most time:

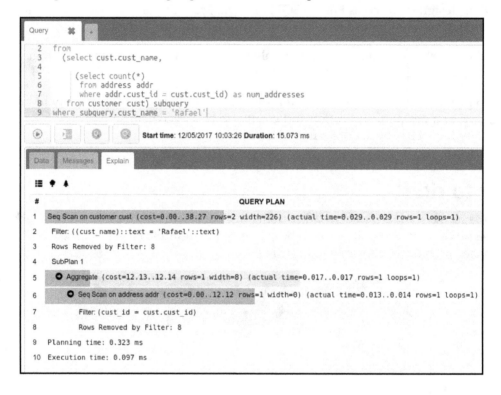

Or, if you prefer the command-line feel, try the **Console** tab:

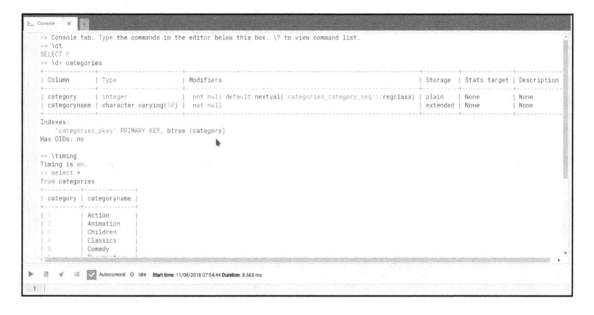

You can also visualize the query plan:

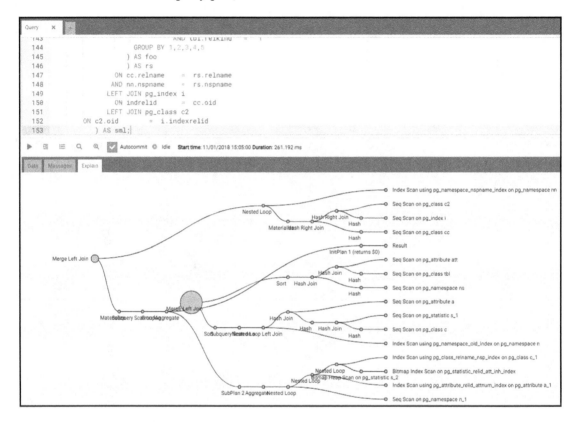

Administrators in OmniDB can manage users graphically. The interface gives you the ability to add, edit, and remove users, along with the ability to make someone a *superuser*. These users can then create connections to PostgreSQL, MySQL, MariaDB, and Oracle—all managed through a unified web page. Connections can also be made via SSH tunnels:

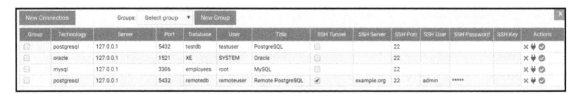

Group	Technology	Server	Port	Database	User	Title	SSH Tunnel	SSH Server	SSH Port	SSH User	SSH Password	SSH Key	Actions
	postgresql	127.0.0.1	5432	testdb	testuser	PostgreSQL			22				✕ ⬇ ✓
	oracle	127.0.0.1	1521	XE	SYSTEM	Oracle			22				✕ ⬇ ✓
	mysql	127.0.0.1	3306	employees	root	MySQL			22				✕ ⬇ ✓
	postgresql	127.0.0.1	5432	remotedb	remoteuser	Remote PostgreSQL	✔	example.org	22	admin	*****		✕ ⬇ ✓

In order to ease the process of developing code in PL/pgSQL, OmniDB provides a powerful, full-featured debugger. The debugger works as an inner tab of the SQL Editor and provides insights into parameters, variables, result, messages, and statistics in five tabs:

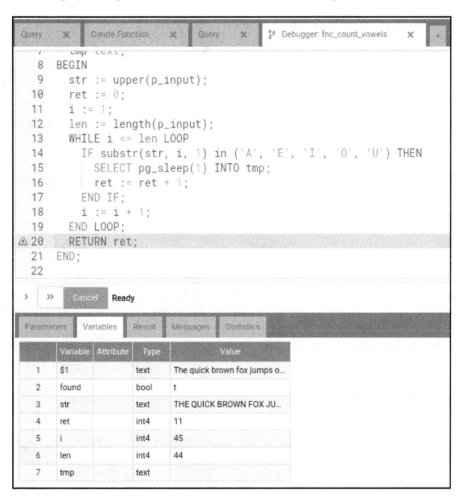

Another useful feature in OmniDB is the monitoring dashboard. The dashboard gives you real-time statistics of important metrics you might want to monitor, such as system **Memory Usage**, **CPU Usage**, and **Locks**:

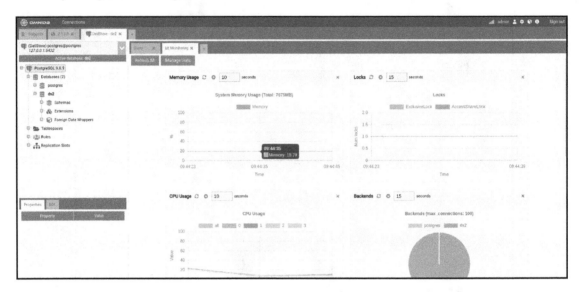

OmniDB has been designed to be a flexible and an extensible tool. Though it comes with several default charts, you can use Python and JSON to write new ones or use the existing ones as templates to enhance and expand. OmniDB provides a plugin API, allowing users to write and distribute their own plugins for expanded capabilities.

See also

You may also be interested in commercial tools of various kinds for PostgreSQL. A full listing is given in the PostgreSQL software catalog at http://www.postgresql.org/download/products/1.

Using the psql query and scripting tool

psql is the query tool supplied as a part of the core distribution of PostgreSQL, so it is available in all environments, and works similarly in all of them. This makes it an ideal choice for developing portable applications and techniques.

psql provides features for use as both an interactive query tool and as a scripting tool.

Getting ready

From here on, we will assume that the `psql` command is enough to allow you access to the PostgreSQL server. This assumes that all your connection parameters are defaults, which may not be true.

Written in full, the connection parameters would be either of these options:

```
psql -h myhost -p 5432 -d mydb -U myuser
psql postgresql://myuser@myhost:5432/mydb
```

The default value for the port (-p) is 5432. By default, `mydb` and `myuser` are both identical to the operating system's username. The default `myhost` on Windows is localhost, while on Unix, we use the default directory for Unix socket connections. The location of such directories varies across distributions and is set at compile time. However, note that you don't actually need to know its value, because on local connections, both the server and the client are normally compiled together, so they use the same default.

How to do it...

The command that executes a single SQL command and prints the output is the easiest, as shown here:

```
$ psql -c "SELECT current_time"
      timetz
-----------------
 18:48:32.484+01
(1 row)
```

The -c command is non-interactive. If we want to execute multiple commands, we can write those commands in a text file and then execute them using the -f option. This command loads a very small and simple set of examples:

```
$ psql -f examples.sql
```

It produces the following output when successful:

```
SET
SET
SET
SET
SET
SET
DROP SCHEMA
```

```
CREATE SCHEMA
SET
SET
SET
CREATE TABLE
CREATE TABLE
COPY 5
COPY 3
```

The `examples.sql` script is very similar to a dump file produced by PostgreSQL backup tools, so this type of file and the output it produces are very common. When a command is executed successfully, PostgreSQL outputs a `command` tag equal to the name of that command; this is how the preceding output was produced.

The `psql` tool can also be used with both the `-c` and `-f` modes together; each one can be used multiple times. In this case, it will execute all the commands consecutively:

```
$ psql -c "SELECT current_time" -f examples.sql -c "SELECT current_time"
    timetz
------------------
 18:52:15.287+01
(1 row)
    ...output removed for clarity...
    timetz
------------------
 18:58:23.554+01
(1 row)
```

The `psql` tool can also be used in interactive mode, which is the default, so it requires no option:

```
$ psql
postgres=#
```

The first interactive command you'll need is the following:

```
postgres=# help
```

You can then enter SQL or other commands. The following is the last interactive command you'll need:

```
postgres=# \quit
```

Unfortunately, you cannot type `quit` on its own, nor can you type `\exit`, or other options. Sorry, just `\quit`, or `\q` for short!

How it works...

In psql, you can enter the following two types of commands:

- psql meta-commands
- SQL

A meta-command is a command for the psql client, whereas SQL is sent to the database server. An example of a meta-command is \q, which tells the client to disconnect. All lines that begin with \ (backslash) as the first nonblank character are presumed to be meta-commands of some kind.

If it isn't a meta-command, it's SQL. We keep reading SQL until we find a semicolon, so we can spread SQL across many lines and format it any way we find convenient.

The help command is the only exception. We provide this for people who are completely lost, which is a good thought; so let's start from there ourselves.

There are two types of help commands, which are as follows:

- \?: This provides help on psql meta-commands
- \h: This provides help on specific SQL commands

Consider the following snippet as an example:

```
postgres=# \h DELETE
Command: DELETE
Description: delete rows of a table
Syntax:
[ WITH [ RECURSIVE ] with_query [, ...] ]
DELETE FROM [ ONLY ] table [ [ AS ] alias ]
    [ USING usinglist ]
    [ WHERE condition | WHERE CURRENT OF cursor_name ]
    [ RETURNING * | output_expression [ AS output_name ] [,]]
```

I find this a great way to discover and remember options and syntax. You'll also appreciate having the ability to scroll back through the previous command history.

You'll get a lot of benefits from tab completion, which will fill in the next part of the syntax when you press the *Tab* key. This also works for object names, so you can type in just the first few letters and then press *Tab*; all the options will be displayed. Thus, you can type in just enough letters to make the object name unique, and then hit *Tab* to get the rest of the name.

One-line comments begin with two dashes, as follows:

```
-- This is a single-line comment
```

Multiline comments are similar to those in C and Java:

```
/*
 * Multiline comment
 */
```

You'll probably agree that psql looks a little daunting at first, with strange backslash commands. I do hope you'll take a few moments to understand the interface and keep digging for more information. The `psql` tool is one of the most surprising parts of PostgreSQL, and it is incredibly useful for database administration tasks when used alongside other tools.

There's more...

`psql` works across releases and works well with older versions. It may not work at all with newer server versions, so use the latest client level of server you are accessing.

See also

Check out some other useful features of psql, which are as follows:

- Information functions
- Output formatting
- Execution timing using the `\timing` command
- Input/output and editing commands
- Automatic startup files, such as `.psqlrc`
- Substitutable parameters (variables)
- Access to the OS command line
- Crosstab views
- Conditional execution

Changing your password securely

If you are using password authentication, then you may wish to change your password from time to time.

How to do it...

The most basic method is to use the `psql` tool. The `\password` command will prompt you once for a new password and again to confirm. Connect to the `psql` tool and type the following:

```
SET password_encryption = 'scram-sha-256';
\password
```

Enter a new password. This causes psql to send a SQL statement to the PostgreSQL server, which contains an already encrypted password string. An example of the SQL statement sent is as follows:

```
ALTER USER postgres PASSWORD 'SCRAM-
SHA-256$4096:H45+UIZiJUcEXrB9SHlv5Q==$I0mc87UotsrnezRKv9Ijqn/zjWMGPVdy1zHPA
RAGfVs=:nSjwT9LGDmAsMo+GqbmC2X/9LMgowTQBjUQsl45gZzA=';
```

Make sure you use SCRAM-SHA-256 encryption, not the older and easily compromised md5 encryption. Whatever you do, don't use `postgres` as your password. This will make you vulnerable to idle hackers, so make it a little more difficult than that!

Make sure you don't forget your password either. It may prove difficult to maintain your database if you can't access it.

How it works...

As changing the password is just a SQL statement, any interface can do this. Other tools also allow this, such as the following:

- pgAdmin4
- phpPgAdmin

If you don't use one of the main routes to change the password, you can still do it yourself, using SQL from any interface. Note that you need to encrypt your password, because if you do submit a password in plain text, such as the following, it will be shipped to the server in plain text:

```
ALTER USER myuser PASSWORD 'secret'
```

Luckily, the password in this case will still be stored in an encrypted form. But it will also be recorded in plain text in psql's history file, as well as in any server and application logs, depending on the actual log-level settings.

PostgreSQL doesn't enforce a password change cycle, so you may wish to use more advanced authentication mechanisms, such as GSSAPI, SSPI, LDAP, or RADIUS.

Avoiding hardcoding your password

We can all agree that hardcoding your password is a bad idea. This recipe shows you how to keep your password in a secure password file.

Getting ready

Not all database users need passwords; some databases use other means of authentication. Don't perform this step unless you know you will be using password authentication, and you know your password.

First, remove the hardcoded password from where you set it previously. Completely remove the `password = xxxx` text from the connection string in a program. Otherwise, when you test the password file, the hardcoded setting will override the details you are about to place in the file. Keeping the password hardcoded and in the password file is not any better. Using `PGPASSWORD` is not recommended either, so remove that also.

If you think someone may have seen the password, change your password before placing it in the secure password file.

How to do it...

A password file contains the usual five fields that we require when connecting, as shown here:

```
host:port:dbname:user:password
```

Change this to the following:

```
myhost:5432:postgres:sriggs:moresecure
```

The password file is located using an environment variable named PGPASSFILE. If PGPASSFILE is not set, a default filename and location must be searched for, as follows:

- On *nix systems, look for ~/.pgpass
- On Windows systems, look for %APPDATA%\postgresql\pgpass.conf, where %APPDATA% is the application data subdirectory in the path (for me, that would be C:\)

> Don't forget to set the file permissions on the file, so that security is maintained. File permissions are not enforced on Windows, though the default location is secure. On *nix systems, you must issue the following command: chmod 0600 ~/.pgpass.
> If you forget to do this, the PostgreSQL client will ignore the .pgpass file. While the psql tool will issue a clear warning, many other clients will just fail silently, so don't forget!

How it works...

Many people name the password file .pgpass, whether or not they are on Windows, so don't get confused if they do this.

The password file can contain multiple lines. Each line is matched against the requested host:port:dbname:user combination until we find a line that matches. Then, we use that password.

Each item can be a literal value or *, a wildcard that matches anything. There is no support for partial matching. With appropriate permissions, a user can potentially connect to any database. Using the wildcard in the dbname and port fields makes sense, but it is less useful in other fields. The following are a few examples of wildcards:

- myhost:5432:*:sriggs:moresecurepw
- myhost:5432:perf:hannu:okpw
- myhost:*:perf:gianni:sicurissimo

There's more...

This looks like a good improvement if you have a few database servers. If you have many different database servers, you may want to think about using a connection service file instead (see the *Using a connection service file* recipe), or perhaps even storing details on a **Lightweight Directory Access Protocol** (**LDAP**) server.

Using a connection service file

As the number of connection options grows, you may want to consider using a connection service file.

The connection service file allows you to give a single name to a set of connection parameters. This can be accessed centrally, to avoid the need for individual users to know the host and port of the database, and it is more resistant to future change.

You can set up a system-wide file as well as individual per-user files. The default file paths for these files are /etc/pg_service.conf and ~/.pg_service.conf, respectively.

A system-wide connection file controls service names for all users from a single place, while a per-user file applies only to that particular user. Keep in mind that the per-user file overrides the system-wide file—if a service is defined in both the files, then the definition in the per-user file will prevail.

How to do it...

First, create a file named pg_service.conf with the following content:

```
[dbservice1]
host=postgres1
port=5432
dbname=postgres
```

You can then copy it to either /etc/pg_service.conf or another agreed upon central location. You can then set the PGSYSCONFDIR environment variable to that directory location.

Alternatively, you can copy it to `~/.pg_service.conf`. If you want to use a different name, set `PGSERVICEFILE`. Either way, you can then specify a connection string, such as the following:

```
service=dbservice1 user=sriggs
```

The service can also be set using an environment variable named `PGSERVICE`.

How it works...

This feature applies to `libpq` connections only, so it does not apply to JDBC.

The connection service file can also be used to specify the user, though that would mean that the username would be shared.

The `pg_service.conf` and `.pgpass` files can work together, or you can use just one of the two. Note that the `pg_service.conf` file is shared, so it is not a suitable place for passwords. The per-user connection service file is not shared, but in any case, it seems best to keep things separate and confine passwords to `.pgpass`.

Troubleshooting a failed connection

This recipe is all about what you should do when things go wrong.

Bear in mind that 90% of problems are just misunderstandings, and you'll quickly be on track again.

How to do it...

Here, we've made a checklist to be followed if a connection attempt fails:

- Check whether the database name and the username are accurate. You may be requesting a service on one system when the database you require is on another system. Recheck your credentials; ensure that you haven't mixed things up and that you are not using the database name as the username, or vice versa. If you receive too many connections, then you may need to disconnect another session before you can connect, or wait for the administrator to re-enable the connections.

- Check for explicit rejections. If you receive the `pg_hba.conf rejects connection for host...` error message, it means your connection attempt has been explicitly rejected by the database administrator for that server. You will not be able to connect from the current client system using those credentials. There is little point in attempting to contact the administrator, as you are violating an explicit security policy with what you are attempting to do.
- Check for implicit rejections. If the error message you receive is `no pg_hba.conf entry for...`, it means there is no explicit rule that matches your credentials. This is likely an oversight on the part of the administrator and is common in very complex networks. Contact the administrator and request a ruling on whether your connection should be allowed (hopefully) or explicitly rejected in the future.
- Check whether the connection works with psql. If you're trying to connect to PostgreSQL from anything other than the psql command-line utility, switch to that now. If you can make psql connect successfully, but cannot make your main connection work correctly, the problem may be in the local interface you are using.
- PostgreSQL 9.3 and later versions ship the `pg_isready` utility, which checks the status of a database server, either local or remote, by establishing a minimal connection. Only the hostname and port are mandatory, which is great if you don't know the database name, username, or password. The following outcomes are possible:
    - The server is running and accepting connections.
    - The server is running but not accepting connections (because it is starting up, shutting down, or in recovery).
    - A connection attempt was made, but it failed.
    - No connection attempt was made because of a client problem (invalid parameters, out of memory).
    - Check whether the server is up. If a server is shut down, you cannot connect. The typical problem here is simply mixing up the server to which you are connecting. You need to specify the hostname and port, so it's possible that you are mixing up those details.
    - Check whether the server is up and accepting new connections. A server that is shutting down will not accept new connections, apart from superusers. Also, a standby server may not have the `hot_standby` parameter enabled, preventing you from connecting.

- Check whether the server is listening correctly, and check the port to which the server is actually listening. Confirm that the incoming request is arriving on the interface listed in the `listen_addresses` parameter. Check whether it is set to * for remote connections and `localhost` for local connections.
- Check whether the database name and username exist. It's possible that the database or user no longer exists.
- Check the connection request; that is, check whether the connection request was successful and was somehow dropped following the connection. You can confirm this by looking at the server log when the following parameters are enabled:

```
log_connections = on
log_disconnections = on
```

- Check for other reasons for disconnection. If you are connecting to a standby server, it is possible that you have been disconnected because of Hot Standby conflicts. See `Chapter 12`, *Replication and Upgrades*, for more information.

There's more...

Client authentication and security are the rapidly changing areas in subsequent major PostgreSQL releases. You will also find differences between maintenance release levels. The PostgreSQL documents on this topic can be viewed at
`http://www.postgresql.org/docs/current/interactive/client-authentication.html`.

Always check which release level you are using before consulting the manual or asking for support. Many problems are caused simply by confusing the capabilities between release levels.

2
Exploring the Database

To understand PostgreSQL, you need to see it in use. An empty database is like a ghost town without houses.

For now, we will assume that you already have a database. There are over a thousand books on how to design your own database from nothing. So, here, we aim to help people who are still learning to use the PostgreSQL database management system with handy routines to explore the database.

The best way to start is by asking some simple questions to orient yourself and begin the process of understanding. Incidentally, these are also questions you'll need to answer if you ask someone else for help.

In this chapter, we'll cover the following recipes:

- What type of server is this?
- What version is the server?
- What is the server uptime?
- Locating the database server files
- Locating the database server's message log
- Locating the database's system identifier
- Listing databases on the database server
- How many tables are there in a database?
- How much disk space does a database use?
- How much disk space does a table use?
- Which are my biggest tables?
- How many rows are there in a table?
- Quickly estimating the number of rows in a table
- Listing extensions in this database
- Understanding object dependencies

What type of server is this?

PostgreSQL is an open source **object-relational database management system** (**ORDBMS**) distributed under a very permissive license, and developed by an active community.

There are a number of PostgreSQL-related services and software (`https://wiki.` `postgresql.org/wiki/PostgreSQL_derived_databases`), either open source or not, that are provided by other software companies. Here, we discuss how to recognize which one you are using.

It is not so easy to detect the variant of PostgreSQL from the name; many of the products and services involving PostgreSQL include the word **Postgres** or **PostgreSQL**.

However, if you need to check the documentation, or to buy services such as support and consulting, you need to find out exactly what type your server is, as the available options will vary.

If you are paying a license fee or a cloud service subscription, you will already know the name of the company you are paying, and of the specific variant of PostgreSQL you are subscribed to. But, it's not rare to have multiple servers of different types, so it is still useful to be able to tell them apart.

How to do it...

Unfortunately, there isn't a single function or parameter that works on each *variant* of PostgreSQL and at the same time is able to answer that question. The closest you can get is the `version()` function that is used in the next recipe, *What version is the server?*, which returns a textual description of the version you are running, including (but not limited to) the version number.

In some cases, this is enough, but otherwise, you have to determine the specific version from other clues, such as the following:

- The version number for stable releases of community PostgreSQL is either $X.Y$ (with $X=10$ or above) or $X.Y.Z$ (up to $X=9$). An extra number usually indicates that you are running a variant of PostgreSQL.
- The presence of certain objects that are available only on a specific variant, for instance an extension. More details on how to work with extensions can be found in the *Listing extensions in this database* recipe in this chapter.

There's more...

Some of the PostgreSQL-based services on the cloud will return the same value of version() as community PostgreSQL does. While this is correct, in the sense that they are indeed running that version of PostgreSQL, it doesn't mean that you have the same level of control. For instance, you might not be given a superuser account, and you will probably be unable to install extensions freely.

What version is the server?

PostgreSQL has internal version numbers for the data file format, database catalog layout, and crash recovery format. Each of these is checked as the server runs to ensure that the data doesn't become corrupt. PostgreSQL doesn't change these internal formats for a single release; they only change across releases.

From a user's perspective, each release differs in terms of the way the server behaves. If you know your application well, then it should be possible to assess the differences simply by reading the release notes for each version. In many cases, a retest of the application is the safest thing to do.

If you experience any general problems related to setup and configuration with your database, then you'll need to double-check which version of the server you have. This will help you to report a fault or to consult the correct version of the manual.

How to do it...

We will find out the version by directly querying the database server:

1. Connect to the database and issue the following command:

```
postgres # SELECT version();
```

2. You'll get a response that looks something like this:

```
PostgreSQL 11.2 on x86_64-apple-darwin16.7.0,
compiled by Apple LLVM version 9.0.0 (clang-900.0.39.2), 64-bit
```

That's probably too much information all at once!

Some other ways of checking the version number are as follows:

```
bash # psql --version
psql (PostgreSQL) 11.2
```

However, be wary that this shows the client software version number, which may differ from the server software version number. You should check the server version directly by using the following command:

```
bash # cat $PGDATA/PG_VERSION
```

Here, you must set PGDATA to the actual data directory. Refer to the *Locating the database server files* recipe for more information.

Notice that the preceding command does not show the maintenance release number.

How it works...

The current PostgreSQL server version format is composed of two numbers; the first number indicates the major release, and the second one denotes subsequent maintenance releases for that major release. It is common to mention just the major release when discussing what features are supported, as they are unchanged on a maintenance release.

11.0 is the first release of PostgreSQL 11, and subsequent maintenance releases will be 11.1, 11.2, 11.3, and so on. In the preceding example, we see that 11.2 is the version of that PostgreSQL server.

For each major release, there is a separate version of the manual, since the feature set is not the same. If something doesn't work exactly the way you think it should, make sure you are consulting the correct version of the manual.

There's more...

Prior to release 10, PostgreSQL used a three-part numbering series, meaning that the feature set and compatibility related to the first two numbers, while maintenance releases were denoted by the third number. For instance, version 9.4 contains more additional features and compatibility changes when compared to version 9.3; version 9.4.0 was the initial release of 9.4, and version 9.4.1 was a later maintenance release.

The release support policy for PostgreSQL is available at http://www.postgresql.org/support/versioning/. This article explains that each release will be supported for a period of five years. Since we release one major version per year, this means five major releases.

Support for all releases up to and including 9.3, ended in September 2018. So, by the time you're reading this book, only PostgreSQL 9.4 and higher versions will be supported. The earlier versions are still robust, though many performance and enterprise features are missing from those releases. The future end-of-support dates are as follows:

Version	Last supported date
PostgreSQL 9.4	December 2019
PostgreSQL 9.5	January 2021
PostgreSQL 9.6	September 2021
PostgreSQL 10	September 2022
PostgreSQL 11	October 2023

What is the server uptime?

You may wonder, how long has it been since the server started?

For instance, you might want to verify that there was no server crash if your server is not monitored; or to see when the server was last restarted, for instance, to change the configuration. We will find this out by asking the database server.

How to do it...

Issue the following SQL from any interface:

```
postgres=# SELECT date_trunc('second', current_timestamp -
pg_postmaster_start_time()) as uptime;
```

You should get the output as follows:

```
        uptime
-------------------------------------
 2 days 02:48:04
```

How it works...

Postgres stores the server start time, so we can access it directly, as follows:

```
postgres=# SELECT pg_postmaster_start_time();
pg_postmaster_start_time
--------------------------------------------------
2018-01-01 19:37:41.389134+00
```

Then, we can write a SQL query to get the uptime, like this:

```
postgres=# SELECT current_timestamp - pg_postmaster_start_time();

?column?
------------------------------------------------------
2 days 02:50:02.23939
```

Finally, we can apply some formatting:

```
postgres=# SELECT date_trunc('second', current_timestamp -
pg_postmaster_start_time()) as uptime;
    uptime
------------------------------
2 days 02:51:18
```

See also

This is simple stuff. Further monitoring and statistics are covered in `Chapter 8`, *Monitoring and Diagnosis*.

Locating the database server files

Database server files are initially stored in a location referred to as the **data directory**. Additional data files may also be stored in tablespaces, if any exist.

In this recipe, you will learn how to find the location of these directories on a given database server.

Getting ready

You'll need to get operating system access to the database system, which is what we call the platform on which the database runs.

How to do it...

The following are the system default `data` directory locations:

- Debian or Ubuntu systems: `/var/lib/postgresql/MAJOR_RELEASE/main`
- Red Hat RHEL, CentOS, and Fedora: `/var/lib/pgsql/data/`
- Windows: `C:\Program Files\PostgreSQL\MAJOR_RELEASE\data`

`MAJOR_RELEASE` is composed of just one number (for release 10 and above) or by two (for releases up to 9.6).

On Debian or Ubuntu systems, the configuration files are located in `/etc/postgresql/MAJOR_RELEASE/main/`, where `main` is just the name of a database server. Other names are also possible. For the sake of simplicity, we assume that you only have a single installation, although the point of including the release number and database server name as components of the directory path is to allow multiple database servers to coexist on the same host.

> The `pg_lsclusters` utility is specific to Debian/Ubuntu, and displays a list of all the available database servers, including information, such as the following, for each server:
>
> - Major release number
> - Port
> - Status (for example, online and down)
> - Data directory
> - Log file
>
> The `pg_lsclusters` utility is part of the `postgresql-common` Debian/Ubuntu package, which provides a structure under which multiple versions of PostgreSQL can be installed, and multiple clusters can be maintained, at one time.

In the packages distributed with Red Hat RHEL, CentOS, and Fedora, the default data directory location also contains the configuration files (`*.conf`) by default. However, note that the packages distributed by the PostgreSQL community use a different default location `/var/lib/pgsql/MAJOR_RELEASE/data/`.

Again, that is just the default location. You can create additional data directories using the `initdb` utility.

The `initdb` utility populates the given data directory with the initial content. The directory will be created for convenience if it is missing, but for safety, the utility will stop if the `data` directory is not empty. The `initdb` utility will read the `data` directory name from the `PGDATA` environment variable unless the `-d` command-line option is used.

How it works...

Even though the Debian/Ubuntu and Red Hat file layouts are different, they both follow the Linux **Filesystem Hierarchy Standard** (**FHS**), so neither layout is wrong.

The Red Hat layout is simpler and easier to understand. The Debian/Ubuntu layout is more complex, but it has different and more adventurous goals. The Debian/Ubuntu layout is similar to the **Optimal Flexible Architecture** (**OFA**) of other database systems. As pointed out earlier, the goals are to provide a file layout that will allow you to have multiple PostgreSQL database servers on one system and to allow many versions of the software to exist in the filesystem at once.

Again, the layouts for the Windows and OS X installers are different. Multiple database clusters are possible, but they are also more complex than on Debian/Ubuntu.

I recommend that you follow the Debian/Ubuntu layout on whichever platform you are using. It doesn't really have a name, so I call it the **PostgreSQL Flexible Architecture** (**PFA**). Clearly, if you are using Debian or Ubuntu, then the Debian/Ubuntu layout is already being used. If you do this on other platforms, you'll need to lay things out yourself, but it does pay off in the long run. To implement PFA, you can set the following environment variables to name parts of the file layout:

```
export PGROOT=/var/lib/pgsql/
export PGRELEASE=10
export PGSERVERNAME=mamba
export PGDATA=$PGROOT/$PGRELEASE/$PGSERVERNAME
```

In this example, `PGDATA` is `/var/lib/pgsql/10/mamba`.

Finally, you must run `initdb` to actually initialize the `data` directory, as noted earlier, and custom administration scripts should be prepared to automate actions, such as starting or stopping the database server, when the system undergoes similar procedures.

Note that server applications such as initdb can only work with one major PostgreSQL version. On distributions that allow several major versions, such as Debian or Ubuntu, these applications are placed in dedicated directories, which are not put in the default command path. This means that if you just type initdb, the system will not find the executable, and you will get an error message.

This may look like a bug, but in fact it is the desired behavior. Instead of directly accessing initdb, you are supposed to use the pg_createcluster utility from postgresql-common, which will select the right initdb utility depending on the major version you specify.

If you plan to run more than one database server on the same host, you must set the preceding variables differently for each server, as they determine the name of the data directory. For instance, you can set them in the script that you use to start or stop the database server, which would be enough, because PGDATA is mostly used only by the database server process.

There's more...

Once you've located the data directory, you can look for the files that comprise the PostgreSQL database server. The layout is as follows:

Subdirectory	Purpose
base	This is the main table storage. Beneath this directory, each database has its own directory, within which are the files for each database table or index.
global	Here are the tables that are shared across all databases, including the list of databases.
pg_commit_ts	Here we store transaction commit timestamp data (from 9.5 onward).
pg_dynshmem	This includes dynamic shared memory information (from 9.4 onward).
pg_logical	This includes logical decoding status data.
pg_multixact	This includes files used for shared row-level locks.
pg_notify	This includes the LISTEN/NOTIFY status files.
pg_replslot	This includes information about replication slots (from 9.4 onward).
pg_serial	This includes information on committed serializable transactions.
pg_snapshots	This includes exported snapshot files.
pg_stat	This includes permanent statistics data.
pg_stat_tmp	This includes transient statistics data.
pg_subtrans	This includes subtransaction status data.
pg_tblspc	This includes symbolic links to tablespace directories.

`pg_twophase`	This includes state files for prepared transactions.
`pg_wal`	This includes the transaction log or **Write-Ahead Log** (**WAL**) (formerly `pg_xlog`).
`pg_xact`	This includes the transaction status files (formerly `pg_clog`).

None of the aforementioned directories contain user-modifiable files, nor should any of the files be manually deleted in order to save space, or for any other reason. *Don't touch it, because you'll break it, and you may not be able to fix it!* It's not even sensible to copy files in these directories without carefully following the procedures described in Chapter 11, *Backup and Recovery*. Keep off the grass!

We'll talk about tablespaces later in the book. We'll also discuss a performance enhancement that involves putting the transaction log on its own set of disk drives in Chapter 10, *Performance and Concurrency*.

The only things you are allowed to touch are configuration files, which are all `*.conf` files, and server message log files. Server message log files may or may not be in the data directory. For more details on this, refer to the next recipe, *Locating the database server's message log*.

Locating the database server's message log

The database server's message log is a record of all messages recorded by the database server. This is the first place to look if you have server problems, and a good place to check regularly.

This log will include messages that look something like the following:

```
2016-09-01 19:37:41 GMT [2507-1] LOG:   database system was shut down at
2016-09-01 19:37:38 GMT

2016-09-01 19:37:41 GMT [2506-1] LOG:   database system is ready to accept
connections
```

We'll explain some more about these logs once we've located the files.

Getting ready

You'll need to get operating system access to the database system, which is what we call the platform on which the database runs.

The server log can be in a few different places, so let's list all of them first so that we can locate the log or decide where we want it to be placed:

- The server log may be in a directory beneath the data directory.
- It may be in a directory elsewhere on the filesystem.
- It may be redirected to `syslog`.
- There may be no server log at all. In this case, it's time to add a log soon.

If not redirected to `syslog`, the server log consists of one or more files. You can change the names of these files, so it may not always be the same on every system.

How to do it...

The following are the default server log locations:

- Debian or Ubuntu systems: `/var/log/postgresql`
- Red Hat, RHEL, CentOS, and Fedora: `/var/lib/pgsql/data/pg_log`
- Windows systems: The messages are sent to the Windows Event Log

The current server log file is named `postgresql-MAJOR_RELEASE-SERVER.log`, where `SERVER` is the name of the server (by default, `main`), and `MAJOR_RELEASE` represents the major release of the server, for example, 9.6 or 11 (as we mentioned in a prior recipe, from release 10 onward the major release is composed by just one number). An example is `postgresql-11-main.log`, while older log files are numbered as `postgresql-11-main.log.1`. The higher the final number, the older the file, since they are being rotated by the `logrotate` utility.

How it works...

The server log is just a file that records messages from the server. Each message has a severity level, the most typical of them being `LOG`, though there are others, as shown in the following table:

PostgreSQL severity	Meaning	Syslog severity	Windows Event Log
DEBUG 1 to DEBUG 5	This comprises the internal diagnostics.	DEBUG	INFORMATION
INFO	This is the command output for the user.	INFO	INFORMATION
NOTICE	This is helpful information.	NOTICE	INFORMATION
WARNING	This warns of likely problems.	NOTICE	WARNING

ERROR	This is the current command that is aborted.	WARNING	ERROR
LOG	This is useful for sysadmins.	INFO	INFORMATION
FATAL	This is the event that disconnects one session only.	ERR	ERROR
PANIC	This is the event that crashes the server.	CRIT	ERROR

Watch out for FATAL and PANIC. This shouldn't happen in most cases during normal server operation, apart from certain cases related to replication, so you should also check out Chapter 12, *Replication and Upgrades*.

You can adjust the number of messages that appear in the log by changing the log_min_messages server parameter. You can also change the amount of information that is displayed for each event by changing the log_error_verbosity parameter. If the messages are sent to a standard log file, then each line in the log will have a prefix of useful information that can also be controlled by the system administrator, with a parameter named log_line_prefix.

You can also alter the *what* and the *how much* that goes into the logs by changing other settings such as log_statements, log_checkpoints, log_connections/log_disconnections, log_verbosity, and log_lock_waits.

There's more...

The log_destination parameter controls where the log messages are stored. The valid values are stderr, csvlog, syslog, and eventlog (the latter is only on Windows).

The logging collector is a background process that writes to a log file everything that the PostgreSQL server outputs to stderr. This is probably the most reliable way to log messages in case of problems, since it depends on fewer services.

Log rotation can be controlled with settings such as log_rotation_age and log_rotation_size if you are using the logging collector. Alternatively, it is possible to configure the logrotate utility to perform log rotation, which is the default on Debian and Ubuntu systems.

See also

In general, monitoring activities are covered in Chapter 8, *Monitoring and Diagnosis*, and examining the message log is just one part of it. Refer to the *Producing a daily summary of log file errors* recipe in Chapter 8, *Monitoring and Diagnosis*, for more details.

Locating the database's system identifier

Each database server has a system identifier assigned when the database is initialized (created). The server identifier remains the same if the server is backed up, cloned, and so on.

Many actions on the server are keyed to the system identifier, and you may be asked to provide this information when you report a fault.

In this recipe, you will learn how to display the system identifier.

Getting ready

You need to connect as the Postgres OS user, or another user with execute privileges on the server software.

How to do it...

In order to display the system identifier, we just need to launch the following command:

```
pg_controldata <data-directory> | grep "system identifier"
Database system identifier:          5558338346489861223
```

Note that the preceding syntax will not work on Debian or Ubuntu systems, for the same reasons explained for initdb in the *Locating the database server files* recipe. However, in this case, there is no postgresql-common alternative, so if you must run pg_controldata, you need to specify the full path to the executable, as in this example:

```
/usr/lib/postgresql/11/bin/pg_controldata $PGDATA
```

Don't use -D in front of the data directory name. This is the only PostgreSQL server application where you don't need to do that.

How it works...

The pg_controldata utility is a PostgreSQL server application that shows the content of a server's control file. The control file is located within the data directory of a server, and it is created at database initialization time. Some of the information within it is updated regularly, and some is only updated when certain major events occur.

The full output of pg_controldata looks like the following (some values may change over time as the server runs):

```
pg_control version number: 1100
Catalog version number: 201809051
Database system identifier: 6678846522653464085
Database cluster state: in production
pg_control last modified: Sun Apr 14 22:37:42 2019
Latest checkpoint location: 0/B29DDF8
... (not shown in full)
```

Never edit the PostgreSQL control file. If you do, the server probably won't start correctly, or you may mask other errors. And if you do that, people will be able to tell, so fess up as soon as possible!

Listing databases on the database server

When we connect to PostgreSQL, we always connect to just one specific database on any database server. If there are many databases on a single server, it can get confusing, so sometimes you may just want to find out which databases are parts of the database server.

This is also confusing because we can use the word database in two different, but related, contexts. Initially, we start off by thinking that PostgreSQL is a database in which we put data, referring to the whole database server by just the word *database*. In PostgreSQL, a database server (also known as **cluster**) is potentially split into multiple, individual databases, so, as you get more used to working with PostgreSQL, you'll start to separate the two concepts.

How to do it...

If you have access to `psql`, you can type the following command:

```
bash $ psql -l
                            List of databases
    Name     | Owner  | Encoding |   Collate   |    Ctype    | Access
privileges
-----------+--------+----------+-------------+-------------+---------------
----
 postgres   | sriggs | UTF8     | en_GB.UTF-8 | en_GB.UTF-8 |
 template0  | sriggs | UTF8     | en_GB.UTF-8 | en_GB.UTF-8 | =c/sriggs
+
            |        |          |             |             |
sriggs=CTc/sriggs
 template1  | sriggs | UTF8     | en_GB.UTF-8 | en_GB.UTF-8 | =c/sriggs
+
            |        |          |             |             |
sriggs=CTc/sriggs
(3 rows)
```

You can also get the same information while running `psql` by simply typing `\l`.

The information that we just looked at is stored in a PostgreSQL catalog table named `pg_database`. We can issue a SQL query directly against that table from any connection to get a simpler result, as follows:

```
postgres=# select datname from pg_database;
datname
-----------
template1
template0
postgres
(3 rows)
```

How it works...

PostgreSQL starts with three databases: `template0`, `template1`, and `postgres`. The main user database is `postgres`.

You can create your own databases as well, like this:

```
CREATE DATABASE my_database;
```

You can do the same from the command line, using the following expression:

```
bash $ createdb my_database
```

After you've created your databases, be sure to secure them properly, as discussed in `Chapter 6`, *Security*.

When you create another database, it actually takes a copy of an existing database. Once it is created, there is no further link between the two databases.

The `template0` and `template1` databases are known as **template databases**. The `template1` database can be changed to allow you to create a localized template for any new databases that you create. The `template0` database exists so that, when you alter `template1`, you still have a pristine copy on which to fall back on. In other words, if you break `template1`, then you can drop it and recreate it from `template0`.

You can drop the database named `postgres`. But don't, okay? Similarly, don't try to touch `template0`, because you won't be allowed to do anything with it, except use it as a template. On the other hand, the `template1` database exists to be modified, so feel free to change it.

There's more...

The information that we just saw is stored in a PostgreSQL catalog table named `pg_database`. We can look at this directly to get some more information. In some ways, the output is less useful as well, as we need to look up some of the code in other tables:

```
postgres=# \x
postgres=# select * from pg_database;
-[ RECORD 1 ]-+-------------------------------
datname       | template1
datdba        | 10
encoding      | 6
datcollate    | en_GB.UTF-8
datctype      | en_GB.UTF-8
datistemplate | t
datallowconn  | t
datconnlimit  | -1
datlastsysoid | 11620
datfrozenxid  | 644
dattablespace | 1663
datacl        | {=c/sriggs,sriggs=CTc/sriggs}
-[ RECORD 2 ]-+-------------------------------
datname       | template0
```

```
datdba        | 10
encoding      | 6
datcollate    | en_GB.UTF-8
datctype      | en_GB.UTF-8
datistemplate | t
datallowconn  | f
datconnlimit  | -1
datlastsysoid | 11620
datfrozenxid  | 644
dattablespace | 1663
datacl        | {=c/sriggs,sriggs=CTc/sriggs}
-[ RECORD 3 ]-+-------------------------------
datname       | postgres
datdba        | 10
encoding      | 6
datcollate    | en_GB.UTF-8
datctype      | en_GB.UTF-8
datistemplate | f
datallowconn  | t
datconnlimit  | -1
datlastsysoid | 11620
datfrozenxid  | 644
dattablespace | 1663
datacl        |
```

First of all, look at the use of the \x command. It makes the output in psql appear as one column per line, rather than one row per line.

We've already discussed templates. The other interesting things are that we can turn connections on and off for a database, and we can set connection limits for them, as well.

Also, you can see that each database has a default tablespace. Therefore, data tables get created inside one specific database, and the data files for that table get placed in one tablespace.

You can also see that each database has a collation sequence, which is the way that various language features are defined. We'll cover more on that in the *Choosing good names for database objects* recipe in Chapter 5, *Tables and Data*.

How many tables are there in a database?

The number of tables in a relational database is a good measure of the complexity of a database, so it is a simple way to get to know any database. But the complexity of what? Well, a complex database may have been designed to be deliberately flexible in order to cover a variety of business situations, or a complex business process may have a limited portion of its details covered in the database. So, a large number of tables might likely reveal a complex business process, or just a complex piece of software.

In this recipe, we will show you how to compute the number of tables.

How to do it...

From any interface, type the following SQL command:

```
SELECT count(*) FROM information_schema.tables
WHERE table_schema NOT IN ('information_schema','pg_catalog');
```

You can also look at the list of tables directly, and judge whether the list is a small or large number.

In `psql`, you can see your own tables by using the following command:

```
$ psql -c "\d"
        List of relations
 Schema |   Name   | Type  |  Owner
--------+----------+-------+----------
 public | accounts | table | postgres
 public | branches | table | postgres
```

In **pgAdmin 4**, you can see the tables in the tree view on the left-hand side, as shown in the following screenshot:

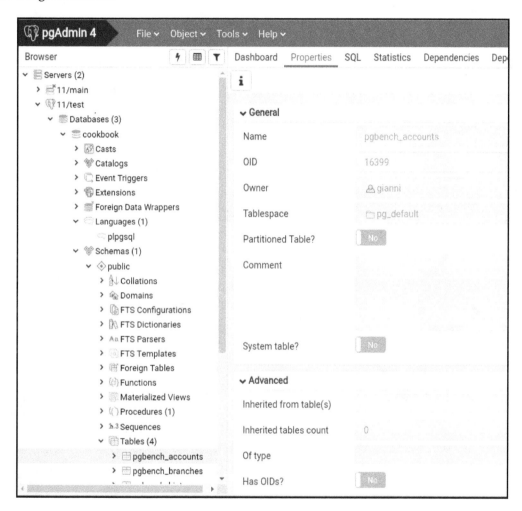

How it works...

PostgreSQL stores information about the database in catalog tables. They describe every aspect of the way the database has been defined. There is a main set of catalog tables stored in a schema, called `pg_catalog`. There is a second set of catalog objects called the **information schema**, which is the SQL standard way of accessing information in a relational database.

We want to exclude both of these schemas from our query. Otherwise, we'll get too much information. We excluded them in the preceding query using the NOT IN phrase in the WHERE clause.

 Note that this query shows only the number of tables in one of the databases on the PostgreSQL server. You can only see the tables in the database to which you are currently connected, so you'll need to run the same query on each database in turn.

There's more...

The highest number of distinct, major tables I've ever seen in a database is 20,000, without counting partitions, views, and work tables. That clearly rates as a very complex system:

Number of distinct tables (entities)	Complexity rating
20,000	This is incredibly complex. You're either counting wrong or you have a big team to manage this.
2,000	This is a complex business database. Usually, not many of these are seen.
200	This is a typical modern business database.
20	This is a simple business database.
2	This is a database with a single, clear purpose, strictly designed for performance or some other goal.
0	This tells you that you haven't loaded any data yet!

Of course, you can't always easily tell which tables are entities, so we just need to count the tables. Some databases use a lot of partitions or similar tables, so the numbers can grow dramatically. I've seen databases with up to 200,000 tables (of any kind). That's not recommended, however, as the database catalog tables then begin to become awfully large.

How much disk space does a database use?

It is very important to allocate sufficient disk space for your database. If the disk gets full, it will not corrupt the data, but it might lead to database server panic and then consequent shutdown.

For planning or space monitoring, we often need to know how big the database is.

How to do it...

We can do this in the following ways:

- Look at the size of the files that make up the database server.
- Run a SQL request to confirm the database size.

If you look at the size of the actual files, you'll need to make sure that you include the data directory and all subdirectories, as well as all other directories that contain tablespaces. This can be tricky, and it is also difficult to break out all the different pieces.

The easiest way is to ask the database a simple query, like this:

```
SELECT pg_database_size(current_database());
```

However, this is limited to only the current database. If you want to know the size of all the databases together, then you'll need a query such as the following:

```
SELECT sum(pg_database_size(datname)) from pg_database;
```

How it works...

The database server knows which tables it has loaded. It also knows how to calculate the size of each table, so the `pg_database_size()` function just looks at the file sizes.

How much disk space does a table use?

The maximum supported table size is 32 TB and it does not require large file support from the operating system. The file system size limits do not impact the large tables, as they are stored in multiple 1 GB files.

Large tables can suffer performance issues. Indexes can take much longer to update and query performance can degrade. In this recipe, we will see how to measure the size of a table.

How to do it...

We can see the size of a table by using this command:

```
postgres=# select pg_relation_size('pgbench_accounts');
```

The output of this command is as follows:

```
pg_relation_size
------------------
        13582336
(1 row)
```

We can also see the total size of a table, including indexes and other related spaces, as follows:

```
postgres=# select pg_total_relation_size('pgbench_accounts');
```

The output is as follows:

```
pg_total_relation_size
------------------------
        15425536
(1 row)
```

We can also use a `psql` command, like this:

```
postgres=# \dt+ pgbench_accounts
                       List of relations
 Schema |       Name       | Type  | Owner  | Size  | Description
--------+------------------+-------+--------+-------+-------------
 gianni | pgbench_accounts | table | gianni | 13 MB |
(1 row)
```

How it works...

In PostgreSQL, a table is made up of many relations. The main relation is the data table. In addition, there are a variety of additional data files. Each index created on a table is also a relation. Long data values are placed in a secondary table named TOAST, so, in most cases, each table also has a TOAST table and a TOAST index.

Each relation consists of multiple data files. The main data files are broken into 1 GB pieces. The first file has no suffix; others have a numbered suffix (such as .2). There are also files marked _vm and _fsm, which represent the visibility map and free space map, respectively. They are used as part of maintenance operations. They stay fairly small, even for very large tables.

There's more...

The preceding functions, which measure the size of a relation, output the number of bytes, which is normally too large to be immediately clear. You can apply the pg_size_pretty() function to format that number nicely, as shown in the following example:

```
SELECT pg_size_pretty(pg_relation_size('pgbench_accounts'));
```

This yields the following output:

```
pg_size_pretty
----------------
13 MB
(1 row)
```

TOAST stands for **The Oversized-Attribute Storage Technique**. As the name implies, this is a mechanism used to store long column values. PostgreSQL allows many data types to store values up to 1 GB in size. It transparently stores large data items in many smaller pieces, so the same data type can be used for data ranging from 1 byte to 1 GB. When appropriate, values are automatically compressed and decompressed before they are split and stored, so the actual limit will vary, depending on compressibility.

You may also see files ending in _init; they are used by unlogged tables and their indexes, for restoring them after a crash. Unlogged objects are called this way because they do not produce WAL. So, they support faster writes, but in the event of a crash they must be truncated, that is, restored to an empty state.

Which are my biggest tables?

We've looked at getting the size of a specific table, so now it's time to widen the problem to related areas. Rather than having an absolute value for a specific table, let's look at the relative sizes.

How to do it...

The following basic query will tell us the 10 biggest tables:

```
SELECT table_name,pg_relation_size(table_schema || '.' || table_name) as
size
FROM information_schema.tables
WHERE table_schema NOT IN ('information_schema', 'pg_catalog')
ORDER BY size DESC
LIMIT 10;
```

The tables are shown in descending order of size, with at the most 10 rows displayed. In this case, we look at all the tables in all the schemas, apart from the tables in information_schema or pg_catalog, like we did in the *How many tables are in the database?* recipe.

How it works...

PostgreSQL provides a dedicated function, pg_relation_size, to compute the actual disk space used by a specific table or index. We just need to provide the table name. In addition to the main data files, there are other files (called **forks**) that can be measured by specifying an optional second argument. These include the **Visibility Map (VM)**, the **Free Space Map (FSM)**, and the **initialization fork** for unlogged objects.

How many rows are there in a table?

There is no limit on the number of rows in a table but it is limited to available disk space and memory/swap space. If you are storing rows that exceed 2 KB aggregated data size, then the maximum number of rows may be limited to 4 billion or less.

Counting is one of the easiest SQL statements, so it is also many people's first experience of a PostgreSQL query.

How to do it...

From any interface, the SQL command used to count rows is as follows:

```
SELECT count(*) FROM table;
```

This will return a single integer value as the result.

In `psql`, the command looks like the following:

```
postgres=# select count(*) from orders;
 count
-------
   345
(1 row)
```

How it works...

PostgreSQL can choose between two techniques available to compute the SQL count (*) function. Both are available in all the currently supported versions:

- The first is called **sequential scan**. We access every data block in the table one after the other, reading the number of rows in each block. If the table is on the disk, it will cause a beneficial disk access pattern, and the statement will be fairly fast.
- The other technique is known as **index-only scan**. It requires an index on the table, and it covers a more general case than optimizing SQL queries with count (*), so we will cover it in more detail in Chapter 10, *Performance and Concurrency*.

Some people think that the count SQL statement is a good test of the performance of a DBMS. Some DBMS have specific tuning features for the count SQL statement, and Postgres optimizes this using index-only scans. The PostgreSQL project has talked about this many times, but few people thought we should try to optimize this. Yes, the count function is frequently used within applications, but without any WHERE clause, it is not that useful. Therefore, the index-only scans feature has been implemented, which applies to more real-world situations, as well as this recipe.

We scan every block of the table because of a major feature of Postgres, named **Multiversion Concurrency Control** (**MVCC**). MVCC allows us to run the count SQL statement at the same time that we are inserting, updating, or deleting data from the table. That's a very cool feature, and we went to a lot of trouble in Postgres to provide it for you.

MVCC requires us to record information on each row of a table, stating when that change was made. If the changes were made after the SQL statement began to execute, then we just ignore those changes. This means that we need to carry out visibility checks on each row in the table to allow us to work out the results of the count SQL statement. The optimization provided by index-only scans is the ability to skip such checks on the table blocks that are already known to be visible to all current sessions. Rows in these blocks can be counted directly on the index, which is normally smaller than the table, and is, therefore, faster.

If you think a little deeper about this, you'll see that the result of the count SQL statement is just the value at a moment in time. Depending on what happens to the table, that value could change a little or a lot while the count SQL statement is executing. So, once you've executed this, all you really know is that, at a particular point in the past, there were exactly x rows in the table.

Quickly estimating the number of rows in a table

We don't always need an accurate count of rows, especially on a large table that may take a long time to execute. Administrators often need to estimate how big a table is so that they can estimate how long other operations may take.

How to do it...

We can get a quick estimate of the number of rows in a table using roughly the same calculation that Postgres optimizer uses:

```
SELECT (CASE WHEN reltuples > 0 THEN
pg_relation_size(oid)*reltuples/(8192*relpages)
ELSE 0
END)::bigint AS estimated_row_count
FROM pg_class
WHERE oid = 'mytable'::regclass;
```

This gives us the following output:

```
estimated_count
---------------------
            293
(1 row)
```

It returns a row count very quickly, no matter how large the table that we are examining is. You may want to create a SQL function for the preceding calculation, so you won't need to retype the SQL code every now and then.

The following function estimates the total number of rows using a mathematical procedure called **extrapolation**. In other words, we take the average number of bytes per row resulting from the last statistics collection, and we apply it to the current table size:

```
CREATE OR REPLACE FUNCTION estimated_row_count(text)
RETURNS bigint
LANGUAGE sql
AS $$
SELECT (CASE WHEN reltuples > 0 THEN
               pg_relation_size($1)*reltuples/(8192*relpages)
            ELSE 0
            END)::bigint
FROM pg_class
WHERE oid = $1::regclass;
$$;
```

How it works...

We saw the `pg_relation_size()` function earlier, so we know that it brings back an accurate value for the current size of the table.

When we vacuum a table in Postgres, we record two pieces of information in the `pg_class` catalog entry for the table. These two items are the number of data blocks in the table (`relpages`) and the number of rows in the table (`reltuples`). Some people think they can use the value of `reltuples` in `pg_class` as an estimate, but it could be severely out of date. You will also be fooled if you use information in another table named `pg_stat_user_tables`, which is discussed in more detail in `Chapter 10`, *Performance and Concurrency*.

The Postgres optimizer uses the `relpages` and `reltuples` values to calculate the average rows per block, which is also known as the **average tuple density**.

If we assume that the average tuple density remains constant over time, then we can calculate the number of rows using this formula: *Row estimate = number of data blocks * rows per block*.

We include some code to handle cases where the `reltuples` or `relpages` fields are zero. The Postgres optimizer actually works a little harder than we do in that case, so our estimate isn't very good.

The `WHERE oid = 'mytable'::regclass;` syntax introduces the concept of object identifier types. They just use a shorthand trick to convert the name of an object to the object identifier number for that object. The best way to understand this is to think of that syntax as meaning the same as a function named `relname2relid()`.

There's more...

The good thing about the aforementioned recipe is that it returns a value in about the same time, no matter how big the table is. The bad thing about it is that `pg_relation_size()` requests a lock on the table, so if any other user has an `AccessExclusiveLock` lock on the table, then the table size estimate will wait for the lock to be released before returning a value.

Err... so what is an `AccessExclusiveLock` lock? While performing a SQL maintenance action, such as changing the data type of a column, PostgreSQL will lock out all other actions on that table, including `pg_relation_size`, which takes a lock in the `AccessShareLock` mode. For me, a typical case is when I issue some form of SQL maintenance action, such as `ALTER TABLE`, and the statement takes much longer than I thought it would. At that point, I think, *Oh, was that table bigger than I thought? How long will I be waiting?* Yes, it's better to calculate that beforehand, but hindsight doesn't get you out of the hole you are in right now. So, we need a way to calculate the size of a table without needing the lock.

My solution is to look at the operating system files that Postgres uses to store data, and figure out how large they are.

Now, this can get somewhat difficult. If the table is locked, PostgreSQL is probably doing something to the table, so trying to look at the files might well be fruitless or give wrong answers. The following are the steps we need to perform:

1. First, get some details on the table from `pg_class`:

   ```
   SELECT reltablespace, relfilenode FROM pg_class
   WHERE oid = 'mytable'::regclass;
   ```

2. Then, confirm the `databaseid` in which the table resides:

   ```
   SELECT oid as databaseid FROM pg_database
   WHERE datname = current_database();
   ```

Together, `reltablespace`, `databaseid`, and `relfilenode` are the three things we need to locate the underlying data files within the `data` directory.

If `reltablespace` is zero, then the files will be at the following location:

```
$PGDATADIR/base/{databaseid}/{relfilenode}*
```

The bigger the table, the more files you see. If `reltablespace` is not zero, then the files will be at the following location:

```
$PGDATADIR/pg_tblspc/{reltablespace}/{databaseid}/{relfilenode}*
```

Every file should be 1 GB in size, apart from the last file.

The preceding discussion glossed over a few other points, as follows:

- Postgres uses the terms data blocks and pages to refer to the same concept. Postgres also does that with the terms tuple and row.
- A data block is 8,192 bytes in size, by default. You can change that if you recompile the server yourself, and create a new database.

Here is a function that does what `pg_relation_size` does, more or less, without taking any locks. Because of this, it is always fast, but it may give an incorrect result if the table is being heavily altered at the same time:

```
CREATE OR REPLACE FUNCTION pg_relation_size_nolock(tablename regclass)
RETURNS BIGINT
LANGUAGE plpgsql
AS $$
DECLARE
    classoutput  RECORD;
    tsid         INTEGER;
    rid          INTEGER;
    dbid         INTEGER;
    filepath     TEXT;
    filename     TEXT;
    datadir      TEXT;
    i            INTEGER := 0;
    tablesize    BIGINT;
BEGIN
    --
    -- Get data directory
    --
    EXECUTE 'SHOW data_directory' INTO datadir;
    --
    -- Get relfilenode and reltablespace
    --
    SELECT
      reltablespace as tsid, relfilenode as rid
    INTO classoutput
```

```
        FROM pg_class
        WHERE oid = tablename
        AND relkind = 'r';
        --
        -- Throw an error if we can't find the tablename specified
        --
        IF NOT FOUND THEN
          RAISE EXCEPTION 'tablename % not found', tablename;
        END IF;
        tsid := classoutput.tsid;
        rid := classoutput.rid;
        --
        -- Get the database object identifier (oid)
        --
        SELECT oid INTO dbid
        FROM pg_database
        WHERE datname = current_database();
        --
        -- Use some internals knowledge to set the filepath
        --
        IF tsid = 0 THEN
  filepath := datadir || '/base/' || dbid || '/' || rid;
        ELSE
  filepath := datadir || '/pg_tblspc/' || tsid || '/'
              || dbid || '/' || rid;
        END IF;
        --
        -- Look for the first file. Report if missing
        --
        SELECT (pg_stat_file(filepath)).size
        INTO tablesize;
        --
        -- Sum the sizes of additional files, if any
        --
        WHILE FOUND LOOP
  i := i + 1;
  filename := filepath || '.' || i;
            --
            -- pg_stat_file returns ERROR if it cannot see file
            -- so we must trap the error and exit loop
            --
        BEGIN
        SELECT tablesize + (pg_stat_file(filename)).size
            INTO tablesize;
        EXCEPTION
            WHEN OTHERS THEN
            EXIT;
        END;
```

```
    END LOOP;
    RETURN tablesize;
END;
$$;
```

This function can also work on Windows with a few minor changes, which are left as an exercise for you.

Listing extensions in this database

Every PostgreSQL database contains some objects that are automatically brought in when the database is created. Every user will find a `pg_database` system catalog that lists databases, as shown in the *Listing databases on this database server* recipe. There is little point in checking whether these objects exist, because even superusers are not allowed to drop them.

On the other hand, PostgreSQL comes with tens of collections of optional objects, called **modules**, or equivalently **extensions**. The database administrator can install or uninstall these objects, depending on the requirements. They are not automatically included in a newly created database, because they might not be required by every use case. Users will install only the extensions they actually need, when they need them; an extension can be installed while a database is up and running.

In this recipe, we will explain how to list extensions that have been installed on the current database. This is important to get to know the database better, and also because certain extensions affect the behavior of the database.

How to do it...

In PostgreSQL, there is a catalog table recording the list of installed extensions, so this recipe is quite simple. Issue the following command:

```
cookbook=> SELECT * FROM pg_extension;
```

This results in the following output:

> Note that the format is expanded, as if the \x meta command has been
> previously issued.

```
-[ RECORD 1 ]--+---------
extname        | plpgsql
extowner       | 10
extnamespace   | 11
extrelocatable | f
extversion     | 1.0
extconfig      |
extcondition   |
```

To get the same list with fewer technical details, you can use the \dx meta command, as
when listing databases.

How it works...

A PostgreSQL extension is represented by a control file, <extension name>.control,
located in the SHAREDIR/extension directory, plus one or more files containing the actual
extension objects. The control file specifies the extension name, version, and other
information that is useful for the extension infrastructure. Each time an extension is
installed, uninstalled, or upgraded to a new version, the corresponding row in the
pg_extension catalog table is inserted, deleted, or updated, respectively.

There's more...

In this recipe, we only mentioned extensions distributed with PostgreSQL, and solely for
the purpose of listing which ones are being used in the current database. The infrastructure
for extensions will be described in greater detail in Chapter 3, *Configuration*. We will talk
about the version number of an extension, and we will show you how to install, uninstall,
and upgrade extensions, including those distributed independently of PostgreSQL.

See also

To get an idea of which extensions are available, you can browse the list of additional modules shipped together with PostgreSQL, which are almost all extensions, at https://www.postgresql.org/docs/current/static/contrib.html.

Understanding object dependencies

In most databases, there will be dependencies between objects in the database. Sometimes, we need to understand these dependencies to figure out how to perform certain actions, such as modifying or deleting existing objects. Let's look at this in detail.

Getting ready

We'll use the following simple database to understand and investigate them:

1. Create two tables as follows:

```
CREATE TABLE orders (
orderid integer PRIMARY KEY
);
CREATE TABLE orderlines (
orderid integer
,lineid smallint
,PRIMARY KEY (orderid, lineid)
);
```

2. Now, we add a link between them to enforce what is known as **referential integrity**, as follows:

```
ALTER TABLE orderlines ADD FOREIGN KEY (orderid)
REFERENCES orders (orderid);
```

3. If we try to drop the referenced table, we get the following message:

```
DROP TABLE orders;
ERROR: cannot drop table orders because other objects depend on it
DETAIL: constraint orderlines_orderid_fkey on table orderlines
depends on table orders
HINT: Use DROP ... CASCADE to drop the dependent objects too.
```

Be very careful! If you follow the hint, you may accidentally remove all the objects that have any dependency on the `orders` table. You might think that this would be a great idea, but it is not the right thing to do. It might work, but we need to ensure that it will work.

Therefore, you need to know what dependencies are present on the `orders` table, and then review them. Then, you can decide whether it is okay to issue the CASCADE version of the command, or whether you should reconcile the situation manually.

How to do it...

You can use the following command from `psql` to display full information about a table, the constraints that are defined upon it, and the constraints that reference it:

```
\d+ orders
```

You can also get specific details of the constraints by using the following query:

```
SELECT * FROM pg_constraint
WHERE confrelid = 'orders'::regclass;
```

The aforementioned queries only covered constraints between tables. This is not the end of the story, so read the *There's more...* section.

How it works...

When we create a foreign key, we add a constraint to the catalog table, known as `pg_constraint`. Therefore, the query shows us how to find all the constraints that depend upon the `orders` table.

There's more...

With Postgres, there's always a little more when you look beneath the surface. In this case, there's a lot more, and it's important.

We didn't discuss dependencies with other kinds of objects. Two important types of object that might have dependencies on tables are views and functions.

Consider the following command:

```
DROP TABLE orders;
```

If you issue this, the dependency on any of the views will prevent the table from being dropped. So, you need to remove those views and then drop the table.

The story with function dependencies is not as useful. Relationships between functions and tables are not recorded in the catalog, nor is the dependency information between functions. This is partly due to the fact that most PostgreSQL procedural languages allow dynamic query execution, so you wouldn't be able to tell which tables or functions a function would access until it executes. That's only partly the reason, because most functions clearly reference other tables and functions, so it should be possible to identify and store those dependencies. However, right now, we don't do that. So, make a note that you need to record the dependency information for your functions manually, so that you'll know if and when it's okay to remove or alter a table or other objects that the functions depend on.

Configuration

3

I get asked many questions about parameter settings in PostgreSQL. Everybody's busy, and most people want a five-minute tour of how things work. That's exactly what a cookbook does, so we'll do our best.

Some people believe that there are some magical parameter settings that will improve their performance, and spend hours combing the pages of books to glean insights. Others feel comfortable because they have found a website somewhere that *explains everything*, and they *know* they have their database configured OK.

For the most part, the settings are easy to understand. Finding the best setting can be difficult, and the optimal setting may change over time. This chapter is mostly about knowing how, when, and where to change parameter settings.

In this chapter, we will cover the following recipes:

- Reading the fine manual
- Planning a new database
- Changing parameters in your programs
- Finding the current configuration settings
- Which parameters are at non-default settings?
- Updating the parameter file
- Setting parameters for particular groups of users
- The basic server configuration checklist
- Adding an external module to PostgreSQL
- Using an installed module
- Managing installed extensions

Reading the fine manual

Reading the fine manual (**RTFM**) is often (rudely) used to mean *don't bother me; I'm busy,* or it is used as a stronger form of abuse. The strange thing is that asking you to read a manual is most often very good advice. Don't force the advisor—instead, take the advice! The most important point to remember is that you should refer to a manual whose release version matches that of the server on which you are operating.

The PostgreSQL manual is very well-written and comprehensive in its coverage of specific topics. However, one of its main failings is that the documents aren't organized in a way that helps somebody who is trying to learn PostgreSQL. They are organized from the perspective of people checking specific technical points so that they can decide whether their difficulty is a user error. It sometimes answers *what?* But it seldom answers *why?* And it seldom answers *how?*

I've helped write sections of the PostgreSQL documents, so I'm not embarrassed to steer you toward reading them. There are, nonetheless, many things to read here that are useful.

How to do it...

The main documents for each PostgreSQL release are available at `http://www.postgresql.org/docs/manuals/`.

The most frequently accessed parts of the documents are as follows:

- The SQL command reference, as well as client and server tools reference: `http://www.postgresql.org/docs/current/interactive/reference.html`
- Configuration: `http://www.postgresql.org/docs/current/interactive/runtime-config.html`
- Functions: `http://www.postgresql.org/docs/current/interactive/functions.html`

You can also grab yourself a PDF version of the manual, which can allow for easier searching in some cases. Don't print it! The documents are more than 2,000 pages of A4-sized sheets.

How it works...

The PostgreSQL documents are written in **Standard Generalized Markup Language** (**SGML**), which is similar to, but not the same as, XML. These files are then processed to generate HTML files, PDFs, and so on. This ensures that all the formats have exactly the same content. Then, you can choose the format you prefer, and you can even compile it in other formats, such as EPUB, INFO, and so on.

Moreover, the PostgreSQL manual is actually a subset of the PostgreSQL source code, so it evolves together with the software. It is written by the same people who make PostgreSQL, which gives you even more reasons to read it!

There's more...

More information is also available at `http://wiki.postgresql.org`.

Many distributions offer packages that install static versions of the HTML documentation. For example, on Debian and Ubuntu, the docs for the most recent stable PostgreSQL version is named `postregsql-doc-11`.

Planning a new database

Planning a new database can be a daunting task. It's easy to get overwhelmed by it, so here we will present some planning ideas. It's also easy to charge headlong at the task, thinking that whatever you know is all you'll ever need to consider.

Getting ready

You are ready. Don't wait to be told what to do. If you haven't been told what the requirements are, then write down what you think they are, clearly labeling them as *assumptions* rather than *requirements*; you must not confuse the two.

Iterate until you get some agreement, and then build a prototype.

How to do it...

Write a document that covers the following items:

- Database design—plan your database design.
- Calculate the initial database sizing.
- Transaction analysis—how will we access the database?
- Look at the most frequent access paths (for example, queries).
- What are the requirements for the response times?
- Hardware configuration.
- Initial performance thoughts—will all of the data fit into the available RAM?
- Choose the operating system and filesystem types.
- How do we partition the disk?
- Localization plan.
- Decide the server encoding, locale, and the time zone.
- Access and security plan.
- Identify client systems and specify the required drivers.
- Create roles according to a plan for access control.
- Specify `pg_hba.conf`.
- Monitoring—are there PostgreSQL plugins for the monitoring solution you are already using (usually yes)? What are the business-specific metrics we need to monitor?
- Maintenance plan—who will keep it working? How?
- Availability plan—consider the availability requirements.
- `checkpoint_timeout` (for more details on this parameter, see the *Understanding and controlling crash recovery* recipe in `Chapter 11`, *Backup and Recovery*).
- Plan your backup mechanism and test it.
- High-availability plan.
- Decide which form of replication you'll need, if any.

How it works...

One of the most important reasons for planning your database ahead of time is that retrofitting some things is difficult. This is especially true of server encoding and locale, which can cause much downtime and exertion if we need to change them later. Security is also much more difficult to set up after the system is live.

There's more...

Planning always helps. You may know what you're doing, but others may not. Tell everybody what you're going to do before you do it to avoid wasting time. If you're not sure yet, then build a prototype to help you decide. Approach the administration framework as if it were a development task. Make a list of things you don't know yet, and work through them one by one.

This is deliberately a very short recipe. Everybody has their own way of doing things, and it's very important not to be too prescriptive about how to do things. If you already have a plan, great! If you don't, think about what you need to do, make a checklist, and then do it.

Changing parameters in your programs

PostgreSQL allows you to set some parameter settings for each session or transaction.

How to do it...

Execute the following steps to set custom parameters settings:

1. You can change the value of a setting during your session, like this:

   ```
   SET work_mem = '16MB';
   ```

2. This value will then be used for every future transaction. You can also change it only for the duration of the current transaction:

   ```
   SET LOCAL work_mem = '16MB';
   ```

3. The setting will last until you issue this command:

   ```
   RESET work_mem;
   ```

4. Alternatively, you can issue the following command:

   ```
   RESET ALL;
   ```

The SET and RESET commands are SQL commands that can be issued from any interface. They apply only to PostgreSQL server parameters, but this does not mean that they affect the entire server. In fact, the parameters you can change with SET and RESET apply only to the current session. Also, note that there may be other parameters, such as JDBC driver parameters, that cannot be set in this way. Refer to the *Connecting to the PostgreSQL server* recipe in Chapter 1, *First Steps,* for help with those parameters.

How it works...

Suppose you change the value of a setting during your session, for example, by issuing this command:

```
SET work_mem = '16MB';
```

Then, the following will show up in the pg_settings catalog view:

```
postgres=# SELECT name, setting, reset_val, source FROM pg_settings WHERE
source = 'session';
    name    | setting | reset_val | source
-----------+---------+-----------+---------
 work_mem  | 16384   | 4096      | session
```

This will show until you issue this command:

```
RESET work_mem;
```

After issuing it, the setting returns to reset_val and the source returns to the default:

```
    name    | setting | reset_val | source
-----------+---------+-----------+---------
 work_mem  | 4096    | 4096      | default
```

There's more...

You can change the value of a setting during your transaction as well, like this:

```
SET LOCAL work_mem = '16MB';
```

This results in the following output:

```
WARNING: SET LOCAL can only be used in transaction blocks
SET
```

In order to understand what the warning means, we can look that setting up in the pg_settings catalog view:

```
postgres=# SELECT name, setting, reset_val, source FROM pg_settings WHERE
source = 'session';
   name    | setting | reset_val | source
-----------+---------+-----------+---------
 work_mem  |  4096   |   4096    | session
```

Huh? What happened to your parameter setting? The SET LOCAL command takes effect only for the transaction in which it was executed, which was just the SET LOCAL command in our case. We need to execute it inside a transaction block to be able to see the setting take hold, as follows:

```
BEGIN;
SET LOCAL work_mem = '16MB';
```

Here is what shows up in the pg_settings catalog view:

```
postgres=# SELECT name, setting, reset_val, source
                   FROM pg_settings WHERE source = 'session';
   name    | setting | reset_val | source
-----------+---------+-----------+---------
 work_mem  |  16384  |   4096    | session
```

You should also note that the value of source is session rather than transaction, as you might have been expecting.

Finding the current configuration settings

At some point, it will occur to you to ask, *What are the current configuration settings?*

Most settings can be changed in more than one way, and some ways do not affect all users or all sessions, so it is quite possible to get confused.

How to do it...

Your first thought is probably to look in postgresql.conf, which is the configuration file, and is described in detail in the *Updating the parameter file* recipe. That works, but only as long as there is only one parameter file. If there are two, then maybe you're reading the wrong file! How would you know? So, the cautious and accurate way is to not trust a text file, but to trust the server itself.

Moreover, you learned in the previous recipe, *Changing parameters in your programs*, that each parameter has a scope that determines when it can be set. Some parameters can be set through `postgresql.conf`, but others can be changed afterwards. So, the current values of the configuration settings may have been subsequently changed.

We can use the SHOW command like this:

```
postgres=# SHOW work_mem;
```

Its output is as follows:

```
work_mem
----------
4MB
(1 row)
```

However, remember that it reports the current setting at the time it is run, and that can be changed in many places.

Another way of finding the current settings is to access a PostgreSQL catalog view named `pg_settings`:

```
postgres=#  \x
Expanded display is on.
postgres=# SELECT * FROM pg_settings WHERE name = 'work_mem';
[ RECORD 1 ] -----------------------------------------------------------
name       | work_mem
setting    | 4096
unit       | kB
category   | Resource Usage / Memory
short_desc | Sets the maximum memory to be used for query workspaces.
extra_desc | This much memory can be used by each internal sort operation
and hash table before switching to temporary disk files.
context    | user
vartype    | integer
source     | default
min_val    | 64
max_val    | 2147483647
enumvals   |
boot_val   | 4096
reset_val  | 4096
sourcefile |
sourceline |
```

Thus, you can use the SHOW command to retrieve the value for a setting, or you can access the full details using the catalog table.

The actual location of each configuration file can be asked directly to the PostgreSQL server, as shown in this example:

```
postgres=# SHOW config_file;
```

This returns the following output:

```
                config_file
------------------------------------------
 /etc/postgresql/11/main/postgresql.conf
(1 row)
```

The other configuration files can be located by querying similar variables, that is, hba_file and ident_file.

How it works...

Each parameter setting is cached within each session so that we can get quick access to the parameter settings. This allows us to access the parameter settings with ease.

Remember that the values displayed are not necessarily settings for the server as a whole. Many of those parameters will be specific to the current session. That's different than what you experience with many other types of database software, and it is also very useful.

Which parameters are at non-default settings?

Often, we need to check which parameters have been changed, or whether our changes have taken effect correctly.

In the previous two recipes, we have seen that parameters can be changed in several ways, and with different scopes. You learned how to inspect the value of one parameter or get the full list of parameters.

In this recipe, we will show you how to use SQL capabilities to list only those parameters whose value in the current session differs from the system-wide default value.

This list is valuable for several reasons. First, it includes only a few of the 200+ available parameters, so it is more immediate. Also, it is difficult to remember all our past actions, especially in the middle of a long or complicated session.

PostgreSQL also supports the ALTER SYSTEM syntax, which we will describe in the next recipe, *Updating the parameter file*. From the viewpoint of this recipe, the behavior of this syntax is quite different compared to the other setting-related commands: you run it from within your session, and it changes the default value, but not the value in your session.

How to do it...

We write an SQL query that lists all parameter values, excluding those whose current value is either the default or set from a configuration file:

```
postgres=# SELECT name, source, setting
                  FROM pg_settings
                  WHERE source != 'default'
                  AND source != 'override'
                  ORDER by 2, 1;
```

The output is as follows:

name	source	setting
application_name	client	psql
client_encoding	client	UTF8
DateStyle	configuration file	ISO, DMY
default_text_search_config	configuration file	pg_catalog.english
dynamic_shared_memory_type	configuration file	posix
lc_messages	configuration file	en_GB.UTF-8
lc_monetary	configuration file	en_GB.UTF-8
lc_numeric	configuration file	en_GB.UTF-8
lc_time	configuration file	en_GB.UTF-8
log_timezone	configuration file	Europe/Rome
max_connections	configuration file	100
port	configuration file	5460
shared_buffers	configuration file	16384
TimeZone	configuration file	Europe/Rome
max_stack_depth	environment variable	2048

How it works...

From `pg_settings`, you can see which parameters have non-default values, and what the source of the current value is. The `SHOW` command doesn't tell you whether a parameter is set at a non-default value. It just tells you the value, which isn't of much help if you're trying to understand what is set and why. If the source is a configuration file, then the `sourcefile` and `sourceline` columns are also set. These can be useful in understanding where the configuration came from.

There's more...

The `setting` column of `pg_settings` shows the current value, but you can also look at the `boot_val` and `reset_val` parameters. The `boot_val` parameter shows the value that was assigned when the PostgreSQL database cluster was initialized (`initdb`), while `reset_val` shows the value that the parameter will return to if you issue the `RESET` command.

The `max_stack_depth` parameter is an exception, because `pg_settings` says it is set by the environment variable, though it is actually set by `ulimit -s` on Linux and Unix systems. The `max_stack_depth` parameter just needs to be set directly on Windows.

The timezone settings are also picked up from the OS environment, so you shouldn't need to set those directly. They are written to `postgresql.conf` when the `data` directory is initialized, so they show up as configuration files.

Updating the parameter file

The parameter file is the main location that's used for defining parameter values for the PostgreSQL server. All the parameters can be set in the parameter file, which is known as `postgresql.conf`. There are also two other parameter files: `pg_hba.conf` and `pg_ident.conf`. Both of these relate to connections and security, so we'll cover them in the appropriate chapters that follow.

Getting ready

Before we start this recipe, we need to locate `postgresql.conf`, as described in *Finding the current configuration settings* recipe.

How to do it...

Some of the parameters take effect only when the server is first started. A typical example might be `shared_buffers`, which defines the size of the shared memory cache. Many of the parameters can be changed while the server is still running.

After changing the required parameters, we issue a `reload` command to the server, forcing PostgreSQL to re-read the `postgresql.conf` file (and all other configuration files). There are a number of ways to do that, depending on your distribution and OS. The most common is to issue the following command, with the same OS user that runs the PostgreSQL server process:

pg_ctl reload

This assumes the default data directory; otherwise, you have to specify the correct data directory with the `-D` option.

As we previously noted, Debian and Ubuntu have a different multiversion architecture, so you should issue the following command instead:

pg_ctlcluster 11 main reload

On modern distributions, you should use `systemd`, as follows:

sudo systemctl reload postgresql@11-main

> See the *Starting the database server manually* recipe in Chapter 4, *Server Control*, for more details on how to manage PostgreSQL via `systemd`; the *Reloading the server configuration files* recipe, also in Chapter 4, *Server Control*, shows more ways to reload configuration files.

Some other parameters require a restart of the server for changes to take effect—for instance, `max_connections`, `listen_addresses`, and so on. The syntax is very similar to a `reload` operation, as shown here:

pg_ctl restart

For Debian and Ubuntu, use this command:

```
pg_ctlcluster 11 main restart
```

With `system`, use this command:

```
sudo systemctl restart postgresql@11-main
```

Of course, a restart also has some impact on existing connections. See the *Restarting the server quickly* recipe in `Chapter 4`, *Server Control*, for further details.

The `postgresql.conf` file is a normal text file that can be simply edited. Most of the parameters are listed in the file, so you can just search for them and then insert the desired value in the right place.

How it works...

If you set the same parameter twice in different parts of the file, the last setting is what applies. This can cause lots of confusion if you add settings to the bottom of the file, so you are advised against doing it.

A longstanding and good practice is to version-control configuration files by using Git alongside any other code or configuration changes. An even better alternative is to use configuration management software such as Ansible, Chef, or Puppet, rather than editing configuration files directly.

There's more...

The `postgresql.conf` file also supports an `include` directive. This allows the `postgresql.conf` file to reference other files, which can then reference other files, and so on. That may help you organize your parameter settings better, if you don't make it too complicated.

For more on reloading, see the *Reloading the server configuration files* recipe in `Chapter 4`, *Server Control*.

Furthermore, you can change the values stored in the parameter files directly from your session, with syntax such as the following:

```
ALTER SYSTEM SET shared_buffers = '1GB';
```

This command will not actually edit `postgresql.conf`. Instead, it writes the new setting to another file named `postgresql.auto.conf`. The effect is equivalent, albeit in a safer way. The original configuration is never written, so it cannot be damaged in the event of a crash. If you mess up with too many `ALTER SYSTEM` commands, you can always delete `postgresql.auto.conf` manually and reload the configuration or restart PostgreSQL, depending on what parameters you changed.

 PostgreSQL 11 now supports up to 7 TB of cache, if you have that much memory.

Setting parameters for particular groups of users

PostgreSQL supports a variety of ways of defining parameter settings for various user groups. This is very convenient, especially for managing user groups that have different requirements.

How to do it...

Follow these steps to set parameters at various levels as per the requirements:

1. For all users in the `saas` database, use the following commands:

```
ALTER DATABASE saas
SET configuration_parameter = value1;
```

2. For a user named `simon` connected to any database, use the following commands:

```
ALTER ROLE simon
SET configuration_parameter = value2;
```

3. Alternatively, you can set a parameter for a user only when they're connected to a specific database, as follows:

```
ALTER ROLE simon
IN DATABASE saas
SET configuration_parameter = value3;
```

The user won't know that these have been executed specifically for them. These are default settings, and in most cases they can be overridden if the user requires non-default values.

How it works...

You can set parameters for each of the following:

- Database
- User (also called role by `postgreSQL`)
- Database and user combination

Each of the parameter defaults is overridden by the one following it.

In the preceding three SQL statements, the following apply:

- If `gianni` connects to the `saas` database, then `value1` will apply
- If `simon` connects to a database other than `saas`, then `value2` will apply
- If `simon` connects to the `saas` database, then `value3` will apply

PostgreSQL implements this in exactly the same way as if the user had manually issued the equivalent `SET` statements immediately after connecting.

The basic server configuration checklist

PostgreSQL arrives configured for use on a shared system, though many people want to run dedicated database systems. The PostgreSQL project wishes to ensure that PostgreSQL will play nicely with other server software, and will not assume that it has access to the full server resources. If you, as the system administrator, know that there is no other important server software running on the system, then you can crank the values up much higher.

Getting ready

Before we start, we need to know two sets of information:

- The size of the physical RAM that will be dedicated to PostgreSQL
- The types of applications for which we will use PostgreSQL

How to do it...

If your database is larger than 32 MB, then you'll probably benefit from increasing `shared_buffers`. You can increase this to a much larger value, but remember that running out of memory induces many problems.

For instance, PostgreSQL is able to store information on disk when the available memory is too small, and it employs sophisticated algorithms to treat each case differently and to place each piece of data on the disk or in memory, depending on each use case.

On the other hand, overstating the amount of available memory confuses such abilities and results in suboptimal behavior. For instance, if the memory is swapped to disk, then PostgreSQL will inefficiently treat all data as if it were the RAM. Another unfortunate circumstance is when the Linux **Out-Of-Memory (OOM)** killer terminates one of the various processes spawned by the PostgreSQL server. So, it's better to be conservative. It is good practice to set a low value in your `postgresql.conf` and increment slowly to ensure that you get the benefits from each change.

If you increase `shared_buffers` and you're running on a non-Windows server, you will almost certainly need to increase the value of the `SHMMAX` OS parameter (and on some platforms, other parameters as well).

On Linux, macOS, and FreeBSD, you will need to either edit the `/etc/sysctl.conf` file or use `sysctl -w` with the following values:

- For Linux, use `kernel.shmmax=value`
- For macOS, use `kern.sysv.shmmax=value`
- For FreeBSD, use `kern.ipc.shmmax=value`

There's more...

For more information, you can refer to
`http://www.postgresql.org/docs/11/static/kernel-resources.html#SYSVIPC`.

For example, on Linux, add the following line to `/etc/sysctl.conf`:

```
kernel.shmmax=value
```

Don't worry about setting `effective_cache_size`. It is much less important a parameter than you might think. There is no need for too much fuss when selecting the value.

If there is heavy write activity, you may want to set `wal_buffers` to a much higher value than the default. In fact, `wal_buffers` is automatically set from the value of `shared_buffers`, following a rule that fits most cases. However, it is always possible to specify an explicit value that overrides the computation for the very few cases where the rule is not good enough.

If you're doing heavy write activity and/or large data loads, you may want to set `max_wal_size` and `min_wal_size` higher than the default to avoid wasting I/O in excessively frequent checkpoints. You may also wish to set `checkpoint_timeout` and `checkpoint_completion_target`.

PostgreSQL tries its best to decouple query latency from storage performance: synchronous writes are limited to the WAL directory, and most calculations are carried out in memory buffers. However, there are cases where a query will need to use the disk before returning (for example, for reading data that was not already cached), meaning that fewer checkpoints will actually improve query latency.

If your database has many large queries, you may wish to set `work_mem` to a value higher than the default. However, remember that such a limit applies to *each* node separately in the query plan, so there is a real risk of over-allocating memory, with all the problems we discussed earlier.

Ensure that `autovacuum` is turned on, unless you have a very good reason to turn it off; most people don't. See later chapters for more information on `autovacuum`; in particular, see `Chapter 9`, *Regular Maintenance*.

Leave the settings as they are for now. Don't fuss too much about getting the settings right. You can change most of them later, so you can take an iterative approach to improving things.

And, remember, don't touch the `fsync` parameter. It's keeping you safe.

Adding an external module to PostgreSQL

Another strength of PostgreSQL is its **extensibility**. Extensibility was one of the original design goals, going back to the late 1980s. Now, in PostgreSQL 11, there are many additional modules that plug into the core PostgreSQL server.

There are many kinds of additional module offerings, such as the following:

- Additional functions
- Additional data types
- Additional operators
- Additional index types

Note that many tools and client interfaces work with PostgreSQL without any special installation. Here, we are discussing modules that extend and alter the behavior of the server beyond its normal range of SQL standard syntax, functions, and behavior.

The procedure that makes a module usable is actually a two-step process. First, you install the module's files on your system so that they become available to the database server. Next, you connect to the database (or databases) where you want to use the module, and create the required objects. The first step is discussed in this recipe. For the second step, refer to the next recipe, *Using an installed module*.

In this book, we will use the words *extension* and *module* as synonyms, as we did in the PostgreSQL documentation. Note, however, that the SQL commands that manage extensions, which we'll describe in the next recipe, are as follows:

- CREATE EXTENSION myext;
- ALTER EXTENSION myext UPDATE;

In particular, commands such as CREATE MODULE won't work at all!

Getting ready

First, you'll need to select an appropriate module to install.

The journey toward a complete, automated package management system for PostgreSQL is not over yet, so you need to look in more than one place for the available modules, such as the following:

- **Contrib**: The PostgreSQL core includes many functions. There is also an official section for add-in modules, known as `contrib` modules. They are always available for your database server, but are not automatically enabled in every database, because not all users might need them. In PostgreSQL Version 11, we have 45 such modules. These are documented at `http://www.postgresql.org/docs/11/static/contrib.html`.
- **PGXN**: This is the PostgreSQL Extension Network, a central distribution system dedicated to sharing PostgreSQL extensions. The website started in 2010 as a repository dedicated to the sharing of extension files. As of November 2018, there were 279 extensions from 317 different authors. You can learn more about it at `http://pgxn.org/`.
- **Separate projects**: These are large external projects, such as PostGIS, offering extensive and complex PostgreSQL modules. For more information, take a look at `http://www.postgis.org/`.

How to do it...

There are several ways to make additional modules available for your database server, as follows:

- Using a software installer
- Installing from PGXN
- Installing from a manually downloaded package
- Installing from source code

Often, a particular module will be available in more than one way, and users are free to choose their favorite, exactly like PostgreSQL itself, which can be downloaded and installed through many different procedures.

Installing modules using a software installer

Certain modules are available exactly like any other software packages that you may want to install in your server. All main Linux distributions provide packages for the most popular modules, such as PostGIS, SkyTools, procedural languages other than those distributed with the core, and so on.

Modules can sometimes be added during installation if you're using a standalone installer application, for example, the OneClick installer, or tools such as `rpm`, `apt-get`, and `YaST` on Linux distributions. The same procedure can also be followed after the PostgreSQL installation, when the need for a certain module arrives. We will actually describe this case, which is very common.

For example, let's say that you need to manage a collection of Debian package files and that one of your tasks is to be able to pick the latest version of one of them. You start by building a database that records all package files. Clearly, you need to store the version number of each package. However, Debian version numbers are much more complex than what we usually call numbers. For instance, on my Debian laptop, I currently have the `11.1-1.pgdg90+1` version of the PostgreSQL client package. Despite being complicated, that string follows a clearly defined specification, which includes many bits of information, including how to compare two versions to establish which of them is older.

Since this recipe discusses extending PostgreSQL with custom data types and operators, you might have already guessed that I will now consider a custom data type for Debian version numbers that is capable of tasks such as understanding the Debian version number format, sorting version numbers, choosing the latest version number in a given group, and so on. It turns out that somebody else already did the work of creating the required PostgreSQL data type, endowed with all the useful accessories: comparison operators, input/output functions, support for indexes, and maximum/minimum aggregates. All of this has been packaged as a PostgreSQL extension, as well as a Debian package (not a big surprise), so it is just a matter of installing the `postgresql-11-debversion` package with a Debian tool such as `apt-get`, `aptitude`, or `synaptic`. On my laptop, that boils down to the following command:

```
apt-get install postgresql-11-debversion
```

This will download the required package and unpack all the files in the right locations, making them available to my PostgreSQL server.

Installing modules from PGXN

The **PostgreSQL Extension Network**, **PGXN** for short, is a website (http://pgxn.org) that was launched in late 2010 with the purpose of providing a central distribution system for open source PostgreSQL extension libraries. Anybody can register and upload their own module, packaged as an extension archive. The website allows you to browse the available extensions and their versions, either via a search interface or from a directory of packages and usernames.

The simple way is to use a command-line utility called `pgxnclient`. It can be easily installed in most systems; see the PGXN website for how to do this. Its purpose is to interact with PGXN and take care of administrative tasks, such as browsing available extensions, downloading the package, compiling the source code, installing files in the proper places, and removing installed package files. Alternatively, you can download the extension files from the website and place them in the right place by following the installation instructions.

PGXN is different compared to the official repositories because it serves another purpose. Official repositories usually contain only seasoned extensions, because they accept new software only after a certain amount of evaluation and testing. On the other hand, anybody can ask for a PGXN account and upload their own extensions, so there is no filter except requiring that the extension has an open source license and a few files that any extension must have.

Installing modules from source code

In many cases, useful modules may not have full packaging. In these cases, you may need to install the module manually. This isn't very hard, and it's a useful exercise that will help you understand what happens.

Each module will have different installation requirements. There are generally two aspects of installing a module. They are as follows:

- Building the libraries (only for modules that have libraries)
- Installing the module files in the appropriate locations

You need to follow the instructions for the specific module in order to build the libraries, if any are required. Installation will then be straightforward, and usually there will be a suitably prepared configuration file for the `make` utility, so you just need to type the following command:

```
make install
```

Each file will be copied to the right directory. Remember that you normally need to be a system superuser in order to install files on the system's directories.

Once a library file is in the directory expected by the PostgreSQL server, it will be loaded automatically as soon as requested by a function. Modules such as `auto_explain` do not provide any additional user-defined functions, so they won't be auto-loaded; that needs to be done manually by a superuser with a `LOAD` statement.

How it works...

PostgreSQL can dynamically load libraries in the following ways:

- Using the explicit LOAD command in a session
- Using the shared_preload_libraries parameter in postgresql.conf at the server start
- At the session start, using the local_preload_libraries parameter for a specific user, as set using ALTER ROLE

PostgreSQL functions and objects can reference code in these libraries, allowing extensions to be bound tightly to the running server process. The tight binding makes this method suitable for use in even very high-performance applications, and there's no significant difference between additionally supplied features and native features.

Using an installed module

In this recipe, we will explain how to enable an installed module so that it can be used in a particular database. The additional types, functions, and so on will exist only in those databases where we have carried out this step.

 Although most modules require this procedure, there are actually a couple of notable exceptions. For instance, the auto_explain module we mentioned earlier, which is shipped together with PostgreSQL, does not create any function, type, or operator. To use it, you must load its object file using the LOAD command. From that moment, all statements longer than a configurable threshold will be logged together with their execution plan. In the rest of this recipe, we will cover all the other modules. They do not require a LOAD statement, because PostgreSQL can automatically load the relevant libraries when they are required.

As we mentioned in the previous recipe, *Adding an external module to PostgreSQL*, specially packaged modules are called **extensions** in PostgreSQL. They can be managed with dedicated SQL commands.

Getting ready

Suppose that you have chosen to install a certain module among those available for your system (see the previous recipe, *Adding an external module to PostgreSQL*); all you need to know is the extension name.

How to do it...

Each extension has a unique name, so it is just a matter of issuing the following command:

```
CREATE EXTENSION myextname;
```

This will automatically create all the required objects inside the current database.

For security reasons, you need to do so as a database superuser. For instance, if you want to install the dblink extension, type this:

```
CREATE EXTENSION dblink;
```

How it works...

When you issue a CREATE EXTENSION command, the database server looks for a file named EXTNAME.control in the SHAREDIR/extension directory. That file tells PostgreSQL some properties of the extension, including a description, some installation information, and the default version number of the extension (which is unrelated to the PostgreSQL version number). Then, a creation script is executed in a single transaction; thus, if it fails, the database is unchanged. The database server also notes down the extension name and all the objects that belong to it in a catalog table.

Managing installed extensions

In the last two recipes, we showed you how to install external modules in PostgreSQL to augment its capabilities.

In this recipe, we will show you some more capabilities that are offered by the extension infrastructure.

How to do it...

The following are the steps to manage the extensions:

1. First, we list all the available extensions:

```
postgres=# \x on
Expanded display is on.
postgres=# SELECT *
postgres-# FROM pg_available_extensions
postgres-# ORDER BY name;
-[ RECORD 1 ]-----+-----------------------------------------------
--
name              | adminpack
default_version   | 2.0
installed_version |
comment           | administrative functions for PostgreSQL
-[ RECORD 2 ]-----+-----------------------------------------------
--
name              | pg_stat statements
default_version   | 1.6
installed_version |
comment           | track execution statistics of all SQL
statements executed
(...)
```

In particular, if the dblink extension is installed, then we see a record such as this:

```
-[ RECORD 10 ]----+-----------------------------------------------
--
name              | dblink
default_version   | 1.2
installed_version | 1.2
comment           | connect to other PostgreSQL databases from
within a database
```

2. Now, we can list all the objects in the dblink extension, as follows:

```
postgres=# \x off
Expanded display is off.
postgres=# \dx+ dblink
                      Objects in extension "dblink"
                        Object Description
----------------------------------------------------------------
--
 function dblink_build_sql_delete(text,int2vector,integer,text[])
 function
```

```
dblink_build_sql_insert(text,int2vector,integer,text[],text[])
 function
dblink_build_sql_update(text,int2vector,integer,text[],text[])
 function dblink_cancel_query(text)
 function dblink_close(text)
 function dblink_close(text,boolean)
 function dblink_close(text,text)
(...)
```

3. Objects created as parts of extensions are not special in any way, except that you can't drop them individually. This is done to protect you from mistakes:

```
postgres=# DROP FUNCTION dblink_close(text);
ERROR:  cannot drop function dblink_close(text) because extension
dblink requires it
HINT:  You can drop extension dblink instead.
```

4. Extensions might have dependencies, too. The cube and earthdistance contrib extensions are a good example, since the latter depends on the former:

```
postgres=# CREATE EXTENSION earthdistance;
ERROR:  required extension "cube" is not installed
HINT: Use CREATE EXTENSION ... CASCADE to install required
extensions too.
postgres=# CREATE EXTENSION earthdistance CASCADE;
NOTICE: installing required extension "cube"
CREATE EXTENSION
```

Note how the CASCADE keyword was used to automatically create all the other extensions that the extension being created depends on, as clearly reminded by the HINT message.

5. As you can reasonably expect, dependencies are taken into account when dropping objects, just like for other objects:

```
postgres=# DROP EXTENSION cube;
ERROR:  cannot drop extension cube because other objects depend on
it
DETAIL:  extension earthdistance depends on extension cube
HINT:  Use DROP ... CASCADE to drop the dependent objects too.
postgres=# DROP EXTENSION cube CASCADE;
NOTICE:  drop cascades to extension earthdistance
DROP EXTENSION
```

How it works...

The `pg_available_extensions` system view shows one row for each extension control file in the `SHAREDIR/extension` directory (see the *Using an installed module* recipe). The `pg_extension` catalog table records only the extensions that have actually been created.

The `psql` command-line utility provides the `\dx` meta-command to examine the extensions. It supports an optional plus sign (+) to control verbosity, and an optional pattern for the extension name to restrict its range. Consider the following command:

```
\dx+ db*
```

This will list all extensions whose names start with `db`, together with all their objects.

The `CREATE EXTENSION` command creates all objects belonging to a given extension and then records the dependency of each object on the extension in `pg_depend`. That's how PostgreSQL can ensure that you cannot drop one such object without dropping its extension.

The extension control file admits an optional line, `requires`, that names one or more extensions on which the current one depends. The implementation of dependencies is still quite simple; for instance, there is no way to specify a dependency on a specific version number of other extensions.

As a general PostgreSQL rule, the `CASCADE` keyword tells the `DROP` command to delete all objects that depend on `cube`, which is the `earthdistance` extension in this example.

There's more...

Another system view, `pg_available_extension_versions`, shows all the versions that are available for each extension. It can be valuable when there are multiple versions of the same extension available at the same time—for example, when making preparations for an extension upgrade.

When a more recent version of an already installed extension becomes available to the database server, for instance, because of a distribution upgrade that installs updated package files, the superuser can perform an upgrade by issuing the following command:

```
ALTER EXTENSION mytext UPDATE TO '1.1';
```

This assumes that the author of the extension taught it how to perform the upgrade.

Extensions interact nicely with logical backup and restore nicely, a topic that will be fully discussed in Chapter 11, *Backup and Recovery*. As an example, if your database contains the cube extension, then you will surely want a single line (CREATE EXTENSION cube) in the dump file instead of lots of lines recreating each object individually, which is inefficient and also dangerous.

The use of CASCADE in a CREATE statement only applies to extensions, because for other object types, the dependency is not predefined in the object metadata, and only exists after creating a specific object (for example, a foreign key).

Remember that CREATE EXTENSION ... CASCADE will only work if all the extensions it tries to install have already been placed in the appropriate location.

4
Server Control

In this chapter, we will cover the following recipes:

- Starting the database server manually
- Stopping the server safely and quickly
- Stopping the server in an emergency
- Reloading the server configuration files
- Restarting the server quickly
- Preventing new connections
- Restricting users to only one session each
- Pushing users off the system
- Deciding on a design for multitenancy
- Using multiple schemas
- Giving users their own private database
- Running multiple servers on one system
- Setting up a connection pool
- Accessing multiple servers using the same host and port

Introduction

PostgreSQL consists of a set of server processes, the group leader of which is named the **postmaster**. Starting the server is the act of creating these processes, and stopping the server is the act of terminating those processes.

Each postmaster listens for client connection requests on a defined port number. Multiple concurrently running postmasters cannot share that port number. The port number is often used to uniquely identify a particular postmaster and hence also the database server that it leads.

When we start a database server, we refer to a data directory, which contains the heart and soul—or at least the data—of our database. Subsidiary tablespaces may contain some data outside the main `data` directory, so the `data` directory is just the main central location, and not the only place where data for that database server is held. Each running server has at minimum of one `data` directory, and one `data` directory can have, at the most, one running server (or instance).

To perform any action for a database server, we must know the `data` directory for that server. The basic actions we can perform on the database server are starting and stopping. We can also perform a restart, though that is just a stop followed by a start. In addition, we can reload the server, which means that we can reread the server's configuration files.

We should also mention a few other points.

The default port number for PostgreSQL is 5432. That has been registered with the **Internet Assigned Numbers Authority** (**IANA**), and so it should already be reserved for PostgreSQL's use in most places. Because each PostgreSQL server requires a distinct port number, the normal convention is to use subsequent numbers for any additional server—for example, 5433, 5434, and so on. Subsequent port numbers might not be as easily recognized by the network infrastructure, which might, in some cases, make life more difficult for you in large enterprises, especially in more security-conscious ones.

Port number 6432 has been registered with IANA for **PgBouncer**, the connection pooler that we will describe in the *Setting up a connection pool* recipe. This happened only recently, and many installations are using non-standard port numbers such as 6543 only because they were deployed earlier.

A database server is also sometimes referred to as a **database cluster**. I don't recommend this term for normal usage because it makes people think about multiple nodes and not one database server on one system.

Starting the database server manually

Typically, the PostgreSQL server will start automatically when the system boots. You may have opted to stop and start the server manually, or you may need to start it up or shut it down for various operational reasons.

Getting ready

First, you need to understand the difference between the service and the server. The word *server* refers to the database server and its processes. The word *service* refers to the operating system wrapper by which the server gets called. The server works in essentially the same way on every platform, whereas each operating system and distribution has its own concept of a service.

Moreover, the way services are managed has changed recently: for instance, at the time of publication, most Linux distributions have adopted the systemd service manager. This means that you need to know which *distribution* and *release* you are using to find the correct variant of this recipe.

With systemd, a PostgreSQL server process is represented by a **service unit**, which is managed via the systemctl command. The systemd command syntax is the same on all distributions, but the name of the service unit unfortunately isn't; for example, it will have to be adjusted depending on your distribution.

In other cases, you need to type the actual **data directory** path as part of the command line to start the server. More information on how to find out the data directory path is available in the *Locating the database server files* recipe in Chapter 2, *Exploring the Database*.

How to do it...

On each platform, there is a specific command to start the server.

If you are using a modern Linux distribution, you are probably using systemd. In this case, PostgreSQL can be started with the following command:

```
sudo systemctl start SERVICEUNIT
```

This must be issued with OS superuser privileges, after replacing SERVICEUNIT with the appropriate systemd service unit name.

> The systemctl command must always be issued with operating system superuser privileges. Remember that, throughout this book, we will always prepend systemctl invocations with sudo.

There are a couple of things to keep in mind:

- This will work only if the user executing the command has been previously granted appropriate `sudo` privileges by the system administrator.
- If the command is executed from a superuser account, then the `sudo` keyword is unnecessary, although not harmful.

As we mentioned previously, the service-unit name depends on what distribution you are using, as follows:

- On Ubuntu and Debian, there is a service unit called this:

```
postgresql@RELEASE-CLUSTERNAME
```

- For each database server instance, there is another service unit called just `postgresql`, and that can be used to manage all the database servers at once. Therefore, you can issue the following command:

```
sudo systemctl start postgresql
```

- To start all the available instances, and to start only the default version 11 instance, use the following:

```
sudo systemctl start postgresql@11-main
```

- Default Red Hat/Fedora packages call the service unit simply `postgresql`, so the syntax is as follows:

```
sudo systemctl start postgresql
```

- Red Hat/Fedora packages from the PostgreSQL Yum repository create a service unit called `postgresql--RELEASE`, so we can start version 11 as follows:

```
sudo systemctl start postgresql-11
```

As we noted previously, `systemctl` is part of `systemd`, which is only available on Linux and is normally used by most of the recent distributions.

The following commands can be used where `systemd` is not available.

- On Debian and Ubuntu releases, you must invoke the PostgreSQL-specific utility `pg_ctlcluster`, as follows:

```
pg_ctlcluster 11 main start
```

This command will also work when `systemd` is available; it will just redirect the start request to `systemctl` and print a message on the screen so that the next time you will remember to use `systemctl` directly.

For Red Hat/Fedora, you can use this command:

```
service postgresql start
```

For Windows, the command is as follows:

```
net start postgres
```

For Red Hat/Fedora, you can also use the following command:

```
pg_ctl -D $PGDATA start
```

Here `PGDATA` is set to the data directory path.

In fact, this command works on most distributions, including **macOS**, **Solaris**, and **FreeBSD**, although bear in mind the following points:

- It is recommended to use, whenever possible, the distribution-specific syntax we described previously.
- You may have to specify the full path to the `pg_ctl` executable if it's not in your path already. This is normally the case with multi-version directory schemes such as Debian/Ubuntu, where distribution-specific scripts pick the appropriate executable for your version.

How it works...

On Ubuntu/Debian, the `pg_ctlcluster` wrapper is a convenient utility that allows multiple servers to coexist more easily, which is especially good when you have servers with different versions. This capability is very useful and is transposed on `systemd`, as shown in the examples using @ in the name of the service unit, where @ denotes the usage of a service file template.

Another interesting `systemd` feature is the capability to `enable`/ `disable` a service unit to specify whether it will be started automatically on the next boot, with a syntax such as the following:

```
sudo systemctl enable postgresql@11-main
```

This can be very useful to set the appropriate behavior based on the purpose of each instance.

A similar feature is implemented on Ubuntu and Debian by the `start.conf` file, located next to the other configuration files (that is, in the same directory). Apart from the informational comments, it contains only a single word, with the following meaning:

- `auto`: The server will be started automatically on boot. This is the default when creating a new server. It is suitable for frequently used servers, such as those powering live services or those being used for everyday development activities.
- `manual`: The server will not be started automatically on boot, but it can be started with `pg_ctlcluster`. This is suitable for custom servers that are seldom used.
- `disabled`: The server is not supposed to be started. This setting is only a protection from starting the server accidentally. The `pg_ctlcluster` wrapper won't let you start it, but a skilled user can easily bypass the protection.

If you need to reserve a port for a server not managed by `pg_ctlcluster`, for example, when compiling directly from the source code, then you can create a cluster with `start.conf` set to `disabled` and then use its port. Any new servers will be allocated different ports.

Stopping the server safely and quickly

There are several modes to stop the server, depending on the level of urgency. We'll do a comparison in view of the effects in each mode.

How to do it...

We provide two variants: with and without `systemd`. This is similar to the previous recipe, *Starting the database server manually*, which we'll refer to for further information. For example, what is the exact name of the `systemd` service unit for a given database server on a given GNU/Linux distribution?

When using `systemd`, you can stop PostgreSQL using the *fast* mode by issuing the following after having replaced `SERVICEUNIT` with the appropriate `systemd` service unit name:

```
sudo systemctl stop SERVICEUNIT
```

If systemd is not available, and you are using Debian or Ubuntu, the command is as in the following example, which applies to the default version 11 instance:

```
pg_ctlcluster 11 main stop -m fast
```

The fast mode is the default since PostgreSQL 9.5; the previous default was to use the smart mode, meaning *wait for all users to finish before we exit*. This can take a very long time, and all the while new connections are refused.

On other Linux/Unix distributions, you can issue a database server stop command using the fast mode, as follows:

```
pg_ctl -D datadir -m fast stop
```

How it works...

When you do a fast stop, all users have their transactions aborted and all connections are disconnected. This is not very polite to users, but it still treats the server and its data with care, which is good.

PostgreSQL is similar to other database systems in that it does do a shutdown checkpoint before it closes. This means that the startup that follows will be quick and clean. The more work the checkpoint has to do, the longer it will take to shut down.

One difference between PostgreSQL and some other RDBMSes such as Oracle, DB2, or SQL Server is that the transaction rollback is very quick. On those other systems, if you shut down the server in a mode that rolls back transactions, it can cause the shutdown to take a while, possibly a very long time. This difference is for internal reasons, and isn't in any way unsafe. Debian and Ubuntu's pg_ctlcluster supports the --force option, which is rather nice because it first attempts a fast shutdown, and if that fails, it performs an immediate shutdown. After that, it kills the postmaster.

See also

The technology that provides immediate rollback for PostgreSQL is called **Multiversion Concurrency Control** (**MVCC**). More information on this is provided in the *Identifying and fixing bloated tables and indexes* recipe in Chapter 9, *Regular Maintenance*.

Stopping the server in an emergency

If nothing else is working, we may need to stop the server quickly, without caring about disconnecting the clients gently.

Break the glass in case of emergency!

How to do it...

1. The basic command to perform an emergency stop on the server is the following:

   ```
   pg_ctl -D datadir stop -m immediate
   ```

2. On Debian/Ubuntu, you can also use the following:

   ```
   pg_ctlcluster 11 main stop -m immediate
   ```

As we mentioned in the previous recipe, this is just a wrapper around pg_ctl. From this example, we can see that it can pass through the -m immediate option.

> In the previous recipe, we have seen examples where the systemctl command was used to stop a server safely; however, that command cannot be used to perform an emergency stop.

How it works...

When you do an immediate stop, all users have their transactions aborted and all connections are disconnected. There is no clean shutdown, nor is there politeness of any kind.

An immediate mode stop is similar to a database crash. Some cached files will need to be rebuilt, and the database itself needs to undergo crash recovery when it comes back up.

Note that for DBAs with Oracle experience, the immediate mode is the same thing as a shutdown abort. The PostgreSQL immediate mode stop is *not* the same thing as shutdown immediate on Oracle.

Reloading the server configuration files

Some PostgreSQL configuration parameters can be changed only by reloading the entire configuration files.

How to do it...

There are two variants of this recipe, depending on whether you are using `systemd`. This is similar to the previous recipes in this chapter, and especially the *Starting the database server manually* recipe. More details are explained there, such as the exact names of `systemd` service units depending on which database server you want to reload, and which GNU/Linux distribution you are working on.

With `systemd`, configuration files can be reloaded with the following syntax:

```
sudo systemctl reload SERVICEUNIT
```

Here, `SERVICEUNIT` must be replaced with the exact name of the `systemd` service unit for the server(s) that you want to reload.

Otherwise, on each platform, there is a specific command to reload the server without using `systemd`. All of these are listed as follows:

- On Ubuntu and Debian, you can issue the following:

```
pg_ctlcluster 11 main reload
```

- On older Red Hat/Fedora, the command is as follows:

```
service postgresql reload
```

- You can also use the following command:

```
pg_ctl -D /var/lib/pgsql/data reload
```

This also works on macOS, Solaris, and FreeBSD, where you replace `/var/lib/pgsql/data` with your actual data directory if it's different.

On all platforms, you can also reload the configuration files while still connected to PostgreSQL. If you are a superuser, this can be done from the following command line:

```
postgres=# select pg_reload_conf();
```

The output is rather short:

```
pg_reload_conf
----------------
 t
```

This function is also often executed from an admin tool, such as **OmniDB**.

If you do this, you should realize that it's possible to implement a new authentication rule that is violated by the current session. It won't force you to disconnect, but when you do disconnect, you may not be able to reconnect.

Any error in a configuration file will be reported in the message log, so we recommend that you look there immediately after reloading. You will quickly notice (and fix!) syntax errors in the parameter file, because they prevent any login even before reloading. Other errors, such as typos in parameter names, or wrong units, will only be reported in the log; moreover, only some non-syntax errors will prevent reloading the whole file, so it's best to always check the log.

How it works...

To reload the configuration files, we send the SIGHUP signal to the postmaster, which then passes that to all connected backends. That's why some people call reloading the server *sigh-up-ing*.

If you look at the pg_settings catalog table, you'll see that there is a column named context. Each setting has a time and a place where it can be changed. Some parameters can only be reset by a server reload, and so the value of context for those parameters will be a sighup. Here are a few of the parameters you'll want to change sometimes during server operation (there are others, however):

```
postgres=#  SELECT name, setting, unit
                      , (source = 'default') as is_default
            FROM pg_settings
            WHERE context = 'sighup'
            AND (name like '%delay' or name like '%timeout')
            AND setting != '0';
            name                        | setting | unit | is_default
 -------------------------------+---------+------+------------
  authentication_timeout        | 60      | s    | t
  autovacuum_vacuum_cost_delay  | 20      | ms   | t
  bgwriter_delay                | 200     | ms   | f
  checkpoint_timeout            | 300     | s    | f
```

```
max_standby_archive_delay     | 30000   | ms  | t
max_standby_streaming_delay   | 30000   | ms  | t
wal_receiver_timeout          | 60000   | ms  | t
wal_sender_timeout            | 60000   | ms  | t
wal_writer_delay              | 200     | ms  | t
(9 rows)
```

There's more...

Since reloading the configuration file is achieved by sending the SIGHUP signal, we can reload the configuration file only for a single backend using the kill command. As you might expect, you may get some strange results from doing this, so don't try it at home.

First, find the PID of the backend using pg_stat_activity. Then, from the OS prompt, issue the following:

```
kill -SIGHUP pid
```

Alternatively, we can do both at once, as shown in this command:

```
kill -SIGHUP \
&& psql -t -c "select pid from pg_stat_activity limit 1";
```

This is only useful with a sensible WHERE clause.

Restarting the server quickly

Some of the database server parameters require you to stop and start the server again fully. Doing this as quickly as possible can be very important in some cases. The best time to do this is usually a quiet time, with lots of planning, testing, and forethought. Sometimes, not everything goes according to plan.

How to do it...

It's now become a habit in many recipes in this chapter that they be presented in two forms: one with systemd and one without. This may look repetitive or boring, but it's unavoidable because the introduction of a new system does not automatically eliminate all existing alternatives, or migrate old installations to new ones.

Like before, the you can find further `systemd` details, including details on service unit names, in the previous recipe, *Starting the database server manually*, of this chapter.

A PostgreSQL server managed by `systemd` can be restarted in *fast* mode by issuing the following command:

```
sudo systemctl restart SERVICEUNIT
```

As before, change `SERVICEUNIT` to the appropriate service unit name—for example, `postgresql@11-main` for a PostgreSQL 10 cluster running in Debian or Ubuntu.

If `systemd` is not available, then you can use the following syntax:

```
pg_ctlcluster 11 main restart -m fast
```

The basic command to restart the server is the following one:

```
pg_ctl -D datadir restart -m fast
```

A `restart` is just a stop that's going to be followed by a start, so it sounds very simple. In many cases, it will be simple, but there are times when you'll need to restart the server while it is fairly busy. That's when we need to start performing some tricks to make that restart happen quicker.

First, the stop performed needs to be a `fast stop`. If we do a default or a `smart` stop, then the server will just wait for everyone to finish. If we do an immediate stop, then the server will crash, and we will need to crash-recover the data, which will be slower overall.

The running database server has a cache full of data blocks, many of which are dirty. PostgreSQL is similar to other database systems in that it does a shutdown checkpoint before it closes. This means that the startup that follows will be quick and clean. The more work the checkpoint has to do, the longer it will take to shut down.

The actual shutdown will happen much quicker if we issue a normal checkpoint first, as the shutdown checkpoint will have much less work to do. So, flush all the dirty shared buffers to disk with the following command, issued by a database superuser:

```
psql -c "CHECKPOINT"
```

The next consideration is that once we restart, the database cache will be empty again and will need to refresh itself. The larger the database cache, the longer it takes for the cache to get warm again, and 30 to 60 minutes is not uncommon before returning to full speed. So, what was a simple restart can actually have a large business impact if handled badly.

There's more...

There is an extension called `pgfincore` that implements a set of functions to manage PostgreSQL data pages in the operating system's file cache. One possible use is to preload some tables so that PostgreSQL will load them quicker when requested. The general idea is that you can provide more detailed information for the operating system cache, which can therefore behave more efficiently.

The `pgfincore` extension is a stable project that was started in 2009. More details about it are available at `https://github.com/klando/pgfincore`, including the source code. However, it should be noted that most distributions include a prebuilt `pgfincore` package, which makes installation easier.

There is also a `contrib` module called `pg_prewarm`, which addresses a similar problem. While there is some overlap with `pgfincore`, the feature sets are not the same; for instance, `pgfincore` can operate on files that aren't in the shared buffer cache, and it can also preload full relations with only a few system calls, taking into account the existing cache; on the other hand, `pg_prewarm` can operate on the PostgreSQL shared buffer cache, and it also works on Windows.

Preventing new connections

In certain emergencies, you may need to lock down the server completely, or just prevent specific users from accessing the database. It's hard to foresee all the situations in which you might need to do this, so we will present a range of options.

How to do it...

Connections can be prevented in a number of ways, as follows:

- Pause and resume the session pool. See the *Setting up a connection pool* recipe later in this chapter on controlling connection pools.
- Stop the server! See the *Stopping the server safely and quickly* and the *Stopping the server in an emergency* recipes, but this is not recommended.
- Restrict the connections for a specific database to zero, by setting the connection limit to zero:

```
ALTER DATABASE foo_db CONNECTION LIMIT 0;
```

- This will limit normal users from connecting to that database, though it will still allow superuser connections.

- Restrict the connections for a specific user to zero by setting the connection limit to zero (see the *Restricting users to only one session each* recipe):

```
ALTER USER foo CONNECTION LIMIT 0;
```

- This will limit normal users from connecting to that database, but it will still allow connections if the user is a superuser, so luckily you cannot shut yourself out accidentally.
- Change the **Host-Based Authentication** (**HBA**) file to refuse all incoming connections and then reload the server:
    - Create a new file named `pg_hba_lockdown.conf`, and add the following two lines to the file. This puts in place rules that will completely lock down the server, including superusers. You should have no doubt that this is a serious and drastic action:

```
# TYPE   DATABASE USER ADDRESS METHOD
  local  all      all                        reject
  host   all      all          0.0.0.0/0   reject
```

    If you still want superuser access, then try something such as the following:

```
# TYPE    DATABASE    USER        ADDRESS         METHOD
  local   all         postgres                    peer
  local   all         all                         reject
  host    all         all         0.0.0.0/0       reject
```

    This will prevent connections to the database by any user except the `postgres` operating system user ID, which connects locally to any database. Be careful not to confuse the second and third columns—the second column is the database and the third column is the username. It's worth keeping the header line just for that reason. The `peer` method should be replaced by other authentication methods if a more complex configuration is in use.

- Copy the existing `pg_hba.conf` file to `pg_hba_access.conf` so that it can be replaced later, if required.
- Copy `pg_hba_lockdown.conf` to `pg_hba.conf`.
- Reload the server by following the recipe earlier in this chapter.

How it works...

The `pg_hba.conf` file is where we specify the host-based authentication rules. We do not specify the authentications themselves; just specify which authentication mechanisms will be used. This is the top-level set of rules for PostgreSQL authentication. The rules are specified in a file and applied by the postmaster process when connections are attempted. To prevent denial-of-service attacks, the HBA rules never involve database access, so we do not know whether a user is a superuser. As a result, you can lock out all users, but note that you can always re-enable access by editing the file and reloading.

Restricting users to only one session each

If resources need to be closely controlled, you may wish to restrict users so that they can only connect to the server once, at most. The same technique can be used to prevent connections entirely for that user.

How to do it...

We can restrict users to only one connection using the following command:

```
postgres=# ALTER ROLE fred CONNECTION LIMIT 1;
ALTER ROLE
```

This will then cause any additional connections to receive the following error message:

```
FATAL: too many connections for role "fred".
```

You can eliminate this restriction by setting the value to -1.

It's possible to set the limit to zero or any positive integer. You can set this to a number other than `max_connections`, though it is up to you to make sense of that if you do.

Setting the value to zero will completely restrict normal connections. Note that even if you set the connection limit to zero for superusers, they will still be able to connect.

How it works...

The connection limit is applied during the session connection. Raising this limit will never affect any connected users. Lowering the limit doesn't have any effect either, unless they try to disconnect and reconnect.

So, if you lower the limit, you should immediately check to see whether there are more sessions connected than the new limit you just set. Otherwise, there may be some surprises if there is a crash:

```
postgres=> SELECT rolconnlimit
              FROM pg_roles
              WHERE rolname = 'fred';
  rolconnlimit
----------------
             1
(1 row)
postgres=> SELECT count (*)
              FROM pg_stat_activity
              WHERE usename = 'fred';
  count
-------
      2
(1 row)
```

If you have more connected sessions than the new limit, you can ask users politely to disconnect, or you can apply the next recipe, *Pushing users off the system*.

Users can't raise or lower their own connection limit, just in case you are worried that they might be able to override this somehow.

Pushing users off the system

Sometimes, we may need to remove groups of users from the database server for various operational reasons. Here's how to do it.

How to do it...

You can terminate a user's session with the `pg_terminate_backend()` function included with PostgreSQL. This function takes the PID, or the process ID, of the user's session on the server. This process is known as the **backend**, and it is a different system process from the program that runs the client.

To find the PID of a user, we can look at the `pg_stat_activity` view. We can use it in a query, like this:

```
SELECT pg_terminate_backend(pid)
FROM pg_stat_activity
WHERE ...
```

There are a couple of things to note if you run this query. If the `WHERE` clause doesn't match any sessions, then you won't get any output from the query. Similarly, if it matches multiple rows, you will get a fairly useless result, that is, a list of Boolean `true` values. Unless you are careful enough to exclude your own session from the query, you will disconnect yourself! What's even funnier is that you'll disconnect yourself halfway through disconnecting the other users, as the query will run `pg_terminate_backend()` in the order in which sessions are returned from the outer query.

Therefore, I suggest a safer and more useful query that gives a useful response in all cases, which is as follows:

```
postgres=# SELECT count(pg_terminate_backend(pid))
FROM pg_stat_activity
WHERE usename NOT IN
(SELECT usename
 FROM pg_user
WHERE usesuper);
 count
--------
     1
```

This is assuming that superusers are performing administrative tasks.

Other good filters might be the following:

```
WHERE application_name = 'myappname'
WHERE wait_event_type IS NOT NULL AND wait_event_type != 'Activity'
WHERE state = 'idle in transaction'
WHERE state = 'idle'
```

How it works...

The `pg_terminate_backend()` function sends a signal directly to the operating system process for that session.

It's possible that the session may have closed by the time `pg_terminate_backend()` is named. As PID numbers are assigned by the operating system, it could even happen that you try to terminate a given session (let's call it *session A*), but you actually terminate another session (let's call it *session B*).

Here is how it could happen. Suppose you take note of the PID of session A and decide to disconnect it. Before you actually issue `pg_terminate_backend()`, session A disconnects, and right after, a new session, session B, is given exactly the same PID. So, when you terminate that PID, you hit session B instead.

On the one hand, you need to be careful. On the other hand, this case is really unlikely, and is only mentioned for completeness. For it to happen, all the following events must happen as well:

- One of the sessions you are trying to close must terminate independently in the very short interval between the moment `pg_stat_activity` is read and the moment `pg_terminate_backend()` is executed.
- Another session on the same database server must be started in the even-shorter interval between the old session closing and the execution of `pg_terminate_backend()`.
- The new session must get exactly the same PID value as the old session, which is less than one chance in 32,000 on a 32-bit Linux machine.

Nonetheless, probability theory is tricky, even for experts. Therefore, it's better to be aware that there is a tiny risk, especially if you use the query many times per day over a long period of time, in which case the probability of getting caught at least once builds up.

It's also possible that new sessions could start after we get the list of active sessions. There's no way to prevent this other than by following the *Preventing new connections* recipe.

Finally, remember that superusers can terminate any session, while a non-superuser can only terminate a session that belongs to the same user.

Deciding on a design for multitenancy

There are many reasons why we might want to split groups of tables or applications: security, resource control, convenience, and so on. Whatever the reason, we often need to separate groups of tables (I avoid saying the word *database*, just to avoid various kinds of confusion).

This topic is frequently referred to as **multitenancy**, though this is not a fully accepted term yet.

The purpose of this recipe is to discuss the options and lead to other, more detailed recipes.

How to do it...

If you want to run multiple physical databases on one server, then you have four main options, which are as follows:

- **Option 1**: Run multiple sets of tables in different schemas in one database of a PostgreSQL instance (covered in the *Using multiple schemas* recipe)
- **Option 2**: Run multiple databases in the same PostgreSQL instance (covered in the *Giving users their own private database* recipe)
- **Option 3**: Run multiple PostgreSQL instances on the same virtual/physical system (covered in the *Running multiple servers on one system* recipe)
- **Option 4**: Run separate PostgreSQL instances in separate virtual machines on the same physical server

Which is best? Well, that's certainly a question many people ask, and something on which many views exist. The answer lies in looking at the specific requirements, which are as follows:

- If our goal is the separation of physical resources, then option 3 or option 4 works best. Separate database servers can be easily assigned different disks, individual memory allocations can be assigned, and we can take the servers up or down without impacting the others.
- If our goal is security, then option 2 is sufficient.
- If our goal is merely the separation of tables for administrative clarity, then option 1 or option 2 can be useful.

Option 2 allows complete separation for security purposes. This does, however, prevent someone with privileges on both groups of tables from performing a join between those tables. So, if there is a possibility of future cross-analytics, it might be worth considering option 1. However, it might also be argued that such analytics should be carried out on a separate data warehouse, not by co-locating production systems.

Option 3 has a difficulty in many of the PostgreSQL distributions: the default installation uses a single location for the database, making it a little harder to configure that option. Ubuntu/Debian handles that aspect particularly well, making it more attractive in that environment.

Option 4 can be applied using virtualization technology, but that is outside the scope of this book.

How it works...

I've seen people who use PostgreSQL with thousands of databases, but it is my opinion that the majority of people use only one database, such as `postgres` (or at least, only a few databases). I've also seen people with a great many schemas.

One thing you will find is that almost all admin GUI tools become significantly less useful if there are hundreds or thousands of items to display. In most cases, administration tools use a tree view, which doesn't cope gracefully with a large number of items.

Using multiple schemas

We can separate groups of tables into their own namespaces, referred to as **schemas** by PostgreSQL. In many ways, they can be thought of as being similar to directories, though that is not a precise description.

Getting ready

Make sure you've read the *Deciding on a design for multitenancy* recipe so that you're certain that this is the route you wish to take. Other options exist, and they may be preferable in some cases.

How to do it...

1. Schemas can be easily created using the following commands:

```
CREATE SCHEMA finance;
CREATE SCHEMA sales;
```

2. We can then create objects directly within those schemas using *fully qualified* names, like this:

```
CREATE TABLE finance.month_end_snapshot (.....)
```

The default schema in which an object is created is known as `current_schema`. We can find out which is our current schema by using the following query:

```
postgres=# select current_schema;
```

This returns an output like the following:

```
current_schema
----------------
 public
(1 row)
```

3. When we access database objects, we use the user-settable `search_path` parameter to identify the schemas to search for. The `current_schema` is the first schema in the `search_path` parameter. There is no separate parameter for the `current_schema`.

So, if we want to let only a specific user look at certain sets of tables, we can modify their `search_path` parameter. This parameter can be set for each user so that the value will be set when they connect. The SQL queries for this would be something like the following:

```
ALTER ROLE fiona SET search_path = 'finance';
ALTER ROLE sally SET search_path = 'sales';
```

The public schema is not mentioned on `search_path`, so it will not be searched. All tables created by `fiona` will go into the `finance` schema by default, whereas all tables created by `sally` will go into the `sales` schema by default.

4. The users for `finance` and `sales` will be able to see that the other schema exists and change `search_path` to use it, but we will be able to GRANT or REVOKE privileges so that they can neither create objects nor read data in other people's schemas:

```
REVOKE ALL ON SCHEMA finance FROM public;
GRANT ALL ON SCHEMA finance TO fiona;
REVOKE ALL ON SCHEMA sales FROM public;
GRANT ALL ON SCHEMA sales TO sally;
```

An alternate technique is to grant user create privileges on only one schema, but grant usage rights on all other schemas. We can set up that arrangement like this:

```
REVOKE ALL ON SCHEMA finance FROM public;
GRANT USAGE ON SCHEMA finance TO fiona;
GRANT CREATE ON SCHEMA finance TO fiona;
REVOKE ALL ON SCHEMA sales FROM public;
GRANT USAGE ON SCHEMA sales TO sally;
GRANT CREATE ON SCHEMA sales TO sally;
GRANT USAGE ON SCHEMA sales TO fiona;
GRANT USAGE ON SCHEMA finance TO sally
```

5. Note that you need to grant the privileges for usage on the schema, as well as specific rights on the objects in the schema. So, you will also need to issue specific grants for objects, as shown here:

```
GRANT SELECT ON month_end_snapshot TO public;
```

You can also set default privileges so that they are picked up when objects are created by using the following command:

```
ALTER DEFAULT PRIVILEGES FOR USER fiona IN SCHEMA finance
GRANT SELECT ON TABLES TO PUBLIC;
```

How it works...

Earlier, I said that schemas work like directories, or at least a little.

The PostgreSQL concept of `search_path` is similar to the concept of a PATH environment variable.

The PostgreSQL concept of the current schema is similar to the concept of the current working directory. There is no `cd` command to change the directory. The current working directory is changed by altering `search_path`.

A few other differences exist; for example, PostgreSQL schemas are not arranged in a hierarchy like filesystem directories.

Many people create a user of the same name as the schema to make this work in a way similar to other RDBMSes, such as Oracle.

 Both the `finance` and `sales` schemas exist within the same PostgreSQL database, and they run on the same database server. They use a common buffer pool, and there are many global settings that tie the two schemas fairly close together.

Giving users their own private database

Separating data and users is a key part of administration. There will always be a need to give users a private, secure, or simply risk-free area (sandbox) to use the database. Here's how.

Getting ready

Again, make sure you've read the *Deciding on a design for multitenancy* recipe so that you're certain this is the route you wish to take. Other options exist, and they may be preferable in some cases.

How to do it...

Follow these steps to create a database with restricted access to a specific user:

1. We can create a database for a specific user with some ease. From the command line, as a superuser, these actions would be as follows:

```
postgres=# create user fred;
CREATE ROLE
postgres=# create database fred owner fred;
CREATE DATABASE
```

2. As the database owners, users have login privileges, so they can connect to any database by default. There is a command named `ALTER DEFAULT PRIVILEGES`; however, this does not currently apply to databases, tablespaces, or languages. The `ALTER DEFAULT PRIVILEGES` command also currently applies only to roles (that is, users) that already exist.

So, we need to revoke the privilege to connect to our new database from everybody except the designated user. There isn't a `REVOKE ... FROM PUBLIC EXCEPT` command. Therefore, we need to revoke everything and then just re-grant everything we need, all in one transaction, such as in the following code:

```
postgres=# BEGIN;
BEGIN
postgres=# REVOKE connect ON DATABASE  fred FROM public;
REVOKE
postgres=# GRANT connect ON DATABASE fred TO fred;
GRANT
postgres=# COMMIT;
COMMIT
postgres=# create user bob;
CREATE ROLE
```

3. Then, try to connect as `bob` to the `fred` database:

```
os $ psql -U bob fred
psql: FATAL:  permission denied for database "fred"
DETAIL:  User does not have CONNECT privilege.
```

This is exactly what we wanted.

How it works...

If you didn't catch it before, PostgreSQL allows transactional DDL in most places, so either both of the `REVOKE` and `GRANT` commands in the preceding section work or neither works. This means that the `fred` user never loses the ability to connect to the database. Note that `CREATE DATABASE` cannot be performed as part of a transaction, though nothing serious happens as a result.

There's more...

Superusers can still connect to the new database, and there is no way to prevent them from doing so. No other users can see the tables that were created in the new database, nor can they know the names of any of the objects. The new database can be seen to exist by other users, and they can also see the name of the user who owns the database.

See also

See `Chapter 6`, *Security*, for more details on these issues.

Running multiple servers on one system

Running multiple PostgreSQL servers on one physical system is possible if it is convenient for your needs.

Getting ready

Once again, make that sure you've read the *Deciding on a design for multitenancy* recipe so that you're certain this is the route you wish to take. Other options exist, and they may be preferable in some cases.

How to do it...

Core PostgreSQL easily allows multiple servers to run on the same system, but there are a few wrinkles to be aware of.

Some installer versions create a PostgreSQL data directory named `data`. It then gets a little difficult to have more than one `data` directory without using different directory structures and names.

Debian/Ubuntu packagers chose a layout specifically designed to allow multiple servers potentially running with different software release levels. You might remember this from the *Locating the database server files* recipe in `Chapter 2`, *Exploring the Database*.

Starting from `/var/lib/postgresql`, which is the home directory of the postgres user, there is a subdirectory for each major version, for example, `10` or `9.3`, inside which the individual data directories are placed. When installing PostgreSQL server packages, a data directory is created with the default name of `main`. Configuration files are separately placed in `/etc/postgresql/<version>/<name>`, and log files are created in `/var/log/postgresql/postgresql-<version>-<name>.log`.

Thus, not all files will be found in the `data` directory. As an example, let's create an additional `data` directory:

1. We start by running this command:

   ```
   sudo -u postgres pg_createcluster 11 main2
   ```

2. The new database server can then be started using the following command:

   ```
   sudo -u postgres pg_ctlcluster 11 main2 start
   ```

This is sufficient to create and start an additional database cluster in version `11`, named `main2`. The data and configuration files are stored inside the `/var/lib/postgresql/11/main2/` and `/etc/postgresql/11/main2/` directories, respectively, giving the new database the next unused port number, for example, `5433` if this is the second PostgreSQL server on that machine.

Local access to multiple PostgreSQL servers has been simplified as well. PostgreSQL client programs, such as `psql`, are wrapped by a special script that takes the cluster name as an additional parameter and automatically uses the corresponding port number. Hence, you don't really need the following command:

```
psql --port 5433 -h /var/run/postgresql ...
```

Instead, you can refer to the database server by name, as shown here:

```
psql --cluster 11/main2 ...
```

This has its advantages, especially if you wish (or need) to change the port in the future. I find this extremely convenient, and it works with other utilities such as `pg_dump`, `pg_restore`, and so on.

With Red Hat systems, you will need to run `initdb` directly, selecting your directories carefully:

1. First, initialize your `data` directory with something such as the following:

   ```
   sudo -u postgres initdb -D /var/lib/pgsql/datadir2
   ```

2. Then, modify the `port` parameter in the `postgresql.conf` file and start using the following command:

```
sudo -u postgres pg_ctl -D /var/lib/pgsql/datadir2 start
```

This will create an additional database server at the default server version, with files stored in `/var/lib/pgsql/datadir2`.

You can also set up the server with the `chkconfig` utility to ensure it starts on boot, if your distribution supports it.

How it works...

PostgreSQL servers are controlled using `pg_ctl`. Everything else is a wrapper of some kind around this utility. The only constraints on running multiple versions of PostgreSQL come from file locations and naming conventions, assuming (of course) that you have enough resources, such as disk space, memory, and so on. Everything else is straightforward. Having said that, the Debian/Ubuntu design is currently the only design that makes it actually easy to run multiple servers.

Setting up a connection pool

A **connection pool** is a term that's used for a collection of already-connected sessions that can be used to reduce the overhead of connection and reconnection.

There are various ways by which connection pools can be provided, depending on the software stack in use. The best option is to look at the server-side connection pool software because that works for all connection types, not just within a single software stack.

Here, we're going to look at **PgBouncer**, which is designed as a very lightweight connection pool. The name comes from the idea that the pool can be paused and resumed to allow the server to be restarted, or *bounced*.

Getting ready

First of all, decide where you're going to store the PgBouncer parameter files, log files, and PID files. PgBouncer can manage more than one database server's connections at the same time, though that probably isn't wise for simple architectures. If you keep PgBouncer files associated with the database server, then it should be easy to manage.

How to do it...

Carry out the following steps to configure PgBouncer:

1. Create a `pgbouncer.ini` file, as follows:

```
;
; pgbouncer configuration example
;
[databases]
postgres = port=5432 dbname=postgres
[pgbouncer]

listen_addr = 127.0.0.1
listen_port = 6432
admin_users = postgres
;stats_users = monitoring userid
auth_type = any
; put these files somewhere sensible:
auth_file = users.txt
logfile = pgbouncer.log
pidfile = pgbouncer.pid

server_reset_query = DISCARD ALL;
; default values
pool_mode = session
default_pool_size = 20
log_pooler_errors = 0
```

2. Create a `users.txt` file. This must contain the minimum users mentioned in `admin_users` and `stats_users`. Its format is very simple: a collection of lines with a username and a password. Consider the following as an example:

```
"postgres"      ""
```

3. PgBouncer also supports MD5 authentication. To use that effectively, you need to copy the MD5 encrypted passwords from the database server into the `users.txt` file.

Note that, at the time of publication, pgBouncer doesn't support `scram-sha-256` encryption.

4. You may wish to create the `users.txt` file by directly copying the details from the server. This can be done by using the following `psql` script:

```
postgres=> \o users.txt
postgres=> \t
postgres=> SELECT '"'||rolname||'"' "'||rolpassword||'"'
postgres-> FROM pg_authid;
postgres=> \q
```

5. Launch `pgbouncer`:

```
pgbouncer -d pgbouncer.ini
```

6. Test the connection; it should respond to `reload`:

```
psql -p 6432 -h 127.0.0.1 -U postgres pgbouncer -c "reload"
```

7. Finally, verify that PgBouncer's `max_client_conn` parameter does not exceed the `max_connections` parameter on PostgreSQL.

How it works...

PgBouncer is a great piece of software. Its feature set is very carefully defined to ensure that it is simple, robust, and very quick. PgBouncer is not multithreaded, so it runs in a single process, and, thus, on a single CPU. It is very efficient, but very large data transfers will take more time and reduce concurrency, so create those data dumps using a direct connection.

PgBouncer provides connection pooling. If you set `pool_mode = transaction`, then PgBouncer will also provide connection concentration. This allows hundreds or even thousands of incoming connections to be managed, while only a few server connections are made.

As new connections, transactions, or statements arrive, the pool will increase in size up to the user-defined maximum values. Those connections will stay around until the `server_idle_timeout` value before the pool releases them.

PgBouncer also releases sessions every `server_lifetime`. This allows the server to free backends in rotation in order to avoid issues with very long-lived session connections.

The earlier query that creates `users.txt` only includes database users that have a password. All other users will have a null `rolpassword` field, so the whole string evaluates to `NULL`, and the line is omitted from the password file. This is intentional; users without a password represent a security risk, unless they are closely guarded. An example of this is the `postgres` system user connecting from the same machine, which bypasses PgBouncer, and is used only for maintenance by responsible and trusted people.

It is possible to use an HBA file with the same syntax as `pg_hba.conf`. This allows for more flexibility when enabling TLS encryption (which includes SSL) only for connections to remote servers, while using the more efficient peer authentication for local servers.

There's more...

Instead of retrieving passwords from the `userlist.txt` file, PgBouncer can retrieve them directly from PostgreSQL, using the optional `auth_user` and `auth_query` parameters. If `auth_user` is set, PgBouncer will connect to the database using that user and run `auth_query` every time it needs to retrieve the password of some user trying to log in. The default value of `auth_query` is as follows:

```
SELECT usename, passwd FROM pg_shadow WHERE usename=$1
```

This default is just a minimal functioning example, which illustrates the idea of `auth_query`; however, it requires giving PgBouncer superuser access to PostgreSQL. Hence, it is good practice to use the more sophisticated approach of creating a `SECURITY DEFINER` function that can retrieve the username and password, possibly making some checks on the username to allow only applicative connections. This is a good restriction because database administration connections should not go through a connection pooler.

It's also possible to connect to PgBouncer itself to issue commands. This can be done interactively, as if you were entering `psql`, or it can be done using single commands or scripts.

To shut down PgBouncer, we can just type `SHUTDOWN` or enter a single command, as follows:

```
psql -p 6432 pgbouncer -c "SHUTDOWN"
```

You can also use the RELOAD command to make PgBouncer reload (which means reread) the parameter files, as we did to test that everything is working.

If you are doing a switchover, you can use the WAIT_CLOSE command, followed by RELOAD or RECONNECT, to wait until the respective configuration change has been fully activated.

If you are using pool_mode = transaction or pool_mode = statement, then you can use the PAUSE command. This waits for the current transaction to complete before holding further work on that session. Thus, it allows you to perform DDL more easily or restart the server.

PgBouncer also allows you to use the SUSPEND mode, which waits for all server-side buffers to flush.

The PAUSE or SUSPEND modes should eventually be followed by RESUME when the work is done.

In addition to the PgBouncer control commands, there are many varieties of SHOW commands, as listed here:

SHOW command	Result set.
SHOW STATS	Traffic stats, total and average requests, query duration, bytes sent/received, and so on. Also, take a look at SHOW STATS_TOTALS and SHOW STATS_AVERAGES.
SHOW SERVERS	One row per connection to the database server.
SHOW CLIENTS	One row per connection from the client.
SHOW POOLS	One row per pool of users.
SHOW LISTS	Gives a good summary of resource totals.
SHOW USERS	Lists users in users.txt.
SHOW DATABASES	Lists databases in pgbouncer.ini.
SHOW CONFIG	Lists configuration parameters.
SHOW FDS	Shows file descriptors.
SHOW SOCKETS	Shows file sockets.
SHOW VERSION	Shows the PgBouncer version.

Accessing multiple servers using the same host and port

We will now show you one simple, yet important, application of the previous recipe, *Setting up a connection pool*. In that recipe, you saw how to reuse connections with PgBouncer, and thus reduce the cost of disconnecting and reconnecting.

Here, we will demonstrate another way to use PgBouncer—one instance can connect to databases hosted by different database servers at the same time. These databases can be on separate hosts, and can even have different major versions of PostgreSQL!

Getting ready

Suppose we have three database servers, each one hosting one database. All you need to know beforehand is the connection string for each database server.

More complex arrangements are possible, but those are left to you as an exercise.

Before you try this recipe, you should have already gone through the previous recipe. These two recipes have many steps in common, but we've kept them separate because they have clearly different goals.

How to do it...

Each database is completely identified by its connection string. PgBouncer will read this information from its configuration file. Just follow these steps:

1. All you need to do is to set up PgBouncer like you did in the previous recipe, by replacing the databases section of pgbouncer.ini with the following:

   ```
   [databases]
   myfirstdb = port=5432 host=localhost
   anotherdb = port=5437 host=localhost
   sparedb = port=5435 host=localhost
   ```

2. Once you have started PgBouncer, you can connect to the first database:

   ```
   $ psql -p 6432 -h 127.0.0.1 -U postgres myfirstdb
   psql (11.1)
   Type "help" for help.
   ```

```
myfirstdb=# show port;
port
------
5432
(1 row)

myfirstdb=# show server_version;
server_version
-----------------
11.1
(1 row)
```

3. Now, you can connect to the `anotherdb` database as if it were on the same server:

```
myfirstdb=# \c anotherdb
psql (11.1, server 9.5.15)
You are now connected to database "anotherdb" as user "postgres".
```

4. The server's greeting message suggests that we have landed on a different server, so we check the port and the version:

```
anotherdb=# show port;
 port
------
 5437
(1 row)

anotherdb=# show server_version;
server_version
-----------------
       9.5.15
(1 row)
```

There's more...

The *Listing databases on this database server* recipe in `Chapter 2`, *Exploring the Database*, shows you how to list the available databases on the current database server, using either the `\l` meta-command or a couple of equivalent variations. Unfortunately, that doesn't work when using PgBouncer, for the very good reason that the current database server cannot know the answer.

We need to ask PgBouncer instead, and we do so by using the SHOW command when connected to the pgbouncer special administrative database:

```
myfirstdb=# \c pgbouncer
psql (10.1, server 1.8.1/bouncer)
You are now connected to database "pgbouncer" as user "postgres".
pgbouncer=# show databases;
    name     |    host     | port | database  | force_user | pool_size |
reserve_pool
-------------+-------------+------+-----------+------------+-----------+-------
--------
 anotherdb  | localhost   | 5437 | anotherdb |            |        20 |
0
 myfirstdb  | localhost   | 5432 | myfirstdb |            |        20 |
0
 pgbouncer  |             | 6432 | pgbouncer | pgbouncer  |         2 |
0
 sparedb    | localhost   | 5435 | sparedb   |            |        20 |
0
(4 rows)
```

Tables and Data

5

This chapter covers a range of general recipes for your tables and for working with the data they contain. Many of the recipes contain general advice, though with specific PostgreSQL examples.

Some system administrators I've met work only on the external aspects of the database server. What's actually in the database is someone else's problem.

Look after your data, and your database will look after you. Keep your data clean, and your queries will run faster and cause fewer application errors. You'll also gain many friends in the business. Getting called in the middle of the night to fix data problems just isn't cool.

In this chapter, we will cover the following recipes:

- Choosing good names for database objects
- Handling objects with quoted names
- Enforcing the same name and definition for columns
- Identifying and removing duplicates
- Preventing duplicate rows
- Finding a unique key for a set of data
- Generating test data
- Randomly sampling data
- Loading data from a spreadsheet
- Loading data from flat files
- Making bulk data changes using server-side procedures with transactions

Choosing good names for database objects

The easiest way to help other people understand a database is to ensure that all the objects have a meaningful name.

What makes a name meaningful?

Getting ready

Take some time to reflect on your database to make sure you have a clear view of its purpose and main use cases. This is because all the items in this recipe describe certain naming choices that you need to consider carefully in view of your specific circumstances.

How to do it...

Here are the points you should consider when naming your database objects:

- The name follows the existing standards and practices in place. Inventing new standards isn't helpful; enforcing existing standards is.
- The name clearly describes the role or table contents.
- For major tables, use short, powerful names.
- Name lookup tables after the table to which they are linked, such as `account_status`.
- For associative or linked tables, use all the names of the major tables to which they relate, such as `customer_account`.
- Make sure that the name is clearly distinct from other similar names.
- Use consistent abbreviations.
- Use underscores. Casing is not preserved by default, so using camel case names, such as `customerAccount`, as used in Java, will just leave them unreadable. See the *Handling objects with quoted names* recipe.
- Use consistent plurals, or don't use them at all.
- Use suffixes to identify the content type or domain of an object. PostgreSQL already uses suffixes for automatically generated objects.
- Think ahead. Don't pick names that refer to the current role or location of an object. So don't name a table `London`, because it exists on a server in London. That server might get moved to Los Angeles.

12. Think ahead. Don't pick names that imply that an entity is the only one of its kind, such as a table named `TEST`, or a table named `BACKUP_DATA`. On the other hand, such information can be put in the database name, which is not normally used from within the database.

13. Avoid using acronyms in place of long table names. For example, `money_allocation_decision` is much better than `MAD`. This is especially important when PostgreSQL translates the names into lowercase, so the fact that it is an acronym may not be clear.

14. The table name is commonly used as the root for other objects that are created, so don't add the `table` suffix or similar ideas.

There's more...

The standard names for indexes in PostgreSQL are as follows:

```
{tablename}_{columnname(s)}_{suffix}
```

Here, the suffix is one of the following:

- `pkey`: This is used for a primary key constraint
- `key`: This is used for a unique constraint
- `excl`: This is used for an exclusion constraint
- `idx`: This is used for any other kind of index

The standard suffix for all sequences is `seq`.

Tables can have multiple triggers fired on each event. Triggers are executed in alphabetical order, so trigger names should have some kind of action name to differentiate them and to allow the order to be specified. It might seem a good idea to put `INSERT`, `UPDATE`, or `DELETE` in the trigger name, but that can get confusing if you have triggers that work on both `UPDATE` and `DELETE`, and all of this may end up as a mess.

The alphabetical order for trigger names always follows the C locale, regardless of your actual locale settings. If your trigger names use non-ASCII characters, then the actual ordering might not be what you expect.

The following example shows how the è and é characters are ordered in the C locale. You can change the locale and/or the list of strings to explore how different locales affect ordering:

```
WITH a(x) AS (
  VALUES ('è'), ('é')
) SELECT *
FROM a
ORDER BY x
COLLATE "C";
```

A useful naming convention for triggers is as follows:

```
{tablename}_{actionname}_{after|before}_trig
```

If you do find yourself with strange or irregular object names, it will be a good idea to use the RENAME subcommands to get things tidy again. Here is an example of this:

```
ALTER INDEX badly_named_index RENAME TO tablename_status_idx;
```

Handling objects with quoted names

PostgreSQL object names can contain spaces and mixed-case characters if we enclose the table names in double quotes. This can cause some difficulties, so this recipe is designed to help you if you get stuck with this kind of problem.

Case sensitivity issues can often be a problem for people more used to working with other database systems, such as MySQL, or for people who are facing the challenge of migrating code away from MySQL.

Getting ready

First, let's create a table that uses a quoted name with mixed cases, such as the following:

```
CREATE TABLE "MyCust"
AS
SELECT * FROM cust;
```

How to do it...

If we try to access these tables without the proper case, we get this error:

```
postgres=# SELECT count(*) FROM mycust;
ERROR:   relation "mycust" does not exist LINE 1: SELECT * FROM mycust;
```

So, we write it in the correct case:

```
postgres=# SELECT count(*) FROM MyCust;
ERROR:   relation "mycust" does not exist
LINE 1: SELECT * FROM mycust;
```

This still fails, and in fact gives the same error.

If you want to access a table that was created with quoted names, then you must use quoted names, such as the following:

```
postgres=# SELECT count(*) FROM "MyCust";
```

The output is as follows:

```
 count
-------
     5
(1 row)
```

The usage rule is that, if you create your tables using quoted names, then you need to write your SQL using quoted names. Alternatively, if your SQL uses quoted names, then you will probably have to create the tables using quoted names as well.

How it works...

PostgreSQL folds all names to lowercase when used within an SQL statement. Consider this command:

```
SELECT * FROM mycust;
```

This is exactly the same as the following command:

```
SELECT * FROM MYCUST;
```

It is also exactly the same as this command:

```
SELECT * FROM MyCust;
```

However, it is not the same thing as the following command:

```
SELECT * FROM "MyCust";
```

There's more...

If you are extracting values from a table that is being used to create object names, then you may need to use a handy function named `quote_ident()`. This function puts double quotes around a value if PostgreSQL requires that for an object name, as shown here:

```
postgres=# SELECT quote_ident('MyCust');
 quote_ident
-------------
 "MyCust"
(1 row)
postgres=# SELECT quote_ident('mycust');
 quote_ident
-------------
 mycust
(1 row)
```

The `quote_ident()` function may be especially useful if you are creating a table based on a variable name in a PL/pgSQL function, as follows:

```
EXECUTE 'CREATE TEMP TABLE ' || quote_ident(tablename) ||
                   '(col1            INTEGER);'
```

Enforcing the same name and definition for columns

Sensibly designed databases have smooth, easy-to-understand definitions. This allows all users to understand the meaning of data in each table. It is an important way of removing data quality issues.

Getting ready

If you want to run the queries in this recipe as a test, then use the following examples. Alternatively, you can just check for problems in your own database:

```
CREATE SCHEMA s1;
CREATE SCHEMA s2;
CREATE TABLE s1.X(col1 smallint,col2 TEXT);
CREATE TABLE s2.X(col1 integer,col3 NUMERIC);
```

How to do it...

First, we will show you how to identify columns that are defined in different ways in different tables, using a query against the catalog. We use an information_schema query, as follows:

```
SELECT
 table_schema
,table_name
,column_name
,data_type
  ||coalesce(' ' || text(character_maximum_length), '')
  ||coalesce(' ' || text(numeric_precision), '')
  ||coalesce(',' || text(numeric_scale), '')
  as data_type
FROM information_schema.columns
WHERE column_name IN
(SELECT
 column_name
FROM
(SELECT
  column_name
 ,data_type
 ,character_maximum_length
 ,numeric_precision
 ,numeric_scale
 FROM information_schema.columns
 WHERE table_schema NOT IN ('information_schema', 'pg_catalog')
 GROUP BY
  column_name
 ,data_type
 ,character_maximum_length
 ,numeric_precision
 ,numeric_scale
) derived
GROUP BY column_name
```

```
HAVING count(*) > 1
)
AND table_schema NOT IN ('information_schema', 'pg_catalog')
ORDER BY column_name
;
```

The query gives an output as follows:

```
table_schema | table_name | column_name |    data_type
-------------+------------+-------------+----------------
s1           | x          | col1        | smallint 16,0
s2           | x          | col1        | integer 32,0
(2 rows)
```

Comparing two given tables is more complex, as there are so many ways that the tables might be similar and yet a little different. The following query looks for all tables of the same name (and hence, in different schemas) that have different definitions:

```
WITH table_definition as
( SELECT table_schema
       , table_name
       , string_agg( column_name || ' ' || data_type
                   , ',' ORDER BY column_name
                   ) AS def
    FROM information_schema.columns
   WHERE table_schema NOT IN ( 'information_schema'
                             , 'pg_catalog')
   GROUP BY table_schema
          , table_name
)
   , unique_definition as
( SELECT DISTINCT table_name
       , def
    FROM table_definition
)
   , multiple_definition as
( SELECT table_name
    FROM unique_definition
   GROUP BY table_name
  HAVING count( * ) > 1
)
SELECT table_schema
     , table_name
     , column_name
     , data_type
    FROM information_schema.columns
   WHERE table_name
         IN ( SELECT table_name
```

```
            FROM multiple_definition )
   ORDER BY table_name
          , table_schema
          , column_name
  ;
```

Here is its output:

```
table_schema | table_name | column_name | data_type
-------------+------------+-------------+-----------
 s1          | x          | col1        | smallint
 s1          | x          | col2        | text
 s2          | x          | col1        | integer
 s2          | x          | col3        | numeric
(4 rows)
```

How it works...

The definitions of tables are held within PostgreSQL, and can be accessed using the Information Schema catalog views.

There might be valid reasons why the definitions differ. We've excluded PostgreSQL's own internal tables because there are similar names between the two catalogs: PostgreSQL's implementation of the SQL Standard Information Schema and PostgreSQL's own internal pg_catalog schema.

Those queries are fairly complex. In fact, there is even more complexity that we could add to those queries to compare all sorts of things such as default values or constraints. The basic idea can be extended in various directions from here.

There's more...

We can compare the definitions of any two tables using the following function:

```
CREATE OR REPLACE FUNCTION diff_table_definition
(t1_schemaname text
,t1_tablename text
,t2_schemaname text
,t2_tablename text)
RETURNS TABLE
(t1_column_name text
,t1_data_type text
,t2_column_name text
,t2_data_type text
```

```
)
LANGUAGE SQL
as
$$
SELECT
 t1.column_name
,t1.data_type
,t2.column_name
,t2.data_type
FROM
  (SELECT column_name, data_type
   FROM information_schema.columns
   WHERE table_schema = $1
       AND table_name = $2
  ) t1
  FULL OUTER JOIN
  (SELECT column_name, data_type
   FROM information_schema.columns
   WHERE table_schema = $3
       AND table_name = $4
  ) t2
  ON t1.column_name = t2.column_name
  AND t1.data_type = t2.data_type
WHERE t1.column_name IS NULL OR t2.column_name IS NULL
;
$$;
```

Here is its usage with output:

```
# select diff_table_definition('s1','x','s2','x');
 diff_table_definition
----------------------
 (col1,smallint,,)
 (col2,text,,)
 (,,col3,numeric)
 (,,col1,integer)
(4 rows)
```

Identifying and removing duplicates

Relational databases work on the idea that items of data can be uniquely identified. However hard we try, there will always be bad data arriving from somewhere. This recipe shows you how to diagnose that and clean up the mess.

Getting ready

Let's start by looking at our example table, `cust`. It has a duplicate value in `customerid`:

```
postgres=# SELECT * FROM cust;
 customerid | firstname | lastname | age
------------+-----------+----------+-----
          1 | Philip    | Marlowe  |  38
          2 | Richard   | Hannay   |  42
          3 | Holly     | Martins  |  25
          4 | Harry     | Palmer   |  36
          4 | Mark      | Hall     |  47
(5 rows)
```

Before you delete duplicate data, remember that sometimes it isn't the data that is wrong: it is your understanding of it. In those cases, it may be that you haven't properly normalized your database model, and that you need to include additional tables to account for the shape of the data. You might also find that duplicate rows are caused because of your decision to exclude a column somewhere earlier in a data load process. Check twice, and delete once.

How to do it...

First, identify the duplicates using a query such as the following:

```
CREATE UNLOGGED TABLE dup_cust AS
SELECT *
FROM cust
WHERE customerid IN
  (SELECT customerid
   FROM cust
   GROUP BY customerid
   HAVING count(*) > 1);
```

We save the list of duplicates in a separate table because the query can be very slow if the table is big, so we don't want to run it more than once.

 An UNLOGGED table can be created with less I/O because it does not write WAL. It is better than a temporary table, because it doesn't disappear if you disconnect and then reconnect. The other side of the coin is that you lose its contents after a crash, but this is not too bad, because if you are using an unlogged table then you are telling PostgreSQL that you are able to recreate the contents of that table in the (unlikely) event of a crash.

The results can be used to identify the bad data manually, and you can resolve the problem by carrying out the following steps:

1. Merge the two rows to give the best picture of the data, if required. This might use values from one row to update the row you decide to keep, as shown here:

```
UPDATE cust
SET age = 47
WHERE customerid = 4
AND lastname = 'Palmer';
```

2. Delete the remaining undesirable rows:

```
DELETE FROM cust
WHERE customerid = 4
AND lastname = 'Hall';
```

In some cases, the data rows might be completely identical, as in the new_cust table, which looks like the following:

```
postgres=# SELECT * FROM new_cust;
 customerid
------------
          1
          2
          3
          4
          4
(5 rows)
```

Unlike the preceding case, we can't tell the data apart at all, so we cannot remove duplicate rows without any manual process. SQL is a set-based language, so picking only one row out of a set is slightly harder than most people want it to be.

In these circumstances, we should use a slightly different procedure to detect duplicates. We will use a hidden column named ctid. It denotes the physical location of the row you are observing; for example, duplicate rows will all have different ctid values. The steps are as follows:

1. First, we start a transaction:

```
BEGIN;
```

2. Then, we lock the table in order to prevent any INSERT, UPDATE, or DELETE operations, which would alter the list of duplicates and/or change their ctid values:

```
LOCK TABLE new_cust IN SHARE ROW EXCLUSIVE MODE;
```

3. Now we locate all duplicates, keeping track of the minimum ctid value so that we don't delete that value:

```
CREATE TEMPORARY TABLE dups_cust AS
SELECT customerid, min(ctid) AS min_ctid
FROM new_cust
GROUP BY customerid
HAVING count(*) > 1;
```

4. Then we can delete each duplicate, with the exception of the duplicate with the minimum ctid value:

```
DELETE FROM new_cust
USING dups_cust
WHERE new_cust.customerid = dups_cust.customerid
AND new_cust.ctid != dups_cust.min_ctid;
```

5. We commit the transaction, which also releases the lock we previously took:

```
COMMIT;
```

6. Finally, we clean up the table after the deletions:

```
VACUUM new_cust;
```

How it works...

The first query works by grouping together the rows on the unique column and counting rows. Anything with more than one row must be caused by duplicate values. If we're looking for duplicates of more than one column (or even all columns), then we have to use a SQL of the following form:

```
SELECT *
FROM mytable
WHERE  (col1, col2, ... ,colN) IN
(SELECT col1, col2, ... ,colN
 FROM mytable
 GROUP BY  col1, col2, ... ,colN
 HAVING count(*) > 1);
```

Here, col1, col2, and so on up until colN are the columns of the key.

Note that this type of query may need to sort the complete table on all the key columns. That will require sort space equal to the size of the table, so you'd better think first before running that SQL on very large tables. You'll probably benefit from a large work_mem setting for this query, probably 128 MB or more.

The DELETE FROM ... USING query that we showed, only works with PostgreSQL because it uses the ctid value, which is the internal identifier of each row in the table. If you wanted to run that query against more than one column, as we did earlier in the chapter, you'd need to extend the queries in *step 3*, as follows:

```
SELECT customerid, customer_name, ..., min(ctid) AS min_ctid
FROM ...
GROUP BY customerid, customer_name, ...
...;
```

Then, extend the query in *step 4*, like this:

```
DELETE FROM new_cust
...
WHERE new_cust.customerid = dups_cust.customerid
AND new_cust.customer_name = dups_cust.customer_name
AND ...
AND new_cust.ctid != dups_cust.min_ctid;
```

The preceding query works by grouping together all the rows with similar values and then finding the row with the lowest ctid value. The lowest will be closer to the start of the table, so duplicates will be removed from the far end of the table. When we run VACUUM, we may find that the table gets smaller, because we have removed rows from the far end.

The BEGIN and COMMIT commands wrap the LOCK and DELETE commands into a single transaction, which is required. Otherwise, the lock will be released immediately after being taken.

Another reason to use a single transaction is that we can always roll back if anything goes wrong, which is a good thing when we are removing data from a live table.

There's more...

Locking the table against changes for long periods may not be possible while we remove duplicate rows. That creates some fairly hard problems with large tables. In that case, we need to do things slightly differently:

1. Identify the rows to be deleted, and save them in a side table.
2. Build an index on the main table to speed up access to rows (maybe using the CONCURRENTLY keyword, as explained in the *Maintaining indexes* recipe in Chapter 9, *Regular Maintenance*).
3. Write a program that reads the rows from the side table in a loop, performing a series of smaller transactions.
4. Start a new transaction.
5. From the side table, read a set of rows that match.
6. Select those rows from the main table for updates, relying on the index to make those accesses happen quickly.
7. Delete the appropriate rows.
8. Commit, and then loop again.

The aforementioned program can't be written as a database function, as we can't have multiple transactions in a function. We need multiple transactions to ensure that we hold locks on each row for the shortest possible duration.

Preventing duplicate rows

Preventing duplicate rows is one of the most important aspects of data quality for any database. PostgreSQL offers some useful features in this area, extending beyond most relational databases.

Getting ready

Identify the set of columns that you wish to make unique. Does this apply to all rows, or just a subset of rows?

Let's start with our example table:

```
postgres=# SELECT * FROM new_cust;
 customerid
------------
          1
          2
          3
          4
(4 rows)
```

How to do it...

To prevent duplicate rows, we need to create a unique index that the database server can use to enforce uniqueness of a particular set of columns. We can do this in the following three similar ways for basic data types:

1. Create a primary key constraint on the set of columns. We are allowed only one of these per table. The values of the data rows must not be NULL, as we force the columns to be NOT NULL if they aren't already:

    ```
    ALTER TABLE new_cust ADD PRIMARY KEY(customerid);
    ```

2. This creates a new index named new_cust_pkey.
3. Create a unique constraint on the set of columns. We can use these instead of/or with a primary key. There is no limit on the number of these per table. NULL values are allowed in the columns:

    ```
    ALTER TABLE new_cust ADD UNIQUE(customerid);
    ```

4. This creates a new index named new_cust_customerid_key.
5. Create a unique index on the set of columns:

    ```
    CREATE UNIQUE INDEX ON new_cust (customerid);
    ```

6. This creates a new index named new_cust_customerid_idx.

All of these techniques exclude duplicates, just with slightly different syntaxes. All of them create an index, but only the first two create a formal *constraint*. Each of these techniques can be used when we have a primary key or unique constraint that uses multiple columns.

The last method is important because it allows you to specify a WHERE clause on the index. This can be useful if you know that the column values are unique only in certain circumstances. The resulting index is then known as a **partial index**.

Suppose our data looked like this:

```
postgres=# SELECT * FROM partial_unique;
```

This gives the following output:

```
customerid | status | close_date
-----------+--------+------------
         1 | OPEN   |
         2 | OPEN   |
         3 | OPEN   |
         3 | CLOSED | 2010-03-22
(4 rows)
```

Then we can put a partial index on the table to enforce uniqueness of customerid only for status = 'OPEN', like this:

```
CREATE UNIQUE INDEX ON partial_unique (customerid)
    WHERE status = 'OPEN';
```

If your uniqueness constraint needs to be enforced across more complex data types, then you may need to use a more advanced syntax. A few examples will help here.

Let's start with the simplest example: create a table of boxes and put sample data in it. This may be the first time you're seeing PostgreSQL's data type syntax, so bear with me:

```
postgres=# CREATE TABLE boxes (name text, position box);
CREATE TABLE
postgres=# INSERT INTO boxes VALUES
                        ('First', box '((0,0), (1,1))');
INSERT 0 1
postgres=# INSERT INTO boxes VALUES
                        ('Second', box '((2,0), (2,1))');
INSERT 0 1
postgres=# SELECT * FROM boxes;
  name   |   position
---------+--------------
 First   | (1,1),(0,0)
 Second  | (2,1),(2,0)
(2 rows)
```

We can see two boxes that neither touch nor overlap, based on their x and y coordinates.

To enforce uniqueness here, we want to create a constraint that will throw out any attempt to add a position that overlaps with any existing box. The overlap operator for the box data type is defined as &&, so we use the following syntax to add the constraint:

```
ALTER TABLE boxes ADD EXCLUDE USING gist (position WITH &&);
```

This creates a new index named `boxes_position_excl`:

```
#\d boxes_position_excl
 Index "public.boxes_position_excl"
  Column | Type | Key? | Definition
----------+------+------+------------
 position | box | yes | "position"
gist, for table "public.boxes"
```

We can use the same syntax even with the basic data types. So, a fourth way of performing our first example would be as follows:

```
ALTER TABLE new_cust ADD EXCLUDE (customerid WITH =);
```

This creates a new index named `new_cust_customerid_excl` and duplicates are excluded:

```
# insert into new_cust VALUES (4);
ERROR: conflicting key value violates exclusion constraint
"new_cust_customerid_excl"
DETAIL: Key (customerid)=(4) conflicts with existing key (customerid)=(4).
```

How it works...

Uniqueness is always enforced by an index.

Each index is defined with a data type operator. When a new row is inserted or the set of column values is updated, we use the operator to search for existing values that conflict with the new data.

So, to enforce uniqueness, we need an index and a search operator defined on the data types of the columns. When we define normal UNIQUE constraints, we simply assume that we mean the equality operator (=) for the data type. The EXCLUDE syntax offers a richer syntax to allow us to express the same problem with different data types and operators.

There's more...

Unique and exclusion constraints can be marked as deferrable, meaning that the user can choose to postpone the check to the end of the transaction, a nice way to relax constraints without reducing data integrity.

Duplicate indexes

Note that PostgreSQL allows you to have multiple indexes with exactly the same definition. This is useful in some contexts, but can also be annoying if you accidentally create multiple indexes, as each index has its own cost in terms of writes. You can also have constraints defined using each of the aforementioned different ways. Each of these ways enforces, essentially, the same constraint, so take care.

Uniqueness without indexes

It's possible to have uniqueness in a set of columns without creating an index. That might be useful if all we want is to ensure uniqueness rather than allow index lookups.

To do that, you can do either of the following:

- Use a serial data type
- Manually alter the default to be the `nextval()` function of a sequence

Each of these will provide a unique value for use as a row's key. The uniqueness is not enforced, nor will there be a unique constraint defined. So, there is still a possibility that someone might reset the sequence to an earlier value, which will eventually cause duplicate values.

Consider, also, that this method provides the unique value as a default, which is not used when the user specifies an explicit value. An example of this is as follows:

```
CREATE TABLE t(id serial, descr text);
INSERT INTO t(descr) VALUES ('First value');
INSERT INTO t(id,descr) VALUES (1,'Cheating!');
```

Finally, you might also wish to have mostly unique data, such as using the `clock_timestamp()` function to provide ascending times to microsecond resolution.

Real-world example – IP address range allocation

The problem is about assigning ranges of IP addresses, while at the same time ensuring that we don't allocate (or potentially allocate) the same addresses to different people or purposes. This is easy to do if we keep track of each individual IP address, and much harder to do if we want to deal solely with ranges of IP addresses.

Initially, you may think of designing the database as follows:

```
CREATE TABLE iprange
  (iprange_start inet
  ,iprange_stop inet
  ,owner text);
INSERT INTO iprange VALUES
        ('192.168.0.1','192.168.0.16', 'Simon');
INSERT INTO iprange VALUES
        ('192.168.0.17','192.168.0.24', 'Gianni');
INSERT INTO iprange VALUES
        ('192.168.0.32','192.168.0.64', 'Gabriele');
```

However, you'll realize that there is no way to create a unique constraint that enforces the model constraint of avoiding overlapping ranges. You could create an after trigger that checks existing values, but it's going to be messy.

PostgreSQL offers a better solution, based on *range types*. In fact, every data type that supports a btree operator class (that is, a way of ordering any two given values) can be used to create a range type. In our case, the SQL is as follows:

```
CREATE TYPE inetrange AS RANGE (SUBTYPE = inet);
```

This command creates a new data type that can represent ranges of inet values, that is, of IP addresses. Now we can use this new type when creating a table:

```
CREATE TABLE iprange2
(iprange inetrange
,owner text);
```

This new table can be populated as usual. We just have to group the extremes of each range into a single value, as follows:

```
INSERT INTO iprange2
VALUES ('[192.168.0.1,192.168.0.16]', 'Simon');
INSERT INTO iprange2
VALUES ('[192.168.0.17,192.168.0.24]', 'Gianni');
INSERT INTO iprange2
VALUES ('[192.168.0.32,192.168.0.64]', 'Gabriele');
```

Now we can create a *unique exclusion constraint* on the table, using the following syntax:

```
ALTER TABLE iprange2
 ADD EXCLUDE USING GIST (iprange WITH &&);
```

If we try to insert a range that overlaps with any of the existing ranges, then PostgreSQL will stop us:

```
INSERT INTO iprange2
VALUES ('[192.168.0.10,192.168.0.20]', 'Somebody else');
ERROR:   conflicting key value violates exclusion constraint
"iprange2_iprange_excl"
DETAIL:   Key (iprange)=([192.168.0.10,192.168.0.20]) conflicts with
existing key (iprange)=([192.168.0.1,192.168.0.16]).
```

Real-world example – range of time

In many databases, there will be historical data tables with data that has a START_DATE value and an END_DATE value, or something similar. As in the previous example, we can solve this example elegantly with a range type. Actually, this example is even shorter – we don't need to create the range type since the most common cases are already built-in, and, to be precise, include integers, decimal values, dates, and timestamps with and without a time zone.

Real-world example – prefix ranges

Another common problem involves assigning credit card numbers or telephone numbers. For example, with credit card numbers, we may need to perform additional checking for certain financial institutions, assuming that each institution is assigned a given range. In that case, we must check efficiently if a given credit card number belongs to a certain range.

The prefix range data type has been specifically designed to address this class of problems. This is available as a PostgreSQL extension at http://github.com/dimitri/prefix.

> A warning: despite the similar name, prefix ranges cannot be implemented as range types.

Finding a unique key for a set of data

Sometimes, it can be difficult to find a unique set of key columns that describe the data.

Getting ready

Let's start with a small table, where the answer is fairly obvious:

```
postgres=# select * from ord;
```

We assume that the output is as follows:

```
 orderid  | customerid |  amt
----------+------------+--------
   10677 |          2 |   5.50
    5019 |          3 | 277.44
    9748 |          3 |  77.17
(3 rows)
```

How to do it...

First of all, there's no need to do this through a brute-force approach. Checking all the permutations of columns to see which is unique might take you a long time.

Let's start by using PostgreSQL's own optimizer statistics. Run the following command on our table to get a fresh sample of statistics:

```
postgres=# analyze ord;
ANALYZE
```

This runs quickly, so we don't have to wait too long. Now we can examine the relevant columns of the statistics:

```
postgres=# SELECT attname, n_distinct
                  FROM pg_stats
                  WHERE schemaname = 'public'
                  AND tablename = 'ord';
   attname    | n_distinct
--------------+------------
 orderid      |         -1
 customerid   |  -0.666667
 amt          |         -1
(3 rows)
```

The preceding example was chosen because we have two potential answers. If the value of `n_distinct` is −1, then the column is thought to be unique within the sample of rows examined.

We would then need to use our judgment to decide whether one or both of these columns are unique by chance, or as part of the design of the database that created them.

It's possible that there is no single column that uniquely identifies the rows. Multiple column keys are fairly common. If none of the columns were unique, then we should start looking for unique keys that are combinations of the most unique columns. The following query shows a frequency distribution for the table such that a value occurs twice in one case, and another value occurs only once:

```
postgres=# SELECT num_of_values, count(*)
            FROM (SELECT customerid, count(*) AS num_of_values
                    FROM ord
                    GROUP BY customerid) s
            GROUP BY num_of_values
            ORDER BY count(*);
 num_of_values | count
---------------+-------
             2 |     1
             1 |     1
(2 rows)
```

We can change the query to include multiple columns, like this:

```
SELECT num_of_values, count(*)
FROM (SELECT   customerid, orderid, amt
               ,count(*) AS num_of_values
               FROM ord
               GROUP BY customerid, orderid, amt
               ) s
GROUP BY num_of_values
ORDER BY count(*);
```

This query will result in only one row, once we find a set of columns that is unique.

As we get closer to finding the key, we will see that the distribution gets tighter and tighter.

So, the procedure is as follows:

1. Choose one column to start with.
2. Compute the corresponding frequency distribution.
3. If the outcome is multiple rows, then add one more column and repeat from step 2. Otherwise, it means you have found a set of columns satisfying a uniqueness constraint.

Now you must verify that the set of columns is minimal; for example, check whether it is possible to remove one or more columns without violating the unique constraint. This can be done using the frequency distribution as a test. To be precise, do the following:

1. Test each column by computing the frequency distribution on all the other columns.
2. If the frequency distribution has one row, then the column is not needed in the uniqueness constraint. Remove it from the set of columns and repeat from *step 1*. Otherwise, you have found a minimal set of columns, which is also called a key for that table.

How it works...

Finding a unique key is possible for a program, but in most cases, a human can do this much faster by looking at things such as column names, foreign keys, or business understanding to reduce the number of searches required by the brute-force approach.

The ANALYZE command works by taking a sample of the table data, and then performing a statistical analysis of the results. The n_distinct value has two different meanings, depending on its sign: if positive, it is the estimate of the number of distinct values for the column; if negative, it is the estimate of the density of such distinct values, with the sign changed. For example, n_distinct = -0.2 means that a table of one million rows is expected to have 200,000 distinct values, while n_distinct = 5 means that we expect just five distinct values.

Generating test data

DBAs frequently need to generate test data for a variety of reasons, whether it's for setting up a test database or just for generating a test case for a SQL performance issue.

How to do it...

To create a table of test data, we need the following:

- Some rows
- Some columns
- Some order

The steps are as follows:

1. First, generate a lot of rows of data. We use something named a `set-returning` function. You can write your own, though PostgreSQL includes a couple of very useful ones.

2. You can generate a sequence of rows using a query like the following:

```
postgres=# SELECT * FROM generate_series(1,5);
 generate_series
-----------------
               1
               2
               3
               4
               5
(5 rows)
```

3. Alternatively, you can generate a list of dates, like this:

```
postgres=# SELECT date(t)
FROM generate_series(now(),
  now() + '1 week', '1 day') AS f(t);
    date
------------
 2018-04-24
 2018-04-25
 2018-04-26
 2018-04-27
 2018-04-28
 2018-04-29
 2018-04-30
 2018-05-01
(8 rows)
```

4. Then, we want to generate a value for each column in the `test` table. We can break that down into a series of functions, using the following examples as a guide:

   - Either of these functions can be used to generate both rows and reasonable primary key values for them
   - For a random `integer` value, this is the function:

   ```
   (random()*(2*10^9))::integer
   ```

   - For a random `bigint` value, the function is as follows:

   ```
   (random()*(9*10^18))::bigint
   ```

5. For random `numeric` data, the function is the following:

   ```
   (random()*100.)::numeric(5,2)
   ```

   - For a random-length string, up to a maximum length, this is the function:

   ```
   repeat('1',(random()*40)::integer)
   ```

   - For a random-length substring, the function is as follows:

   ```
   substr('abcdefghijklmnopqrstuvwxyz',1,
   (random()*25)::integer)
   ```

   - Here is the function for a random string from a list of strings:

   ```
   (ARRAY['one','two','three'])[0.5+random()*3]
   ```

6. Finally, we can put both techniques together to generate our table:

   ```
   postgres=# SELECT key
                     ,(random()*100.)::numeric(4,2)
                     ,repeat('1',(random()*25)::integer)
   FROM generate_series(1,10) AS f(key);
   key | numeric |          repeat
   -----+---------+-------------------------------
     1 |   83.05 | 1111
     2 |    5.28 | 11111111111111
     3 |   41.85 | 111111111111111111111111
     4 |   41.70 | 11111111111111111
     5 |   53.31 | 1
     6 |   10.09 | 1111111111111111
     7 |   68.08 | 111
   ```

```
  8 |   19.42 | 1111111111111111
  9 |   87.03 | 1111111111111111111
 10 |   70.64 | 11111111111111
(10 rows)
```

7. Alternatively, we can use random ordering:

```
postgres=# SELECT key
                 ,(random()*100.)::numeric(4,2)
                 ,repeat('1',(random()*25)::integer)
                 FROM generate_series(1,10) AS f(key)
                 ORDER BY random() * 1.0;
 key | numeric |        repeat
-----+---------+-------------------------
   4 |   86.09 | 1111
  10 |   28.30 | 11111111
   2 |   64.09 | 111111
   8 |   91.59 | 111111111111111
   5 |   64.05 | 11111111
   3 |   75.22 | 11111111111111111
   6 |   39.02 | 1111
   7 |   20.43 | 1111111
   1 |   42.91 | 1111111111111111111111
   9 |   88.64 | 1111111111111111111111111
(10 rows)
```

How it works...

To set returning functions, literally return a set of rows. That allows them to be used in either the FROM clause, as if they were a table, or the SELECT clause. The generate_series() set of functions returns either dates or integers, depending on the data types of the input parameters you use.

The :: operator is used to cast between data types. The *random string from a list of strings* example uses PostgreSQL arrays. You can create an array using the ARRAY constructor syntax, and then use an integer to reference one element in the array. In our case, we used a random subscript.

There's more...

There are also some commercial tools used to generate application-specific test data for PostgreSQL. They are available
at `http://www.sqlmanager.net/products/postgresql/datagenerator` and
`http://www.datanamic.com/datagenerator/index.html`.

The key features for any data generator are as follows:

- The ability to generate data in the right format for custom data types
- The ability to add data to multiple tables, while respecting foreign key constraints between tables
- The ability to add data to non-uniform distributions

The tools and tricks shown here are cool and clever, though there are some problems hiding here as well. Real data has so many strange things in it that it can be very hard to simulate. One of the most difficult things is generating data that follows realistic distributions. For example, if we had to generate data for people's heights, then we'd want to generate data to follow a normal distribution. If we were generating customer bank balances, we'd want to use a ZIP distribution, or for the number of reported insurance claims, perhaps a Poisson distribution (or perhaps not). Replicating the real quirks in data can take some time.

Finally, note that casting a float into an integer rounds it to the nearest integer, so the distribution of integers is not uniform on each extreme. For instance, the probability of `(random()*10)::int` being 0 is just 5%, as is its probability of being 10, while each integer between 1 and 9 occurs with a probability of 10%. This is why we put 0.5 in the last example, which is simpler than using the `floor()` function.

See also

- You can use existing data to generate test databases using sampling. That's the subject of our next recipe, *Randomly sampling data*.

Randomly sampling data

DBAs may be asked to set up a test server and populate it with test data. Often, that server will be old hardware, possibly with smaller disk sizes. So, the subject of data sampling raises its head.

The purpose of sampling is to reduce the size of the dataset and improve the speed of later analysis. Some statisticians are so used to the idea of sampling that they may not even question whether its use is valid or if it can cause further complications.

The SQL standard way to perform sampling is by adding the TABLESAMPLE clause to the SELECT statement.

How to do it...

In this section, we will take a random sample of a given collection of data (for example, a given table). First, you should realize that there isn't a simple tool to slice off a sample of your database. It would be neat if there were, but there isn't. You'll need to read all of this to understand why:

1. We first consider using SQL to derive a sample. Random sampling is actually very simple because we can use the TABLESAMPLE clause. Consider the following example:

```
postgres=# SELECT count(*) FROM mybigtable;
 count
-------
 10000
(1 row)
postgres=# SELECT count(*) FROM mybigtable
                        TABLESAMPLE BERNOULLI(1);
 count
-------
   106
(1 row)
postgres=# SELECT count(*) FROM mybigtable
                        TABLESAMPLE BERNOULLI(1);
 count
-------
    99
(1 row)
```

2. Here, the TABLESAMPLE clause applies to mybigtable, and tells SELECT to consider only a random sample, while the BERNOULLI keyword denotes the sampling method used, and the number 1 between parentheses represents the percentage of rows that we want to consider in the sample, that is, 1%. Quite easy!

3. Now we need to get the sampled data out of the database, which is tricky for a few reasons. Firstly, there is no option to specify a WHERE clause for pg_dump. Secondly, if you create a view that contains the WHERE clause, pg_dump dumps only the view definition, not the view itself.

4. You can use pg_dump to dump all databases, apart from a set of tables, so you can produce a sampled dump like this:

```
pg_dump --exclude-table=mybigtable > db.dmp
pg_dump --table=mybigtable --schema-only > mybigtable.schema
psql -c '\copy (SELECT * FROM mybigtable
                 TABLESAMPLE BERNOULLI (1)) to mybigtable.dat'
```

5. Then reload onto a separate database using the following commands:

```
psql -f db.dmp
psql -f mybigtable.schema
psql -c '\copy mybigtable from mybigtable.dat'
```

Overall, my advice is to use sampling with caution. In general, it is easier to apply it to a few very large tables only, in view of both the mathematical issues surrounding the sample design and the difficulty of extracting the data.

How it works...

The extract mechanism shows off the capabilities of the PostgreSQL command-line tools, psql and pg_dump, as pg_dump allows you to include or exclude objects and dump the entire table (or only its schema), whereas psql allows you to dump out the result of an arbitrary query into a file.

The BERNOULLI clause specifies the sampling method, that is, PostgreSQL takes the random sample by performing a full table scan, and then selecting each row with the required probability, here 1%.

Another built-in sampling method is SYSTEM, which reads a random sample of table pages, and then includes all rows in these pages; this is generally faster, given that samples are normally quite a bit smaller than the original, but the randomness of the selection is affected by how rows are physically arranged on disk, which makes it suitable for some applications only.

Here is an example that shows what the problem is. Suppose you take a dictionary, rip out a few pages, and then select all the words in them; you will get a random sample composed of a few *clusters* of consecutive words. This is good enough if you want to estimate the average length of a word, but not for analyzing the average number of words for each initial letter. The reason is that the initial letter of a word is strongly correlated with how the words are arranged in pages, while the length of a word is not.

We haven't discussed how random the TABLESAMPLE clause is. This isn't the right place for such details; however, it is reasonably simple to extend PostgreSQL with extra functions or sampling methods, so if you prefer another mechanism, you can find an external random number generator, and create a new sampling method for the TABLESAMPLE clause. PostgreSQL includes two extra sampling methods, tsm_system_rows and tsm_system_time,, as contrib extensions: they are excellent examples to start from.

The tsm_system_rows method does not work with percentages; instead, the numeric argument is interpreted as the number of rows to be returned. Similarly, the tsm_system_time method will regard its argument as the number of milliseconds to spend retrieving the random sample.

These two methods include the word system in their name because they use block-level sampling, like the built-in system sampling method; hence, their randomness is affected by the same *clustering* limitation as described previously.

The sampling method shown earlier is a simple random sampling technique that has an **equal probability of selection (EPS)** design.

EPS samples are considered useful because the variance of the sample attributes is similar to the variance of the original dataset. However, bear in mind that this is useful only if you are considering variances.

Simple random sampling can make the eventual sample biased towards more frequently occurring data. For example, if you have a 1% sample of data on which some kinds of data occur only 0.001% of the time, you may end up with a dataset that doesn't have any of that outlying data.

What you might wish to do is to pre-cluster your data and take different samples from each group to ensure that you have a sampled dataset that includes many more outlying attributes. A simple method might be to do the following:

- Include 1% of all normal data
- Include 25% of outlying data

Note that if you do this, then it is no longer an EPS sample design.

Undoubtedly, there are statisticians who will be apoplectic after reading this. You're welcome to use the facilities of the SQL language to create a more accurate sample. Just make sure that you know what you're doing and/or check out some good statistical literature, websites, or textbooks.

Loading data from a spreadsheet

Spreadsheets are the most obvious starting place for most data stores. Studies within a range of businesses consistently show that more than 50% of smaller data stores are held in spreadsheets or small desktop databases. Loading data from these sources is a frequent and important task for many DBAs.

Getting ready

Spreadsheets combine data, presentation, and programs all into one file. That's perfect for power users wanting to work quickly. Like other relational databases, PostgreSQL is mainly concerned with the lowest level of data, so extracting just the data from these spreadsheets can present some challenges.

We can easily handle spreadsheet data if that spreadsheet's layout follows a very specific form, as follows:

- Each spreadsheet column becomes one column in one table
- Each row of the spreadsheet becomes one row in one table
- Data is only in one worksheet of the spreadsheet
- Optionally, the first row is a list of column descriptions/titles

This is a very simple layout, and more often there will be other things in the spreadsheet, such as titles, comments, constants for use in formulas, summary lines, macros, and images. If you're in this position, the best thing to do is to create a new worksheet within the spreadsheet in the pristine form described earlier, and then set up cross-worksheet references to bring in the data. An example of a cross-worksheet reference would be =Sheet2.A1. You'll need a separate worksheet for each set of data that will become one table on PostgreSQL. You can load multiple worksheets into one table, however.

Some spreadsheet users will say that all of this is unnecessary, and is evidence of the problems of databases. The real spreadsheet gurus do actually advocate this type of layout – data in one worksheet and calculation and presentation in other worksheets. So, it is actually best practice to design spreadsheets in this way; however, we must work with the world the way it is.

How to do it...

Here, we will show you an example where data in a spreadsheet is loaded into a database:

1. If your spreadsheet data is neatly laid out in a single worksheet, as shown in the following screenshot, then you can go to **File** | **Save As** and then select **CSV** as the file type to be saved:

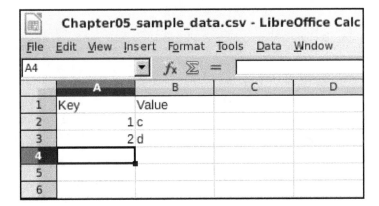

2. This will export the current worksheet to a file, like the following:

```
"Key","Value"
1,"c"
2,"d"
```

3. We can then load it into an existing PostgreSQL table, using the following `psql` command:

```
postgres=# \COPY sample FROM sample.csv CSV HEADER
postgres=# SELECT * FROM sample;
 key | value
-----+-------
   1 | c
   2 | d
```

4. Alternatively, from the command line, this would be as follows:

```
psql -c '\COPY sample FROM sample.csv CSV HEADER'
```

5. Note that the file can include a full file path if the data is in a different directory. The `psql` `\COPY` command transfers data from the client system where you run the command through to the database server, so the file is on the client.
6. If you are submitting SQL through another type of connection, then you should use the following SQL statement:

```
COPY sample FROM '/mydatafiledirectory/sample.csv' CSV HEADER;
```

Note that the preceding SQL statement runs on the database server and can only be executed by a super user. So, you need to ensure that the server process is allowed to read that file, then transfer the data yourself to the server, and finally load the file. The `COPY` statement shown in the preceding SQL statement uses an absolute path to identify data files, which is required.

The `COPY` (or `\COPY`) command does not create the table for you; that must be done beforehand. Note also that the `HEADER` option does nothing but ignore the first line of the input file, so the names of the columns from the `.csv` file don't need to match those of the `Postgres` table. If it hasn't occurred to you yet, this is also a problem. If you say `HEADER` and the file does not have a header line, then all it does is ignore the first data row. Unfortunately, there's no way for PostgreSQL to tell whether the first line of the file is truly a header or not. Be careful!

There isn't a standard tool to load data directly from the spreadsheet to the database. It's fairly simple to write a spreadsheet macro to automate the aforementioned tasks, but that's not a topic for this book.

How it works...

The `\COPY` command executes a `COPY` SQL statement, so the two methods described earlier are very similar. There's more to be said about `COPY`, so we'll cover that in the next recipe.

There's more...

There are many data extraction and loading tools available out there, some cheap and some expensive. Remember that the hardest part of loading data from any spreadsheet is separating the data from all the other things it contains. I've not yet seen a tool that can help with that.

Loading data from flat files

Loading data into your database is one of the most important tasks. You need to do this accurately and quickly. Here's how.

Getting ready

You'll need a copy of `pgloader`, which is commonly available in all main software distribution.

At the time of writing, the current stable version is 3.4.1. The 3.x series is a major rewrite, with many additional features, and the 2.x series is now considered obsolete.

How to do it...

PostgreSQL includes a command named `COPY` that provides the basic data load/unload mechanism. The `COPY` command doesn't do enough when loading data, so let's skip the basic command and go straight to `pgloader`.

To load data, we need to understand our requirements, so let's break this down into a step-by-step process, as follows:

1. Identify the data files and where they are located. Make sure that `pgloader` is installed at the location of the files.
2. Identify the table into which you are loading, ensure that you have the permissions to load, and check the available space. Work out the file type (examples include fixed-size fields, delimited text, and CSV) and check the encoding.

3. Specify the mapping between columns in the file and columns on the table being loaded. Make sure you know which columns in the file are not needed – pgloader allows you to include only the columns you want. Identify any columns in the table for which you don't have data. Do you need them to have a default value on the table, or does pgloader need to generate values for those columns through functions or constants?

4. Specify any transformations that need to take place. The most common issue is date formats, although, possibly, there may be other issues.

5. Write the pgloader script.

6. The pgloader script will create a log file to record whether the load has succeeded or failed, and another file to store rejected rows. You need a directory with sufficient disk space if you expect them to be large. Their size is roughly proportional to the number of failing rows.

7. Finally, consider what settings you need for performance options. This is definitely last, as fiddling with things earlier can lead to confusion when you're still making the load work correctly.

8. You must use a script to execute pgloader. This is not a restriction; actually, it is more like best practice, because it makes it much easier to iterate towards something that works. Loads never work the first time, except in the movies!

Let's look at a typical example from pgloader's quick start documentation, the csv.load file.

Define the required operations in a command and save it in a file, say csv.load:

```
LOAD CSV
     FROM '/tmp/file.csv' (x, y, a, b, c, d)
     INTO postgresql://postgres@localhost:5432/postgres?csv (a, b, d, c)

     WITH truncate,
          skip header = 1,
          fields optionally enclosed by '"',
          fields escaped by double-quote,
          fields terminated by ','

      SET client_encoding to 'latin1',
          work_mem to '12MB',
          standard_conforming_strings to 'on'

     BEFORE LOAD DO
      $$ drop table if exists csv; $$,
      $$ create table csv (
          a bigint,
```

```
        b bigint,
        c char(2),
        d text
    );
$$;
```

This command allows loading the following CSV file content. Save this in a file, say `file.csv` under the `/tmp` directory:

```
Header, with a © sign
"2.6.190.56","2.6.190.63","33996344","33996351","GB","United Kingdom"
"3.0.0.0","4.17.135.31","50331648","68257567","US","United States"
"4.17.135.32","4.17.135.63","68257568","68257599","CA","Canada"
"4.17.135.64","4.17.142.255","68257600","68259583","US","United States"
"4.17.143.0","4.17.143.15","68259584","68259599","CA","Canada"
"4.17.143.16","4.18.32.71","68259600","68296775","US","United States"
```

We can use the following `load` script:

```
pgloader csv.load
```

Here's what gets loaded in the PostgreSQL database:

```
postgres=# select * from csv ;
    a     |    b     | c  |       d
----------+----------+----+-----------------
 33996344 | 33996351 | GB | United Kingdom
 50331648 | 68257567 | US | United States
 68257568 | 68257599 | CA | Canada
 68257600 | 68259583 | US | United States
 68259584 | 68259599 | CA | Canada
 68259600 | 68296775 | US | United States
(6 rows)
```

How it works...

`pgloader` copes gracefully with errors. The `COPY` command loads all rows in a single transaction, so only a single error is enough to abort the load. `pgloader` breaks down an input file into reasonably sized chunks, and loads them piece by piece. If some rows in a chunk cause errors, then `pgloader` will split it iteratively until it loads all the good rows and skips all the bad rows, which are then saved in a separate rejects file for later inspection. This behavior is very convenient if you have large data files with a small percentage of bad rows; for instance, you can edit the rejects, fix them, and, finally, load them with another `pgloader` run.

Versions from the 2.x iteration of `pgloader` were written in Python and connected to PostgreSQL through the standard Python client interface. Version 3.x is written in Common Lisp. Yes, `pgloader` is less efficient than loading data files using a `COPY` command, but running a `COPY` command has many more restrictions: the file has to be in the right place on the server, has to be in the right format, and must be unlikely to throw errors on loading. `pgloader` has additional overhead, but it also has the ability to load data using multiple parallel threads, so it can be faster to use as well. pgloader's ability to reformat the data via user-defined functions is often essential; straight `COPY` is just too simple.

`pgloader` also allows loading from fixed-width files, which `COPY` does not.

There's more...

If you need to reload the table completely from scratch, then specify the `-WITH TRUNCATE` clause in the `pgloader` script.

There are also options to specify SQL to be executed before and after loading the data. For instance, you may have a script that creates the empty tables before, or you can add constraints after, or both.

After loading, if we have load errors, then there will be some junk loaded into the PostgreSQL tables. It is not junk that you can see, or that gives any semantic errors, but think of it more like fragmentation. You should think about whether you need to add a `VACUUM` command after the data load, though this will possibly make the load take much longer.

We need to be careful to avoid loading data twice. The only easy way of doing that is to make sure that there is at least one unique index defined on every table that you load. The load should then fail very quickly.

String handling can often be difficult, because of the presence of formatting or non-printable characters. The default setting for PostgreSQL is to have a parameter named `standard_conforming_strings` set to `off`, which means that backslashes will be assumed to be escape characters. Put another way, by default, the `\n` string means line feed, which can cause data to appear truncated. You'll need to turn `standard_conforming_strings` to `on`, or you'll need to specify an escape character in the load-parameter file.

If you are reloading data that has been unloaded from PostgreSQL, then you may want to use the pg_restore utility instead. The pg_restore utility has an option to reload data in parallel, -j number_of_threads, though this is only possible if the dump was produced using the custom pg_dump format. Refer to the recipes in Chapter 11, *Backup and Recovery*, for more details. This can be useful for reloading dumps, though it lacks almost all of the other pgloader features discussed here.

If you need to use rows from a read-only text file that does not have errors, then you may consider using the file_fdw contrib module. The short story is that it lets you create a *virtual* table that will parse the text file every time it is scanned. This is different from filling a table once and for all, either with COPY or pgloader; therefore, it covers a different use case. For example, think about an external data source that is maintained by a third party and needs to be shared across different databases.

Making bulk data changes using server-side procedures with transactions

In some cases, you'll need to make bulk changes to your data. In many cases, you need to scroll through the data making changes according to a complex set of rules. You have a few choices in that case:

- Write a single SQL statement that can do everything
- Open a cursor and read the rows out, then make changes with a client-side program
- Write a procedure that uses a cursor to read the rows and make changes using server-side SQL

Writing a single SQL statement that does everything is sometimes possible, but, if you need to do more than just UPDATE then it becomes difficult very quickly. The main difficulty is that the SQL statement isn't restartable, so, if you need to interrupt it then you lose all of your work.

Reading all the rows back to a client-side program can be very slow – if you need to write this kind of program, it is better to do it all on the database server.

How to do it...

We're going to write a Procedure in PL/pgSQL. A Procedure is similar to a Function, except that it doesn't return any value or object. We use a Procedure because it allows you to run multiple server-side transactions. By using procedures in this way, we are able to break the problem down into a set of smaller transactions that cause less of a problem with database bloat and long running transactions.

As an example, let's consider a case where we need to update all employees with the A2 job grade, giving each person a 2% pay rise:

```
CREATE PROCEDURE annual_pay_rise ()
LANGUAGE plpgsql AS $$
DECLARE
c CURSOR FOR
SELECT * FROM employee
    WHERE job_code = 'A2';
BEGIN
FOR r IN c LOOP
UPDATE employee
SET salary = salary * 1.02
WHERE empid = r.empid;
  IF mod (r.empid, 100) = 0 THEN
COMMIT;
END IF;
END LOOP;
END;
$$;
```

Execute the preceding procedure like this:

```
CALL annual_pay_rise();
```

We want to issue regular commits as we go. The preceding procedure is coded so it issues commits roughly every 100 rows. There's nothing magical about that number: we just want to break it down into smaller pieces whether it is number of rows scanned or rows updated.

There's more...

You can use both COMMIT and ROLLBACK in a procedure. Each new transaction will see the changes from prior transactions and any other concurrent commits that have occurred.

What happens if your Procedure is interrupted? Since we are using multiple transactions to complete the task, we wouldn't expect the whole task to be atomic. If the execution is interrupted, we would need to re-run the parts that didn't execute successfully. What happens if we accidentally re-run parts that have already been executed? We would give some people a double pay rise, but not everyone.

To cope, let's invent a simple job restart mechanism. This uses a persistent table to track changes as they are made, accessed by a simple API:

```
CREATE TABLE job_status
(id bigserial not null primary key,status text not null,restartdata
bigint);
CREATE OR REPLACE FUNCTION job_start_new ()
 RETURNS bigint
 LANGUAGE plpgsql
 AS $$
 DECLARE
  p_id BIGINT;
BEGIN
  INSERT INTO job_status (status, restartdata)
    VALUES ('START', 0)
   RETURNING id INTO p_id;
  RETURN p_id;
 END; $$;

CREATE OR REPLACE FUNCTION job_get_status (jobid bigint)
RETURNS bigint
LANGUAGE plpgsql
AS $$
DECLARE
 rdata BIGINT;
BEGIN
  SELECT restartdata INTO rdata
    FROM job_status
    WHERE status != 'COMPLETE' AND id = jobid;
  IF NOT FOUND THEN
    RAISE EXCEPTION 'job id does not exist';
  END IF;
  RETURN rdata;
END; $$;
CREATE OR REPLACE PROCEDURE
job_update (jobid bigint, rdata bigint)
```

```
LANGUAGE plpgsql
AS $$
BEGIN
  UPDATE job_status
    SET status = 'IN PROGRESS'
        ,restartdata = rdata
    WHERE id = jobid;
END; $$;
CREATE OR REPLACE PROCEDURE job_complete (jobid bigint)
LANGUAGE plpgsql
AS $$
BEGIN
  UPDATE job_status SET status = 'COMPLETE'
    WHERE id = jobid;
END; $$;
```

First of all, we start a new job:

```
SELECT job_start_new();
```

Then we execute our procedure, passing the job number to it. Let's say this returns 8474:

```
CALL annual_pay_rise(8474);
```

If the procedure is interrupted, we will restart from the correct place, without needing to specify any changes:

```
CALL annual_pay_rise(8474);
```

The existing procedure needs to be modified to use the new restart API, as shown in the following code block. Note, also, that the cursor has to be modified to use an ORDER BY clause to make the procedure sensibly repeatable:

```
CREATE OR REPLACE PROCEDURE annual_pay_rise (job bigint)
LANGUAGE plpgsql AS $$
DECLARE
        job_empid bigint;
        c NO SCROLL CURSOR FOR
                SELECT * FROM employee
                WHERE job_code='A2'
                AND empid > job_empid
                ORDER BY empid;
BEGIN
        SELECT job_get_status(job) INTO job_empid;
        FOR r IN c LOOP
                UPDATE employee
                SET salary = salary * 1.02
                WHERE empid = r.empid;
```

```
                IF mod (r.empid, 100) = 0 THEN
                        CALL job_update(job, r.empid);
                        COMMIT;
                END IF;
        END LOOP;
        CALL job_complete(job);
    END; $$;
```

For extra practice, follow execution using the debugger in pgAdmin or OmniDB.

The CALL statement can also be used to call functions that return void, but, other than that, functions and Procedures are separate concepts. Procedures also allow you to execute transactions in PL/Python and PL/perl.

6
Security

In this chapter, we will cover the following recipes:

- The PostgreSQL superuser
- Revoking user access to a table
- Granting user access to a table
- Granting user access to specific columns
- Granting user access to specific rows
- Creating a new user
- Temporarily preventing a user from connecting
- Removing a user without dropping their data
- Checking whether all users have a secure password
- Giving limited superuser powers to specific users
- Auditing database access
- Always knowing which user is logged in
- Integrating with **Lightweight Directory Access Protocol** (**LDAP**)
- Connecting using SSL
- Using SSL certificates to authenticate
- Mapping external usernames to database roles
- Encrypting sensitive data

Introduction

First, set up access rules into the database server. PostgreSQL allows you to control access based upon the host that is trying to connect, using the pg_hba.conf file. You can specify SSL connections if needed or skip that if the network is secure. You can specify the use of SCRAM authentication using 256 bit keys, as well as many other mechanisms.

Next, set up the role and privileges for accessing your data. Databases are mostly used to store data, with several restrictions on how it can be used. Some records or tables can only be seen by certain users, and even those tables that are visible to everyone can have restrictions in terms of who can insert new data or change the existing data. All of this is managed by a privilege system, where users are granted different privileges for different tables or other database objects, such as schemas or functions.

It is good practice not to grant these privileges directly to users, but to use an intermediate role to collect a set of privileges. Then, instead of granting all of the same privileges to the actual user, the entire role is granted to users needing these privileges. For example, a clerk role may have the right to both insert data and update existing data in the user_account table, but may have the right to only insert data in the transaction_history table.

Fine-grained control over access can be managed using the **Row-Level Security** (**RLS**) feature, which allows a defined policy on selected tables.

Another aspect of database security concerns the management of this access to the database: making sure that only the right people can access the database; that one user can't see what other users are doing (unless they are an administrator or auditor); and deciding whether users can or cannot pass on the roles granted to them.

You should consider auditing the actions of administrators using pgaudit.

Typical user role

The minimal production database setup contains at least two types of users, namely administrators and end users, where administrators can do everything (they are superusers), and end users can only do very little, usually just modifying the data in only a few tables and reading from a few more.

It is not a good idea to let ordinary users create or change database object definitions, meaning that they should not have the CREATE privilege on any schema, including PUBLIC.

There can be more roles for different types of end users, such as analysts, who can only select from a single table or view, or some maintenance script users who see no data at all and just have the ability to execute a few functions.

Alternatively, there can also be a manager role, which can grant and revoke roles for other users but is not supposed to do anything else.

The PostgreSQL superuser

In this recipe, you will learn how to grant the right to a user to become a superuser.

A PostgreSQL superuser is a user that bypasses all permission checks, except the right to log in. This is a dangerous privilege and should not be used carelessly. Many cloud databases do not allow this level of privilege to be granted. It is normal to place strict controls on users of this type.

How to do it...

Follow the steps to add or remove superuser privileges for any user:

1. A user becomes a superuser when it is created with the SUPERUSER attribute set:

   ```
   CREATE USER username SUPERUSER;
   ```

2. A user can be deprived of its superuser status by removing the SUPERUSER attribute using this command:

   ```
   ALTER USER username NOSUPERUSER;
   ```

3. A user can be restored to superuser status later using the following command:

   ```
   ALTER USER username SUPERUSER;
   ```

4. When neither SUPERUSER nor NOSUPERUSER is given in the CREATE USER command, then the default is to create a user who is not a superuser.

How it works...

The rights to some operations in PostgreSQL are not available by default and need to be granted specifically to users. They must be performed by a special user who has this special attribute set. The preceding commands set and reset this attribute for the user.

There's more...

The PostgreSQL system comes set up with at least one superuser. Most commonly, this superuser is named `postgres`, but occasionally it adopts the same name as the system user who owns the database directory and with whose rights the PostgreSQL server runs.

Other superuser-like attributes

In addition to `SUPERUSER`, there are two lesser attributes—`CREATEDB` and `CREATEUSER`—which give the user only some of the power reserved for superusers, namely creating new databases and users. See the *Giving limited superuser powers to specific users* recipe for more information on this.

Attributes are never inherited

Later, you will learn about granting one role to another user—role inheritance—and how privileges can be granted through these intermediate group roles. None of this applies to attributes—to perform superuser-only operations, you must be that user.

See also

Also check out the *Always knowing which user is logged in* recipe in this chapter.

 All of the following recipes assume a non-superuser unless it is explicitly mentioned that they apply to or need a superuser.

Revoking user access to a table

This recipe answers the question: how do I make sure that user X cannot access table Y?

Getting ready

The current user must either be a superuser, the owner of the table, or a user with a `GRANT` option for the table.

Also, bear in mind that you can't revoke rights from a user who is a superuser.

How to do it...

To revoke all rights on the `table1` table from the `user2` user, you must run the following SQL command:

```
REVOKE ALL ON table1 FROM user2;
```

However, if `user2` has been granted another role that gives them some rights on `table1`, say `role3`, this command is not enough; you must also choose one of the following options:

- Fix the user—that is, revoke `role3` from `user2`
- Fix the role—that is, revoke privileges on `table1` from `role3`

Both choices are imperfect because of their side-effects. The former will revoke all of the privileges associated to `role3`, not just the privileges concerning `table1`; the latter will revoke the privileges on `table1` from all of the other users that have been granted `role3`, not just from `user2`.

It is normally better to avoid damaging other legitimate users, so we opt for the first solution. The following is a working example.

Using `psql`, display the list of roles that have been granted at least one privilege on `table1` by issuing `\z table1`. For instance, you can obtain the following output (an extra column about column privileges has been removed from the right-hand side because it was not relevant here):

```
                     Access privileges
 Schema |  Name  | Type  |      Access privileges     |  ...
--------+--------+-------+----------------------------+ ...
 public | table1 | table | postgres=arwdDxt/postgres+|  ...
        |        |       | role3=r/postgres         +|  ...
        |        |       | role5=a/postgres          |  ...
(1 row)
```

Then, we check whether `user2` is a member of any of those roles by typing `\du user2`:

```
              List of roles
 Role name | Attributes |   Member of
-----------+------------+---------------
 user2     |            | {role3, role4}
```

In the previous step, we notice that `role3` had been granted the SELECT privilege (*r* for *read*) by the `postgres` user, so we must revoke it, as follows:

```
REVOKE role3 FROM user2;
```

We must also inspect `role4`. Even if it doesn't have privileges on `table1`, in theory, it could be a member of one of the three roles that have privileges on that table. We issue `\du role4` and get the following output:

```
              List of roles
  Role name |   Attributes   | Member of
 -----------+----------------+-----------
  role4     | Cannot login   | {role5}
```

Our suspicion was well founded: `user2` can get the INSERT privilege (*a* for *append*) on `table1`, first via `role4` and then via `role5`. So we must break this two-step chain as follows:

```
REVOKE role4 FROM user2;
```

 This example may seem too unlikely to be true. We unexpectedly gain access to the table via a chain of two different role memberships, which was made possible by the fact that a non-login role, such as `role4`, was made a member of another non-login role, that is, `role5`. In most real-world cases, superusers will know whether such chains exist at all, so there will be no surprises; however, the goal of this recipe is to make sure that the user cannot access the table, meaning we cannot exclude less-likely options.

How it works...

The `\z` command, as well as its synonym, `\dp`, display all privileges granted on tables, views, and sequences. If the `Access privileges` column is empty, it means **default privileges**, that is, all privileges are given to the owner (and the superusers, as always).

The `\du` command shows you the attributes and roles that have been granted to roles.

Both commands accept an optional name or pattern to restrict the display.

There's more...

Here, we'll cover some good practices on user and role management.

Database creation scripts

For production systems, it is usually a good idea to always include GRANT and REVOKE statements in the database creation script so that you can be sure that only the right set of users has access to the table. If this is done manually, it is easy to forget. Also, in this way, you can be sure that the same roles are used in development and testing environments so that there are no surprises at deployment time.

The following is a sample extract from the database creation script:

```
CREATE TABLE table1(
...
);
GRANT SELECT ON table1 TO webreaders;
GRANT SELECT, INSERT, UPDATE, DELETE ON table1 TO editors;
GRANT ALL ON table1 TO admins;
```

Default search path

It is always good practice to use a fully qualified name when revoking or granting rights; otherwise, you may be inadvertently working with the wrong table.

To see the effective search path for the current database, run the following:

```
pguser=# show search_path ;
   search_path
-----------------
 "$user",public
(1 row)
```

To see which table will be affected if you omit the schema name, run the following in PSQL:

```
pguser=# \d x
      Table "public.x"
 Column | Type | Modifiers
--------+------+-----------
```

The public.x table name in the response contains the full name, including the schema.

Securing views

It is a common technique to use a view to disclose only some parts of a secret table; however, a clever attacker can use access to the view to display the rest of the table using log messages. For instance, consider the following example:

```
CREATE VIEW for_the_public AS
  SELECT * FROM reserved_data WHERE importance < 10;
GRANT SELECT ON for_the_public TO PUBLIC;
```

A malicious user could define the following function:

```
CREATE FUNCTION f(text)
RETURNS boolean
COST 0.00000001
LANGUAGE plpgsql AS $$
BEGIN
  RAISE INFO '$1: %', $1;
  RETURN true;
END;
$$;
```

They could use it to filter rows from the view:

```
SELECT * FROM for_the_public x WHERE f(x :: text);
```

The PostgreSQL optimizer will then internally rearrange the query, expanding the definition of the view and then combining the two filter conditions into a single WHERE clause. The trick here is that the function has been told to be very cheap using the COST keyword, so the optimizer will choose to evaluate that condition first. In other words, the function will access all of the rows in the table, as you will realize when you see the corresponding INFO lines on the console if you run the code yourself.

This security leak can be prevented using the security_barrier attribute:

```
ALTER VIEW for_the_public SET (security_barrier = on);
```

This means that the conditions that define the view will always be computed first, irrespective of cost considerations.

The performance impact of this fix can be mitigated by the LEAKPROOF attribute for functions. In short, a function that cannot leak information other than its output value can be marked as LEAKPROOF by a superuser so the planner will know that it's secure enough to compute the function before the other view conditions.

Granting user access to a table

A user needs to have access to a table in order to perform any actions on it.

Getting ready

Make sure that you have the appropriate roles defined, and that privileges are revoked from the PUBLIC role:

```
CREATE GROUP webreaders;
CREATE USER tim;
CREATE USER bob;
REVOKE ALL ON SCHEMA someschema FROM PUBLIC;
```

How to do it...

We had to grant access to the schema in order to allow access to the table. This suggests that access to a given schema can be used as a fast and extreme way of preventing any access to any object in that schema. Otherwise, if you want to allow some access, you must use specific GRANT and REVOKE statements as needed:

```
GRANT USAGE ON SCHEMA someschema TO webreaders;
```

It is often desirable to give a group of users similar permissions to a group of database objects. To do this, you first assign all the permissions to a proxy role (also known as a **permission group**), and then assign the group to selected users, as follows:

```
GRANT SELECT ON someschema.pages TO webreaders;
GRANT INSERT ON someschema.viewlog TO webreaders;
GRANT webreaders TO tim, bob;
```

Now, both tim and bob have the SELECT privilege on the pages table and INSERT on the viewlog table. You can also add privileges to the group role after assigning it to users. Consider the following command:

```
GRANT INSERT, UPDATE, DELETE ON someschema.comments TO webreaders;
```

After running this command, both bob and tim have all of the aforementioned privileges on the comments table.

This assumes that both the `bob` and `tim` roles were created with the `INHERIT` default setting. Otherwise, they do not automatically inherit the rights of roles but need to explicitly set their role to the granted user to make use of the privileges granted to that role.

We can grant privileges on all objects of a certain kind in a specific schema, as follows:

```
GRANT SELECT ON ALL TABLES IN SCHEMA someschema TO bob;
```

You still need to grant the privileges on the schema itself in a separate `GRANT` statement.

How it works...

The preceding sequence of commands first grants access to a schema for a group role, then gives appropriate viewing (`SELECT`) and modifying (`INSERT`) rights on certain tables to the role, and finally grants membership in that role to two database users.

There's more...

There is no requirement in PostgreSQL to have some privileges in order to have others. This means that you may well have write-only tables, where you are allowed to insert but you can't select. This can be used to implement a mail-queue-like functionality, where several users post messages to one user, but they can't see what other users have posted.

Alternatively, you could set up a situation where you can write a record, but you can't change or delete it. This is useful for auditing log-type tables, where all changes are recorded but cannot be tampered with.

Granting user access to specific columns

A user can be given access to only some table columns.

Getting ready

We will continue the example from the previous recipe, so we assume that there is already a schema called `someschema` and a role called `somerole` with `USAGE` privileges on it. We create a new table on which we will grant column-level privileges:

```
CREATE TABLE someschema.sometable2(col1 int, col2 text);
```

How to do it...

1. We want to grant `somerole` the ability to view existing data and insert new data; we also want to provide the ability to amend existing data, limited to column `col2` only. We use the following self-evident statements:

   ```
   GRANT SELECT, INSERT ON someschema.sometable2 TO somerole;
   GRANT UPDATE (col2) ON someschema.sometable2 TO somerole;
   ```

2. Let's assume the identity of the `somerole` role and test these privileges with the following commands:

   ```
   SET ROLE TO somerole;
   INSERT INTO someschema.sometable2 VALUES (1, 'One');
   SELECT * FROM someschema.sometable2 WHERE col1 = 1;
   ```

3. As expected, we are able to insert a new row and to view its contents. Let's now check our ability to update individual columns. We start with the second column, which we have authorized:

   ```
   UPDATE someschema.sometable2 SET col2 = 'The number one';
   ```

4. This command returns the familiar output:

   ```
   UPDATE 1
   ```

5. This means that we were able to successfully update that column in one row. Now, we try to update the first column:

   ```
   UPDATE someschema.sometable2 SET col1 = 2;
   ```

6. This time, we get the following error message:

   ```
   ERROR:  permission denied for relation sometable2
   ```

   This confirms that, as planned, we only authorized updates to the second column.

How it works...

The GRANT command has been extended to allow for specifying a list of columns, meaning that the privilege is granted on that list of columns, rather than on the whole table.

There's more...

Consider a table, t, with columns, c1, c2, and c3; there are two different ways of authorizing user u to perform the following query:

```
SELECT * FROM t;
```

The first is by granting a table-level privilege, as follows:

```
GRANT SELECT ON TABLE t TO u;
```

The alternative way is by granting column-level privileges, as follows:

```
GRANT SELECT (c1,c2,c3) ON TABLE t TO u;
```

Despite these two methods having overlapping effects, table-level privileges are distinct from column-level privileges, which is correct since the meaning of each is different. Granting privileges on a table means giving them *to all columns present and future*, while column-level privileges require the explicit indication of columns and, therefore, don't extend automatically to new columns.

The way privileges work in PostgreSQL means that a given role will be allowed to perform a given action if it matches one of its privileges. This creates some ambiguity in overlapping areas. For example, consider the following command sequence:

```
GRANT SELECT ON someschema.sometable2 TO somerole;
REVOKE SELECT (col1) ON someschema.sometable2 FROM
somerole;
```

The outcome, somehow surprisingly, will be that somerole is allowed to view all of the columns of that table using the table-level privilege granted by the first command. The second command was ineffective because it tried to revoke a column-level privilege (SELECT on col1) that was never granted in the first place.

Granting user access to specific rows

PostgreSQL supports granting users privileges on some rows only.

Getting ready

This recipe uses RLS, which is available only in PostgreSQL version 9.5 or later, so start by checking that you are not using an older version.

As for the previous recipe, we assume that there is already a schema called `someschema` and a role called `somerole` with `USAGE` privileges on it. We create a new table to experiment with row-level privileges:

```
CREATE TABLE someschema.sometable3(col1 int, col2 text);
```

RLS must also be enabled on that table:

```
ALTER TABLE someschema.sometable3 ENABLE ROW LEVEL SECURITY;
```

How to do it...

First, we grant `somerole` the privilege to view the contents of the table, as we did in the previous recipe:

```
GRANT SELECT ON someschema.sometable3 TO somerole;
```

Let's assume that the contents of the table are as shown by the following command:

```
SELECT * FROM someschema.sometable3;
 col1 |    col2
------+-----------
    1 | One
   -1 | Minus one
(2 rows)
```

In order to grant the ability to access some rows only, we create a policy specifying what is allowed and on which rows. For instance, this way, we can enforce the condition that `somerole` is only allowed to select rows with positive values of `col1`:

```
CREATE POLICY example1 ON someschema.sometable3
FOR SELECT
TO somerole
USING (col1 > 0);
```

The effect of this command is that the rows that do not satisfy the policy are silently skipped, as shown when `somerole` issues the following command:

```
SELECT * FROM someschema.sometable3;
 col1 |    col2
------+-----------
    1 | One
(1 row)
```

What if we want to introduce a policy on the INSERT clause? The preceding policy shows how the USING clause specifies which rows are affected. There is also a WITH CHECK clause that can be used to specify which inserts are accepted. More generally, the USING clause applies to pre-existing rows, while WITH CHECK applies to rows that are generated by the statement being analyzed. So, the former works with SELECT, UPDATE, and DELETE, while the latter works with INSERT and UPDATE.

Coming back to our example, we may want to allow inserts only where col1 is positive:

```
CREATE POLICY example2 ON someschema.sometable3
FOR INSERT
TO somerole
WITH CHECK (col1 > 0);
```

We must also remember to allow the INSERT commands on the table, as we did before with SELECT:

```
GRANT INSERT ON someschema.sometable3 TO somerole;
SELECT * FROM someschema.sometable3;
 col1 |    col2
------+-----------
    1 | One
(1 row)
```

Now we are able to insert a new row and to see it afterward:

```
INSERT INTO someschema.sometable3 VALUES (2, 'Two');
SELECT * FROM someschema.sometable3;
 col1 |    col2
------+-----------
    1 | One
    2 | Two
(2 rows)
```

How it works...

RLS policies are created and dropped on a given table using the CREATE POLICY syntax. The RLS policy itself must also be enabled explicitly on the given table, because it is disabled by default.

In the previous example, we needed to grant privileges on the table or on the columns, in addition to creating the RLS policy. This is because RLS is not one more privilege to be added to the other; rather, it works like an additional check. In this sense, it is convenient that it is off by default, as we have to create policies only on the tables where our access logic depends on the row contents.

There's more...

RLS can lead to very complex configurations for a variety of reasons, as in the following instances:

- An UPDATE policy can specify both the rows on which we act and what changes can be accepted
- UPDATE and DELETE policies, in some cases, require visibility as granted by an appropriate SELECT policy
- UPDATE policies are also applied to INSERT ... ON CONFLICT DO UPDATE

We recommend reading the finer details at the following URL: https://www.postgresql. org/docs/11/static/ddl-rowsecurity.html.

Creating a new user

In this recipe, we will show you two ways of creating a new database user, one with a dedicated command-line utility and one using SQL commands.

Getting ready

To create new users, you must either be a superuser or have the CREATEROLE or CREATEROLE privilege.

How to do it...

From the command line, you can run the `createuser` command:

```
pguser@hvost:~$ createuser bob
```

If you add the `--interactive` command-line option, you activate the interactive mode, which means you will be asked some questions, as follows:

```
pguser@hvost:~$ createuser --interactive alice
Shall the new role be a superuser? (y/n) n
Shall the new role be allowed to create databases? (y/n) y
Shall the new role be allowed to create more new roles? (y/n) n
```

Without `--interactive`, the preceding questions get no as the default answer; you can change that with the `-s`, `-d`, and `-r` command-line options.

In interactive mode, questions are asked only if they make sense. One example is when the user is a superuser; no other questions are asked because a superuser is not subject to privilege checks. Another example is when one of the preceding options is used to specify a non-default setting; the corresponding question will not be asked.

How it works...

The `createuser` program is just a shallow wrapper around the executing SQL against the database cluster. It connects to the `postgres` database and then executes SQL commands for user creation. To create the same users through SQL, you can issue the following commands:

```
CREATE USER bob;
CREATE USER alice CREATEDB;
```

There's more...

You can check the attributes of a given user in `psql`, as follows:

```
pguser=# \du alice
```

This gives you the following output:

```
                List of roles
  Role name | Attributes | Member of
-----------+------------+-----------
  alice     | Create DB  | {}
```

The CREATE USER and CREATE GROUP commands are actually variations of CREATE ROLE. The CREATE USER username; statement is equivalent to CREATE ROLE username LOGIN;, and the CREATE GROUP groupname; statement is equivalent to CREATE ROLE groupname NOLOGIN;.

Temporarily preventing a user from connecting

Sometimes, you need to temporarily revoke a user's connection rights without actually deleting the user or changing the user's password. This recipe presents the ways of doing this.

Getting ready

To modify other users, you must either be a superuser or have the CREATEROLE privilege (in the latter case, only non-superuser roles can be altered).

How to do it...

Follow the steps to temporarily prevent and reissue the logging in capability to a user:

1. To temporarily prevent the user from logging in, run this command:

   ```
   pguser=# alter user bob nologin;
   ALTER ROLE
   ```

2. To let the user connect again, run the following:

   ```
   pguser=# alter user bob login;
   ALTER ROLE
   ```

How it works...

This sets a flag in the system catalog, telling PostgreSQL not to let the user log in. It does not kick out already connected users.

There's more...

Here are some additional remarks.

Limiting the number of concurrent connections by a user

The same result can be achieved by setting the connection limit for that user to 0:

```
pguser=# alter user bob connection limit 0;
ALTER ROLE
```

To allow 10 concurrent connections for the bob user, run this command:

```
pguser=# alter user bob connection limit 10;
ALTER ROLE
```

To allow an unlimited number of connections for this user, run the following:

```
pguser=# alter user bob connection limit -1;
ALTER ROLE
```

Note that unlimited connections to PostgreSQL concurrently could allow a **Denial of Service** (**DoS**) attack by exhausting connection resources; also, a system could fail or degrade by an overload of legitimate users.

To reduce these risks, we should always limit the number of concurrent sessions per user.

Forcing NOLOGIN users to disconnect

In order to make sure that all users whose login privileges have been revoked are disconnected right away, run the following SQL statement as a superuser:

```
SELECT pg_terminate_backend(pid)
  FROM pg_stat_activity a
   JOIN pg_roles r ON a.usename = r.rolname AND NOT rolcanlogin;
```

This disconnects all users who no longer are allowed to connect by terminating the backends opened by these users.

Removing a user without dropping their data

When trying to drop a user who owns some tables or other database objects, you get the following error, and the user is not dropped:

```
testdb=# drop user bob;
ERROR:  role "bob" cannot be dropped because some objects depend on it
DETAIL:  owner of table bobstable
owner of sequence bobstable_id_seq
```

This recipe presents two solutions to this problem.

Getting ready

To modify users, you must either be a superuser or have the CREATEROLE privilege.

How to do it...

The easiest solution to this problem is to refrain from dropping the user and use the trick from a previous recipe to prevent the user from connecting:

```
pguser=# alter user bob nologin;
ALTER ROLE
```

This has the added benefit of the original owner of the table being available later, if needed, for auditing or debugging purposes (*Why is this table here? Who created it?*).

Then, you can assign the rights of the deleted user to a new user, using the following code:

```
pguser=# GRANT bob TO bobs_replacement;
GRANT
```

How it works...

As noted previously, a user is implemented as a role with the login attribute set. This recipe works by removing that attribute from the user, which is then kept just as a role.

If you really need to get rid of a user, you have to assign all ownership to another user. To do so, run the following query, which is a PostgreSQL extension to standard SQL:

```
REASSIGN OWNED BY bob TO bobs_replacement;
```

It does exactly what it says: it assigns ownership of all database objects currently owned by the bob role to the bobs_replacement role.

However, you need to have privileges on both the old and the new roles to do that, and you need to do it in all databases where bob owns any objects, as the REASSIGN OWNED command works only on the current database.

After this, you can delete the original user, bob.

Checking whether all users have a secure password

PostgreSQL has no built-in facilities to make sure that you are using strong passwords.

The best you can do is to make sure that all user passwords are encrypted, and that your pg_hba.conf file does not allow logins with a plain password; that is, always use the SCRAM-SHA-256 login method for users, which was added in PostgreSQL 10. Any servers upgrading from earlier versions should upgrade from md5 to SCRAM-SHA-256 password encryption.

For client applications connecting from trusted private networks, either real or virtual (VPN), you may use host-based access, provided you know that the machine on which the application is running is not used by some non-trusted individuals. For remote access over public networks, it may be a better idea to use SSL client certificates.

How to do it...

To see which users don't yet have SCRAM encrypted passwords, use this query:

```
test2=# select usename,passwd from pg_shadow where passwd
not like 'SCRAM%' or passwd is null;
 usename   |     passwd
-----------+--------------
 tim       | weakpassword
 asterisk  | md5chicken
(2 rows)
```

To enable SCRAM-SHA-256 for encrypted passwords, use the following:

```
test2=# SET password_encryption = 'scram-sha-256';
test2=# ALTER USER bob ENCRYPTED PASSWORD 'whatever';
 ALTER USER
```

How it works...

The password_encryption parameter decides how the ALTER USER statement will encrypt the password. This should be set globally in the postgresql.conf file.

Having the passwords encrypted in the database is just half of the equation. The bigger problem is making sure that users actually use passwords that are hard to guess. Passwords such as password, secret, or test are out of the question, and most common words are not good passwords either.

If you don't trust your users to select strong passwords, you can write a wrapper application that checks the password strength and makes them use that when changing passwords. A contrib module lets you do this for a limited set of cases (the password is sent from client to server in plain text). Visit http://www.postgresql.org/docs/11/static/passwordcheck.html for more information on this.

Giving limited superuser powers to specific users

The superuser role has some privileges that can also be granted to non-superuser roles separately.

To give the bob role the ability to create new databases, run this:

```
ALTER ROLE BOB WITH CREATEDB;
```

To give the bob role the ability to create new users, run the following:

```
ALTER ROLE BOB WITH CREATEROLE;
```

It is also possible to give ordinary users more fine-grained and controlled access to an action reserved for superusers using security definer functions. The same trick can also be used to pass partial privileges between different users.

Getting ready

First, you must have access to the database as a superuser in order to delegate powers. Here, we assume the use of the default superuser named postgres.

We will demonstrate two ways to make some superuser-only functionality available to a selected ordinary user.

How to do it...

An ordinary user cannot tell PostgreSQL to copy table data from a file. Only a superuser can do that, as follows:

```
pguser@hvost:~$ psql -U postgres
test2
...
test2=# create table lines(line text);
CREATE TABLE
test2=# copy lines from '/home/bob/names.txt';
COPY 37
test2=# SET ROLE to bob;
SET
test2=> copy lines from '/home/bob/names.txt';
ERROR:  must be superuser to COPY to or from a file
HINT:  Anyone can COPY to stdout or from stdin. psql's \copy command also
works for anyone.
```

To let `bob` copy directly from the file, the superuser can write a special wrapper function for `bob`, as follows:

```
create or replace function copy_from(tablename text, filepath text)
returns void
security definer
as
$$
 declare
 begin
       execute 'copy ' || quote_ident(tablename)
                || ' from ' || quote_literal(filepath) ;
 end;
$$ language plpgsql;
```

It is usually a good idea to restrict the use of such a function to the intended user only:

```
revoke all on function copy_from( text,   text) from public;
grant execute on function copy_from( text,   text) to bob;
```

You may also want to verify that `bob` imports files only from his home directory.

Unfortunately, this solution is not completely secure against superuser privilege escalation by a malicious attacker. This is because the execution of the COPY command inside the function will also cause the execution, as the `postgres` user, of all side-effects, such as the execution of any INSERT trigger, the computation of any CHECK constraint, the computation of any functional index, and more.

In other words, if the user wants to execute a given function as the superuser, it's enough to put that function inside any of the preceding functions.

There are a few workarounds for this security hole, none of which are optimal.

You can require that the table has no triggers and CHECK constraints and functional indexes.

Instead of running COPY on the given table, create a new table with the same structure using the CREATE newtable(LIKE oldtable) syntax. Run COPY against the new table, drop the old table, and give the new table the same name as the old one.

How it works...

When a function defined with `security definer` is called, PostgreSQL changes the session's rights to those of the user who defined the function while that function is being executed.

So, when `bob` executes the `copy_from(tablename, filepath)` function, `bob` is effectively promoted to a superuser when the function is running.

This behavior is similar to the `setuid` flag in Unix systems, where you can have a program that can be run by anybody (with `execute` access) as the owner of that program. It also carries similar risks.

There's more...

There are other operations that are reserved for PostgreSQL superusers, such as setting certain parameters.

Writing a debugging_info function for developers

Several of the parameters controlling logging are reserved for superusers.

If you want to allow some of your developers to set logging, you can write a function for them to do exactly that:

```
create or replace function debugging_info_on()
returns void
security definer
as
$$
  begin
    set client_min_messages to 'DEBUG1';
    set log_min_messages to 'DEBUG1';
    set log_error_verbosity to 'VERBOSE';
    set log_min_duration_statement to 0;
  end;
$$ language plpgsql;
revoke all on function debugging_info_on() from public;
grant execute on function debugging_info_on() to bob;
```

You may also want to have a function go back to the default logging state by assigning `DEFAULT` to all of the variables involved:

```
create or replace function debugging_info_reset()
returns void
security definer
as
$$
  begin
    set client_min_messages to DEFAULT;
    set log_min_messages to DEFAULT;
    set log_error_verbosity to DEFAULT;
    set log_min_duration_statement to DEFAULT;
  end;
$$ language plpgsql;
```

There's no need for `GRANT` and `REVOKE` statements here, as setting them back to the default does not pose a security risk. Instead of `SET xxx to DEFAULT`, you can also use a shorter version of the same command, namely `RESET xxx`.

Alternatively, you can simply end your session, as the parameters are valid only for the current session.

Auditing database access

Auditing database access is a much bigger topic than you might expect because it can cover a whole range of requirements.

Getting ready

First, decide which of these you want and look at the appropriate subsection:

- What were the SQL statements executed? *Auditing SQL*
- What were the tables accessed? *Auditing table access*
- What were the data rows changed? *Auditing data changes*
- What were the data rows viewed? Not described here, usually too much data

Auditing just SQL produces the lowest volume of audit log information, especially if you choose to log only DDL. Higher levels accumulate more information very rapidly, so you may quickly decide not to do this in practice. Read each section to understand the benefits and trade-offs.

Auditing SQL

There are two main ways to log SQL:

- Using the PostgreSQL `log_statement` parameter
- Using the `pgaudit` extension's `pgaudit.log` parameter

The `log_statement` parameter can be set to one of the following options:

- `ALL`: Logs all SQL statements executed at top level
- `MOD`: Logs all SQL statements for `INSERT`, `UPDATE`, `DELETE`, and `TRUNCATE`
- `ddl`: Logs all SQL statements for DDL commands
- `NONE`: No statements logged

For example, to log all DDL commands, edit your `postgresql.conf` file to set the following:

```
log_statement = 'ddl'
```

The `log_statement` SQL statements are explicitly given in top-level commands. It is still possible to perform SQL without it being logged by this setting if you use any of the PL languages, either through `DO` statements or by calling a function that includes SQL statements.

Was the change committed? It is possible to have some statements recorded in the log file but not be visible in the database structure. Most DDL commands in PostgreSQL can be rolled back, so what is in the log is just a list of commands executed by PostgreSQL—not what was actually committed. The log file is not transactional, and it keeps commands that were rolled back. It is possible to display the transaction identifier on each log line by including `%x` in the `log_line_prefix` setting, though that has some difficulties in terms of usage.

Who made the changes? To be able to know which database user made the DDL changes, you have to make sure that this information is logged as well. In order to do so, you may have to change the `log_line_prefix` parameter to include the `%u` format string.

A recommended minimal `log_line_prefix` format string for auditing DDL is `%t  %u  %d`, which tells PostgreSQL to log the timestamp, database user, and database name at the start of every log line.

The pgaudit extension provides two levels of audit logging: session and object levels. The session level has been designed to solve some of the problems of log_statement. pgaudit will log all access, even if it is not executed as a top-level statement, and it will log all dynamic SQL. pgaudit.log can be set to include zero or more of the following settings:

- READ: SELECT and COPY
- WRITE: INSERT, UPDATE, DELETE, TRUNCATE, and COPY
- FUNCTION: Function calls and DO blocks
- ROLE: GRANT, REVOKE, CREATE/ALTER/DROP ROLE
- DDL: All DDL not already included in the ROLE category
- MISC: Miscellaneous—DISCARD, FETCH, CHECKPOINT, VACUUM, and so on

For example, to log all DDL commands, edit your postgresql.conf file to set the following:

```
pgaudit.log = 'role, ddl'
```

You should set these parameters to reduce the overhead of logging:

```
pgaudit.log_catalog = off
pgaudit.log_relation = off
pgaudit.log_statement_once = on
```

The pgaudit extension was originally written by Simon Riggs and Abhijit Menon-Sen of 2ndQuadrant as part of the AXLE project for the EU. The next version was designed by Simon Riggs and David Steele to provide object-level logging. The original version was deprecated and is no longer available. The new version is fully supported and has been adopted by the US DoD as the tool of choice for PostgreSQL audit logging.

pgaudit is available in binary form via postgresql.org repositories.

Auditing table access

pgaudit can log access to each table. So, if an SQL table touches three tables, then it can generate three log records, one for each table. This is important because otherwise, you might have to try and parse the SQL to find out which tables it touched, which would be difficult without access to the schema and the search_path settings.

To make it easier to access the audit log per table, adjust these settings:

```
pgaudit.log_relation = on
pgaudit.log_statement_once = off
```

If you want even finer-grained auditing, `pgaudit` allows you to control which tables are audited. The user cannot tell which tables are logged and which are not, so it is possible for investigators to quietly enhance the level of logging once they are alerted to a suspect or a potential attack.

First, set the role that will be used by the auditor:

```
pgaudit.role = 'investigator'
```

Then, you can define logging through the privilege system, like the following command:

```
GRANT INSERT, UPDATE, DELETE on <vulnerable_table> TO investigator;
```

Remove it again when no longer required.

Privileges may be set at individual column level to protect **Personally Identifiable Information (PII)**.

Managing the audit log

Both `log_statement` and `pgaudit` output audit log records to the server log. This is the most flexible approach since the log can be routed in various ways to ensure it is safe and separate from normal log entries.

If you allow the log entries to go the normal server log, you can find all occurrences of the CREATE, ALTER, and DROP commands in the log:

```
postgres@hvost:~$ egrep -i "create|alter|drop" \
/var/log/postgresql/postgresql-11-main.log
```

If log rotation is in effect, you may need to use `grep` on older logs as well.

If the available logs are too new and you haven't saved the older logs in some other place, you are out of luck.

The default settings in the `postgresql.conf` file for log rotation are as follows:

```
log_filename = 'postgresql-%Y-%m-%d_%H%M%S.log'
log_rotation_age = 1d
log_rotation_size = 10MB
```

Log rotation can also be implemented with third-party utilities. For instance, the default behavior on Debian and Ubuntu distributions is to use the `logrotate` utility to compress or delete old log files, according to the rules specified in the `/etc/logrotate.d/postgresql-common` file.

To make sure you have the full history of DDL commands, you may want to set up a cron job that saves the DDL statements extracted from the main PostgreSQL log to a separate DDL audit log. You would still want to verify that the logs are not rotating too fast for this to catch all DDL statements.

If you use `syslog`, then you can route audit messages using various OS utilities.

Alternatively, you can use the `pgaudit` analyze extension to load data back into a special audit log database. Various other options exist.

Auditing data changes

This recipe provides different ways of collecting changes to data contained in the tables for auditing purposes.

First, you must make the following decisions:

- Do you need to audit all changes or only some?
- What information about the changes do you need to collect? Only the fact that the data has changed?
- When recording the new value of a field or tuple, do you also need to record the old value?
- Is it enough to record which user made the change, or do you also need to record the IP address and other connection information?
- How secure (tamper-proof) must the auditing information be? For example, does it need to be kept separately, away from the database being audited?

Changes can be collected using triggers which collect new (and if needed, old) values from tuples, and save them to auditing table(s). Triggers can be added to whichever tables need to be tracked.

The `audit_trigger` extension provides a handy universal audit trigger so you do not need to write your own. It logs both old and new values of rows in any table, serialized as `hstore` data type values. The latest version and its documentation are both available at `https://github.com/2ndQuadrant/audit-trigger`.

The extension creates a schema called `audit`, into which all of the other components of the audit trigger code are placed, after which we can enable auditing on specific tables.

As an example, we create standard `pgbench` tables by running the `pgbench` utility:

```
pgbench -i
```

Next, we connect to PostgreSQL as a superuser, and issue the following SQL to enable auditing on the `pgbench_account` table:

```
SELECT  audit.audit_table('pgbench_accounts');
```

Now, we perform some write activity to see how it is audited. The easiest choice is to run the `pgbench` utility again, this time to perform some transactions, as follows:

```
pgbench -t 1000
```

We expect the audit trigger to have logged the actions on `pgbench_accounts`, as we have enabled auditing on it. In order to verify this, we connect again with psql and issue the following SQL:

```
cookbook=# SELECT count(*) FROM audit.logged_actions;
count
-------
1000
(1 row)
```

This confirms that we have indeed logged 1,000 actions. Let's inspect the information that is logged by reading one row of the `logged_actions` table. First, we enable expanded mode, as the query produces a large number of columns:

```
cookbook=# \x on
```

Then, we issue the following command:

```
cookbook=# SELECT * FROM audit.logged_actions LIMIT 1;
-[ RECORD 1 ]-----+----------------------------------------------------------------------
-----------
event_id          | 1
schema_name       | public
table_name        | pgbench_accounts
relid             | 246511
session_user_name | gianni
action_tstamp_tx  | 2017-01-18 19:48:05.626299+01
action_tstamp_stm | 2017-01-18 19:48:05.626446+01
action_tstamp_clk | 2017-01-18 19:48:05.628488+01
```

```
transaction_id     | 182578
application_name    | pgbench
client_addr         |
client_port         |
client_query        | UPDATE pgbench_accounts SET abalance = abalance + -758
WHERE aid = 86061;
action              | U
row_data            | "aid"=>"86061", "bid"=>"1", "filler"=>"   ",
"abalance"=>"0"
changed_fields      | "abalance"=>"-758"
statement_only      | f
```

Always knowing which user is logged in

In the preceding recipes, we just logged the value of the user variable in the current PostgreSQL session to log the current user role.

This does not always mean that this particular user was the user that was actually authenticated at the start of the session. For example, a superuser can execute the SET ROLE TO ... command to set its current role to any other user or role in the system. As you might expect, non-superusers can assume only those roles that they own.

It is possible to differentiate between the logged-in role and the assumed role using the current_user and session_user session variables:

```
postgres=# select current_user, session_user;
current_user | session_user
-------------+--------------
postgres     | postgres

postgres=# set role to bob;
SET
postgres=> select current_user, session_user;
current_user | session_user
-------------+--------------
bob          | postgres
```

Sometimes, it is desirable to let each user log in with their own username and just assume the role needed on a case-by-case basis.

Getting ready

Prepare the required group roles for different tasks and access levels by granting the necessary privileges and options.

How to do it...

The steps are as follows:

1. Create user roles with no privileges and with the NOINHERIT option:

   ```
   postgres=# create user alice noinherit;
   CREATE ROLE
   postgres=# create user bob noinherit;
   CREATE ROLE
   ```

2. Then, create roles for each group of privileges that you need to assign:

   ```
   postgres=# create group sales;
   CREATE ROLE
   postgres=# create group marketing;
   CREATE ROLE
   postgres=# grant postgres to marketing;
   GRANT ROLE
   ```

3. Now, grant each user the roles it may need:

   ```
   postgres=# grant sales to alice;
   GRANT ROLE
   postgres=# grant marketing to alice;
   GRANT ROLE
   postgres=# grant sales to bob;
   GRANT ROLE
   ```

After you do this, the alice and bob users have no rights after login, but they can assume the sales role by executing SET ROLE TO sales, and alice can additionally assume the superuser role.

How it works...

If a role or user is created with the NOINHERIT option, this user will not automatically get the rights that have been granted to the other roles that have been granted to itself. To claim these rights from a specific role, it has to set its role to one of those other roles.

In some sense, this works a bit like the su (set user) command in Unix and Linux systems. That is, you (may) have the right to become that user, but you do not automatically have the rights of the aforementioned user.

This setup can be used to get better audit information, as it lets you know who the actual user was. If you just allow each user to log in as the role needed for a task, there is no good way to know later which of the users was really logged in as clerk1 when a $100,000 transfer was made.

There's more...

The SET ROLE command works both ways, that is, you can both gain and lose privileges. A superuser can set its role to any user defined in the system. To get back to your original login role, just use RESET ROLE.

Not inheriting user attributes

Not all rights come to users via GRANT commands. Some important rights are given via user attributes (SUPERUSER, CREATEDB, and CREATEROLE), and these are never inherited.

If your user has been granted a superuser role and you want to use the superuser powers of this granted role, you have to use SET ROLE To mysuperuserrole before anything that requires the superuser attribute to be set.

In other words, the user attributes always behave as if the user had been a NOINHERIT user.

Integrating with LDAP

This recipe shows you how to set up your PostgreSQL system so that it uses the LDAP for authentication.

Getting ready

Ensure that the usernames in the database and your LDAP server match, as this method works for user authentication checks of users who are already defined in the database.

How to do it...

In the PostgreSQL authentication file, `pg_hba.conf`, we define some address ranges to use LDAP as an authentication method, and we configure the LDAP server for this address range:

```
host       all         all          10.10.0.1/16            ldap \
ldapserver=ldap.our.net ldapprefix="cn=" ldapsuffix=",
    dc=our,dc=net"
```

How it works...

This setup makes the PostgreSQL server check passwords from the configured LDAP server.

User rights are not queried from the LDAP server but have to be defined inside the database using the ALTER USER, GRANT, and REVOKE commands.

There's more...

We have shown you how PostgreSQL can use an LDAP server for password authentication. It is also possible to use some more information from the LDAP server, as shown in the next two examples.

Setting up the client to use LDAP

If you are using the `pg_service.conf` file to define your database access parameters, you may define some to be queried from the LDAP server by including a line similar to the following in your `pg_service.conf` file:

```
ldap://ldap.mycompany.com/dc=mycompany,dc=com?uniqueMember?one?(cn=mydb)
```

Replacement for the User Name Map feature

Although we cannot use the User Name Map feature with LDAP, we can achieve a similar effect on the LDAP side. Use `ldapsearchattribute` and the search + bind mode to retrieve the PostgreSQL role name from the LDAP server.

See also

- For server setup, including the search + bind mode, visit `http://www.postgresql.org/docs/11/static/auth-methods.html#AUTH-LDAP`
- For client setup, visit `http://www.postgresql.org/docs/11/static/libpq-ldap.html`

Connecting using SSL

Here, we will demonstrate how to enable PostgreSQL to use SSL for the protection of database connections by encrypting all of the data passed over that connection. Using SSL makes it much harder to sniff the database traffic, including usernames, passwords, and other sensitive data. Otherwise, everything that is passed unencrypted between a client and the database can be observed by someone listening to a network somewhere between them. An alternative to using SSL is running the connection over a **Virtual Private Network (VPN)**.

Using SSL makes the data transfer on the encrypted connection a little slower, so you may not want to use it if you are sure that your network is safe. The performance impact can be quite large if you are creating lots of short connections, as setting up an SSL connection is quite CPU heavy. In this case, you may want to run a local connection pooling solution, such as PgBouncer, to which the client connects without encryption, and then configure PgBouncer for server connections using SSL. Older versions of PgBouncer did not support SSL; the solution was to channel server connections through stunnel, as described in the PgBouncer FAQ at `https://pgbouncer.github.io/faq.html`.

Getting ready

Get, or generate, an SSL server key and certificate pair for the server, and store these in the `data` directory of the current database instance as the `server.key` and `server.crt` files.

On some platforms, this is unnecessary; the key and certificate pair may already be generated by the packager. For example, in Ubuntu, PostgreSQL is set up to support SSL connections by default.

How to do it...

Set `ssl` = `on` in `postgresql.conf` and restart the database.

How it works...

If `ssl` = `on` is set, then PostgreSQL listens to both plain and SSL connections on the same port (`5432` by default) and determines the type of connection from the first byte of a new connection. Then, it proceeds to set up an SSL connection if an incoming request asks for it.

There's more...

You can leave the choice of whether or not to use SSL up to the client, or you can force SSL usage from the server side.

To let the client choose, use a line of the following form in the `pg_hba.conf` file:

```
host database  user   IP-address/IP-mask  auth-method
```

If you want to allow only SSL clients, use the `hostssl` keyword instead of `host`.

The contents of `pg_hba.conf` can be seen using the `pg_hba_file_rules` view.

The following fragment of `pg_hba.conf` enables both non-SSL and SSL connections from the `192.168.1.0/24` local subnet, but requires SSL from everybody accessing the database from other networks:

```
host       all       all       192.168.1.0/24      md5
hostssl    all       all       0.0.0.0/0           md5
```

Getting the SSL key and certificate

For web servers, you must usually get your SSL certificate from a recognized **Certificate Authority** (**CA**), as most browsers complain if the certificate is not issued by a known CA. They warn the user of the most common security risks and require confirmation before connecting to a server with a certificate issued by an unknown CA.

For your database server, it is usually sufficient to generate the certificate yourself using OpenSSL. The following commands generate a self-signed certificate for your server:

```
openssl genrsa 2048 > server.key
openssl req -new -x509 -key server.key -out server.crt
```

 Read more on X.509 keys and certificates by visiting OpenSSL's HOWTO pages at `https://github.com/openssl/openssl/tree/master/doc/HOWTO`.

Setting up a client to use SSL

The behavior of the client application regarding SSL is controlled by an environment variable, `PGSSLMODE`. This can have the following values, as defined in the official PostgreSQL documentation:

SSL mode	Eavesdropping protection	MITM protection	Statement
disabled	No	No	I don't care about security, and I don't want to pay the overhead of encryption.
allow	Maybe	No	I don't care about security, but I will pay the overhead of encryption if the server insists on it.
prefer	Maybe	No	I don't care about encryption, but I will to pay the overhead of encryption if the server supports it.
require	Yes	No	I want my data to be encrypted, and I accept the overhead. I trust that the network will ensure that I always connect to the server I want.
verify-ca	Yes	Depends on the CA policy	I want my data encrypted, and I accept the overhead. I want to be sure that I connect to a server that I trust.
verify-full	Yes	Yes	I want my data encrypted, and I accept the overhead. I want to be sure that I connect to a server I trust, and that the server is the one I specify.

MITM in the preceding table means **man-in-the-middle** attack, that is, someone posing as your server, perhaps by manipulating DNS records or IP routing tables, but who actually just observes and forwards the traffic.

For this to be possible with an SSL connection, this person needs to have obtained a certificate that your client considers valid.

Checking server authenticity

The last two SSL modes allow you to be reasonably sure that you are actually talking to your server by checking the SSL certificate presented by the server.

In order to enable this useful security feature, the following files must be available on the client side. On Unix systems, they are located in the client home directory, in a subdirectory named `~/.postgresql`. On Windows, they are in `%APPDATA%\postgresql\`:

File	Contents	Effect
`root.crt`	Certificates of one or more trusted CAs	PostgreSQL verifies that the server certificate is signed by a trusted CA
`root.crl`	Certificates revoked by CAs	The server certificate must not be on this list

Only the `root.crt` file is required for the client to authenticate the server certificate. It can contain multiple root certificates against which the server certificate is compared.

Using SSL certificates to authenticate

This recipe shows you how to set up your PostgreSQL system so that it *requires* clients to present a valid X.509 certificate before allowing them to connect.

This can be used as an additional security layer, using double authentication, where the client must both have a valid certificate to set up the SSL connection and know the database user's password. It can also be used as the sole authentication method, where the PostgreSQL server will first verify the client connection using the certificate presented by the client, and then retrieve the username from the same certificate.

Getting ready

Get, or generate, a root certificate and a client certificate to be used by the connecting client.

How to do it...

For testing purposes, or for setting up a single trusted user, you can use a self-signed certificate:

```
openssl genrsa 2048 > client.key
openssl req -new -x509 -key server.key -out client.crt
```

In the server, set up a line in the pg_hba.conf file with the hostssl method and the clientcert option set to 1:

```
hostssl all    all    0.0.0.0/0         md5 clientcert=1
```

Put the client root certificate in the root.crt file in the server data directory ($PGDATA/root.crt). This file may contain multiple trusted root certificates.

If you are using a central certificate authority, you probably also have a certificate revocation list, which should be put in a root.crl file and regularly updated.

In the client, put the client's private key and certificate in ~/.postgresql/postgresql.key and ~/.postgresql/postgresql.crt. Make sure that the private key file is not world-readable or group-readable by running the following command:

```
chmod 0600 ~/.postgresql/postgresql.key
```

In a Windows client, the corresponding files are %APPDATA%\postgresql\postgresql.key and %APPDATA%\postgresql\postgresql.crt. No permission check is done, as the location is considered secure.

If the client certificate is not signed by the root CA but by an intermediate CA, then all of the intermediate CA certificates up to the root certificate must be placed in the postgresql.crt file as well.

How it works...

If the clientcert=1 option is set for a hostssl row in pg_hba.conf, then PostgreSQL accepts only connection requests accompanied by a valid certificate.

The validity of the certificate is checked against certificates present in the root.crt file in the server data directory.

If there is a `root.crl` file, then the presented certificate is searched for in this file and, if found, is rejected.

After the client certificate is validated and the SSL connection is established, the server proceeds to validate the actual connecting user using whatever authentication method is specified in the corresponding `hostssl` line.

In the following example, clients from a special address can connect as any user when using an SSL certificate, and they must specify a `SCRAM-SHA-256` password for non-SSL connections. Clients from all of the other addresses must present a certificate and use `md5` password authentication:

```
host      all   all   10.10.10.10/32   md5
hostssl   all   all   10.10.10.10/32   trust            clientcert=1
hostssl   all   all   all              scram-sha-256    clientcert=1
```

There's more...

In this section, we provide some additional content, describing an important optimization for an SSL-only database server, plus two extensions of the basic SSL configuration.

Avoiding duplicate SSL connection attempts

In the *Setting up a client to use SSL* section of the previous *Connecting using SSL* recipe, we saw how the client's SSL behavior is affected by environment variables. Depending on how the `SSLMODE` environment variable is set on the client (either via compile-time settings, the `PGSSLMODE` environment variable, or the `sslmode` connection parameter), the client may attempt to connect without SSL first, and then attempt an SSL connection only after the server rejects the non-SSL connection. This duplicates a connection attempt every time a client accesses an SSL-only server.

To make sure that the client tries to establish an SSL connection on the first attempt, `SSLMODE` must be set to `prefer` or higher.

Using multiple client certificates

You may sometimes need different certificates to connect to different PostgreSQL servers.

The location of the certificate and key files in `postgresql.crt` and `postgresql.key` in the table from the *Checking server authenticity* section is just the default and can be overridden by specifying alternative file paths using the `sslcert` and `sslkey` connection parameters or the `PGSSLCERT` and `PGSSLKEY` environment variables.

Using the client certificate to select the database user

It is possible to use the client certificate for two purposes at once: proving that the connecting client is a valid one and selecting the database user to be used for the connection.

To do this, you set the authentication method to `cert` in the `hostssl` line:

```
hostssl   all   all   0.0.0.0/0          cert
```

As you can see, the `clientcert=1` option used with `hostssl` to require client certificates is no longer required, as it is implied by the `cert` method itself.

When using the `cert` authentication method, a valid client certificate is required, and the `cn` (short for common name) attribute of the certificate will be compared to the requested database username. The login will be allowed only if they match.

It is possible to use a User Name Map to map the common names in the certificates to database usernames by specifying the `map` option:

```
hostssl   all   all   0.0.0.0/0          cert    map=x509cnmap
```

Here, `x509cnmap` is the name that we have arbitrarily chosen for our mapping. More details on User Name Maps are provided in the *Mapping external usernames to database roles* recipe.

See also

To understand more about SSL in general, and the OpenSSL library used by PostgreSQL in particular, visit `http://www.openssl.org` or get a good book about SSL.

To get started with the generation of simple SSL keys and certificates, see `https://github.com/openssl/openssl/blob/master/doc/HOWTO/certificates.txt`.

There is also a nice presentation named *Encrypted PostgreSQL* explaining these issues at PGCon 2009. The slides are available at `http://www.pgcon.org/2009/schedule/events/120.en.html`.

Mapping external usernames to database roles

In some cases, the authentication username is different from the PostgreSQL username. For instance, this can happen when using an external system for authentication, such as certificate authentication, as described in the previous recipe, or any other external or single sign-on system authentication method from `http://www.postgresql.org/docs/11/static/auth-methods.html` (GSSAPI, SSPI, Kerberos, Radius, or PAM). You may just need to enable an externally authenticated user to connect as multiple database users. In such cases, you can specify rules to map the external username to the appropriate database role.

Getting ready

Prepare a list of usernames from the external authentication system and decide which database users they are allowed to connect as—that is, which external users map to which database users.

How to do it...

Create a `pg_ident.conf` file in the usual place (`PGDATA`), with lines in the following format:

```
map-name system-username database-username
```

Here, `map-name` is the value of the `map` option from the corresponding line in `pg_hba.conf`, `system-username` is the username that the external system authenticated the connection as, and `database-username` is the database user this system user is allowed to connect as. The same system user may be allowed to connect as multiple database users, so this is not a 1:1 mapping, but rather a list of allowed database users for each system user.

If `system-username` starts with a slash (`/`), then the rest of it is treated as a regular expression rather than a directly matching string, and it is possible to use the `\1` string in `database-username` to refer to the part captured by the parentheses in the regular expression. For example, consider the following lines:

```
salesmap    /^(.*)@sales\.comp\.com$      \1
salesmap    /^(.*)@sales\.comp\.com$    sales
salesmap    manager@sales.comp.com     auditor
```

These will allow any user authenticated with a @sales.comp.com email address to connect both as a database user equal to the name before the @ sign in their email address and as the sales user. They will additionally allow anager@sales.comp.com to connect as the auditor user. Then, edit the pg_hba.conf line to specify the map=salesmap option.

How it works...

After authenticating the connection using an external authentication system, PostgreSQL will usually proceed to check that the externally authenticated username matches the database username that the user wishes to connect as and rejects the connection if these two do not match.

If there is a map= parameter specified for the current line in pg_hba.conf, then the system will scan the map line by line and will let the client proceed with connecting if a match is found.

There's more...

By default, the map file is called pg_ident.conf (because it was first used for the ident authentication method).

Nowadays, it is possible to change the name of this file via the ident_file configuration parameter in postgresql.conf. It can also be located outside the PGDATA directory by setting ident_file to a full path.

A relative path can also be used, but since it is relative to where the postgres process is started, this is usually not a good idea.

Encrypting sensitive data

This recipe shows you how to encrypt data using the pgcrypto contrib package.

Getting ready

Make sure you (and/or your database server) are in a country where encryption is not illegal—it still is in some countries.

In order to create and manage PGP keys, you also need the well-known GnuPG command-line utility, which is available on practically all distributions.

pgcrypto is part of the contrib collection. Starting from version 10, on Debian and Ubuntu it is part of the main postgresql-10 server package, while in previous versions there was a separate package, for example, postgresql-contrib-9.6.

Install it on the database in which you want to use it, following the *Adding an external module to PostgreSQL* recipe from Chapter 3, *Configuration*.

You also need to have PGP keys set up:

```
pguser@laptop:~$ gpg --gen-key
```

Answer some questions here (the defaults are OK, unless you are an expert), select the key type as DSA and Elgamal, and enter an empty password.

Now, export the keys:

```
pguser@laptop:~$ gpg -a --export "PostgreSQL User (test key for PG
Cookbook) <pguser@somewhere.net>" > public.key
pguser@laptop:~$ gpg -a --export-secret-keys "PostgreSQL User (test key for
PG Cookbook) <pguser@somewhere.net>" > secret.key
```

Make sure only you and the postgres database user have access to the secret key:

```
pguser@laptop:~$ sudo chgrp postgres secret.key
pguser@laptop:~$ chmod 440 secret.key
pguser@laptop:~$ ls -l *.key
-rw-r--r-- 1 pguser pguser   1718 2016-03-26 13:53 public.key
-r--r----- 1 pguser postgres 1818 2016-03-26 13:54 secret.key
```

Last but not least, make a copy of the public and the secret key; if you lose them, you'll lose the ability to encrypt/decrypt.

How to do it...

To ensure that the secret keys are never visible in database logs, write a wrapper function to get the keys from the file. You need to do it in an untrusted embedded language, such as PL/PythonU, as only untrusted languages can access the filesystem. You need to be a PostgreSQL superuser in order to create functions in untrusted languages. It's not difficult to write a PostgreSQL function that reads a text file. For convenience, here is an example that requires PL/PythonU:

```
create or replace function get_my_public_key() returns text as $$
return open('/home/pguser/public.key').read()
$$
language plpythonu;
revoke all on function get_my_public_key() from public;
create or replace function get_my_secret_key() returns text as $$
return open('/home/pguser/secret.key').read()
$$
language plpythonu;
revoke all on function get_my_secret_key() from public;
```

This can also be fully implemented in PL/pgSQL using the built-in PostgreSQL system function, `pg_read_file` (filename), and you don't have to bother with PL/PythonU at all. However, to use this function, you must place the files in the `data` directory as required by that function for additional security, so the database superuser is not allowed to access the rest of the filesystem directly.

If you don't want other database users to be able to see the keys, you also need to write wrapper functions for encryption and decryption and then give access to these wrapper functions to end users.

The `encryption` function can be like this:

```
create or replace function encrypt_using_my_public_key(
    cleartext text,
    ciphertext out bytea
)
AS $$
DECLARE
    pubkey_bin bytea;
BEGIN
    -- text version of public key needs to be passed through function
dearmor() to get to raw key
    pubkey_bin := dearmor(get_my_public_key());
```

```
        ciphertext := pgp_pub_encrypt(cleartext, pubkey_bin);
END;
$$ language plpgsql security definer;
revoke all on function encrypt_using_my_public_key(text) from public;
grant execute on function encrypt_using_my_public_key(text) to bob;
```

The `decryption` function can be as follows:

```
create or replace function decrypt_using_my_secret_key(
    ciphertext bytea,
    cleartext out text
)
AS $$
DECLARE
    secret_key_bin bytea;
BEGIN
    -- text version of secret key needs to be passed through function
dearmor() to get to raw binary key
    secret_key_bin := dearmor(get_my_secret_key());

    cleartext := pgp_pub_decrypt(ciphertext, secret_key_bin);
END;
$$ language plpgsql security definer;
revoke all on function decrypt_using_my_secret_key(bytea) from public;
grant execute on function decrypt_using_my_secret_key(bytea) to bob;
```

Finally, we test the encryption:

```
test2=# select encrypt_using_my_public_key('X marks the spot!');
```

This function returns a `bytea` (that is, raw binary) result that looks something like the following:

```
encrypt_using_my_public_key |
\301\301N\003\223o\215\2125\203\252;\020\007\376-z\233\211H...
```

To see that it actually works, you must go both ways:

```
test2=# select decrypt_using_my_secret_key(encrypt_using_my_public_key('X
marks the spot!'));
 decrypt_using_my_secret_key
-----------------------------
 X marks the spot!
(1 row)
```

Yes, we got back our initial string!

How it works...

What we have done here is the following:

- Hidden the keys from non-superuser database users
- Provided wrappers for authorized users to use encryption and decryption functionalities

To ensure that your sensitive data is not stolen while in transit between the client and the database server, make sure you connect to PostgreSQL either using an SSL-encrypted connection or from localhost.

You also have to trust your server administrators and all of the other users with superuser privileges to be sure that your encrypted data is safe. And, of course, you must trust the safety of the entire environment; PostgreSQL can decrypt the data, so any other user or software that has access to the same files can do the same.

There's more...

A higher level of security is possible, with more complex procedures and architecture, as shown in the next sections. We also mention a limited `pgcrypto` version that does not use OpenSSL.

For really sensitive data

For some data, you wouldn't want to risk keeping the decryption password on the same machine as the encrypted data.

In those cases, you can use **public-key cryptography**, also known as **asymmetric cryptography**, and carry out only the encryption part on the database server. This also means that you only have the encryption key on the database host and not the key needed for decryption. Alternatively, you can deploy a separate, extra-secure encryption server in your server infrastructure that provides just the encrypting and decrypting functionality as a remote call.

This solution is secure because, in asymmetric cryptography, the private (that is, decryption) key cannot be derived from the corresponding public (that is, encryption) key, hence the names `public` and `private`, which denote the appropriate dissemination policies.

If you wish to prove the identity of the author of a file, the correct method is to use a digital signature, which is an entirely different application of cryptography. Note that this is not currently supported by `pgcrypto`, so you must implement your own methods as C functions or in a procedural language capable of using cryptographic libraries.

For really, really, really sensitive data

For even more sensitive data, you may never want the data to leave the client computer unencrypted. Therefore, you need to encrypt the data before sending it to the database. In that case, PostgreSQL receives already encrypted data and never sees the unencrypted version. This also means that the only useful indexes you can have are for use in `WHERE encrypted_column = encrypted_data` and for ensuring uniqueness.

Even these forms can be used only if the encryption algorithm always produces the same ciphertext (output) for the same plaintext (input), which is true only for weaker encryption algorithms. For example, it would be easy to determine the age or sex of a person if the same value were always encrypted into the same ciphertext. To avoid this vulnerability, strong encryption algorithms are able to produce a different ciphertext for the same value.

The versions of `pgcrypto` are usually compiled to use the *OpenSSL library* (http://www.openssl.org). If, for some reason, you don't have OpenSSL, or just don't want to use it, it is possible to compile `pgcrypto` without it, with a smaller number of supported encryption algorithms and a slightly reduced performance.

See also

- The page on `pgcrypto` in the PostgreSQL online documentation, available at http://www.postgresql.org/docs/11/static/pgcrypto.html
- The OpenSSL web page, accessed at http://www.openssl.org/
- The *GNU Privacy Handbook* at http://www.gnupg.org/gph/en/manual.html

Database Administration
7

In Chapter 5, *Tables and Data*, we looked at the contents of tables and various complexities. Now we'll turn our attention to larger administration tasks that we need to perform from time to time, such as creating things, moving things around, storing things neatly, and removing them when they're no longer required.

The most sensible way to perform major administrative tasks is to write a script to do what you think is required. If you're unsure, you can always run the script on a system test server, and then run it again on the production server once you're happy. Manically typing commands against production database servers isn't wise. Worse, using an admin tool can lead to serious issues if that tool doesn't show you the SQL you're about to execute. If you haven't dropped your first live table yet, don't worry; you will. Perhaps you might want to read Chapter 11, *Backup and Recovery*, first, eh? Back it up using scripts.

Scripts are great because you can automate common tasks, and there's no need to sit there with a mouse, working your way through hundreds of changes. If you're drawn to the discussion about the command line versus GUI, then my thoughts and reasons are completely orthogonal to that. I want to encourage you to avoid errors and save time by performing repetitive and automatic execution of small administration programs or scripts. If it were safe or easy to do the equivalent of mouse movements in a script, then that would be an option, but it's definitely not. The only viable way to write a repeatable script is by writing text SQL commands. Which scripting tool to use is a more interesting debate. We consider psql here because if you've got PostgreSQL, then you've certainly got it, without needing to install additional software. So, we're on solid ground to provide examples that way.

Let's move on to the recipes! First, we'll start by looking at some scripting techniques that are valuable in PostgreSQL.

In this chapter, we will cover the following recipes:

- Writing a script that either succeeds entirely or fails entirely
- Writing a psql script that exits on the first error

- Using psql variables
- Placing query output into psql variables
- Writing a conditional psql script
- Investigating a psql error
- Performing actions on many tables
- Using pgAdmin for DBA tasks
- Using OmniDB for DBA tasks
- Adding/removing columns on a table
- Changing the data type of a column
- Changing the definition of a data type
- Adding/removing schemas
- Moving objects between schemas
- Adding/removing tablespaces
- Moving objects between tablespaces
- Accessing objects in other PostgreSQL databases
- Accessing objects in other foreign databases
- Updatable views
- Using materialized views

Writing a script that either succeeds entirely or fails entirely

Database administration often involves applying a coordinated set of changes to the database. One of PostgreSQL's great strengths is its transaction system, wherein almost all actions can be executed inside a transaction. This allows us to build a script with many actions that will either all succeed or all fail. This means that if any of these actions fail, then all the other actions in the script are rolled back and never become visible to any other user, which can be critically important on a production system. This property is referred to as **atomicity** in the sense that the script is intended as a single unit that cannot be split. This is the meaning of the *A* in the **ACID** properties of database transactions.

Transactions definitely apply to **Data Definition Language** (**DDL**), which refers to the set of SQL commands used to define, modify, and delete database objects. The term DDL goes back many years, but it persists because that subset is a useful short name for the commands that most administrators need to execute: CREATE, ALTER, DROP, and so on.

Although most commands in PostgreSQL are transactional, there are a few that cannot be. The most common example is of commands that use sequences. They cannot be transactional because when a new sequence number is allocated, the effect of having *consumed* that number must become visible immediately, without waiting for that transaction to be committed. Otherwise, the same number will be given to another transaction, which is contrary to what sequences are supposed to do.

How to do it...

The basic way to ensure that we get all commands successful or none at all is to literally wrap our script into a transaction, as follows:

```
BEGIN;
command 1;
command 2;
command 3;
COMMIT;
```

Writing a transaction control command involves editing the script, which you may not want to do or even have access to. There are, however, other ways as well.

From psql, you can do this by simply using the -1 or --single-transaction command-line options, as follows:

```
bash $ psql -1 -f myscript.sql
bash $ psql --single-transaction -f myscript.sql
```

The -1 option is short, but I recommend using --single-transaction, as it's much clearer which option is being selected.

How it works...

The entire script will fail if, at any point, one of the commands gives an error (or higher) message. Almost all of the SQL used to define objects (DDL) provides a way to avoid throwing errors. More precisely, commands that begin with the DROP keyword have an IF EXISTS option. This allows you to execute the DROP keyword, regardless of whether or not the object already exists.

Thus, by the end of the command, that object will not exist:

```
DROP VIEW IF EXISTS cust_view;
```

Similarly, most commands that begin with the CREATE keyword have the optional OR REPLACE suffix. This allows the CREATE statement to overwrite the definition if one already exists, or add the new object if it doesn't exist yet, like this:

```
CREATE OR REPLACE VIEW cust_view AS SELECT * FROM cust;
```

In the cases where both the DROP IF EXISTS and CREATE OR REPLACE options exist, you might think that CREATE OR REPLACE is usually sufficient. However, if you change the output definition of a function or a view, then using OR REPLACE is not sufficient. In that case, you must use DROP and recreate it, as shown in the following example:

```
postgres=# CREATE OR REPLACE VIEW cust_view AS
SELECT col as title1 FROM cust;
CREATE VIEW
postgres=# CREATE OR REPLACE VIEW cust_view
AS SELECT col as title2 FROM cust;
ERROR:  cannot change name of view column "title1" to "title2"
```

Also, note that CREATE INDEX does not have an OR REPLACE option. If you run it twice, you'll get two indexes on your table, unless you specifically name the index. There is a DROP INDEX IF EXISTS option, but it may take a long time to drop and recreate an index. An index exists just for the purpose of optimization, and it does not change the actual result of any query, so this different behavior is actually very convenient. This is also reflected in the fact that the SQL standard doesn't mention indexes at all, even though they exist in practically all database systems, because they do not affect the logical layer.

PostgreSQL does not support nested transaction control commands, which can lead to unexpected behavior. For instance, consider the following code, written in a **nested transaction** style:

```
postgres=# BEGIN;
BEGIN
postgres=# CREATE TABLE a(x int);
CREATE TABLE
postgres=# BEGIN;
WARNING:  there is already a transaction in progress
BEGIN
postgres=# CREATE TABLE b(x int);
CREATE TABLE
postgres=# COMMIT;
COMMIT
postgres=# ROLLBACK;
```

```
NOTICE:   there is no transaction in progress
ROLLBACK
```

A hypothetical author of such code probably meant to create table a first, and then create table b. Then, they changed their mind and rolled back both the *inner* transaction and the *outer* transaction. However, what PostgreSQL does is discard the second BEGIN statement so that the COMMIT statement is matched with the first BEGIN statement and the inner transaction becomes a top-level transaction. Hence, right after the COMMIT statement, we are outside a transaction block, so the next statement is assigned its own transaction. When ROLLBACK is issued as the next statement, PostgreSQL notices that the transaction is actually empty.

The danger in this particular example is that the user inadvertently committed a transaction, thus waving the right to roll it back; however, we should say that a careful user would have noticed the warning and paused to think before going ahead.

From this example, you have learned a valuable lesson: if you have used transaction control commands in your script, then wrapping them again in a higher-level script or command can cause problems of the worst kind, such as committing stuff that you wanted to roll back. This is important enough to deserve a boxed warning.

 PostgreSQL accepts nested transactional control commands, but does not act on them. After the first commit, the commands will be assumed to be transactions in their own right and will persist, should the script fail. Be careful!

There's more...

The following commands cannot be included in a script that uses transactions in the way we just described:

- CREATE DATABASE/DROP DATABASE
- CREATE TABLESPACE/DROP TABLESPACE
- CREATE INDEX CONCURRENTLY
- VACUUM
- REINDEX DATABASE/REINDEX SYSTEM
- CLUSTER

None of these actions need to be run manually on a regular basis within complex programs, so this shouldn't be a problem for you.

Also, note that these commands do not substantially alter the *logical* content of a database; that is, they don't create new user tables or alter any rows, so there's less need to use them inside complex transactions.

While PostgreSQL does not support nested transaction commands, it supports the notion of SAVEPOINT, which can be used to achieve the same behavior. Suppose we wanted to implement the following pseudocode:

```
(begin transaction T1)
  (statement 1)
  (begin transaction T2)
    (statement 2)
  (commit transaction T2)
  (statement 3)
(commit transaction t1)
```

The effect we seek has the following properties:

- If statements 1 and 3 succeed, and statement 2 fails, then statements 1 and 3 will be committed
- If all three statements succeed, then they will all be committed
- Otherwise, no statement will be committed

These properties also hold with the following PostgreSQL commands:

```
BEGIN;
    (statement 1)
  SAVEPOINT T2;
    (statement 2)
  RELEASE SAVEPOINT T2; /* we assume that statement 2 does not fail */
    (statement 3)
COMMIT;
```

This form, as noted in the code, applies only if statement 2 does not fail. If it fails, we must replace RELEASE SAVEPOINT with ROLLBACK TO SAVEPOINT, or we will get an error. This is a slight difference between top-level transaction commands; a COMMIT statement is silently converted into a ROLLBACK when the transaction is in a failed state.

Writing a psql script that exits on the first error

The default mode for the `psql` script tool is to continue processing when it finds an error. This sounds dumb, but it exists for historical compatibility only. There are some easy and mostly permanent ways to avoid this, so let's look at them.

Getting ready

Let's start with a simple script, with a command we know will fail:

```
$ $EDITOR test.sql
mistake1;
mistake2;
mistake3;
```

Execute the following script using `psql` to see what the results look like:

```
$ psql -f test.sql
psql:test.sql:1: ERROR:    syntax error at or near "mistake1"
LINE 1: mistake1;
        ^
psql:test.sql:2: ERROR:    syntax error at or near "mistake2"
LINE 1: mistake2;
        ^
psql:test.sql:3: ERROR:    syntax error at or near "mistake3"
LINE 1: mistake3;
        ^
```

How to do it...

We will perform the following steps:

1. To exit the script on the first error, we can write the following command:

   ```
   $ psql -f test.sql -v ON_ERROR_STOP=on
   psql:test.sql:1: ERROR:    syntax error at or near "mistake1"
   LINE 1: mistake1;
           ^
   ```

2. Alternatively, we can edit the `test.sql` file with the initial line that's shown here:

```
$ $EDITOR test.sql
\set ON_ERROR_STOP on
mistake1;
mistake2;
mistake3;
```

3. Note that the following command will *not* work because we have missed the crucial ON value:

```
$ psql -f test.sql -v ON_ERROR_STOP
```

How it works...

The ON_ERROR_STOP variable is a psql special variable that controls the behavior of psql as it executes in script mode. When this variable is set, a SQL error will generate an OS return code 3, whereas other OS-related errors will return code 1.

There's more...

You can place some psql commands in a profile that will get executed when you run psql. Adding ON_ERROR_STOP to your profile will ensure that this setting is applied to all psql sessions:

```
$ $EDITOR ~/.psqlrc
\set ON_ERROR_STOP
```

You can forcibly override this, and request psql to execute without a profile using -X. This is probably the safest thing to do for the batch execution of scripts so that they always work in the same way, irrespective of the local settings.

ON_ERROR_STOP is one of some special variables that affects the way psql behaves. The full list is available at the following URL: https://www.postgresql.org/docs/11/static/app-psql.html#APP-PSQL-VARIABLES.

Using psql variables

In the previous recipe, we have seen how to use the ON_ERROR_STOP variable. Here, we will show you how to work with any variable, including user-defined ones.

Getting ready

As an example, we will create a script that does some work on a given table. We will keep it simple, because we just want to show how variables work.

For instance, we might want to add a text column to a table, and then set it to a given value. So, we write the following lines into a file called vartest.sql:

```
ALTER TABLE mytable ADD COLUMN mycol text;
UPDATE mytable SET mycol = 'myval';
```

The script can be run as follows:

```
psql -f vartest.sql
```

How to do it...

We change vartest.sql as follows:

```
\set tabname mytable
\set colname mycol
\set colval 'myval'
ALTER TABLE :tabname ADD COLUMN :colname text;
UPDATE :tabname SET :colname = :'colval';
```

How it works...

What do these changes mean? We have defined three variables, setting them to the table name, column name, and column value, respectively. Then, we have replaced the mentions of those specific values with the name of the variable preceded by a colon, which in psql means *replace with the value of this variable*. In the case of colval, we have also surrounded the variable name with single quotes, meaning *treat the value as a string*.

If we want `vartest.sql` to add a different column, we just have to make one change to the top of the script, where all variables are conveniently set. Then, the new column name will be used.

There's more...

This was just one way to define variables. Another is to indicate them in the command line, when running the script:

```
psql -v tabname=mytab2 -f vartest.sql
```

Variables can also be set interactively. The following line will prompt the user, and then set the variable to whatever is typed before hitting *Enter*:

```
\prompt 'Insert the table name: ' tabname
```

In the next recipe, we will see how to set variables using a SQL query.

Placing query output into psql variables

It is also possible to store some values produced by a query into variables—for instance, to reuse them later in other queries.

In this recipe, we will demonstrate this approach with a concrete example.

Getting ready

In the *Controlling automatic database maintenance* recipe of Chapter 9, *Regular Maintenance*, we will describe VACUUM, showing that it runs regularly on each table based on the number of rows that might need vacuuming (**dead rows**).
The VACUUM command will run if that number exceeds a given threshold, which by default is just above 20% of the row count.

In this recipe, we will create a script that picks the table with the largest number of dead rows and runs VACUUM on it.

How to do it...

The script is as follows:

```
SELECT schemaname
, relname
, n_dead_tup
, n_live_tup
FROM pg_stat_user_tables
ORDER BY n_dead_tup DESC
LIMIT 1
\gset
\qecho Running VACUUM on table :"relname" in schema :"schemaname"
\qecho Rows before: :n_dead_tup dead, :n_live_tup live
VACUUM ANALYZE :schemaname.:relname;
\qecho Waiting 1 second...
SELECT pg_sleep(1);
SELECT n_dead_tup AS n_dead_tup_now
,       n_live_tup AS n_live_tup_now
FROM pg_stat_user_tables
WHERE schemaname = :'schemaname'
AND relname = :'relname'
\gset
\qecho Rows after: :n_dead_tup_now dead, :n_live_tup_now live
```

How it works...

You might have noticed that the first query does not end with a semicolon, as usual. This is because we end it with \gset instead, which means *run the query, and assign each returned value to a variable having the same name as the output column.*

This command expects the query to return exactly one row, as you might expect it to, and if not, it does not set any variable.

The script waits one second before reading the updated number of dead and live rows. The reason for the wait is that such statistics are updated after the end of the transaction that makes the changes, which sends a signal to the statistics collector, which then does the update.

There's more...

See the next recipe on how to improve the script with iterations so that it vacuums more than one table.

Writing a conditional psql script

psql supports the conditional meta-commands \if, \elif, \else, and \endif. In this recipe, we will demonstrate some of them.

Getting ready

We want to improve the vartest.sql, script so that it runs VACUUM only if there actually are dead rows in that table.

How to do it...

We add conditional commands to vartest.sql resulting in the following script:

```
SELECT schemaname
, relname
, n_dead_tup
, n_live_tup
, n_dead_tup > 0 AS needs_vacuum
FROM pg_stat_user_tables
ORDER BY n_dead_tup DESC
LIMIT 1
\gset
\if :needs_vacuum
\qecho Running VACUUM on table :"relname" in schema :"schemaname"
\qecho Rows before: :n_dead_tup dead, :n_live_tup live
VACUUM ANALYZE :schemaname.:relname;
\qecho Waiting 1 second...
SELECT pg_sleep(1);
```

```
SELECT n_dead_tup AS n_dead_tup_now
,       n_live_tup AS n_live_tup_now
FROM pg_stat_user_tables
WHERE schemaname = :'schemaname' AND relname = :'relname'
\gset
\qecho Rows after: :n_dead_tup_now dead, :n_live_tup_now live
\else
\qecho Skipping VACUUM on table :"relname" in schema :"schemaname"
\endif
```

How it works...

We have added an extra column, needs_vacuum, to the first query, resulting in one more variable that we can use to make the VACUUM part conditional.

There's more...

Conditional statements are usually part of flow-control statements, which also include iterations.

While iterating is not directly supported by psql, a similar effect can be achieved in other ways, for instance:

- A script called file.sql (for instance) can be iterated by adding some lines at the end, as in the following fragment:

```
SELECT /* add a termination condition as appropriate */ AS do_loop
\gset
\if do_loop
\ir file.sql
\endif
```

- Instead of iterating, you can follow the approach described later in this chapter in the *Performing actions on many tables* recipe.

Investigating a psql error

Error messages can sometimes be cryptic, and you may be left wondering, *Why did this error happen at all?*

For this purpose, `psql` recognizes two variables, VERBOSITY and CONTEXT; valid values are `terse`, `default`, or `verbose` for the former, and `never`, `errors`, or `always` for the latter. A more verbose error message will hopefully specify extra detail, and the context information will be included. Here is an example to show the difference:

```
postgres=# \set VERBOSITY terse
postgres=# \set CONTEXT never
postgres=# select * from missingtable;
ERROR:  relation "missingtable" does not exist at character 15
```

This is quite a simple error, so we don't actually need the extra detail, but it is nevertheless useful for illustrating the extra detail you get when raising verbosity and enabling context information:

```
postgres=# \set VERBOSITY verbose
postgres=# \set CONTEXT errors
postgres=# select * from missingtable;
ERROR:  42P01: relation "missingtable" does not exist
LINE 1: select * from missingtable;
                      ^
LOCATION:  parserOpenTable, parse_relation.c:1159
```

Now you get the SQL error code `42P01`, which you can look up in the PostgreSQL manual, and even a reference to the file and the line in the PostgreSQL source code where this error is raised so that you can investigate it (the beauty of open source!).

However, there is a problem with having to enable verbosity in advance: you need to do it before running the command. If all errors were reproducible, this would not be a huge inconvenience. But in certain cases, you may hit a transient error, such as a **serialization failure**, which is difficult to detect itself, and it could sometimes happen that you struggle to reproduce the error, let alone analyze it.

The `\errverbose` meta command in `psql` was introduced precisely to avoid these problems.

Getting ready

In fact, there isn't much to do, as the point of the `\errverbose` meta-command is precisely to capture information on the error without requiring any prior activity.

How to do it...

Check the following example to understand the usage of the `\errverbose` meta-command.

1. Suppose you hit an error, as in the following query, and `verbose` reporting was not enabled:

```
postgres=# create table wrongname();
ERROR:  relation "wrongname" already exists
```

2. The extra detail that is not displayed is nevertheless remembered by psql, so you can view it as follows:

```
postgres=# \errverbose
ERROR:  42P07: relation "wrongname" already exists
LOCATION:  heap_create_with_catalog, heap.c:1067
```

There's more...

The error and source codes for this recipe can be found in the following links:

- The list of PostgreSQL error codes is available in the manual at the following URL: https://www.postgresql.org/docs/11/static/errcodes-appendix.html
- The PostgreSQL source code can be downloaded or inspected from the following URL https://git.postgresql.org/

Using pgAdmin for DBA tasks

In this recipe, we will show you how to use **pgAdmin** for the administration of your database. PgAdmin is one of the two graphical interfaces that we introduced in the *Using graphical administration tools* recipe in Chapter 1, *First Steps*; the other one is OmniDB, to which we dedicate this next recipe.

Getting ready

You should have already installed pgAdmin as part of the *Using graphical administration tools* recipe from Chapter 1, *First Steps*, which includes website pointers. If you haven't done so, please read it now.

Remember to install pgAdmin 4, which is the last generation of the software; the previous one, pgAdmin 3, is no longer supported and hasn't been for a few years, and will give various errors on PostgreSQL 10 and above.

How to do it...

The first task of a DBA is to get access to the database, and get a first glance of its contents. In that respect, we have already seen how to create a connection, access the dashboard, and display some database statistics. We also mentioned the **Grant Wizard** and the graphical **Explain** tool:

1. The list of schemas in a given database can be obtained by opening a database and selecting **Schemas**:

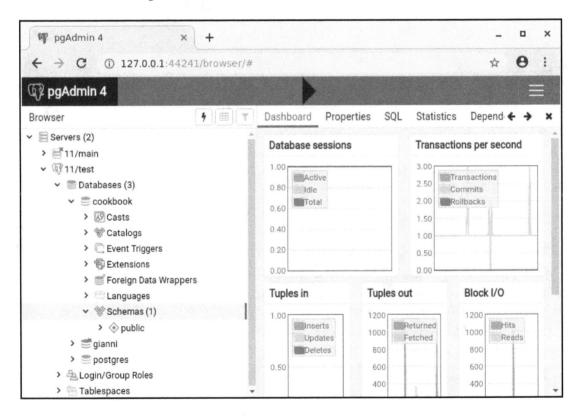

2. If you right-click on an individual schema, you get a number of possible actions. For instance, you can take a backup of that schema only:

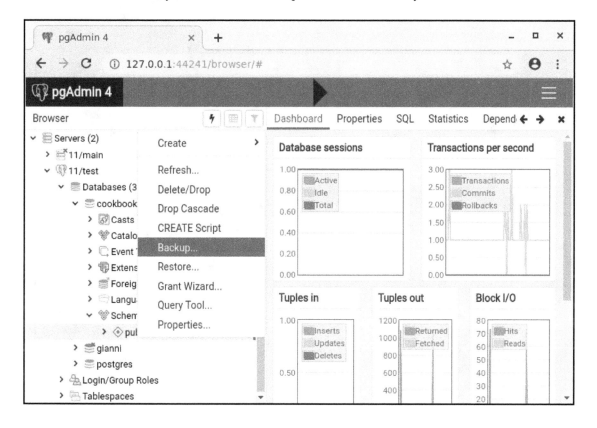

3. Clicking the left button on the mouse will drill down inside the schema and show you a number of object types. You will probably want to start from **Tables**:

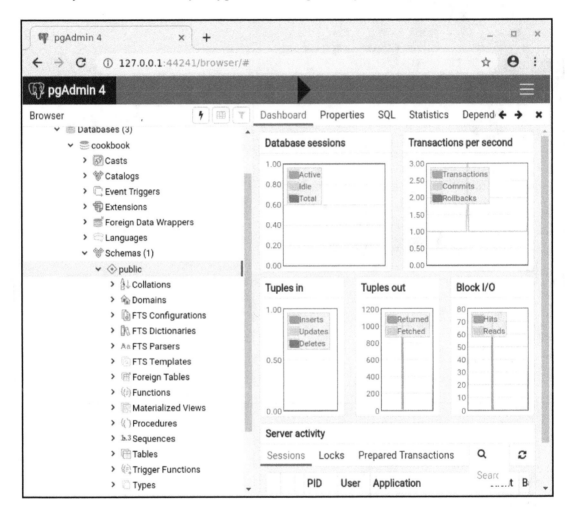

4. A PostgreSQL table supports a wide range of operations. For instance, you can count the number of rows:

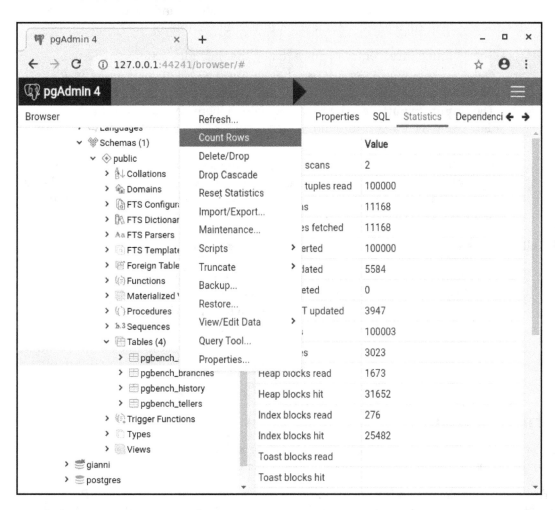

Note that this is just an example of a pgAdmin feature, and we are not suggesting that counting table rows is the best way to gather information on your database; see the *How many rows are there in a table?* recipe in `Chapter 2`, *Exploring the Database*, for a discussion on this topic.

How it works...

PostgreSQL is a complex database system, with many features and even more actions, so we can't discuss them all; we will just mention three table actions of interest:

- The **Maintenance...** entry opens a dialog that includes actions such as VACUUM and ANALYZE, which are discussed in various recipes in Chapter 9, *Regular Maintenance.*
- The **Import/Export...** entry leads to a dialog where you can export and import data using the COPY command, which includes CSV format, as demonstrated in Chapter 5, *Tables and Data.*
- With **View/Edit Data,** you can edit the contents of the table as you would do in a spreadsheet. This is slightly different than the CSV import/export feature because you edit the data directly inside the database without having to export it to another tool.

Finally, we would also like to mention these other three options as well:

- Each server (for example, connection) offers the option to **Backup Globals**, meaning roles (users/groups) and tablespaces
- The **Maintenance...** entry inside **Indexes**, which itself is a sub-entry of **Tables**, allows you to REINDEX or CLUSTER a given index
- You can create SQL scripts to perform some of the specific actions, for example, if you want to execute a procedure, or write an INSERT query on a given table

There's more

As you can see, the general idea of pgAdmin is that a right-click on an object, or on a group of objects, opens a menu presenting a number of actions for that particular object or group.

Browsing available actions is a very good way to get more familiar with what PostgreSQL can do, although not all the actions that are available in PostgreSQL will be reachable through pgAdmin's interface.

Using OmniDB for DBA tasks

Like pgAdmin, OmniDB was introduced first in Chapter 1, *First Steps*, as part of the *Using graphical administration tools* recipe. This recipe shows how it can be used to carry out some database administration tasks.

Getting ready

You should read the recipe we mentioned previously, if you haven't done so already, to get started with OmniDB.

How to do it...

Let's begin by opening the database and looking inside it:

1. You will already have a connection to your local database; if you haven't, you can create one by selecting **New Connection** in the **Connections** tab. This adds a new row with mostly empty fields, which you can fill before selecting **Save Data**:

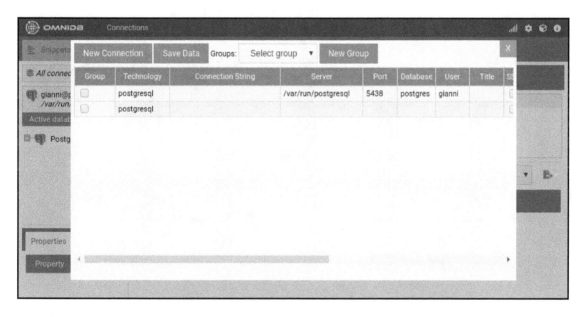

If you open one of your connections, you can access the corresponding database server through the familiar tree view, with a right-click interface that, like pgAdmin, opens a set of available actions on that particular object.

2. Here is an example where we operate on a column of a table:

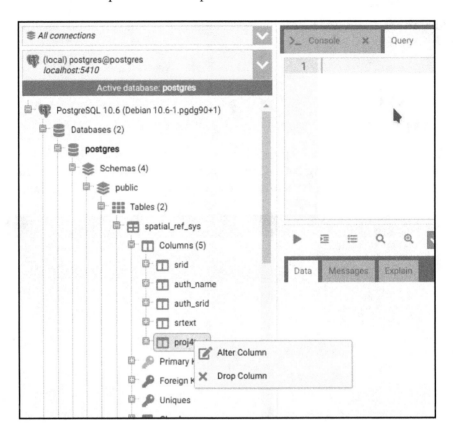

3. More generally, OmniDB offers graphical interfaces for inspecting and managing the various kinds of database objects; we cannot possibly provide a comprehensive list here, and this is probably a good thing because we like to encourage you to test it yourself. Let's provide just one example; here, we are managing the structure of a given table:

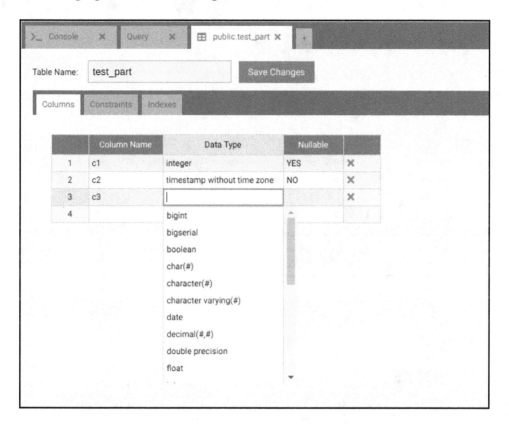

4. Going beyond database object administration, an interesting feature is the ability to remember some metadata about all the queries that you ran through OmniDB, from the **Query History** tab:

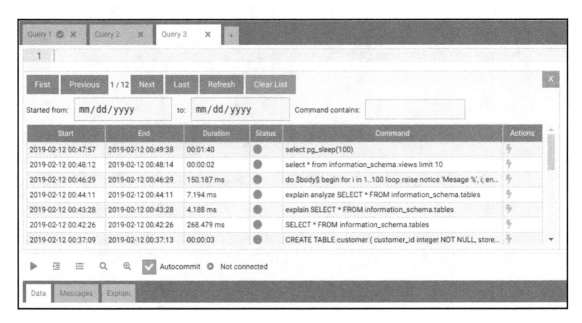

In particular, you don't need to remember the queries that you ran because OmniDB does it for you.

How it works

We close this section by noting that OmniDB has dedicated support for a number of replication solutions related to PostgreSQL, such as the following:

- Native PostgreSQL Logical Replication
- BDR
- pglogical
- Postgres-XL

There's more...

When we mentioned OmniDB's monitoring dashboard, earlier in `Chapter 1`, *First Steps*, we discussed that OmniDB has a plugin API that allows users to expand its capabilities.

This is a general design principle of OmniDB that can also be seen in the feature that allows for the customization of the monitoring dashboard, including adding custom metrics:

Performing actions on many tables

As a database administrator, you will often need to apply multiple commands as part of the same overall task. That task could be one of the following:

- Many different actions on multiple tables
- The same action on multiple tables
- The same action on multiple tables in parallel
- Different actions, one on each table, in parallel

The first is a general case where you need to make a set of coordinated changes. The solution is to *write a script*, as we've already discussed. We can also call this **static scripting** because you write the script manually and then execute it.

The second type of task can be achieved very simply with dynamic scripts, where we write a script that writes another script. This technique is the main topic of this recipe.

Performing actions in parallel sounds really cool, and it would be useful if it were easy. In some ways it is, but trying to run multiple tasks concurrently and trap and understand all the errors is much harder. And if you're thinking it won't matter if you don't check for errors, think again. If you run tasks in parallel, then you cannot run them inside the same transaction, so you definitely need error-checking.

Don't worry! Running in parallel is usually not as bad as it may seem after reading the previous paragraph, and we'll explain it after a few basic examples.

Getting ready

Let's just create a basic schema to run some examples:

```
postgres=# create schema test;
CREATE SCHEMA
postgres=# create table test.a (col1 INTEGER);
CREATE TABLE
postgres=# create table test.b (col1 INTEGER);
CREATE TABLE
postgres=# create table test.c (col1 INTEGER);
CREATE TABLE
```

How to do it...

Our task is to run a SQL statement using this form, with X as the table name, against each of our three test tables:

```
ALTER TABLE X
ADD COLUMN last_update_timestamp TIMESTAMP WITH TIME ZONE;
```

The steps are as follows:

1. Our starting point is a script that lists the tables that we want to perform tasks against—something like the following:

    ```
    postgres=# SELECT relname
            FROM pg_class c
            JOIN pg_namespace n
              ON c.relnamespace = n.oid
            WHERE n.nspname = 'test'
              AND c.relkind = 'r';
    ```

2. This displays the list of tables that we will act upon (so that you can check it):

    ```
    relname
    ---------
      a
      b
      c
    (3 rows)
    ```

3. We then use the preceding SQL to generate the text for a SQL script, substituting the schema name and table name in the SQL text. We then output to a script file named `multi.sql`, as follows:

    ```
    postgres=# \pset format unaligned
    postgres=# \t on
    postgres=# \o multi.sql
    postgres=# SELECT format('ALTER TABLE %I.%I ADD COLUMN
    last_update_timestamp TIMESTAMP WITH TIME ZONE;'
    , n.nspname, c.relname )
    FROM pg_class c
    JOIN pg_namespace n
        ON c.relnamespace = n.oid
    WHERE n.nspname = 'test'
        AND c.relkind = 'r';
    \o
    ```

4. Once we've generated the script, we can check whether all of it looks correct:

    ```
    postgres=# \! cat multi.sql
     ALTER TABLE test.a ADD COLUMN
     last_update_timestamp TIMESTAMP WITH TIME ZONE;
     ALTER TABLE test.b ADD COLUMN
     last_update_timestamp TIMESTAMP WITH TIME ZONE;
     ALTER TABLE test.c ADD COLUMN
     last_update_timestamp TIMESTAMP WITH TIME ZONE;
    ```

5. Finally, we run the script and watch the results (success!):

```
postgres=# \i multi.sql
ALTER TABLE
ALTER TABLE
ALTER TABLE
```

How it works...

Overall, this is just an example of dynamic scripting, and it has been used by DBAs for many decades, even before PostgreSQL was born.

This method can go wrong in various ways, especially if you generate SQL text with syntax errors. Just fix that and carry on.

The `\t` command means *tuples only*, so keeping `\t` to `on` will ensure that there are no headers, command tags, or row counts following the results.

Similarly, we set the output format to unaligned, meaning that psql will not add extra

spaces to make all values the same width.

The `\o` `FILENAME` command redirects the output to a file until the subsequent `\o` command reverts to no redirection.

We use the format function, which takes a template string as its first argument and replaces all occurrences of `%I`, `%L`, and `%s` with the values supplied as additional arguments (in our case, the values of `n.nspname` and `r.relname`). The differences between these three forms is in how the replacement values are quoted:

- `%I` treats the value as an SQL Identifier, adding double quotes as appropriate
- `%L` treats the value as an SQL Literal, adding single quotes as appropriate
- `%s` treats the value as a simple string

Also, note that `%%` is replaced by a single `%` character.

The \! command runs operating system commands, so \! cat will show the file contents on *nix systems.

The \i command redirects the input from a file, or in simpler terms, executes the named file. Running the script in this way may ignore earlier recipes, so I still recommend following those earlier guidelines.

The \ir command does the same as \i; the difference is that \ir is relative to the directory where the current script is, while \i is relative to the *current* directory. This directory is the one where the psql command line was started, and is changed by the \cd command.

Dynamic scripting can also be called a **quick and dirty** approach. The previous scripts didn't filter out views and other objects in the test schema, so you'll need to add that yourself, or not, as required.

There is another way of doing this as well:

```
DO $$
DECLARE t record;
    FOR t IN SELECT c.*, n.nspname
        FROM pg_class c JOIN pg_namespace n
        ON c.relnamespace = n.oid
        WHERE n.nspname = 'test'
        AND c.relkind = 'r'  /* ; not needed */
    LOOP
        EXECUTE format('
        ALTER TABLE %I.%I
        ADD COLUMN last_update_timestamp
        TIMESTAMP WITH TIME ZONE;
        ' , t.nspname, t.relname);
    END LOOP;
END $$;
```

I don't prefer using this method because it executes the SQL directly and doesn't allow you to review it before, or keep the script afterwards.

The preceding syntax with DO is called an **anonymous code block** because it's like a function without a name.

There's more...

Earlier, I said I'd explain how to run multiple tasks in parallel. Some practical approaches to this are possible, with a bit of discussion.

Making tasks run in parallel can be thought of as subdividing the main task so that we run x2, x4, x8, and other subscripts, rather than one large script.

First, you should note that error-checking gets worse when you spawn more parallel tasks, whereas performance improves the most for the first few subdivisions. Also, we're often constrained by CPU, RAM, or I/O resources for intensive tasks. This means that splitting a main task into two to four parallel subtasks isn't practical without some kind of tool to help us manage them.

There are two approaches here, depending on the two types of tasks:

- A task consists of many smaller tasks, all roughly of the same size
- A task consists of many smaller tasks, and the execution times vary according to the size and complexity of the database object

If we have lots of smaller tasks, then we can simply run our scripts multiple times using a simple round-robin split of tasks so that each subscript runs a part of all subtasks. Here is how to do it: each row in pg_class has a hidden column called oid, whose value is a 32-bit number allocated from an internal counter on table creation. Therefore, about half of the tables will have even values of oid, and we can achieve an even split by adding the following clauses:

- **Script 1**: Add WHERE c.oid % 2 = 0.
- **Script 2**: Add WHERE c.oid % 2 = 1.

The task we were performing as an example was to add a column to many tables. In the previous example, we were adding the column with no specified default; so, the new column will have a NULL value, and as a result, it will run very quickly with ALTER TABLE, even on large tables. If we change the ALTER TABLE statement so as to specify a default, then we should choose a non-volatile expression for the default value; otherwise, PostgreSQL will need to rewrite the entire table. So, the runtime will vary according to the table size (approximately, and also according to the number and type of indexes).

Now that our subtasks vary in runtime according to size, we need to be more careful when splitting the subtasks so that we can end up with multiple scripts that will run for about the same time.

If we already know that we have just a few big tables, it's easy to split those manually into their own scripts.

If the database has many large tables, then we can sort SQL statements by table size and then distribute them using round-robin distribution into multiple subscripts that will have approximately the same runtime. The following SQL script, which should be saved in a `make-script.sql` file, is an example of this technique:

```
\t on
\o script-:i.sql
SELECT sql FROM (
SELECT format('ALTER TABLE %I.%I ADD COLUMN
last_update_timestamp TIMESTAMP WITH TIME ZONE
DEFAULT now();' , n.nspname, c.relname) as sql,
row_number() OVER (ORDER BY pg_relation_size(c.oid))
FROM pg_class c
 JOIN pg_namespace n
   ON c.relnamespace = n.oid
WHERE n.nspname = 'test'
  AND c.relkind = 'r'
ORDER BY 2 DESC) as s
WHERE row_number % 2 = :i;
\o
```

Then, we generate the two scripts, as follows:

```
$ psql -v i=0 -f make-script.sql
$ psql -v i=1 -f make-script.sql
```

Finally, we execute the two jobs in parallel, like this:

```
$ psql -f script-0.sql &
$ psql -f script-1.sql &
```

Note how we used `psql` parameters—via the `-v` command-line option—to select different rows using the same script.

Also, note how we used the `row_number()` window function to sort the data by size. Then, we split the data into pieces using the following line:

```
WHERE row_number % N = i;
```

Here, N is the total number of scripts we're producing, and i ranges between 0 and N minus 1 (we are using modular arithmetic to distribute the subtasks).

Adding/removing columns on a table

As designs change, we may want to add or remove columns from our data tables. These are common operations in development, though they need more careful planning on a running production database server, as they take full locks and may run for long periods.

How to do it...

You can add a new column to a table using this command:

```
ALTER TABLE mytable
ADD COLUMN last_update_timestamp TIMESTAMP WITHOUT TIME ZONE;
```

You can drop the same column using the following command:

```
ALTER TABLE mytable
DROP COLUMN last_update_timestamp;
```

You can combine multiple operations when using ALTER TABLE, which then applies the changes in a sequence. This allows you to do a useful trick, which is to add a column unconditionally using IF EXISTS, as follows:

```
ALTER TABLE mytable
DROP COLUMN IF EXISTS last_update_timestamp,ADD COLUMN
last_update_timestamp TIMESTAMP WITHOUT TIME ZONE;
```

Note that this will have almost the same effect as the following command:

```
UPDATE mytable SET last_update_timestamp = NULL;
```

However, ALTER TABLE runs much faster. That's very cool if you want to perform an update, but not much fun if you want to keep the data in the existing column.

How it works...

The ALTER TABLE statement, which is used to add or drop a column, takes a full table lock (at the AccessExclusiveLock lock level) so that it can prevent all other actions on the table. So, we want it to be as fast as possible.

The DROP COLUMN command doesn't actually remove the column from each row of the table; it just marks the column as dropped. This makes DROP COLUMN a very fast operation.

The ADD COLUMN command is also very fast if we are adding a nullable column with a non-volatile default value, for example, a NULL value or a constant. A non-volatile expression always returns the same value, when computed multiple times within the same SQL statement; this means that PostgreSQL can compute the default value once and write it into the table metadata. Conversely, if the default is a volatile expression, then it is not guaranteed to evaluate to the same result for each of the existing rows; therefore, PostgreSQL needs to rewrite every row of the table, which can be quite slow.

The ALTER TABLE command allows us to execute many column operations at once, as shown in the main recipe. The ALTER TABLE command is optimized so that we are able to include all column operations in a single pass of the table, greatly improving the speed for complex sets of changes:

```
ALTER TABLE mytable
ADD COLUMN last_update_userid INTEGER DEFAULT 0,ADD COLUMN
last_update_comment TEXT;
```

If we rewrite the table, then the dropped columns are removed. If not, they may stay there for some time. Subsequent INSERT and UPDATE operations will insert a null value for the dropped column(s). Updates will reduce the size of the stored rows if they were not null already. So, in theory, you just have to wait, and the database will eventually reclaim the space. In practice, this works only if all the rows in the table are updated within a given period of time. Many tables contain historical data, so space may not be reclaimed at all without additional actions.

The PostgreSQL manual recommends changing the data type of a column to the same, which forces the rewriting of every row as a technique to reclaim the space taken by the dropped columns. I don't recommend this because it will completely lock the table for a long period, at least on larger databases. My recommendation is not to drop the column at all, if you can avoid it, when you're in production. Just keep track of the changes you would make if you get time, if ever. If you're looking at alternatives, then VACUUM will not rewrite the table, though a VACUUM FULL or a CLUSTER statement will. Be careful in those cases as well, because they also hold a full table lock.

There's more...

Indexes that depend on a dropped column are automatically dropped as well. All other objects that depend on the column(s), such as foreign keys from other tables, will cause the ALTER TABLE statement to be rejected. You can override this and drop everything in sight using the CASCADE option, as follows:

```
ALTER TABLE x
DROP COLUMN  last_update_timestamp
CASCADE;
```

Adding a column with a non-null default value can be done with ALTER TABLE ... ADD COLUMN ... DEFAULT ..., as we have just shown, but this holds an AccessExclusive lock for the whole duration of the command, which can take a long time if the DEFAULT is a volatile expression, as 100% of the rows must be rewritten.

The script which introduced in the *Using psql variables* recipe in this chapter is an example of how to do the same without holding an AccessExclusive lock for a long time. This lighter solution has only one other tiny difference: it doesn't use a single transaction, which would be pointless, since it would hold the lock until the end.

If any row is inserted by another session between ALTER TABLE and UPDATE and that row has a NULL value for the new column, then that value will be updated together with all the rows that existed before the ALTER TABLE, which is OK in most cases, but not in all, depending on the data model of the application.

A proper solution would involve using two sessions to ensure that no such writes can happen in-between, with a procedure that can be sketched as follows:

1. Open two sessions, and note their PIDs.
2. In session 1, BEGIN a transaction, and then take an ACCESS EXCLUSIVE lock on the table, which will be granted.

3. Immediately after, but in session 2, BEGIN a transaction, then take a SHARE lock on the table, which will hang waiting for session 1.

4. In a third session, display the ordered wait queue for locks on session 1, as follows:

```
SELECT *
FROM pg_stat_activity
WHERE pg_blocking_pids(pid) @> array[pid1]
ORDER BY state_change;
```

Here, pid1 is the PID of session 1. Check that PID2 is the second one in the list; if not, it means that *step 3* was not fast enough, so ROLLBACK both sessions and repeat from *step 1*.

5. In session 1, perform ALTER TABLE and then COMMIT.

6. In session 2 (which will be unblocked by the previous step, and will therefore acquire the SHARE lock straight away), perform the UPDATE and then the COMMIT.

Changing the data type of a column

Thankfully, changing column data types is not an everyday task, but when we need to do it, we must know all the details so that we can perform the conversion on a production system without any errors.

Getting ready

Let's start with a simple example of a table, as follows:

```
postgres=# select * from birthday;
```

This gives the following output:

```
 name  |   dob
-------+---------
 simon | 690926
(1 row)
```

The preceding table was created using this command:

```
CREATE TABLE birthday
( name          TEXT, dob          INTEGER);
```

How to do it...

Let's say we want to change the dob column to another data type. Let's try with a simple example first, as follows:

```
postgres=# ALTER TABLE birthday
postgres-# ALTER COLUMN dob SET DATA TYPE text;
ALTER TABLE
```

This works fine. Let's just change that back to the integer type so that we can try something more complex, such as a date data type:

```
postgres=# ALTER TABLE birthday
postgres-# ALTER COLUMN dob SET DATA TYPE integer;
ERROR:  column "dob" cannot be cast to type integer
```

Oh! What went wrong? Let's try using an explicit conversion with the USING clause, as follows:

```
postgres=# ALTER TABLE birthday
               ALTER COLUMN dob SET DATA TYPE integer
               USING dob::integer;
ALTER TABLE
```

This works as expected. Now, let's try moving to a date type:

```
postgres=# ALTER TABLE birthday
ALTER COLUMN dob SET DATA TYPE date
USING date(to_date(dob::text, 'YYMMDD') -
       (CASE WHEN dob/10000 BETWEEN 16 AND 69 THEN interval '100
         years'
       ELSE interval '0' END));
```

Now, it gives us what we were hoping to see:

```
postgres=# select * from birthday;
 name  |    dob
-------+------------
 simon | 26/09/1969
(1 row)
```

With PostgreSQL, you can also set or drop default expressions, irrespective of whether the NOT NULL constraints are applied:

```
ALTER TABLE foo
ALTER COLUMN col DROP DEFAULT;
ALTER TABLE foo
ALTER COLUMN col SET DEFAULT 'expression';
ALTER TABLE foo
ALTER COLUMN col SET NOT NULL;
ALTER TABLE foo
ALTER COLUMN col DROP NOT NULL;
```

How it works...

Moving from the integer to the date type uses a complex USING expression. Let's break that down step by step so that we can see why, as follows:

```
postgres=# ALTER TABLE birthday
ALTER COLUMN dob SET DATA TYPE date
USING date(to_date(dob::text, 'YYMMDD') -
      (CASE WHEN dob/10000 BETWEEN 16 AND 69
      THEN interval '100 years'
      ELSE interval '0' END));
```

First, we can't move directly from integer to date. We need to convert it into text and then to date. The dob::text statement means *cast to text*.

Once we have text, we use the to_date() function to move to a date type.

This is not enough; our starting data was 690926, which we presume is a date in the YYMMDD format. When PostgreSQL converts this data into a date, it assumes that the two-digit year, 69, is in the current century because it chooses the year nearest to 2020. So, it outputs 2069 rather than 1969. This is why a case statement is added to reduce any year between 16 and 69 to be a date in the previous century by explicitly subtracting an interval of 100 years. We do not need to take away one century for years after 69 because they are already placed in the 20th century.

It is very strongly recommended that you test this conversion by performing a SELECT first. Converting data types, especially to/from dates, always causes some problems, so don't try to do this quickly. Always take a backup of the data first.

There's more...

The USING clause can also be used to handle complex expressions involving other columns. This could be used for data transformations, which might be useful for DBAs in some circumstances, such as migrating to a new database design on a production database server. Let's put everything together in a full, working example. We will start with this table that has to be transformed:

```
postgres=# select * from cust;
 customerid | firstname | lastname | age
------------+-----------+----------+-----
          1 | Philip    | Marlowe  |  38
          2 | Richard   | Hannay   |  42
          3 | Holly     | Martins  |  25
          4 | Harry     | Palmer   |  36
(4 rows)
```

We want to transform it into a table design like the following:

```
postgres=# select * from cust;
 customerid |    custname     | age
------------+-----------------+-----
          1 | Philip Marlowe  |  38
          2 | Richard Hannay  |  42
          3 | Holly Martins   |  25
          4 | Harry Palmer    |  36
(4 rows)
```

We can decide to do it using these simple steps:

```
ALTER TABLE cust ADD COLUMN custname text NOT NULL DEFAULT '';
UPDATE cust SET custname = firstname || ' ' || lastname;
ALTER TABLE cust DROP COLUMN firstname;
ALTER TABLE cust DROP COLUMN lastname;
```

We can also use the SQL commands directly or make them use a tool such as **OmniDB**. Following those steps may cause problems, as the changes aren't within a transaction, meaning that other users can see the changes when they are only half finished. Hence, it would be better to do this in a single transaction using BEGIN and COMMIT. Also, those four changes require us to make two passes over the table.

However, we can perform the entire transformation in one pass using multiple clauses on the ALTER TABLE command. So, instead, we do the following:

```
BEGIN;
ALTER TABLE cust
   ALTER COLUMN firstname SET DATA TYPE text
         USING firstname || ' ' || lastname,
   ALTER COLUMN firstname SET NOT NULL,
   ALTER COLUMN firstname SET DEFAULT '',
   DROP COLUMN lastname;
ALTER TABLE cust RENAME firstname TO custname;
COMMIT;
```

This is a great example of why I personally prefer using scripts to make such changes to large production databases rather than directly making the changes using a GUI.

Some type changes can be performed without actually rewriting rows—for example, if you are casting data from varchar to text, or from NUMERIC(10,2) to NUMERIC(18,2), or simply to NUMERIC. Moreover, foreign key constraints will recognize type changes of this kind on the source table, and will therefore skip the constraint check whenever it is safe.

Changing the definition of a data type

PostgreSQL comes with several data types, but users can create custom types to faithfully represent any value. Data type management is mostly, but not exclusively, a developer's job, and data type design goes beyond the scope of this book. This is a quick recipe that covers only the simpler problem of the need to apply a specific change to an existing data type.

Getting ready

Enumerative data types are defined like this:

```
CREATE TYPE satellites_urani AS ENUM ('titania','oberon');
```

The other popular case is composite data types, which are created as follows:

```
CREATE TYPE node AS
( node_name text,
  connstr text,
  standbys text[]);
```

How to do it...

If you made a mistake in the spelling of some enumerative values, and you realize it too late, you can fix it like so:

```
ALTER TYPE satellites_urani RENAME VALUE 'titania' TO 'Titania';
ALTER TYPE satellites_urani RENAME VALUE 'oberon' TO 'Oberon';
```

This is very useful if the application expects—and uses—the right names.

A more complicated case is when you are upgrading your database to a new version, say because you want to consider some facts that were not available during the initial design, and you need extra values for the enumerative type that we defined in the preceding code. You want to put the new values in a certain position to preserve the correct ordering. For that, you can use an ALTER TYPE syntax, as follows:

```
ALTER TYPE satellites_urani ADD VALUE 'Ariel' BEFORE 'Titania';
ALTER TYPE satellites_urani ADD VALUE 'Umbriel' AFTER 'Ariel';
```

Composite data types can be changed with similar commands. Attributes can be renamed, as in this example:

```
ALTER TYPE node
RENAME ATTRIBUTE slaves TO standbys;
```

And new attributes can be added as follows:

```
ALTER TYPE node
DROP ATTRIBUTE standbys,
ADD ATTRIBUTE async_standbys text[],
ADD ATTRIBUTE sync_standbys text[];
```

This form supports a list of changes, perhaps because composite types are more complex than a list of enumerative values, and can therefore require complicated modifications.

How it works...

Each time you create a table, a composite type is automatically created with the same attribute names, types, and positions. Each ALTER TABLE command that changes table column definitions will silently issue a corresponding ALTER TYPE statement to keep the type in agreement with *its* table definition.

Enumerative values in PostgreSQL are stored in tables as numbers, which are transparently mapped to strings via the `pg_enum` catalog table. In order to allow inserting a new value between two existing ones, enumerative values are indexed by real numbers, which allow decimal points and have the same size in bytes as integer numbers. The motive is to use the numeric ordering to encode the order of values that was specified by the user.

In the `satellites_urani` example, the first two values were `Titania` and `Oberon`, which initially got indexed by the real numbers 1 and 2:

```
postgres=# select * from pg_enum where enumtypid = regtype
'satellites_urani';

 enumtypid | enumsortorder | enumlabel
-----------+---------------+-----------
     38112 |             1 | Titania
     38112 |             2 | Oberon
(2 rows)
```

When we add a third value before `Titania` (that is, 1), the number 0 is taken, as you would probably expect:

```
postgres=# ALTER TYPE satellites_urani ADD VALUE 'Ariel' BEFORE 'Titania';
ALTER TYPE
postgres=# select * from pg_enum where enumtypid = regtype
'satellites_urani';
 enumtypid | enumsortorder | enumlabel
-----------+---------------+-----------
     38112 |             1 | Titania
     38112 |             2 | Oberon
     38112 |             0 | Ariel
(3 rows)
```

And, finally, when adding a fourth value between `Ariel` (0) and `Titania` (1), PostgreSQL can pick the real value, 0.5:

```
postgres=# ALTER TYPE satellites_urani ADD VALUE 'Umbriel' AFTER 'Ariel';

ALTER TYPE

postgres=# select * from pg_enum where enumtypid = regtype
'satellites_urani';
 enumtypid | enumsortorder | enumlabel
-----------+---------------+-----------
     38112 |             1 | Titania
     38112 |             2 | Oberon
     38112 |             0 | Ariel
```

```
     38112 |              0.5 | Umbriel
(4 rows)
```

In order to test the resulting order, we can build a test table with all the possible values, and then sort it:

```
postgres=# CREATE TABLE test(x satellites_urani);
CREATE TABLE

postgres=# INSERT INTO test VALUES ('Ariel'), ('Oberon'), ('Titania'),
('Umbriel');
INSERT 0 4

postgres=# SELECT * FROM test ORDER BY x;
    x
----------
 Ariel
 Umbriel
 Titania
 Oberon
(4 rows)
```

There's more...

When an attribute is removed from a composite data type, the corresponding values will instantly disappear from all the values of that same type stored in any database table. What actually happens is that these values are still inside the tables, but they have become invisible because their attribute is now marked as deleted, and the space they occupy will be reclaimed only when the contents of the composite type are parsed again. This can be forced with a query such as the following:

```
UPDATE mytable SET mynode = mynode :: text :: node;
```

Here, mytable is a table that has a mynode column of the node type. This query converts the values into the text type, displaying only current attribute values, and then back to node. You may have noticed that this behavior is very similar to the example of the dropped column in the previous recipe.

Adding/removing schemas

Separating groups of objects is a good way of improving administration efficiency. You need to know how to create new schemas and remove schemas that are no longer required.

How to do it...

To add a new schema, issue this command:

```
CREATE SCHEMA sharedschema;
```

If you want that schema to be owned by a particular user, then you can add the following option:

```
CREATE SCHEMA sharedschema AUTHORIZATION scarlett;
```

If you want to create a new schema that has the same name as an existing user so that the user becomes the owner, then try this:

```
CREATE SCHEMA AUTHORIZATION scarlett;
```

In many database systems, the schema name is the same as that of the owning user. PostgreSQL allows schemas owned by one user to have objects owned by another user within them. This can be especially confusing when you have a schema that has the same name as the owning user. To avoid this, you should have two types of schema: schemas that are named the same as the owning user should be limited to only objects owned by that user. Other general schemas can have shared ownership.

To remove a schema named `str`, we can issue the following command:

```
DROP SCHEMA str;
```

If you want to ensure that the schema exists in all cases, you can issue the following command:

```
CREATE SCHEMA IF NOT EXISTS str;
```

Clearly, you need to be careful because the outcome of the command depends on the previous state of the database. As an example, try issuing the following:

```
CREATE TABLE str.tb (x int);
```

This can generate an error if the `str` schema contained that table before CREATE SCHEMA IF NOT EXISTS was run. Otherwise, there's no namespace error.

Irrespective of your PostgreSQL version, there isn't a CREATE OR REPLACE SCHEMA command, so when you want to create a schema, regardless of whether it already exists, you can do the following:

```
DROP SCHEMA IF EXISTS newschema;
CREATE SCHEMA newschema;
```

The DROP SCHEMA command won't work unless the schema is empty or unless you use the **Nuclear** option:

```
DROP SCHEMA IF EXISTS newschema CASCADE;
```

The **Nuclear** option kills all known germs and all your database objects (*even the good objects*).

There's more...

In the SQL standard, you can also create a schema and the objects it contains in one SQL statement. PostgreSQL accepts this syntax if you need it:

```
CREATE SCHEMA foo
      CREATE TABLE account
      (id           INTEGER NOT NULL PRIMARY KEY
      ,balance      NUMERIC(50,2))
      CREATE VIEW accountsample AS
      SELECT *
      FROM account
      WHERE random() < 0.1;
```

Mostly, I find this limiting. This syntax exists to allow us to create two or more objects at the same time. This can be achieved more easily using PostgreSQL's ability to allow transactional DDL, which was discussed in the *Writing a script that either succeeds entirely or fails entirely* recipe.

Using schema-level privileges

Privileges can be granted for objects in a schema using the GRANT command, as follows:

```
GRANT SELECT ON ALL TABLES IN SCHEMA sharedschema TO PUBLIC;
```

However, this will only affect tables that already exist. Tables that are created in the future will inherit privileges defined by the ALTER DEFAULT PRIVILEGES command, as follows:

```
ALTER DEFAULT PRIVILEGES IN SCHEMA sharedschema
GRANT SELECT ON TABLES TO PUBLIC;
```

Moving objects between schemas

Once you've created schemas for administration purposes, you'll want to move existing objects to keep things tidy.

How to do it...

To move one table from its current schema to a new schema, use the following:

```
ALTER TABLE cust
SET SCHEMA anotherschema;
```

If you want to move all objects, you can consider renaming the schema itself by using the following query:

```
ALTER SCHEMA existingschema RENAME TO anotherschema;
```

This only works if another schema with that name does not exist. Otherwise, you'll need to run ALTER TABLE for each table you want to move. You can use the earlier recipe in this chapter *Performing actions on many tables,* to achieve that.

Views, sequences, functions, aggregates, and domains can also be moved by ALTER commands with SET SCHEMA options.

How it works...

When you move tables to a new schema, all the indexes, triggers, and rules defined on those tables will also be moved to the new schema. If you've used a SERIAL data type and an implicit sequence has been created, then that also moves to the new schema. Schemas are purely an administrative concept and they do not affect the location of the table's data files. Tablespaces don't work this way, as we will see in later recipes.

Databases, users/roles, languages, and conversions don't exist in a schema. Schemas exist in a particular database. Schemas don't exist within schemas; they are not arranged in a tree or hierarchy. More details can be found in the *Using multiple schemas* recipe in Chapter 4, *Server Control.*

There's more...

Casts don't exist in a schema, though the data types and functions they reference do exist. These things are not typically something we want to move around, anyway. This is just a note if you're wondering how things work.

Adding/removing tablespaces

Tablespaces allow us to store PostgreSQL data across different devices. We might want to do that for performance or administrative ease, or our database might just have run out of disk space.

Getting ready

Before we can create a useful tablespace, we need the underlying devices in a production-ready form.

Think carefully about the speed, volume, and robustness of the disks you are about to use. Make sure that they are configured correctly. Those decisions will affect your life for the next few months and years!

Disk performance is a subtle issue that most people think can be decided in a few seconds. We recommend reading Chapter 10, *Performance and Concurrency*, from this book, as well as additional books on the same topic.

Once you've done all of that, then you can create a directory for your tablespace. The directory must be as follows:

- Empty
- Owned by the PostgreSQL-owning user ID
- Specified with an absolute pathname

On Linux and Unix systems, you shouldn't use a mount point directly. Create a subdirectory and use that instead. That simplifies ownership and avoids some filesystem-specific issues, such as getting lost+found directories.

The directory also needs to follow sensible naming conventions so that we can clearly identify which tablespace goes with which server. Do not be tempted to use something simple, such as data, because it will make later administration more difficult. Be especially careful that test or development servers do not and cannot get confused with production systems.

How to do it...

Once you've created your directory, adding the tablespace is simple:

```
CREATE TABLESPACE new_tablespace
LOCATION '/usr/local/pgsql/new_tablespace';
```

The command to remove the tablespace is also simple and is as follows:

```
DROP TABLESPACE new_tablespace;
```

Every tablespace has a location assigned to it, with the exception of the pg_global and pg_default default tablespaces, for shared system catalogs and all other objects, respectively. They don't have a location because they live in a subdirectory of the data directory.

A tablespace can be dropped only when it is empty, so how do you know when a tablespace is empty?

Tablespaces can contain both permanent and temporary objects. Permanent data objects are tables, indexes, and TOAST objects. We don't need to worry too much about TOAST objects because they are created and always live in the same tablespace as their main table, and you cannot manipulate their privileges or ownership.

Indexes can exist in separate tablespaces as a performance option, though that requires explicit specification in the CREATE INDEX statement. The default is to create indexes in the same tablespace as the table to which they belong.

Temporary objects may also exist in a tablespace. These exist when users have explicitly created temporary tables or there may be implicitly created data files when large queries overflow their work_mem settings. These files are created according to the setting of the temp_tablespaces parameter. This might cause an issue because you can't tell for certain what the setting of temp_tablespaces is for each user. Users can change their setting of temp_tablespaces from the default value specified in the postgresql.conf file to something else.

We can identify the tablespace of each user object using the following query:

```
SELECT spcname
     ,relname
     ,CASE WHEN relpersistence = 't' THEN 'temp '
           WHEN relpersistence = 'u' THEN 'unlogged '
      ELSE '' END ||
      CASE
      WHEN relkind = 'r' THEN 'table'
      WHEN relkind = 'p' THEN 'partitioned table'
      WHEN relkind = 'f' THEN 'foreign table'
      WHEN relkind = 't' THEN 'TOAST table'
      WHEN relkind = 'v' THEN 'view'
      WHEN relkind = 'm' THEN 'materialized view'
      WHEN relkind = 'S' THEN 'sequence'
      WHEN relkind = 'c' THEN 'type'
      ELSE 'index' END as objtype
FROM pg_class c join pg_tablespace ts
ON (CASE WHEN c.reltablespace = 0 THEN
          (SELECT dattablespace FROM pg_database
           WHERE datname = current_database())
     ELSE c.reltablespace END) = ts.oid
WHERE relname NOT LIKE 'pg_toast%'
AND relnamespace NOT IN
     (SELECT oid FROM pg_namespace
      WHERE nspname IN ('pg_catalog', 'information_schema'))
;
```

This displays an output such as the following:

```
       spcname       |   relname   |   objtype
---------------------+-------------+-------------
 new_tablespace      | x           | table
 new_tablespace      | y           | table
 new_tablespace      | z           | temp table
 new_tablespace      | y_val_idx   | index
```

You may also want to look at the spcowner, relowner, relacl, and spcacl columns to determine who owns what and what they're allowed to do. The relacl and spcacl columns refer to the **Access Control List** (**ACL**) that details the privileges available on those objects. The spcowner and relowner columns record the owners of the tablespace and tables/indexes, respectively.

How it works...

A tablespace is just a directory where we store PostgreSQL data files. We use symbolic links from the data directory to the tablespace.

We exclude TOAST tables because they are always in the same tablespace as their parent tables, but remember that TOAST tables are always in a separate schema. You can exclude TOAST tables using the relkind column, but that would still include the indexes on the TOAST tables. TOAST tables and TOAST indexes both start with pg_toast, so we can exclude those easily from our queries.

The preceding query needs to be complex because the pg_class entry for an object will show reltablespace = 0 when an object is created in the database's default tablespace. So, if you directly join pg_class and pg_tablespace, you end up losing rows.

Note that we can see that a temporary object exists, and we can see the tablespace in which it is created, even though we cannot refer to a temporary object in another user's session.

There's more...

Some more notes on best practices follow.

A tablespace can contain objects from multiple databases, so it's possible to be in a position where there are no objects visible in the current database. The tablespace just refuses to go away, giving the following error:

```
ERROR:  tablespace "old_tablespace" is not empty
```

You are strongly advised to make a separate tablespace for each database to avoid confusion. This can be especially confusing if you have the same schema names and table names in the separate databases.

How do you avoid this? If you just created a new tablespace directory, you might want to create subdirectories within that for each database that needs space, and then change the subdirectories to tablespaces instead.

You may also wish to consider giving each tablespace a specific owner by using the following query:

```
ALTER TABLESPACE new_tablespace OWNER TO eliza;
```

This may help smooth administration.

You may also wish to set default tablespaces for a user so that tables are automatically created there by issuing the following query:

```
ALTER USER eliza SET default_tablespace = 'new_tablespace';
```

Putting pg_wal on a separate device

You may seek advice about placing the `pg_wal` directory on a separate device for performance reasons. This sounds very similar to tablespaces, though there is no explicit command to do this once you have a running database, and files in `pg_wal` are frequently written. So, you must perform the steps outlined in the following example:

1. Stop the database server:

   ```
   [postgres@myhost ~]$ pg_ctl stop
   ```

2. Move `pg_wal` to a location supported by a different disk device:

   ```
   [postgres@myhost ~]$ mv $PGDATA/pg_wal   /mnt/newdisk/
   ```

3. Create a symbolic link from the old location to the new location:

   ```
   [postgres@myhost ~]$ ln -s /mnt/newdisk/pg_wal    $PGDATA/pg_wal
   ```

4. Restart the database server:

   ```
   [postgres@myhost ~]$ pg_ctl start
   ```

5. Verify that everything is working by committing any transaction (preferably, a transaction that does not damage the existing workload):

   ```
   [postgres@myhost ~]$ psql -c 'CREATE TABLE all is ok()'
   ```

Tablespace-level tuning

Since each tablespace has different I/O characteristics, we may wish to alter the planner cost parameters for each tablespace. These can be set with the following command:

```
ALTER TABLESPACE new_tablespace SET
(seq_page_cost = 0.05, random_page_cost = 0.1);
```

In this example, settings are roughly appropriate for an SSD drive, and it assumes that the drive is 40 times faster than an HDD for random reads, and 20 times faster for sequential reads.

The values given need more discussion than we have time for here; these are only examples to demonstrate the procedure to change the settings.

Moving objects between tablespaces

Moving data between tablespaces may be required.

Getting ready

First, create your tablespaces. Once the old and new tablespaces exist, we can issue the commands to move them.

How to do it...

Tablespaces can contain both permanent and temporary objects.

Permanent data objects are tables, indexes, and TOAST objects. We don't need to worry too much about TOAST objects because they are created in and always live in the same tablespace as their main table. So, if you alter the tablespace of a table, its TOAST objects will also move:

```
ALTER TABLE mytable SET TABLESPACE new_tablespace;
```

Indexes can exist in separate tablespaces, and moving a table leaves the indexes where they are. Don't forget to run ALTER INDEX commands as well, one for each index, as follows:

```
ALTER INDEX mytable_val_idx SET TABLESPACE new_tablespace;
```

Temporary objects cannot be explicitly moved to a new tablespace, so we need to ensure they are created somewhere else in the future. To do that, you need to do the following:

1. Edit the temp_tablespaces parameter, as shown in the *Updating the parameter file* recipe in Chapter 3, *Configuration*.
2. Reload the server to allow new configuration settings to take effect.

There is no single command to do this that will work for all users.

How it works...

If you want to move a table and its indexes all in one pass, you can issue all the commands in a single transaction, as follows:

```
BEGIN;
ALTER TABLE mytable SET TABLESPACE new_tablespace;
ALTER INDEX mytable_val1_idx SET TABLESPACE new_tablespace;
ALTER INDEX mytable_val2_idx SET TABLESPACE new_tablespace;
COMMIT;
```

Moving tablespaces means the bulk copying of data. Copying happens sequentially, block by block. That works well, but there's no way to avoid the fact that the bigger the table, the longer it will take.

Performance will be optimized if archiving or streaming replication is not active, as no WAL will be written in that case.

You should be aware that the table is fully locked (the `AccessExclusiveLock` lock) while the copy is taking place, so this can cause an effective outage for your application. Be very careful!

If you want to ensure that objects are created in the right place next time you create them, then you can use this query:

```
SET default_tablespace = 'new_tablespace';
```

You can run this automatically for all users that connect to a database using the following query:

```
ALTER DATABASE mydb SET default_tablespace = 'new_tablespace';
```

Take care that you do not run the following command by mistake, however:

```
ALTER DATABASE mydb SET TABLESPACE new_tablespace;
```

This literally moves all objects that do not have an explicitly defined tablespace into `new_tablespace`. For a large database, this will take a very long time, and your database will be completely locked while it runs; not preferred, if you do it by accident!

There's more...

If you just discovered that indexes don't get moved when you move a table, then you may want to check whether any indexes are in tablespaces that are different than their parent tables. Run the following to check:

```
SELECT i.relname as index_name
     , tsi.spcname as index_tbsp
     , t.relname as table_name
     , tst.spcname as table_tbsp
  FROM ( pg_class t /* tables */
           JOIN pg_tablespace tst
             ON t.reltablespace = tst.oid
             OR ( t.reltablespace = 0
                  AND tst.spcname = 'pg_default' )
       )
  JOIN pg_index pgi
    ON pgi.indrelid = t.oid
  JOIN ( pg_class i /* indexes */
           JOIN pg_tablespace tsi
             ON i.reltablespace = tsi.oid
             OR ( i.reltablespace = 0
                  AND tsi.spcname = 'pg_default' )
       )
    ON pgi.indexrelid = i.oid
 WHERE i.relname NOT LIKE 'pg_toast%'
   AND i.reltablespace != t.reltablespace
;
```

If we have one table with an index in a separate tablespace, we might see this as a `psql` definition:

```
postgres=# \d y
      Table "public.y"
 Column | Type | Modifiers
--------+------+-----------
 val    | text |
Indexes:
    "y_val_idx" btree (val), tablespace "new_tablespace"
Tablespace: "new_tablespace2"
```

Running the previously presented query gives the following results:

```
  relname   |       spcname      | relname |     spcname
------------+--------------------+---------+----------------
 y_val_idx  | new_tablespace     | y       | new_tablespace2
(1 row)
```

Accessing objects in other PostgreSQL databases

Sometimes, you may want to access data in other PostgreSQL databases. The reasons may be as follows:

- You have more than one database server, and you need to extract data (such as reference) from one server and load it into the other.
- You want to access data that is in a different database on the same database server, which was split for administrative purposes.
- You want to perform some changes that you do not wish to rollback in the event of an error or transaction abort. These are known as **function side effects** or **autonomous transactions**.

You might also be considering this because you are exploring the scale out, sharding, or load balancing approaches. If so, read the last part of this recipe, the *See also* section, and then skip to Chapter 12, *Replication and Upgrades*.

 PostgreSQL includes two separate mechanisms for accessing external PostgreSQL databases: dblink and the PostgreSQL Foreign Data Wrapper. The latter is more efficient and implements a part of the SQL standard, but does not fully replace dblink; therefore, we provide two variants of this recipe.

Getting ready

First of all, let's make a distinction to prevent confusion:

- The **Foreign Data Wrapper** infrastructure, a mechanism to manage the definition of remote connections, servers, and users, is available in all supported PostgreSQL versions
- The **PostgreSQL Foreign Data Wrapper** is a specific contrib extension that uses the Foreign Data Wrapper infrastructure to connect to remote PostgreSQL servers

In particular, the Foreign Data Wrapper infrastructure will be used to manage definitions in both cases, that is, when using the PostgreSQL Foreign Data Wrapper and when using the dblink module.

Foreign Data Wrapper extensions for other database systems will be discussed in the next recipe, *Accessing objects in other foreign databases.*

How to do it...

We will first describe the variant that uses `dblink`:

1. First, we need to install the `dblink contrib` module. The general procedure is explained in the *Adding an external module to PostgreSQL* recipe of `Chapter 3`, *Configuration.*

2. Then, we create some access definitions. The preferred way is to use the following commands, which are SQL standard (SQL/MED):

```
postgres=# CREATE FOREIGN DATA WRAPPER postgresql
 VALIDATOR postgresql_fdw_validator;
CREATE FOREIGN DATA WRAPPER

postgres=# CREATE SERVER otherdb
 FOREIGN DATA WRAPPER postgresql
 OPTIONS (host 'foo', dbname 'otherdb', port '5432');
CREATE SERVER

postgres=# CREATE USER MAPPING FOR PUBLIC
SERVER otherdb;
CREATE USER MAPPING
```

3. You must create `FOREIGN DATA WRAPPER` only once, though you need one `SERVER` for each PostgreSQL destination database to which you may wish to connect. This is just the connection definition, not the connection itself.

4. Creating a public user mapping with no options seems strange, though it will mean that we use the `libpq` default behavior. It will also mean that we will connect the remote database using the value of `PGUSER`, or if it is not set, use the operating system user. Clearly, if we want to use different credentials, then we must specify them with suitable options, either while creating the mapping or afterwards (`ALTER USER MAPPING`).

The `VALIDATOR` clause specifies a function whose purpose is to validate the parameters. That function is a part of the Foreign Data Wrapper and should have been provided by the author, so you need to create it only if you are developing a new type of Foreign Data Wrapper yourself.

5. Now, connect using an unnamed connection, as follows:

```
SELECT dblink_connect('otherdb');
```

6. This produces the following output:

```
dblink_connect
----------------
OK
(1 row)
```

7. We limit ourselves to unnamed connections for simplicity. It is also possible to create a named connection, that is, a connection that is assigned a string so that it can be referred to directly later. This is obviously useful if we want to manage several connections, but it comes at the price of actually having to manage their life cycle (connection and disconnection).

8. Suppose you want to execute the following command:

```
postgres=#  INSERT  INTO  audit_log  VALUES  (current_user,
now());
```

9. To do so, run it on the unnamed remote connection, like this:

```
postgres=#  SELECT  dblink_exec('INSERT  INTO  audit_log  VALUES'
||
       '  (current_user,  now())',  true);
```

10. This will give the following output:

```
dblink_exec
--------------
 INSERT 0 1
(1 row)
```

11. Notice that the `remote` command returns the command tag and the number of rows that were processed as the return value of the function. The second option means *fail on error*. If you look closely, there's also a subtle error—when the `INSERT` command is executed locally, we use this server's value of `current_user`. But when we execute remotely, we use the remote server's value of `current_user`, which might differ, depending on the user mapping defined previously.

12. Similarly, suppose you want to execute the following query on the unnamed remote connection:

```
SELECT generate_series(1,3)
```

13. We start by typing this:

```
SELECT *
FROM dblink('SELECT generate_series(1,3)')
```

14. This will result in the following error:

```
ERROR:    a  column  definition  list  is  required for functions
returning
"record"
LINE  2:  FROM  dblink('SELECT  generate_series(1,3)');
              ^
```

15. This error message is telling us that we need to specify the list of output columns and output types that we expect from the dblink() function, because PostgreSQL is unable to determine them automatically at parsing time (that is, without running the query).

16. We can add the missing information by providing an alias in the FROM clause, as in the following example:

```
SELECT *
FROM dblink('SELECT generate_series(1,3)')
AS link(col1 integer);
```

17. This will succeed, and result in the following output:

```
col1
------
1
2
3
(3 rows)
```

18. To disconnect from the unnamed connection, you can issue the following:

```
SELECT dblink_disconnect();
```

19. You get the following output:

```
dblink_connect
-----------------
OK
(1 row)
```

Now, we will describe the second variant of this recipe, which uses the PostgreSQL Foreign Data Wrapper instead of `dblink`:

1. The first step is to install the `postgres_fdw contrib` module, which is as simple as this:

   ```
   postgres=# CREATE EXTENSION postgres_fdw;
   ```

2. The result is as follows:

   ```
   CREATE EXTENSION
   ```

3. This extension automatically creates the corresponding Foreign Data Wrapper, as you can check with psql's \dew meta-command:

   ```
   postgres=# \dew
                       List of foreign-data wrappers
          Name     | Owner  |       Handler        |      Validator
   ---------------+--------+----------------------+--------------------
   ----
    postgres_fdw | gianni | postgres_fdw_handler |
   postgres_fdw_validator
   (1 row)
   ```

4. We can now define a server:

   ```
   postgres=# CREATE SERVER otherdb
   FOREIGN DATA WRAPPER postgres_fdw
   OPTIONS (host 'foo', dbname 'otherdb', port '5432');
   ```

5. This produces the following output:

   ```
   CREATE SERVER
   ```

6. Then, we can define the user mapping:

   ```
   postgres=# CREATE USER MAPPING FOR PUBLIC SERVER otherdb;
   ```

7. The output is as follows:

CREATE USER MAPPING

As an example, we will access a portion of a remote table containing (integer, text) pairs:

```
postgres=# CREATE FOREIGN TABLE ft (
 num int ,
 word text )
SERVER otherdb
OPTIONS (
   schema_name 'public' , table_name 't' );
```

The result is quite laconic:

CREATE FOREIGN TABLE

This table can now be operated almost like any other table. We check whether it is empty:

```
postgres=# select * from ft;
```

This is the output:

```
num | word
-----+-------
(0 rows)
```

8. We can insert rows as follows:

```
postgres=# insert into ft(num,word) values
(1,'One'), (2,'Two'),(3,'Three');
```

9. This query produces the following output:

INSERT 0 3

10. Then, we can verify that the aforementioned rows have been inserted:

```
postgres=# select * from ft;
```

11. This is confirmed by the output:

```
num | word
-----+-------
1 | One
2 | Two
3 | Three
(3 rows)
```

 Note that you don't have to manage connections or format text strings to assemble your queries. Most of the complexity is handled automatically by the Foreign Data Wrapper.

How it works...

The `dblink` module establishes a persistent connection with the other database. The `dblink` functions track the details of that connection, so you don't need to worry about doing so yourself. You should be aware that this is an external resource, and so the generic programming problem of **resource leaks** becomes possible. If you forget about your connection and forget to disconnect it, you may experience problems later. The remote connections will be terminated should your session disconnect.

Note that the remote connection persists even across transaction failures and other errors, so there is no need to reconnect.

The `postgres_fdw` extension can manage connections transparently and efficiently, so if your use case does not involve commands other than SELECT, INSERT, UPDATE, and DELETE, then you should definitely go for it.

The `dblink()` module executes the remote query and will assemble the result set in the memory before the local reply begins to be sent. This means that very large queries might fail due to lack of memory, and everybody else will notice that. This isn't a problem; `dblink` is simply not designed to handle bulk data flows. Look at the *Loading data from flat files* recipe in Chapter 5, *Tables and Data*, if that's what you want to do.

Running slightly larger queries can be achieved using cursors. They allow us to bring the answer set back in smaller chunks. Conceptually, we need to open the cursor, loop while fetching rows until we are done, and then close the cursor. An example query for that is as follows:

```
postgres=# SELECT dblink_open('example',
    'SELECT generate_series(1,3)', true);
```

```
dblink_open
--------------
 OK
(1 row)
postgres=# SELECT *
       FROM dblink_fetch('example', 10, true)
        AS link (col1 integer);
 col1
------
    1
    2
    3
(3 rows)
```

Notice that we didn't need to define the cursor when we opened it, though we do need to define the results from the cursor when we fetch from it, just as we did with a normal query. For instance, to fetch 10 rows at a time, we can do this:

```
postgres=# SELECT *
       FROM dblink_fetch('example', 10, true)
        AS link (col1 integer);
 col1
------
(0 rows)
postgres=# SELECT dblink_close('example');
 dblink_close
---------------
 OK(1 row)
```

The `dblink` module also allows you to use more than one connection. Using just one connection is generally not good for modular programming. For more complex situations, it's good practice to assume that the connection you want is not the same as the connection that another part of the program might need. The `dblink` module allows named connections, so you don't need to hope that the default connection is still the right connection. There is also a function named `dblink_get_connections()` that will allow you to see which connections you have active.

There's more...

Remote data sources look as if they can be treated as tables, and, in fact, they are represented as such by Foreign Data Wrappers. Unfortunately, in practice, this doesn't work in all the ways you might hope and expect.

However, by writing your queries and code in the standard way, you give the database usable context information about what you are trying to achieve; future PostgreSQL versions might achieve better optimization on the same SQL code. This is a general advantage over custom solutions, which are usually opaque to the server and thus cannot be optimized further.

Ideally, we would like to use foreign tables interchangeably with local tables, with minimum possible performance penalty and maintenance cost, so it is important to know what already works and what is still on the wish list.

First, here's the good news: foreign tables can have statistics collected, just like ordinary tables, and they can be used as models to create local tables:

```
CREATE TABLE my_local_copy (LIKE my_foreign_table);
```

This is not supported by `dblink`, because it works on statements instead of managing tables. In general, there is no federated query optimizer. If we join a local table and a remote table with `dblink`, then data from the remote database is simply pulled through, even if it would have been quicker to send the data and then pull back matching rows. On the other hand, `postgres_fdw` can share information with the query planner, allowing some optimization, and more improvements are likely to come in the following years, now that the infrastructure has been built.

As of version 11, `postgres_fdw` transparently pushes WHERE clauses to the remote server. Suppose you issue the following:

```
SELECT * FROM ft WHERE num = 2;
```

Then, only the matching rows will be fetched, using any remote index if available. This is a massive advantage in working with selective queries on large tables.

The `dblink` module cannot automatically send a local WHERE clause to the remote database, so a query such as the following would perform poorly:

```
SELECT *
FROM dblink('otherdb',
      'SELECT * FROM bigtable') AS link ( ... )
WHERE filtercolumn > 100;
```

We will need to explicitly add the WHERE clause to the remote query at the application level, as shown here:

```
SELECT *
FROM dblink('otherdb',
     'SELECT * FROM bigtable' ||
     ' WHERE filtercolumn > 100') AS link ( ... );
```

This means that, in general, setting up views of remote data this way isn't very helpful, as it encourages users to think that the table location doesn't matter, whereas, from a performance perspective, it definitely does. This isn't really any different than other federated or remote access database products.

The version of postgres_fdw that's shipped with PostgreSQL 11 can delegate even more activities to the remote node. This includes performing sorts or joins, computing aggregates carrying out entire UPDATE or DELETE statements, and evaluating operators or functions provided by suitable extensions.

There are also a few performance considerations that you may wish to consider. The first is that when the remote query executes, the current session waits for it to complete. You can also execute queries without waiting for them to return by using the following functions:

- dblink_send_query()
- dblink_is_busy()
- dblink_get_result()

If you are concerned about the overhead of connection time, then you may want to consider using a session pool. This will reserve a number of database connections, which will allow you to reduce apparent connection time. For more information, look at the *Setting up a connection pool recipe* in Chapter 4, *Server Control*.

Another—and sometimes easier—way of accessing other databases is with a tool named **PL/Proxy**, available as a PostgreSQL extension. PL/Proxy allows you to create a local database function that is a proxy for a remote database function. PL/Proxy works only for functions, and some people regard this as a restriction in a way similar to postgres_fdw, which operates only on rows in tables. That is why these solutions complement dblink, rather than replacing it.

Creating a local proxy function is simple:

```
CREATE FUNCTION my_task(VOID)
RETURNS SETOF text AS $$
    CONNECT 'dbname=myremoteserver';
    SELECT my_task();
$$ LANGUAGE plproxy;
```

You need a local function, but you don't need to call a remote function; you can use SQL statements directly. The following example shows a parameterized function:

```
CREATE FUNCTION get_cust_email(p_username text)
RETURNS SETOF text AS $$
    CONNECT 'dbname=myremoteserver';
    SELECT email FROM users WHERE username = p_username;
$$ LANGUAGE plproxy;
```

PL/Proxy is specifically designed to allow more complex architecture for sharding and load balancing. The RUN ON command allows us to dynamically specify the remote database on which we will run the SQL statement. So, the preceding example becomes as follows:

```
CREATE FUNCTION get_cust_email(p_username text)
RETURNS SETOF text AS $$
    CLUSTER 'mycluster';
    RUN ON hashtext(p_username);
    SELECT email FROM users WHERE username = p_username;
$$ LANGUAGE plproxy;
```

You'll likely need to read Chapter 12, *Replication and Upgrades*, before you begin designing application architecture using these concepts.

Accessing objects in other foreign databases

In the previous recipe, you saw how to use objects from a different PostgreSQL database, either with dblink or by using the Foreign Data Wrapper infrastructure. Here, we will explore another variant of the latter—using Foreign Data Wrappers to access databases other than PostgreSQL.

There are many Foreign Data Wrappers for other database systems, all of which are maintained as extensions independently from the PostgreSQL project. The **PostgreSQL Extension Network** (**PGXN**) we mentioned in Chapter 3, *Configuration*, is a good place where you can see which extensions are available.

Just note this so that you don't get confused: while you can find Foreign Data Wrappers to access several database systems, there are also other wrappers for different types of data sources, such as text files, web services, and so on. There is even `postgres_fdw`, a backport of the `contrib` module that we covered in the previous recipe, for users of older PostgreSQL versions who do not have it yet.

> When evaluating external extensions, I advise you to carefully examine the `README` file in each extension before making stable choices, as the code maturity varies a lot. Some extensions are still development experiments, while others are production-ready extensions, such as `oracle_fdw`.

Getting ready

For this example, we will use the Oracle Foreign Data Wrapper, `oracle_fdw`, whose current version is 2.1.1.

You must have obtained and installed the required Oracle software as specified in the `oracle_fdw` documentation at `https://github.com/laurenz/oracle_fdw/blob/ORACLE_FDW_2_1_0/README.oracle_fdw#L503`.

The `oracle_fdw` wrapper is available in the PostgreSQL Extension Network, so you can follow the straightforward installation procedure described in the *Installing modules from PGXN* section of the *Adding an external module to PostgreSQL* recipe in `Chapter 3`, *Configuration*.

Obviously, you must have access to an Oracle database server.

How to do it...

Here, we provide the steps to follow regarding how to connect to an Oracle server using `oracle_fdw`:

1. First, we ensure that the extension is loaded:

   ```
   CREATE EXTENSION IF NOT EXISTS oracle_fdw;
   ```

2. Then, we configure the server and the user mapping:

```
CREATE SERVER myserv
FOREIGN DATA WRAPPER oracle_fdw
OPTIONS (dbserver '//myhost/MYDB');
CREATE USER MAPPING FOR myuser
SERVER myserv;
```

3. Then, we create a PostgreSQL foreign table with the same column names as the source table in Oracle, and with compatible column types:

```
CREATE FOREIGN TABLE mytab(id bigint, descr text)
SERVER myserv
OPTIONS (user 'scott', password 'tiger');
```

4. Now, we can try to write to the table:

```
INSERT INTO mytab VALUES (-1, 'Minus One');
```

5. Finally, we are able to read the values that we have inserted:

```
SELECT * FROM mytab WHERE id = -1;
```

This should result in the following output:

```
id |   descr
----+------------
-1 | Minus One
(1 row)
```

How it works...

Our query has a WHERE condition that filters the rows we select from the foreign table. As in the postgres_fdw example from the previous recipe, Foreign Data Wrappers do the clever thing: the WHERE condition is pushed to the remote server, and only the matching rows are retrieved.

This is good in two ways: firstly, we delegate some work to another system, and secondly, we reduce the overall network traffic by not transferring unnecessary data.

We also notice that the WHERE condition is expressed in the PostgreSQL syntax; the Foreign Data Wrapper is able to translate it into whatever form is required by the remote system.

There's more...

PostgreSQL provides the infrastructure for collecting statistics on foreign tables, so the planner will be able to consider such information, provided that the feature is implemented in the specific Foreign Data Wrapper you are using. For example, statistics are supported by `oracle_fdw`.

The latest improvements for foreign tables include trigger support, `IMPORT FOREIGN SCHEMA`, and several improvements to the query planner.

Particularly useful for database administrators is the `IMPORT FOREIGN SCHEMA` syntax, which can be used to create foreign tables for all tables and views in a given remote schema with a single statement.

Among the query planner improvements, we wish to mention **Join Pushdown**. In a nutshell: a query that joins some foreign tables that belong to the same server is able to have the join performed transparently on the remote server. To avoid security issues, this can only happen if these tables are all accessed with the same role.

Another interesting extension is **Multicorn** (`http://multicorn.org`). It helps Python programmers create Foreign Data Wrappers by providing a dedicated interface. Multicorn reduces the creation of a basic Foreign Data Wrapper to the implementation of one Python method. Additional features, such as write access, are available through further optional methods.

Updatable views

PostgreSQL supports the SQL standard `CREATE VIEW` command, which supports automatic `UPDATE`, `INSERT`, and `DELETE` commands, provided they are simple enough.

Note that certain types of updates are forbidden just because it is either impossible or impractical to derive a corresponding list of modifications on the constituent tables. We'll discuss those issues here.

Getting ready

First, you need to consider that only simple views can be made to receive insertions, updates, and deletions easily. The SQL standard differentiates between views that are simple and updatable, and more complex views that cannot be expected to be updatable.

So, before we proceed, we need to understand what a simple updatable view is and what it is not. Let's start from the `cust` table:

```
postgres=# SELECT * FROM cust;
 customerid | firstname | lastname | age
------------+-----------+----------+-----
          1 | Philip    | Marlowe  |  38
          2 | Richard   | Hannay   |  42
          3 | Holly     | Martins  |  25
          4 | Harry     | Palmer   |  36
          4 | Mark      | Hall     |  47
(5 rows)
```

We will create a very simple view on top of it, such as the following:

```
CREATE VIEW cust_view AS
SELECT customerid
     , firstname
     , lastname
     , age
FROM cust;
```

Each row in our view corresponds to one row in a single-source table, and each column is referred to directly without any further processing, except possibly for a column rename. Thus, we expect to be able to make INSERT, UPDATE, and DELETE commands pass through our view into the base table, which is what happens in PostgreSQL.

The following examples are three views where INSERT, UPDATE, and DELETE commands cannot be made to flow to the base table easily, for the reasons just described:

```
CREATE VIEW cust_avg AS
SELECT avg(age)
FROM cust;
CREATE VIEW cust_above_avg_age AS
SELECT customerid
          , substr(firstname, 1, 20) as fname
          , substr(lastname, 1, 20) as lname
          , age -
          (SELECT avg(age)::integer
          FROM cust) as years_above_avg
FROM cust
WHERE age >
     (SELECT avg(age)
      FROM cust);

CREATE VIEW potential_spammers AS
SELECT customerid, spam_score(firstname,lastname)
```

```
FROM cust
ORDER BY spam_score(firstname,lastname) DESC
LIMIT 100;
```

The first view just shows a single row with the average of a numeric column. Changing an average directly doesn't make much sense. For instance, if we want to raise the average age by 1, should we increase all numbers by 1, resulting in an update of each row that is unusual? Or should we change some rows only, by a larger amount? A user who really wants to do this can update the cust table directly.

The second view shows a column called years_above_avg, which is the difference between the age of that customer and the average. Changing that column would be more complex than it seems at first glance: just consider that increasing the age by 10 would not result in increasing years_above_avg by 10, because the average will also be affected.

The third view displays a computed column that can definitely not be updated directly—we can't change the value in the spam_score column without changing the algorithm implemented by the spam_score() function.

Now, we can proceed to the steps to allow any or all of insertions, updates, or deletions to flow from views to base tables, since we've clarified whether this makes sense conceptually.

How to do it...

There is nothing to do for simple views—PostgreSQL will propagate modifications to the underlying table automatically.

Conversely, if the view is not simple enough, but you still have a clear idea of how you would like to propagate changes to the underlying table(s), then you can allow updatable views by telling PostgreSQL how to actually perform **Data Manipulation Language (DML)** statements, which in PostgreSQL means INSERT, UPDATE, DELETE, or TRUNCATE.

PostgreSQL supports two mechanisms to achieve updatable views, namely rewrite rules and INSTEAD OF triggers. The latter provide a mechanism to implement updatable views by creating trigger functions that execute arbitrary code every time a data-modification command is executed on the view.

The INSTEAD OF triggers are part of the SQL standard, and other database systems support them. Conversely, query rewrite rules are specific to PostgreSQL and cannot be found anywhere else in this exact form.

There is no clearly preferable method. On one hand, rules can be more efficient than triggers, but, on the other hand, they can be more difficult to understand than triggers and could result in inefficient execution if the code is badly written (although the latter is not an exclusive property of rules, unfortunately).

To explain this point concretely, we will now provide an example using rules, and then we will re-implement the same example with triggers.

We will start with a table of mountains and their height in meters:

```
CREATE TABLE mountains_m
( name text primary key
, meters int not null
);
```

Then, we will create a view that adds a computed column expressing the height in feet, and that displays the data in descending height order:

```
CREATE VIEW mountains AS
SELECT *, ROUND(meters / 0.3048) AS feet
FROM mountains_m
ORDER BY meters DESC;
```

DML automatically flows to the base table when inserting only columns that are not computed:

```
INSERT INTO mountains(name, meters)
VALUES ('Everest', 8848);
TABLE mountains;
name    | meters | feet
--------+--------+-------
Everest|   8848 | 29029
(1 row)
```

However, when we try to insert data with the height specified in feet, we get the following error:

```
INSERT INTO mountains(name, feet)
VALUES ('K2', 28251);
ERROR:  cannot insert into column "feet" of view "mountains"
DETAIL:  View columns that are not columns of their base relation are not
updatable.
```

So, we create a rule that replaces the update with another query that works all the time:

```
CREATE RULE mountains_ins_rule AS
ON INSERT TO mountains DO INSTEAD
INSERT INTO mountains_m
VALUES (NEW.name, COALESCE (NEW.meters, NEW.feet * 0.3048));
```

Now, we can insert both `meters` and `feet`:

```
INSERT INTO mountains(name, feet)
VALUES ('K 2', 28251);
INSERT INTO mountains(name, meters)
VALUES ('Kangchenjunga', 8586);
TABLE mountains;
name            | meters | feet
----------------+--------+----
Everest         |   8848 | 29029
K 2             |   8611 | 28251
Kangchenjunga   |   8586 | 28169
(3 rows)
```

Updates are also propagated automatically, but only to non-computed columns:

```
UPDATE mountains SET name = 'K2' WHERE name = 'K 2';
TABLE mountains;
name            | meters | feet
----------------+--------+--------
Everest         |   8848 | 29029
 K2             |   8611 | 28251
Kangchenjunga   |   8586 | 28169
(3 rows)
UPDATE mountains SET feet = 29064 WHERE name = 'K2';
ERROR:  cannot update column "feet" of view "mountains"
DETAIL:  View columns that are not columns of their base relation are not
updatable.
```

If we add another rule replacing updates with a query that covers all cases, then the last update will succeed and produce the desired effect:

```
CREATE RULE mountains_upd_rule AS
ON UPDATE TO mountains DO INSTEAD
UPDATE mountains_m
SET name = NEW.name, meters =
CASE
WHEN NEW.meters != OLD.meters
THEN NEW.meters
WHEN NEW.feet != OLD.feet
THEN NEW.feet * 0.3048
```

```
ELSE OLD.meters
END
WHERE name = OLD.name;
UPDATE mountains SET feet = 29064 WHERE name = 'K2';
TABLE mountains;
name            | meters | feet
----------------+--------+--------
K2              |   8859 | 29065
Everest         |   8848 | 29029
Kangchenjunga   |   8586 | 28169
(3 rows)
```

The query that's used in this rule also covers the simpler case of a non-computed column:

```
UPDATE mountains SET meters = 8611 WHERE name = 'K2';
TABLE mountains;
name            | meters | feet
----------------+--------+--------
Everest         |   8848 | 29029
K2              |   8611 | 28251
Kangchenjunga   |   8586 | 28169
(3 rows)
```

The same effect can be achieved by adding the following trigger, which replaces the earlier two rules:

```
CREATE FUNCTION mountains_tf()
RETURNS TRIGGER
LANGUAGE plpgsql
AS $$
BEGIN
IF TG_OP = 'INSERT' THEN
INSERT INTO mountains_m VALUES (NEW.name,
CASE
  WHEN NEW.meters IS NULL
  THEN NEW.feet * 0.3048
  ELSE NEW.meters
  END );
ELSIF TG_OP = 'UPDATE' THEN
UPDATE mountains_m
SET name = NEW.name, meters =
CASE
WHEN NEW.meters != OLD.meters
THEN NEW.meters
WHEN NEW.feet != OLD.feet
THEN NEW.feet * 0.3048
ELSE OLD.meters
END
```

```
WHERE name = OLD.name;
END IF;
RETURN NEW;
END;
$$;
CREATE TRIGGER mountains_tg
INSTEAD OF INSERT OR UPDATE ON mountains
FOR EACH ROW
EXECUTE PROCEDURE mountains_tf();
```

How it works...

In the rule-based example, we use the COALESCE function, which returns the first argument, if not null, or the second one otherwise. When the original INSERT statement does not specify a value in meters, then it uses the value in feet divided by 0.3048.

The second rule sets the value in meters to different expressions—if the value in meters was updated, we use the new one, if the value in feet was updated, we use the new value in feet divided by 0.3048, and otherwise we use the old value in meters (that is, we don't change it).

The logic implemented in the trigger function is similar to the previous one; note that we use the TG_OP automatic variable to handle INSERT and UPDATE separately.

We've just scratched the surface of what you can achieve with rules, though personally I find them too complex for widespread use.

You can do a lot of things with rules; you just need to be sure that everything you do makes sense and has a practical purpose. There are some other important points that I should mention about rules before you dive in and start using them everywhere.

Rules are applied by PostgreSQL after the SQL has been received by the server and parsed for syntax errors, but before the planner tries to optimize the SQL statement.

In the rules in the preceding recipe, we referenced the values of the old or the new row, just as we do within trigger functions, using the old and new keywords. Similarly, there are only new values in an INSERT command and only old values in a DELETE command.

One of the major downsides of using rules is that we cannot bulk load data into the table using the COPY command. Also, we cannot transform a stream of inserts into a single COPY command, nor can we do a COPY operation against the view. Bulk loading requires direct access to the table.

Suppose we have a view such as the following:

```
CREATE VIEW cust_minor AS
SELECT customerid
 ,firstname
,lastname
,age
FROM cust
WHERE age < 18;
```

Then, we have some more difficulties. If we wish to update this view, then you might read the manual and understand that we can use a conditional rule by adding a WHERE clause to match the WHERE clause in the view, as follows:

```
CREATE RULE cust_minor_update AS
ON  update TO cust_minor
WHERE new.age < 18
DO INSTEAD
UPDATE cust SET
 firstname = new.firstname
,lastname = new.lastname
,age = new.age
WHERE customerid = old.customerid;
```

This fails, however, as you can see if you try to update cust_minor. The fix is to add two rules—one as an unconditional rule that does nothing (literally) and needs to exist for internal reasons, and the other to do the work we want:

```
CREATE RULE cust_minor_update_dummy AS ON
update TO cust_minor
DO INSTEAD NOTHING;
CREATE RULE cust_minor_update_conditional AS
ON   update TO cust_minor
WHERE new.age < 18
DO INSTEAD
UPDATE cust SET firstname = new.firstname
,lastname = new.lastname
,age = new.age
WHERE customerid = old.customerid;
```

There's more...

There is yet another question posed by updatable views.

As an example, we shall use the `cust_minor` view we just defined, which does not allow you to perform insertions or updates so that the affected rows fall out of the view itself. For instance, consider this query:

```
UPDATE cust_minor SET age = 19 WHERE customerid = 123;
```

The preceding query will not affect any row because of the `WHERE age < 18` conditions in the rule definition.

The `CREATE VIEW` statement has a `WITH CHECK OPTION` clause; if specified, any update that excludes any row from the view will fail.

If a view includes some updatable columns together with other non-updatable columns (for example expressions, literals, and so on), then updates are allowed if they only change the updatable columns.

Finally, let's show that views are just (empty) tables with a `SELECT` rule. Let's start by creating an empty table, as follows:

```
CREATE TABLE cust_view AS SELECT * FROM cust WHERE false;
```

The `SELECT` rule works only if it is named `_RETURN` and the table is completely empty:

```
postgres # CREATE RULE "_RETURN" AS
               ON SELECT TO cust_view
               DO INSTEAD
               SELECT * FROM cust;
CREATE RULE
postgres=# \d cust_view
```

Huh? So, what is it if it's not a table?

```
postgres # DROP TABLE cust_view;
ERROR:  "cust_view" is not a table
HINT:  Use DROP VIEW to remove a view
postgres # DROP VIEW cust_view;
DROP VIEW
```

Yes, we created a table and then added a rule to it. This turned the table into a view.

Using materialized views

Every time we select rows from a view, we actually select from the result of the underlying query. If that query is slow and we need to use it more than once, then it makes sense to run the query once, save its output as a table, and then select the rows from the latter.

This procedure has been available for a long time, and there is a dedicated syntax, CREATE MATERIALIZED VIEW, which we will describe in this recipe.

Getting ready

Let's create two randomly populated tables, of which one is large:

```
CREATE TABLE dish
( dish_id SERIAL PRIMARY KEY
, dish_description text
);

CREATE TABLE eater
( eater_id SERIAL
, eating_date date
, dish_id int REFERENCES dish (dish_id)
);
INSERT INTO dish (dish_description)
VALUES ('Lentils'), ('Mango'), ('Plantain'), ('Rice'), ('Tea');

INSERT INTO eater(eating_date, dish_id)
SELECT floor(abs(sin(n)) * 365) :: int + date '2014-01-01'
, ceil(abs(sin(n :: float * n))*5) :: int
FROM generate_series(1,500000) AS rand(n);
```

Notice that the data is not truly random. It is generated by a deterministic procedure, so you can get exactly the same result if you copy the preceding code.

How to do it...

Let's create the following view:

```
CREATE VIEW v_dish AS
SELECT dish_description, count(*)
FROM dish JOIN eater USING (dish_id)
GROUP BY dish_description
ORDER BY 1;
```

Then, we'll query it:

```
SELECT * FROM v_dish;
```

We will obtain the following output:

```
dish_description  | count
------------------+--------
 Lentils          |  64236
 Mango            |  66512
 Plantain         |  74058
 Rice             |  90222
 Tea              | 204972
(5 rows)
```

With a very similar syntax, we create a materialized view with the same underlying query:

```
CREATE MATERIALIZED VIEW m_dish AS
SELECT dish_description, count(*)
FROM dish JOIN eater USING (dish_id)
GROUP BY dish_description
ORDER BY 1;
```

The corresponding query yields the same output as before:

```
SELECT * FROM m_dish;
```

The materialized version is much faster than the non-materialized version. On my laptop, their execution times are 0.2 milliseconds versus 300 milliseconds.

How it works...

Creating a non-materialized view is exactly the same as creating an empty table with a SELECT rule, as we discovered from the previous recipe. No data is extracted until the view is actually used.

When creating a materialized view, the default is to run the query immediately and then store its results, as we do for table content.

In short, creating a materialized view is slow, but using it is fast. This is the opposite of standard views, which are created instantly and recomputed at every use.

There's more...

The output of a materialized view is physically stored like a regular table, and the analogy doesn't stop here. In both cases, it is possible to create indexes to speed up queries.

A materialized view will not automatically change when its constituent tables change. For that to happen, you must issue the following:

REFRESH MATERIALIZED VIEW m_dish;

This replaces all the contents of the view with newly computed ones.

It is possible to quickly create an empty materialized view and populate it later. Just add WITH NO DATA at the end of the CREATE MATERIALIZED VIEW statement. Obviously, the view cannot be used before being populated, which you can do with REFRESH MATERIALIZED VIEW, as you just saw.

A materialized view cannot be read while it is being refreshed. For that, you need to use the CONCURRENTLY clause at the expense of a somewhat slower refresh.

As you can see from these paragraphs, currently, there is only a partial advantage in using materialized views, compared to previous solutions such as this:

CREATE UNLOGGED TABLE m_dish AS SELECT * FROM v_dish;

However, when using a declarative language, such as SQL, the same syntax may automatically result in a more efficient algorithm in the case of future improvements to PostgreSQL. For instance, one day, PostgreSQL will be able to perform a faster refresh by simply replacing those rows that changed, instead of recomputing the entire content.

What PostgreSQL already provides is the ability to collect all changes that happen in a given statement, in the form of transition tables that AFTER triggers can use. This can be useful if you have a materialized view, for which you can write a trigger that uses transition tables data to perform the equivalent of an **incremental refresh**.

Finally, remember that you are not allowed to modify a materialized with INSERT, UPDATE, or DELETE commands. Therefore, the simpleset way to use transition tables to implement an incremental refresh is to use an unlogged table.

Monitoring and Diagnosis

8

In this chapter, we will cover the following recipes:

- Providing PostgreSQL information to monitoring tools
- Real-time viewing using pgAdmin or OmniDB
- Checking whether a user is connected
- Checking whether a computer is connected
- Repeatedly executing a query in psql
- Checking which queries are running
- Checking which queries are active or blocked
- Knowing who is blocking a query
- Killing a specific session
- Detecting an in-doubt prepared transaction
- Knowing whether anybody is using a specific table
- Knowing when a table was last used
- Usage of disk space by temporary data
- Understanding why queries slow down
- Investigating and reporting a bug
- Producing a daily summary of log file errors
- Analyzing the real-time performance of your queries

Introduction

In this chapter, you will find recipes for some common monitoring and diagnosis actions that you will want to perform inside your database. They are meant to answer specific questions that you often face when using PostgreSQL.

Databases are not isolated entities. They live on computer hardware using CPUs, RAM, and disk subsystems. Users access databases using networks. Depending on the setup, databases themselves may need network resources to function in any of the following ways: performing some authentication checks when users log in, using disks that are mounted over the network (not generally recommended), or making remote function calls to other databases.

This means that *monitoring only the database is not enough*. As a minimum, you should also monitor everything directly involved in using the database. This means knowing about the following:

- Is the database host available? Does it accept connections?
- How much of the network bandwidth is in use? Have there been network interruptions and dropped connections?
- Is there enough RAM available for the most common tasks? How much of it is left?
- Is there enough disk space available? When will you run out of disk space?
- Is the disk subsystem keeping up? How much more load can it take?
- Can the CPU keep up with the load? How many spare idle cycles do the CPUs have?
- Are other network services the database access depends on (if any) available? For example, if you use Kerberos for authentication, you need to monitor it as well.
- How many context switches are happening when the database is running?
- For most of these things, you are interested in the history; that is, how have things evolved? Was everything mostly the same yesterday or last week?
- When did the disk usage start changing rapidly?
- For any larger installation, you probably have something already in place to monitor the health of your hosts and network.

The two aspects of monitoring are collecting historical data to see how things have evolved, and getting alerts when things go seriously wrong. Tools based on a **Round Robin Database Tool** (**RRDtool**) such as **Munin**, or time series databases such as Graphite's **Carbon**, and **Prometheus**, are quite popular for collecting historical information on all aspects of the servers, and presenting this information in an easy-to-follow graphical form, for which Grafana is a popular tool. Seeing several statistics on the same timescale can really help when trying to figure out why the system is behaving the way it is.

Another aspect of monitoring is getting alerts when something goes really wrong and needs (immediate) attention.

For alerting, one of the most widely used tools is **Icinga** (a fork of **Nagios**), an established solution. The aforementioned trending tools can integrate with it. `check_postgres` is a rather popular Icinga plugin for monitoring many standard aspects of a PostgreSQL database server.

Icinga is a stable and mature solution, based on the long-standing approach where each plugin decides whether a given measurement is a cause for alarm, which means that it's more complex to manage and maintain. A more recent tool is the aforementioned **Prometheus**, based on a design that separates data collection from the centralized alerting logic.

Should you need a solution for both the alerting and trending aspects of a monitoring tool, you might also want to look into **Zabbix**.

Furthermore, if you require integration with a system based on the **Simple Network Management Protocol** (**SNMP**), the `pgsnmpd` project offers some basic support. However, as it is not actively maintained, we recommend switching to one of the other monitoring approaches, if at all possible.

Providing PostgreSQL information to monitoring tools

It's best to use historical monitoring information when all of it is available from the same place and on the same timescale. Most monitoring systems are designed for generic purposes, while allowing application and system developers to integrate their specific checks with the monitoring infrastructure. This is possible through a plugin architecture. Adding new kinds of data inputs to them means installing a plugin. Sometimes, you may need to write or develop this plugin, but writing a plugin for something such as Cacti is easy. You just have to write a script that outputs monitored values in simple text format.

In most common scenarios, the monitoring system is centralized and data is collected directly (and remotely) by the system itself or through some distributed components that are responsible for sending the observed metrics back to the main node.

As far as PostgreSQL is concerned, some useful things to include in graphs are the number of connections, disk usage, number of queries, number of WAL files, most numbers from `pg_stat_user_tables` and `pg_stat_user_indexes`, and so on. One *Swiss Army knife* script, which can be used from both Cacti and Nagios/Icinga, is `check_postgres`. It is available at `http://bucardo.org/wiki/Check_postgres`. It has ready-made reporting actions for a large array of things that are worth monitoring in PostgreSQL.

For Munin, there are some PostgreSQL plugins available at the Munin plugin repository at `https://github.com/munin-monitoring/contrib/tree/master/plugins/postgresql`.

The following screenshot shows a Munin graph about PostgreSQL buffer cache hits for a specific database, where cache hits (the blue line) dominate reads from the disk (the green line):

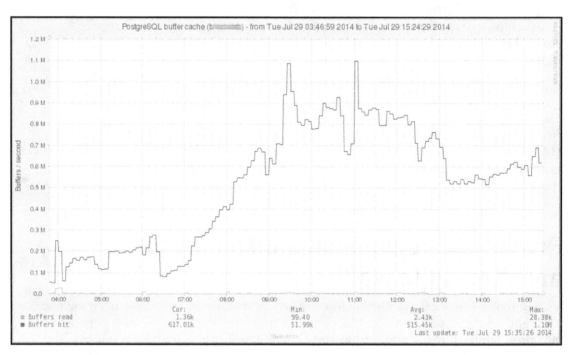

Finding more information about generic monitoring tools

Setting up the tools themselves is a larger topic, and it is beyond the scope of this book. In fact, each of these tools has more than one book written about them. The basic setup information and the tools themselves can be found at the following URLs:

- RRDtool: `http://www.mrtg.org/rrdtool/`
- Cacti: `http://www.cacti.net/`
- Icinga: `http://www.icinga.org`

- **Munin:** `http://munin-monitoring.org/`
- **Nagios:** `http://www.nagios.org/`
- **Zabbix:** `http://www.zabbix.org/`

Real-time viewing using pgAdmin or OmniDB

You can also use a GUI tool such as pgAdmin or OmniDB, which we discussed for the first time in `Chapter 1`, *First Steps*, to get a quick view of what is going on in the database.

Getting ready

If you use pgAdmin, for better control, you need to install the `adminpack` extension in the destination database by issuing the following command:

```
CREATE EXTENSION adminpack;
```

This extension is a part of the additionally supplied modules of PostgreSQL (also known as **contrib**). It provides several administration functions that pgAdmin (and other tools) can use in order to manage, control, and monitor a Postgres server from a remote location.

How to do it...

In this section, we will be covering pgAdmin and OmniDB usage.

Using pgAdmin

This section illustrates the pgAdmin tool.

Once you have installed `adminpack`, connect to the database server; this will open a window similar to the one that's shown in the following screenshot, where you can see a general view plus information on connections, locks, and running transactions:

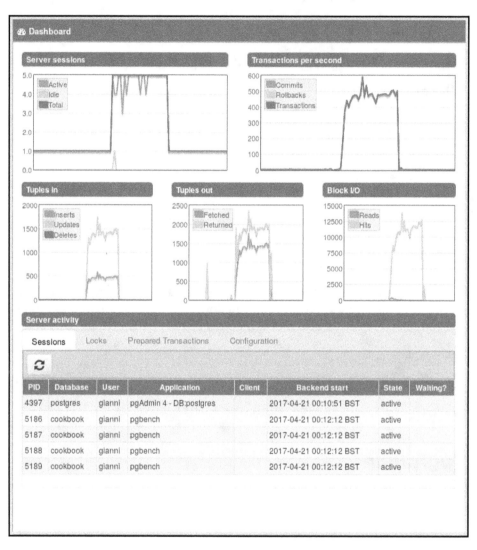

Using OmniDB

This is another section that illustrates the OmniDB tool.

After starting OmniDB and opening a database, a tab called **Monitoring** is automatically displayed, as shown in the following screenshot:

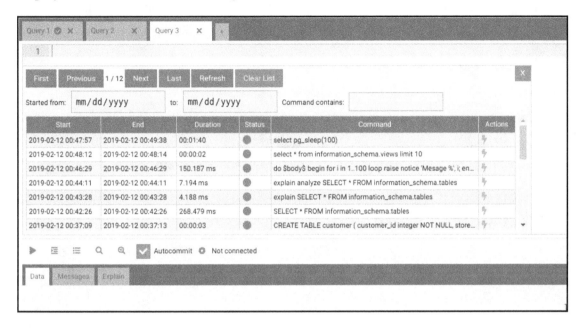

The **Monitoring** tab shows a series of charts and diagrams about sessions, locks, activity, database size, and table size.

The display can be customized by adding/removing charts from a list of predefined templates, or by creating a bespoke chart by modifying the data script and/or the chart script.

The easiest way to add a new type of chart is to take an existing one, understanding what information it displays, and then using it as a starting point to make a different one.

Checking whether a user is connected

Here, we will show you how to learn whether a certain database user is currently connected to the database.

Getting ready

If you are logged in as a superuser, you will have full access to monitoring information.

How to do it...

Issue the following query to see whether the user `bob` is connected:

```
SELECT datname FROM pg_stat_activity WHERE usename = 'bob';
```

If this query returns any rows, then it that means `bob` is connected to the database. The returned value is the name of the database to which the user is connected.

How it works...

PostgreSQL's `pg_stat_activity` system view keeps track of all running PostgreSQL backends. This includes information such as the query that is being currently executed, or the last query that was executed by each backend, who is connected, when the connection, the transaction, and/or the query were started, and so on.

There's more...

Please spend a few minutes reading the PostgreSQL documentation, which contains more detailed information about `pg_stat_activity`, available at http://www.postgresql.org/docs/11/static/monitoring-stats.html#PG-STAT-ACTIVITY-VIEW.

You can find answers to many administration-related questions by analyzing the `pg_stat_activity` view. One common example is outlined in the following recipe.

Checking whether a computer is connected

Often, several different processes may connect as the same database user. In that case, you may actually want to know whether there is a connection from a specific computer.

How to do it...

You can get this information from the `pg_stat_activity` view, as it includes the connected clients' IP address, port, and hostname (where applicable). The port is only needed if you have more than one connection from the same client computer and you need to do further digging to see which process there connects to which database. Run the following command:

```
SELECT datname, usename, client_addr, client_port,
       application_name FROM pg_stat_activity;
```

The `client_addr` and `client_port` parameters help you look up the exact computer and even the process on that computer that has connected to the specific database. You can also retrieve the hostname of the remote computer through the `client_hostname` option (this requires `log_hostname` to be set to `on`).

There's more...

I would always recommend including `application_name` in your reports. This field has become widely recognized and honored by third-party application developers (I advise you to do the same with your own applications).

For information on how to set the application name for your connections, refer to *Database Connection Control Functions* in the PostgreSQL documentation at `http://www.postgresql.org/docs/11/static/libpq-connect.html`.

Repeatedly executing a query in psql

Sometimes, we want to execute a query more than once, repeated at regular intervals; in this recipe, we will look at an interesting `psql` command that does exactly that.

How to do it...

The `\watch` meta-command allows psql users to automatically (and continuously) re-execute a query.

This behavior is similar to the `watch` utility of some Linux and Unix environments.

In the following example, we will run a simple query on `pg_stat_activity` and ask psql to repeat it every 5 seconds. You can exit at any time by pressing *Ctrl + C*:

```
gabriele=> SELECT count(*) FROM pg_stat_activity;
 count
--------
     1
(1 row)

gabriele=> \watch 5
Watch every 5s     Tue Aug 27 21:47:24 2013

 count
--------
     1
(1 row)
<snip>
```

There's more...

For further information about the psql utility, refer to the PostgreSQL documentation at `http://www.postgresql.org/docs/11/static/app-psql.html`.

Checking which queries are running

In this section, we will show you how to check which query is currently running.

Getting ready

You have to make sure that you are logged in as a superuser or as the same database user you want to check out. Also, ensure that the `track_activities = on` parameter is set (which it normally should be, being the default setting). If not, check the *Updating the parameter file* recipe in `Chapter 3`, *Configuration*.

How to do it...

To see which connected users are running at this moment, just run the following code:

```
SELECT datname, usename, state, query
    FROM pg_stat_activity;
```

On systems with a lot of users, you may notice that the majority of backends have `state` set to `idle`. This denotes that no query is actually running, and PostgreSQL is waiting for new commands from the user. The `query` field shows the statement that was last executed by that particular backend.

If, on the other hand, you are interested in active queries only, limit your selection to those records that have `state` set to `active`:

```
SELECT datname, usename, state, query
      FROM pg_stat_activity WHERE state = 'active';
```

How it works...

When `track_activities` = `on` is set, PostgreSQL collects data about all running queries. Users with sufficient rights can then view this data using the `pg_stat_activity` system view.

The `pg_stat_activity` view uses a system function named `pg_stat_get_activity` `(procpid int)`. You can use this function directly to watch for the activity of a specific backend by supplying the process ID as an argument. Giving `NULL` as an argument returns information for all backends.

There's more...

Sometimes, you don't care about getting all queries that are currently running. You may be only interested in seeing some of these, or you may not like to connect to the database just to see what is running.

Catching queries that only run for a few milliseconds

Since most queries on modern **online transaction processing** (**OLTP**) systems take only a few milliseconds to run, it is often hard to catch the active ones when simply probing the `pg_stat_activity` table.

Most likely, you will be able to see only the last executed query for those backends that have `state` different from `active`. In some cases, this can be enough.

In general, if you need to perform a deeper analysis, I strongly recommend installing and configuring the `pg_stat_statements` module, which is described in the *Analyzing the real-time performance of your queries* recipe in this chapter. Another option is to run a post analysis of log files using pgBadger. Depending on the workload of your system, you may want to limit the production of highly granular log files (that is, log all queries) to a short period of time. For further information on pgBadger, refer to the *Producing a daily summary of log file errors* recipe of this chapter.

Watching the longest queries

Another point of interest that you may want to look for is long-running queries. To get a list of running queries ordered by how long they have been executing, use the following code:

```
SELECT
  current_timestamp - query_start AS runtime,
  datname, usename, query
FROM pg_stat_activity
WHERE state = 'active'
ORDER BY 1 DESC;
```

This will return currently running queries, with the longest running queries in the front.

On busy systems, you may want to limit the set of queries that are returned to only the first few queries (add `LIMIT 10` at the end) or only the queries that have been running over a certain period of time. For example, to get a list of queries that have been running for more than a minute, use the following query:

```
SELECT
    current_timestamp - query_start AS runtime,
    datname, usename, query
FROM pg_stat_activity
WHERE state = 'active'
    AND current_timestamp - query_start > '1 min'
ORDER BY 1 DESC;
```

Watching queries from ps

If you want, you can also make queries that are being run show up in process titles, by setting the following configuration in the `postgresql.conf` file:

```
update_process_title = on
```

Although the `ps` and `top` outputs are not the best places for watching database queries, they may make sense in some circumstances.

See also

- The page in PostgreSQL's online documentation that covers the appropriate settings is available at `http://www.postgresql.org/docs/11/static/runtime-config-statistics.html`

Checking which queries are active or blocked

Here, we will show you how to find out whether a query is actually running or waiting for another query.

Getting ready

If you are logged in as superuser, you will have full access to monitoring information.

How to do it...

Follow these steps to check if a query is waiting for another query:

1. Run the following query:

```
SELECT datname, usename, wait_event_type, wait_event, backend_type,
query
FROM pg_stat_activity
WHERE wait_event_type IS NOT NULL
AND wait_event_type NOT IN ('Activity', 'Client');
```

2. You will receive the following output:

```
-[ RECORD 1 ]---+------------------
datname         | postgres
usename         | gianni
wait_event_type | Lock
wait_event      | relation
backend_type    | client backend
query           | select * from t;
```

How it works...

The `pg_stat_activity` system view includes the `wait_event_type` and `wait_event` columns, which are set to the kind of wait, and to the kind of object that is blocked, respectively. The `backend_type` column indicates the type of current backend.

The preceding query uses the `wait_event_type` field to filter out only those queries that are waiting.

There's more...

PostgreSQL provides a version of the `pg_stat_activity` view that's capable of capturing many kinds of waits; however, in older versions, `pg_stat_activity` could only detect waits on locks such as those placed on SQL objects, via the `pg_stat_activity.waiting` field.

Although this is the main cause of waiting when using pure SQL, it is possible to write a query in any of PostgreSQL's embedded languages that can wait on other system resources, such as waiting for an HTTP response, for a file write to get completed, or just waiting on a timer.

As an example, you can make your backend sleep for a certain number of seconds using `pg_sleep(seconds)`. While you are monitoring `pg_stat_activity`, open a new Terminal session with `psql` and run the following statement in it:

```
db=# SELECT pg_sleep(10);
<it "stops" for 10 seconds here>
pg_sleep
----------

(1 row)
```

In older versions of Postgres, it will show up as *not waiting* in the `pg_stat_activity` view, even though the query is, in fact, blocked in the timer.

You will see the following output with newer versions of Postgres where the `wait_event_type` is *Timeout*—the server process is waiting for a timeout to expire and `wait_event` is *PgSleep*—waiting for a process that called `pg_sleep`:

```
-[ RECORD 1 ]---+--------------------
datname         | postgres
usename         | postgres
wait_event_type | Timeout
```

```
wait_event      | PgSleep
backend_type    | client backend
query           | SELECT pg_sleep(10);
```

Knowing who is blocking a query

Once you have found out that a query is being blocked, you need to know who or what is blocking it.

Getting ready

If you are logged in as a superuser, you will have full access to monitoring information.

How to do it...

Perform the following steps:

1. Write the following query:

   ```
   SELECT datname, usename, wait_event_type, wait_event,
   pg_blocking_pids(pid) AS blocked_by, backend_type, query
   FROM pg_stat_activity
   WHERE wait_event_type IS NOT NULL
   AND wait_event_type NOT IN ('Activity', 'Client');
   ```

2. You will receive the following output:

   ```
   -[ RECORD 1 ]---+------------------
   datname         | postgres
   usename         | gianni
   wait_event_type | Lock
   wait_event      | relation
   blocked_by      | {18142}
   backend_type    | client backend
   query           | select * from t;
   ```

This is, in fact, the query we described in the previous recipe, with the addition of the blocked_by column. Recall that the PID is the unique identifier assigned by the operating system to each session; for more details, see Chapter 4, *Server Control*. Here, the PID is used by the pg_blocking_pids(pid) system function to identify blocking sessions.

Parallel queries allow powerful queries using multiple cores, but also increase the number of ways in which one query can be blocked by another. Think how complicated it can be to extract dependencies and display them neatly if there are multiple PIDs for a single session.

How it works...

The query is relatively simple: we just introduced the `pg_blocking_pids()` function, which returns an array that was composed by the PIDs of all the sessions that were blocking the session with the given PID.

Killing a specific session

Sometimes, the only way to let the system continue as a whole is by *surgically* terminating some offending database sessions. Yes, you read it right: surgically. You might indeed be tempted to *reboot* the server, but you should think of that as a last resort in a business continuity scenario.

In this recipe, you will learn how to intervene, from gracefully canceling a query, to brutally killing the actual process from the command line.

How to do it...

You can either run this function as a superuser or with the same user as that of the offending backend (look for the `usename` field in the `pg_stat_activity` view).

Once you have figured out the backend you need to kill, use the `pg_terminate_backend(pid)` function to kill it.

How it works...

When a backend executes the `pg_terminate_backend(pid)` function, it sends a signal, `SIGTERM`, to the backend as an argument after verifying that the process identified by the `pid` argument is actually a PostgreSQL backend.

The backend receiving this signal stops whatever it is doing, and terminates it in a controlled way.

The client using that backend loses the connection to the database. Depending on how the client application is written, it may silently reconnect, or it may show an error to the user.

There's more...

Killing the session may not always be what you really want, so consider other options as well.

It might also be a good idea to look at the *Server Signaling Functions* section in the PostgreSQL documentation at
`http://www.postgresql.org/docs/11/static/functions-admin.html#FUNCTIONS-ADMIN-SIGNAL`.

Try to cancel the query first

First, you may want to try `pg_cancel_backend(pid)`, a milder version of `pg_terminate_backend(pid)`.

The difference between these two is that `pg_cancel_backend()` just cancels the current query, whereas `pg_terminate_backend()` really kills the backend. (Therefore, this can be used for `idle` or `idle in transaction` backends).

What if the backend won't terminate?

If `pg_terminate_backend(pid)` fails to kill the backend and you really need to reset the database state to make it continue processing requests, then you have yet another option: sending `SIGKILL` to the offending backend.

This can be done only from the command line as the `root` or the `postgres` system user, and on the same host the database is running, by executing the following code:

```
kill -9 <backend_pid>
```

This command kills that backend immediately, without giving it a chance to clean up. Consequently, the postmaster is forced to kill all the other backends as well and restart the whole cluster.

Therefore, it actually does not matter which of the PostgreSQL backends you kill.

You must be extremely careful if you have set the `synchronous_commit` parameter to `off`. You may end up losing some supposedly committed transactions if you use `kill -9` on a backend.

Thus, `kill -9` is a last resort, but only if nothing else helps, and not on a regular basis.

Using statement_timeout to clean up queries that take too long to run

Often, you know that you don't have any use for queries running longer than a given time. Maybe your web frontend just refuses to wait for more than 10 seconds for a query to complete and returns a default answer to users if it takes longer, abandoning the query.

In such a case, it might be a good idea to set `statement_timeout = 10 sec`, either in `postgresql.conf` or as a per-user or per-database setting. Once you do so, queries running too long won't consume precious resources and make other queries fail.

The queries terminated by a statement timeout show up in the log, as follows:

```
postgres=# SET statement_timeout TO '3 s';
SET
postgres=# SELECT pg_sleep(10);
ERROR: canceling statement due to statement timeout
```

Killing idle in-transaction queries

Sometimes, people start a transaction, run some queries, and then just leave, without ending the transaction. This can leave some system resources in a state where some housekeeping processes can't be run. They may even have done something more serious, such as locking a table, thereby causing immediate *denial of service* for other users who need that table.

You can use the following query to kill all backends that have an open transaction but have been doing nothing for the last 10 minutes:

```
SELECT pg_terminate_backend(pid)
  FROM pg_stat_activity
WHERE state = 'idle in transaction'
   AND current_timestamp - query_start > '10 min';
```

You can even schedule this to run every minute while you are trying to find the specific frontend application that ignores open transactions, or when you have a lazy administration that leaves a psql connection open, or when a flaky network drops clients without the server noticing it.

Killing the backend from the command line

Another way to terminate a backend is by using a Unix/Linux command named `kill N`. This command orders the `SIGTERM` signal to process `N` on the system where it is running. You have to be either the `root` user or the user running the database backends (usually `postgres`) to be able to send signals to processes.

You can cancel a backend (and simulate the `pg_cancel_backend(pid)` function) by sending a `SIGINT` signal:

```
kill -SIGINT <backend_pid>
```

For more detailed information and the exact syntax, type `man kill` from your favorite shell environment.

Detecting an in-doubt prepared transaction

While using **two-phase commit** (**2PC**), you may end up in a situation where you have something locked but cannot find a backend that holds the locks. This recipe describes how to detect such a case.

How to do it...

Perform the following steps:

1. You need to look up the `pg_locks` table for those entries with an empty `pid` value. Run the following query:

   ```
   SELECT t.schemaname || '.' || t.relname AS tablename,
          l.pid, l.granted
          FROM pg_locks l JOIN pg_stat_user_tables t
          ON l.relation = t.relid;
   ```

2. The output will be something similar to the following:

```
tablename |  pid  | granted
-----------+-------+---------
    db.x   |       | t
    db.x   | 27289 | f
(2 rows)
```

The preceding example shows a lock on the db.x table, which has no process associated with it.

If you need to remove a particular prepared transaction, you can refer to the *Removing old prepared transactions* recipe in Chapter 9, *Regular Maintenance*.

Knowing whether anybody is using a specific table

This recipe helps you when you are in doubt about whether an obscure table is being used anymore, or if it has been left over from past use and is just taking up space.

Getting ready

Make sure that you are a superuser, or at least have full rights to the table in question.

How to do it...

Perform the following steps:

1. To see whether a table is currently in active use (that is, whether anyone is using it while you are watching it), run the following query on the database you plan to inspect:

```
CREATE TEMPORARY TABLE tmp_stat_user_tables AS
    SELECT * FROM pg_stat_user_tables;
```

2. Then, wait a little and see what has changed:

```
SELECT * FROM pg_stat_user_tables n
  JOIN tmp_stat_user_tables t
    ON n.relid=t.relid
   AND (n.seq_scan,n.idx_scan,n.n_tup_ins,n.n_tup_upd,n.n_tup_del)
    <> (t.seq_scan,t.idx_scan,t.n_tup_ins,t.n_tup_upd,t.n_tup_del);
```

How it works...

The `pg_stat_user_tables` view shows the current statistics for table usage.

To see whether a table is being used, you can check for changes in its usage counts.

The previous query selects all the tables where any of the usage counts for SELECT or data manipulation have changed.

There's more...

You can use one of the following approaches to detect usage changes.

The quick-and-dirty way

If you are sure that you have no use for the cumulative statistics gathered by PostgreSQL, you can just reset all table statistics by executing the following command:

```
SELECT pg_stat_reset();
```

This sets all statistics to zero, and you can detect table use by just looking for tables where any usage count is not zero.

Of course, you can make a backup copy of the statistics table first, as follows:

```
CREATE TABLE backup_stat_user_tables AS
      SELECT current_timestamp AS snaptime,*
  FROM pg_stat_user_tables;
```

Collecting daily usage statistics

It is often useful to have historical usage statistics for tables when trying to solve performance problems or understand usage patterns.

For this purpose, you can collect usage data in a regular manner, daily or even more often, using either a cron or a PostgreSQL-specific scheduler such as `pg_agent`. Advanced users can take advantage of background workers to schedule such an activity. For more information on background worker processes, go to `http://www.postgresql.org/docs/11/static/bgworker.html`.

The following query adds a snapshot of current usage statistics with a timestamp to the table we created earlier:

```
INSERT INTO backup_stat_user_tables
      SELECT current_timestamp AS snaptime,*
 FROM pg_stat_user_tables;
```

Knowing when a table was last used

Once you know that a table is not currently being used, the next question is, *When was it last used?*

Getting ready

You need to use a user with appropriate privileges.

How to do it...

PostgreSQL does not have any built-in *last used* information about tables, so you have to use other means to figure it out.

If you have set up a cron job to collect usage statistics, as described in the previous chapter, then it is relatively easy to find out the last date of change using a SQL query.

Other than this, there are basically two possibilities, neither of which give you absolutely reliable answers.

You can either look at the actual timestamps of the files in which the data is stored, or you can use the `xmin` and `xmax` system columns to find out the latest transaction ID that changed the table data.

In this recipe, we will cover the first case and focus on the date information in the table's files.

The following PL/pgSQL function looks for the table's data files to get the value of their last access and modification times:

```
CREATE OR REPLACE FUNCTION table_file_access_info(
    IN schemaname text, IN tablename text,
    OUT last_access timestamp with time zone,
    OUT last_change timestamp with time zone
    ) LANGUAGE plpgsql AS $func$
DECLARE
    tabledir text;
    filenode text;
BEGIN
    SELECT regexp_replace(
        current_setting('data_directory') || '/' ||
pg_relation_filepath(c.oid),
            pg_relation_filenode(c.oid) || '$', ''),
        pg_relation_filenode(c.oid)
      INTO tabledir, filenode
      FROM pg_class c
      JOIN pg_namespace ns
        ON c.relnamespace = ns.oid
       AND c.relname = tablename
       AND ns.nspname = schemaname;
    RAISE NOTICE 'tabledir: % - filenode: %', tabledir, filenode;
    -- find latest access and modification times over all segments
    SELECT max((pg_stat_file(tabledir || filename)).access),
           max((pg_stat_file(tabledir || filename)).modification)
      INTO last_access, last_change
      FROM pg_ls_dir(tabledir) AS filename
      -- only use files matching <basefilename>[.segmentnumber]
     WHERE filename ~ ('^' || filenode || '([.]?[0-9]+)?$');
END;
$func$;
```

Here is the sample output:

```
postgres=# select * from table_file_access_info('public','job_status');
NOTICE: tabledir: /Library/PostgreSQL/11/data/base/13329/ - filenode:
169733
        last_access         |        last_change
----------------------------+----------------------------
 2019-04-19 22:42:00+05:30 | 2019-04-19 09:36:40+05:30
```

How it works...

The `table_file_access_info(schemaname, tablename)` function returns the last access and modification times for a given table, using the filesystem as a source of information.

The last query uses this data to get the latest time any of these files were modified or read by PostgreSQL. Beware that this is not a very reliable way to get information about the latest use of any table, but it gives you a rough upper-limit estimate about when it was last modified or read (for example, consider the autovacuum process for accessing a table).

You can definitely improve and personalize the preceding function. I advise that you look at the PostgreSQL documentation and read about two built-in functions, `pg_ls_dir(dirname text)` and `pg_stat_file(filename text)`.

Another good source of information is the *Database File Layout* page in the PostgreSQL documentation at
`http://www.postgresql.org/docs/11/static/storage-file-layout.html`.

There's more...

Recently, there have been discussions about adding last-used data to the information about tables that PostgreSQL keeps, so it is quite possible that answering the question *when did anybody last use this table?* will be much easier in the next version of PostgreSQL.

Usage of disk space by temporary data

In addition to ordinary persistent tables, you can also create temporary tables.

PostgreSQL may use temporary files for query processing if it can't fit all the necessary data into memory.

So, how do you find out how much data is being used by temporary tables and files? You can do this by using any untrusted embedded language, or directly on the database host.

Getting ready

You have to use an untrusted language, because trusted languages run in a sandbox, which prohibits them from directly accessing the host filesystem.

How to do it...

Perform the following steps:

1. First, check whether your database defines special tablespaces for temporary files, as follows:

```
SELECT current_setting('temp_tablespaces');
```

2. As explained later on in this recipe, if the setting is empty, it means that PostgreSQL is not using temporary tablespaces, and temporary objects will be located in the default tablespace for each database.

3. On the other hand, if `temp_tablespaces` has one or more tablespaces, then your task is easy because all temporary files, both those used for temporary tables and those used for query processing, are inside the directories of these tablespaces. The following query (which uses `WITH` queries and string and array functions) demonstrates how to check the space that's being used by temporary tablespaces:

```
WITH temporary_tablespaces AS (SELECT
 unnest(string_to_array(
  current_setting('temp_tablespaces'), ',')
 ) AS temp_tablespace
)
SELECT tt.temp_tablespace,
pg_tablespace_location(t.oid) AS location,

 pg_tablespace_size(t.oid) AS size
FROM temporary_tablespaces tt
JOIN pg_tablespace t ON t.spcname = tt.temp_tablespace
 ORDER BY 1;
```

The output shows very limited use of temporary space (I ran the preceding query while I had two open transactions that had just created small, temporary tables using random data through `generate_series()`):

```
temp_tablespace  |   location    |  size
-----------------+---------------+---------
 pgtemp1         | /srv/pgtemp1  | 3633152
 pgtemp2         | /srv/pgtemp2  |  376832
(2 rows)
```

Even though you can obtain similar results using different queries, or just by checking the disk usage from the filesystem through `du` (once you know the location of tablespaces), I would like to focus on two functions here:

- `pg_tablespace_location(oid)`: This provides the location of the tablespace with the given `oid`
- `pg_tablespace_size(oid)` or `pg_tablespace_size(name)`: This allows you to check the size being used by a named tablespace directly within PostgreSQL

Because the amount of temporary disk space being used can vary a lot in an active system, you may want to repeat the query several times to get a better picture of how the disk usage changes. (With psql, use \watch, as explained in the *Checking whether a user is connected* recipe.)

 Further information on these functions can be found at
http://www.postgresql.org/docs/11/static/functions-admin.html.

On the other hand, if the `temp_tablespaces` setting is empty, then the temporary tables are stored in the same directory as ordinary tables, and the temporary files that are used for query processing are stored in the `pgsql_tmp` directory inside the main database directory.

Look up the cluster's `home` directory using the following query:

```
SELECT current_setting('data_directory') || '/base/pgsql_tmp'
```

The size of this directory gives the total size of current temporary files for query processing.

The total size of temporary files used by a database can be found in the `pg_stat_database` system view, and specifically in the two fields `temp_files` and `temp_bytes`. The following query returns the cumulative number of temporary files and the space being used by every database since the last reset (`stats_reset`):

```
SELECT datname, temp_files, temp_bytes, stats_reset
  FROM pg_stat_database;
```

The `pg_stat_database` view holds very important statistics. I recommend that you look at the official documentation at http://www.postgresql.org/docs/11/static/monitoring-stats.html#PG-STAT-DATABASE -VIEW for detailed information and to get further ideas on how to improve your monitoring skills.

How it works...

Because all temporary tables and other temporary on-disk data are stored in files, you can use PostgreSQL's internal tables to find the locations of these files, and then determine the total size of these files.

There's more...

While the preceding information about temporary tables is correct, it is not the entire story.

Finding out whether a temporary file is in use anymore

Because temporary files are not as carefully preserved as ordinary tables (this is actually one of the benefits of temporary tables, as less bookkeeping makes them faster), it may sometimes happen that a system crash leaves a few temporary files, which can (in the worst case) take up a significant amount of disk space.

As a rule, you can clean up such files by shutting down the PostgreSQL server and then deleting all files from the `pgsql_tmp` directory.

Logging temporary file usage

If you set `log_temp_files = 0` or a larger value, then the creation of all temporary files that are larger than this value in kilobytes is logged to the standard PostgreSQL log.

If, while monitoring the log and the `pg_stat_database` view, you notice an increase in temporary file activity, you should consider increasing `work_mem`, either globally or (preferably) on a query/session basis.

Understanding why queries slow down

In production environments with large databases and high concurrent access, it might happen that queries that used to run in tens of milliseconds suddenly take several seconds.

Likewise, a summary query for a report that used to run in a few seconds might take half an hour to complete.

Here are some ways to find out what is slowing them down.

Getting ready

Any questions of the type *why is this different today from what it was last week?* are much easier to answer if you have some kind of historical data collection setup.

The tools we mentioned in the earlier recipe, *Providing PostgreSQL information,* to monitor tools so that we can monitor general server characteristics, such as CPU and RAM usage, disk I/O, network traffic, and load average, and so on are very useful for seeing what has changed recently, and for trying to correlate these changes with the observed performance of some database operations.

Also, collecting historical statistics data from `pg_stat_*` tables, whether daily, hourly, or even every five minutes if you have enough disk space, is also very useful for detecting possible causes of sudden changes or a gradual degradation in performance.

If you are gathering both of these, then that's even better. If you have none, then the question is actually: *Why is this query slow?*

But don't despair! There are a few things you can do to try to restore performance.

How to do it...

First, analyze your database using the following code:

```
db_01=# analyse;
ANALYZE
Time: 6231.313 ms
db_01=#
```

This is the first thing to try, as it is usually cheap and is meant to be done quite often anyway.

If this restores the query's performance or at least improves the current performance considerably, then it means that autovacuum is not doing its task well, and the next thing to do is find out why.

You must ensure that the performance improvement is not due to caching of the pages required by the requested query. Make sure that you repeat your query several times before classifying it as slow. Looking at `pg_stat_statements` (which is covered later in this chapter) can help you analyze the impact of a particular query in terms of caching, and is done by inspecting two fields: `shared_blks_hit` and `shared_blks_read`.

How it works...

The `ANALYZE` command updates statistics about data size and data distribution in all tables. If a table size has changed significantly without its statistics being updated, then PostgreSQL's statistics-based optimizer may choose a bad plan. Manually running the `ANALYZE` command updates the statistics for all tables.

There's more...

There are a few other common problems.

Do queries return significantly more data than they did earlier?

If you've initially tested your queries on almost empty tables, it is entirely possible that you are querying much more data than you need.

As an example, if you select all users' items and then show the first 10 items, this query runs very fast when the user has 10 or even 50 items, but not so well when they have 50,000.

Ensure that you don't ask for more data than you need. Use the `LIMIT` clause to return less data to your application (and to give the optimizer at least a chance to select a plan that processes less data when selecting: it may also have a lower startup cost). In some cases, you can evaluate the use of cursors for your applications.

Do queries also run slowly when they run alone?

If you can, then try to run the same slow query when the database has no (or very few) other queries running concurrently. If it runs well in this situation, then it may be that the database host is just overloaded (CPU, memory, or disk I/O) or other applications are interfering with PostgreSQL on the same server. Consequently, a plan that works well under a light load is not very good any more. It may even be that this is not a very good query plan with which to begin, and you were fooled by modern computers being really fast:

```
db=# select count(*) from t;
  count
---------
 1000000
(1 row)
Time: 329.743 ms
```

As you can see, scanning 1 million rows takes just 0.3 seconds on a laptop that is a few years old if these rows are already cached.

However, if you have a few such queries running in parallel, and also other queries competing for memory, this query is likely to slow down an order of magnitude or two.

See `Chapter 10`, *Performance and Concurrency*, for general advice on performance tuning.

Is the second run of the same query also slow?

This test is related to the previous test, and it checks whether the slowdown is caused by some of the necessary data not fitting into the memory or being pushed out of the memory by other queries.

If the second run of the query is fast, then you probably lack enough memory. Again, see `Chapter 10`, *Performance and Concurrency*, for details about this.

Table and index bloat

Table bloat is something that can develop over time if some maintenance processes can't be run properly. In other words, due to the way **Multiversion Concurrency Control** (**MVCC**) works, your table will contain a lot of older versions of rows, if these versions can't be removed in a timely manner.

There are several ways this can develop, but all involve lots of updates or deletes and inserts, while autovacuum is prevented from doing its job of getting rid of old tuples. It is possible that, even after the old versions are deleted, the table stays at its newly acquired and large size, thanks to visible rows being located at the end of the table and preventing PostgreSQL from shrinking the file. There have been cases where a one-row table has grown to several gigabytes in size.

If you suspect that some tables may contain bloat, then run the following query:

```
SELECT pg_relation_size(relid) AS tablesize,schemaname,relname,n_live_tup
FROM pg_stat_user_tables
WHERE relname = <tablename>;
```

Then, see whether the relation of `tablesize` to `n_live_tup` makes sense.

For example, if the table size is tens of megabytes, and there are only a small number of rows, then you have bloat, and proper VACUUM strategies are necessary (as explained in `Chapter 9`, *Regular Maintenance*).

It is important to check that the statistics are up-to-date. You might indeed need to run ANALYSE on the table and run the query again.

See also

- The *Collecting daily usage statistics* section shows one way to collect information on table changes
- `Chapter 9`, *Regular Maintenance*
- `Chapter 10`, *Performance and Concurrency*
- The *How many rows in a table?* recipe in `Chapter 2`, *Exploring the Database*, for an introduction to MVCC
- The `auto_explain` contrib module, at http://www.postgresql.org/docs/11/static/auto-explain.html

Investigating and reporting a bug

When you find out that PostgreSQL is not doing what it should, then it's time to investigate.

Getting ready

It is a good idea to make a full copy of your PostgreSQL installation before you start investigating. This will help you restart several times and be sure that you are actually investigating the results of the bug, and not chasing your own tail by looking at changes that were introduced by your last investigation and debugging attempt.

Do not forget to include your tablespaces in the full copy.

How to do it...

Try to make a minimal repeatable test scenario that exhibits this bug. Sometimes, the bug disappears while doing this, but mostly it is needed to make the process easy. It is almost impossible to fix a bug that you can't observe and repeat at will.

If it is about query processing, then you can usually provide a minimal dump file (the result of running `pg_dump`) of your database, together with a SQL script that exhibits the error.

If you have corrupt data, then you may want to make a subset of the corrupted data files available for people who have the knowledge and time to look at it. Sometimes, you can find such people on the PostgreSQL hackers' list, and sometimes you have to hire someone or even fix it yourself. The more preparatory work you do yourself and the better you formulate your questions, the higher the chance you have of finding help quickly.

If you suspect a data corruption bug and feel adventurous, then you can read about data formats at `http://www.postgresql.org/docs/current/static/storage.html`, and investigate your data tables using the `pageinspect` package from contrib.

When reporting a bug, always include at least the PostgreSQL version you are using and the operating system on which you are using it.

More detailed information on this process is available at the PostgreSQL wiki. By following the official recommendations at
`http://wiki.postgresql.org/wiki/Guide_to_reporting_problems` and
`http://wiki.postgresql.org/wiki/SlowQueryQuestions`, you will have a higher chance of getting your questions answered.

How it works...

If everything works really well, then it goes as follows:

- A user submits a well-researched bug report to the PostgreSQL hackers' list.
- Some discussions follow on the list, and the user may be asked to provide some additional information.
- Somebody finds out what is wrong and proposes a fix.
- The fix is discussed on the hackers' list.
- The bug is fixed. There is a patch for the current version, and the fix is sure to be included in the next version.
- Sometimes, the fix is backported to older versions.

Unfortunately, any step may go wrong due to various reasons, such as nobody feeling that this is their area of expertise, the right people not having time and hoping for someone else to deal with it, and these other people not reading the list at the right moment.

If this happens, follow up your question in a day or two to try and understand why there was no reaction.

Producing a daily summary of log file errors

PostgreSQL can generate gigabytes of logs per day. Lots of data is good if you want to investigate a specific event, but it is not what you will use for daily monitoring of database health.

In this recipe, we'll look at how to perform a post analysis of our log files and get reports (and insights) about what has happened in a given period of time.

A different approach is to perform real-time analysis of queries through the `pg_stat_statements` extension, which will be covered in the next recipe.

Getting ready

Make sure that your PostgreSQL is set up to rotate log files, for example, daily. I personally prefer to integrate PostgreSQL with `rsyslog` and `logrotate` for log management on Linux or Unix systems, but you can use any method that is allowed by PostgreSQL (CSV or standard error, for example).

A typical default setup will divert log messages to `stderr`, and you can set up log rotation directly in PostgreSQL through the `log_rotation_age` configuration option.

Once you have your logs ready, it is time to feed them to a PostgreSQL log-processing program. Here, we will describe how to do so using pgBadger, a multi-platform application written in Perl that has recently become more popular than its famous predecessor, **pgFouine**.

Some of the cool features of pgBadger include multi-file processing, parallel processing, auto-detection of the input format, on-the-fly decompression, as well as very light HTML reports with JavaScript-generated charts (that have zooming capabilities), as shown here:

The following screenshot shows the report of time-consuming queries with pgBadger:

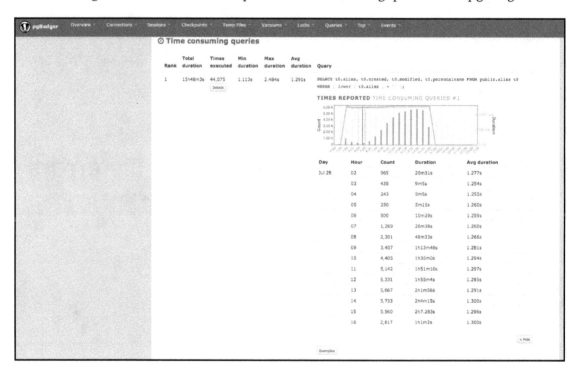

For most Linux systems, you should be able to use your default package manager to install pgBadger. Otherwise, you can simply download its sources.

Configure your PostgreSQL server to produce log files in a format that `pgBadger` understands. Everything is thoroughly described in the online documentation for pgBadger at `https://pgbadger.darold.net/`.

Suppose you are using `syslog` and you want to exclude queries that take less than a second to be executed. You can have a logging configuration of your PostgreSQL server similar to this:

```
log_destination = syslog
syslog_facility = LOCAL0
syslog_ident = 'postgres'
log_line_prefix = 'user=%u,db=%d,client=%h '
log_temp_files = 0
log_statement = ddl
log_min_duration_statement = 1000
log_min_messages = info
log_checkpoints = on
log_lock_waits = on
```

The documentation for pgBadger is a great source of information regarding PostgreSQL configuration in terms of logging. You are advised to read that together with the *Error Reporting and Logging* section of the Postgres documentation, which is available at `http://www.postgresql.org/docs/11/static/runtime-config-logging.html`.

How to do it...

Set up a cron job to run regularly (for example, once every hour, day, or week) and let pgBadger analyze one or more log files. Here, you can find a very simple example that can be used to prepare daily reports every hour.

For the sake of simplicity, the script has been purged of any error checks. Production usage requires the addition of some basic shell controls:

```
#!/bin/bash
outdir=/var/www/reports
begin=$(date +'%Y-%m-%d %H:00:00' -d '-1 day')
end=$(date +'%Y-%m-%d %H:00:00')
outfile="$outdir/daily-$(date +'%H').html"

pgbadger -q -b "$begin" -e "$end" -o "$outfile" \
    /var/log/postgres.log.1 /var/log/postgres.log
```

The preceding script informs `pgbadger` to analyze the current log file (`/var/log/postgresql.log`) and the previously rotated file (`/var/log/postgres.log.1`), to limit the reporting activity to the last 24 hours (see how the `date` command was used to generate timestamps), and then write the output to the `$outfile` HTML file.

Once again, this is just a very simple use case for pgBadger. I strongly advise that you look at the documentation and investigate all the options and possibilities that pgBadger offers.

I want to end this recipe with a practical idea that you can explore with your system administrators. You might have noticed that the output directory has been set as a common default `DocumentRoot` for Apache servers (`/var/www`).

A very practical way to use pgBadger is to integrate it with a web server.

Production environments may benefit from SSL encryption, basic authentication, and the `mod_dir` module, which allows you to make your reports automatically available through the internet (or your intranet).

How it works...

The pgBadger tool condenses and ranks error messages for easy viewing, and produces a nicely formatted report in HTML. From that report, you can find out the most frequent errors.

As a rule, it is good practice not to tolerate errors in database logs if you can avoid them. Once the errors start showing up in the log and report, you should find their cause and fix them.

While it is tempting to leave the errors there and consider them as just a small nuisance because *they do no harm*, simple errors are often an indication of other problems in the application. These problems, if not found and understood, may lead to all kinds of larger problems, such as security breaches or eventual data corruption at the logical level.

Also, if you normally have lots of recurring error messages, you might not notice an important error when it occurs for the first time.

There's more...

If you have only a small number of errors in your log files, then it may be sufficient to run each log file through grep to find errors:

```
user@dbhost: $ egrep "FATAL|ERROR" /var/log/postgres.log
```

Analyzing the real-time performance of your queries

The `pg_stat_statements` extension adds the capability to track execution statistics of queries that are run in a database, including the number of calls, total execution time, total number of returned rows, and internal information on memory and I/O access.

It is evident how this approach opens up new opportunities in PostgreSQL performance analysis by allowing DBAs to get insights directly from the database through SQL and in real time.

Getting ready

The `pg_stat_statements` module is available as a contrib module of PostgreSQL. The extension must be installed as a superuser in the desired databases. It also requires administrators to add the library in the `postgresql.conf` file, as follows:

```
shared_preload_libraries = 'pg_stat_statements'
```

This change requires restarting the PostgreSQL server.

Finally, in order to use it, the extension must be installed in the desired database through the usual CREATE EXTENSION command (run as a superuser):

```
gabriele=# CREATE EXTENSION pg_stat_statements;
CREATE EXTENSION
```

How to do it...

Connect to a database where you have installed the `pg_stat_statements` extension, preferably as a superuser.

You can start by retrieving a list of the most frequent queries:

```
SELECT query FROM pg_stat_statements ORDER BY calls DESC;
```

Alternatively, you can retrieve the queries with the highest average execution time:

```
SELECT query, total_time/calls AS avg, calls
     FROM pg_stat_statements ORDER BY 2 DESC;
```

These are just examples. I strongly recommend that you look at the PostgreSQL documentation at http://www.postgresql.org/docs/44/static/pgstatstatements.html for more detailed information on the structure of the pg_stat_statements view.

How it works...

Since the pg_stat_statements shared library has been loaded by the PostgreSQL server, Postgres starts collecting statistics for every database in the instance.

The extension simply installs the pg_stat_statements view and the pg_stat_statements_reset() function in the current database, allowing the DBA to inspect the available statistics.

By default, read access to the pg_stat_statements view is granted to every user who can access the database (even though standard users are only allowed to see the SQL statements of their queries).

The pg_stat_statements_reset() function can be used to discard the statistics collected by the server up to that moment, and set all the counters to 0. It requires a superuser in order to be run.

There's more...

A very important pg_stat_statements feature is the normalization of queries that can be planned (SELECT, INSERT, DELETE, and UPDATE). You might have indeed noticed some ? characters in the query field being returned by the queries we outlined in the previous section. The normalization process intercepts constants in SQL statements run by users and replaces them with a placeholder (identified by a question mark).

Consider the following queries:

```
SELECT * FROM bands WHERE name = 'AC/DC';
SELECT * FROM bands WHERE name = 'Lynyrd Skynyrd';
```

After the normalization process, these two queries appear as one in `pg_stat_statements`:

```
gabriele=# SELECT query, calls FROM pg_stat_statements;
                query                 | calls
--------------------------------------+-------
 SELECT * FROM bands WHERE name = ?;  |     2
&mldr; <snip> &mldr;
```

This is the expected behavior, isn't it?

The extension comes with a few configuration options, such the maximum number of queries to be tracked.

Regular Maintenance

9

In these busy times, many people believe: *if it ain't broken, don't fix it*. I believe that too, but it isn't an excuse for not taking action to maintain your database servers and be sure that nothing will break.

Database maintenance is about making your database run smoothly.

PostgreSQL prefers regular maintenance, so please read the *Planning maintenance* recipe for more information.

We recognize that you're here for a reason and are looking for a quick solution to your needs. You're probably thinking—*Fix me first, and I'll plan later*. So, off we go!

PostgreSQL provides a utility command named VACUUM, which is a jokey name for a garbage collector that sweeps up all of the bad things and fixes them—or at least, most of them. That's the single most important thing you need to remember to do—I say *single* because closely connected to that is the ANALYZE command, which collects optimizer statistics. It's possible to run VACUUM and ANALYZE as a single joint command, VACUUM ANALYZE, and those actions are automatically executed for you when appropriate by autovacuum, a special background process that runs as part of the PostgreSQL server.

VACUUM performs a range of cleanup activities, some of them too complex to describe without a whole sideline into their internals. VACUUM has been heavily optimized over a 30-year period to take the minimum required lock levels on tables and execute them in the most efficient manner possible, skipping all of the unnecessary work and using L2 cache CPU optimizations when work is required.

Many experienced PostgreSQL DBAs will prefer to execute their own VACUUM commands, though autovacuum now provides a fine degree of control, which—if enabled and controlled—can save much of your time. Using both manual and automatic vacuuming gives you control and a safety net.

In this chapter, we will cover the following recipes:

- Controlling automatic database maintenance
- Avoiding auto-freezing and page corruptions
- Removing issues that cause bloat
- Removing old prepared transactions
- Actions for heavy users of temporary tables
- Identifying and fixing bloated tables and indexes
- Monitoring and tuning a vacuum
- Maintaining indexes
- Adding a constraint without checking existing rows
- Finding unused indexes
- Carefully removing unwanted indexes
- Planning maintenance

Controlling automatic database maintenance

Autovacuum is enabled by default in PostgreSQL and mostly does a great job of maintaining your PostgreSQL database. We say mostly because it doesn't know everything you do about the database, such as the best time to perform maintenance actions. Let's explore the settings that can be tuned so that you can use vacuums efficiently.

Getting ready

Exercising control requires some thinking about what you actually want:

- What are the best times of day to do things? When are system resources more available?
- Which days are quiet, and which are not?
- Which tables are critical to the application, and which are not?

How to do it...

Perform the following steps:

- The first thing to do is make sure that `autovacuum` is switched `on`, which is the default. Check that you have the following parameters enabled in your `postgresql.conf` file:

  ```
  autovacuum = on
  track_counts = on
  ```

- PostgreSQL controls `autovacuum` with more than 40 individually tunable parameters that provide a wide range of options, though it can be a little daunting. The following are the relevant parameters that can be set in `postgresql.conf` to tune the `VACUUM` command:

  ```
  vacuum_cleanup_index_scale_factor
  vacuum_cost_delay
  vacuum_cost_limit
  vacuum_cost_page_dirty
  vacuum_cost_page_hit
  vacuum_cost_page_miss
  vacuum_defer_cleanup_age
  vacuum_freeze_min_age
  vacuum_freeze_table_age
  vacuum_multixact_freeze_min_age
  vacuum_multixact_freeze_table_age
  ```

- There are also parameters that apply specifically to the `autovacuum` process:

  ```
  autovacuum
  autovacuum_analyze_scale_factor
  autovacuum_analyze_threshold
  autovacuum_freeze_max_age
  autovacuum_max_workers
  autovacuum_multixact_freeze_max_age
  autovacuum_naptime
  autovacuum_vacuum_cost_delay
  autovacuum_vacuum_cost_limit
  autovacuum_vacuum_scale_factor
  autovacuum_vacuum_threshold
  autovacuum_work_mem
  log_autovacuum_min_duration
  ```

- The preceding parameters apply to all tables at once. Individual tables can be controlled by storage parameters, which are set using the following command:

```
ALTER TABLE mytable SET (storage_parameter = value);
```

- The storage parameters that relate to maintenance are as follows:

```
autovacuum_enabled
autovacuum_vacuum_cost_delay
autovacuum_vacuum_cost_limit
autovacuum_vacuum_scale_factor
autovacuum_vacuum_threshold
autovacuum_freeze_min_age
autovacuum_freeze_max_age
autovacuum_freeze_table_age
autovacuum_multixact_freeze_min_age
autovacuum_multixact_freeze_max_age
autovacuum_multixact_freeze_table_age
autovacuum_analyze_scale_factor
autovacuum_analyze_threshold
log_autovacuum_min_duration
```

- The `toast` tables can be controlled with the following parameters:

```
toast.autovacuum_enabled
toast.autovacuum_vacuum_cost_delay
toast.autovacuum_vacuum_cost_limit
toast.autovacuum_vacuum_scale_factor
toast.autovacuum_vacuum_threshold
toast.autovacuum_freeze_min_age
toast.autovacuum_freeze_max_age
toast.autovacuum_freeze_table_age
toast.autovacuum_multixact_freeze_min_age
toast.autovacuum_multixact_freeze_max_age
toast.autovacuum_multixact_freeze_table_age
toast.log_autovacuum_min_duration
```

How it works...

If `autovacuum` is set, then it will wake up every `autovacuum_naptime` seconds, and decide whether to run VACUUM, ANALYZE, or both (don't modify that).

There will never be more than `autovacuum_max_workers` maintenance processes running at any time. As these autovacuum workers perform I/O, they accumulate cost points until they hit the `autovacuum_vacuum_cost_limit` value, after which they sleep for an `autovacuum_vacuum_cost_delay` period of time. This is designed to throttle the resource utilization of autovacuum to prevent it from using all of the available disk performance, which it should never do. So, increasing `autovacuum_vacuum_cost_delay` will slow down each VACUUM to reduce the impact on user activity. Autovacuum will run ANALYZE when there have been at least `autovacuum_analyze_threshold` changes and a fraction of the table defined by `autovacuum_analyze_scale_factor` has been inserted, updated, or deleted.

Autovacuum will run VACUUM when there have been at least `autovacuum_vacuum_threshold` changes, and a fraction of the table defined by `autovacuum_vacuum_scale_factor` has been updated or deleted.

The `autovacuum_*` parameters only change vacuums and analyze operations that are executed by autovacuum. User initiated VACUUM and ANALYZE commands are affected by `vacuum_cost_delay` and other `vacuum_*` parameters.

If you set `log_autovacuum_min_duration`, then any autovacuum process that runs for longer than this value will be logged to the server log, like so:

```
2019-04-19 01:33:55 BST (13130) LOG:   automatic vacuum of table
"postgres.public.pgbench_accounts": index scans: 1
     pages: 0 removed, 3279 remain
     tuples: 100000 removed, 100000 remain
     system usage: CPU 0.19s/0.36u sec elapsed 19.01 sec
2019-04-19 01:33:59 BST (13130) LOG:   automatic analyze of table
"postgres.public.pgbench_accounts"
     system usage: CPU 0.06s/0.18u sec elapsed 3.66 sec
```

Most of the preceding global parameters can also be set at the table level. For example, if you think that you don't want a table to be autovacuumed, then you can set the following:

```
ALTER TABLE big_table SET (autovacuum_enabled = off);
```

It's also possible to set parameters for `toast` tables. A `toast` table is the location where the oversized column values get placed, which the documents refer to as *supplementary storage tables*. If there are no oversized values, then the `toast` table will occupy little space. Tables with very wide values often have large `toast` tables. **TOAST** (short for **The Oversized Attribute Storage Technique**) is optimized for UPDATE.

If you have a heavily updated table, the `toast` table is untouched, so it may make sense to turn off autovacuuming for the `toast` table, as follows:

```
ALTER TABLE pgbench_accounts
SET ( toast.autovacuum_enabled = off);
```

 Note that autovacuuming of the `toast` table is performed completely separately from the main table, even though you can't ask for an explicit include or exclude of the `toast` table yourself when running VACUUM.

Use the following query to display the `reloptions` for tables and their `toast` tables:

```
postgres=#
SELECT n.nspname
, c.relname
, array_to_string(
    c.reloptions ||
ARRAY(
SELECT 'toast.' || x
FROM unnest(tc.reloptions) AS x
), ', ')
AS relopts
FROM pg_class c
LEFT JOIN pg_class tc    ON c.reltoastrelid = tc.oid
JOIN pg_namespace n ON c.relnamespace  = n.oid
WHERE c.relkind = 'r'
AND nspname NOT IN ('pg_catalog', 'information_schema');
```

This query gives the following output:

```
nspname |      relname       |      relopts
--------+--------------------+------------------------------
public  | pgbench_accounts   | fillfactor=100,
                               autovacuum_enabled=on,
                               autovacuum_vacuum_cost_delay=20
public  | pgbench_tellers    | fillfactor=100
public  | pgbench_branches   | fillfactor=100
public  | pgbench_history    |
public  | text_archive       | toast.autovacuum_enabled=off
```

VACUUM allows insertions, updates, and deletions while it runs, but it prevents actions such as ALTER TABLE and CREATE INDEX. Autovacuum can detect whether a user has requested a conflicting lock on the table while it runs, and it will cancel itself if it is getting in the user's way. VACUUM doesn't cancel itself since we expect that the DBA would not want it to be canceled.

Note that VACUUM does not shrink a table when it runs, unless there is a large run of space at the end of a table, and nobody is accessing the table when we try to shrink it. To shrink a table properly, you'll need VACUUM FULL, but it locks up the whole table for a long time, and should be avoided if possible. The VACUUM FULL command will literally rewrite every row of the table and completely rebuild all indexes. This process is faster than it used to be, though it still takes a long time for larger tables.

There's more...

The postgresql.conf file also allows include directives, which look like the following:

```
include 'autovacuum.conf'
```

These specify another file that will be read at that point, just as if those parameters had been included in the main file.

This can be used to maintain multiple sets of files for the autovacuum configuration. Let's say we have a website that is busy mainly during the daytime, with some occasional nighttime use. We decide to have two profiles, one for daytime, when we want less aggressive autovacuuming, and another at night, where we can allow more aggressive vacuuming:

1. You need to add the following lines to postgresql.conf:

```
autovacuum = on
autovacuum_max_workers = 3
include 'autovacuum.conf'
```

2. Remove all other autovacuum parameters.
3. Then, create a file named autovacuum.conf.day that contains the following parameters:

```
autovacuum_analyze_scale_factor = 0.1
autovacuum_analyze_threshold = 50
autovacuum_vacuum_cost_delay = 30
autovacuum_vacuum_cost_limit = -1
autovacuum_vacuum_scale_factor = 0.2
autovacuum_vacuum_threshold = 50
```

4. Then, create another file, named autovacuum.conf.night, that contains the following parameters:

```
autovacuum_analyze_scale_factor = 0.05
autovacuum_analyze_threshold = 50
```

```
autovacuum_vacuum_cost_delay = 10
autovacuum_vacuum_cost_limit = -1
autovacuum_vacuum_scale_factor = 0.1
autovacuum_vacuum_threshold = 50
```

5. To swap profiles, simply do the following:

```
$ ln -sf autovacuum.conf.night autovacuum.conf
$ pg_ctl reload
```

The latter is the command to reload the server configuration, and it must be customized depending on your platform.

This then allows us to switch profiles twice per day without needing to edit the configuration files. You can also easily tell which is the active profile simply by looking at the full details of the linked file (using `ls -l`). The exact details of the schedule are up to you. Night and day was just an example, which is unlikely to suit everybody.

See also

The `autovacuum_freeze_max_age` parameter is explained in the next recipe, *Avoiding auto-freezing and page corruptions*, as are the more complex table-level parameters.

Avoiding auto-freezing and page corruptions

There are some aspects of VACUUM whose reason for existence is complex to explain, and occasionally they have negative behaviors. Let's look at these in more details and find some solutions to them.

PostgreSQL uses internal transaction identifiers that are 4 bytes long, so we only have 2^{32} transaction IDs (about four billion). PostgreSQL starts again from the beginning when that wraps around, allocating new identifiers in a circular manner. The reason we do this is that moving to an 8-byte identifier has various other negative effects and costs that we would rather not pay, so we keep the 4-byte transaction identifier, which means we need to do regular sweeps to replace old transaction identifiers with a special value that is not interpreted in a circular way, which is called **frozen transaction ID**; that's why this procedure is known as **freezing**.

How to do it...

There are two routes that a row can take in PostgreSQL—a row version dies and needs to be removed by VACUUM, or a row version gets old enough and needs to be frozen, which is also performed by the VACUUM process.

Why do we care? Suppose that we load a table with 100 million rows, and everything is fine. When those rows have been there long enough to begin being frozen, the next VACUUM operation on that table will rewrite all of them to freeze their transaction identifiers. Put another way, autovacuum will wake up and start using lots of I/O to perform the freezing.

The most obvious way to forestall this problem is to explicitly vacuum a table after a major load. Of course, that doesn't remove the problem entirely, and you might not have time for that.

The knee-jerk reaction for many people is to turn off autovacuum, because it keeps waking up at the most inconvenient times. My way is described in the *Controlling automatic database maintenance* recipe.

Freezing takes place when a transaction identifier on a row becomes more than vacuum_freeze_min_age transactions older than the current next value. Normal VACUUM operations will perform a small amount of freezing as you go, and in most cases, you won't notice that at all. As explained in the previous example, large transactions leave many rows with the same transaction identifiers, so those might cause problems at the freezing time.

The VACUUM command is normally optimized to only look at the chunks of a table that require cleaning, both for normal vacuum and freezing operations.

If you fiddle with those parameters to try to forestall heavy VACUUM operations, then you'll notice that the autovacuum_freeze_max_age parameter controls when the table will be scanned by a forced VACUUM command. To put that another way, you can't turn off the need to freeze rows, but you can get to choose when this happens. My advice is to control autovacuum as we described in the previous recipe or perform explicit VACUUM operations at a time of your choosing.

The VACUUM command is also an efficient way to confirm the absence of page corruptions, so it is worth scanning the whole database, block-by-block, from time to time. To do this, you can run the following command on each of your databases:

```
VACUUM (DISABLE_PAGE_SKIPPING);
```

You can do this table by table, as well. There's nothing special about whole database VACUUM operations anymore; in earlier versions of PostgreSQL, this was important, so you may read that this is a good idea on the web.

If you've never had a corrupt block, then you may only need to scan every two to three months. If you start to get corrupt blocks, then you may want to increase the scan rate to confirm that everything is OK. Corrupt blocks are usually hardware induced, though they show up as database errors. It's possible but rare that the corruption was from a PostgreSQL bug instead.

There's no easy way to fix page corruptions at present. There are, however, ways to investigate and extract data from corrupt blocks, for example, by using the pageinspect contrib utility that Simon wrote. You can also detect them automatically by creating the whole cluster using the following code:

```
initdb --data-checksums
```

This command initializes the data directory and enables data block checksums. This means that, every time something changes in a block, PostgreSQL will compute the new checksum, and then store the resulting block checksums in that same block so that a simple program can detect it.

Removing issues that cause bloat

Bloat can be caused by long-running queries or long-running write transactions that execute alongside write-heavy workloads. Resolving that is mostly down to understanding the workloads running on the server.

Getting ready

Look at the age of the oldest snapshots that are running, like this:

```
postgres=# SELECT now() -
  CASE
  WHEN backend_xid IS NOT NULL
  THEN xact_start
  ELSE query_start END
  AS age
, pid
, backend_xid AS xid
, backend_xmin AS xmin
, state
```

```
FROM  pg_stat_activity
WHERE backend_type = 'client backend'
ORDER BY 1 DESC;
age               |  pid  |   xid    |   xmin    |        state
------------------+-------+----------+-----------+--------------------
00:00:25.791098 | 27624 |          | 10671262 | active
00:00:08.018103 | 27591 |          |          | idle in transaction
00:00:00.002444 | 27630 | 10703641 | 10703639 | active
00:00:00.001506 | 27631 | 10703642 | 10703640 | active
00:00:00.000324 | 27632 | 10703643 | 10703641 | active
00:00:00         | 27379 |          | 10703641 | active
```

The preceding example shows an updated workload of three sessions alongside one session that is waiting in an *idle in transaction* state, plus two other sessions that are only reading data.

How to do it...

If you have sessions stuck in idle in transaction state, then you may want to consider setting the `idle_in_transaction_session_timeout` parameter so that transactions in that mode will be canceled. The default for that is zero, meaning there will be no cancellation.

If not, try running shorter transactions or shorter queries.

If that is not an option, then consider setting `old_snapshot_threshold`. This parameter sets a time delay, after which dead rows are at risk of being removed. If a query attempts to read data that has been removed, then we cancel the query. All queries executing in less time than the `old_snapshot_threshold` parameter will be safe. This is a very similar concept to the way *Hot Standby* works (see `Chapter 12`, *Replication and Upgrades*).

How it works...

VACUUM cannot remove dead rows until they are invisible to all users. The earliest data that's visible to a session is defined by its oldest snapshot's `xmin` value, or if that is not set, then by the backend's `xid` value.

There's more...

A session that is not running any query is in the *idle* state if it's outside of a transaction, or in the *idle in transaction* state if it's inside a transaction, that is, between a BEGIN and the corresponding COMMIT. Recall the *Writing a script that either succeeds entirely or fails entirely* recipe in Chapter 7, *Database Administration*, which was about how BEGIN and COMMIT can be used to wrap several commands into one transaction.

The reason to distinguish between these two states is that locks are released at the end of a transaction. Hence, an *idle in transaction* session is not currently doing anything, but it might be preventing other queries, including VACUUM, from accessing some tables.

Removing old prepared transactions

You may have been routed here from other recipes, so you might not even know what prepared transactions are, let alone what an old prepared transaction looks like.

The good news is that prepared transactions don't just happen; they happen in certain situations. If you don't know what I'm talking about, it's OK! You won't need to, and better still, you probably don't have any prepared transactions either.

Prepared transactions are part of the two-phase commit feature, also known as **2PC**. A transaction commits in two stages rather than one, allowing multiple databases to have synchronized commits. Its typical use is to combine multiple so-called resource managers using the **XA** protocol, which is usually provided by a **Transaction Manager** (**TM**), as used by the **Java Transaction API** (**JTA**) and others. If none of this means anything to you, then you probably don't have any prepared transactions.

Getting ready

First, check the setting of max_prepared_transactions:

```
SHOW max_prepared_transactions;
```

If your setting is more than zero, then check whether you have any prepared transactions. As an example, you may find something like the following:

```
postgres=# SELECT * FROM pg_prepared_xacts;
-[ RECORD 1 ]---------------------------------
transaction | 459812
gid         | prep1
```

```
prepared    | 2017-04-11   13:21:51.912374+01
owner       | postgres
database    | postgres
```

Here, `gid` (global identifier) will usually be automatically generated.

How to do it...

Removing a prepared transaction is also referred to as *resolving in-doubt transactions*. The transaction is literally stuck between committing and aborting. The database or transaction manager may have crashed, leaving the transaction midway through the two-phase commit process.

If you have a connection pool of 100 active connections and something crashes, you'll probably find 1 to 20 transactions stuck in the prepared state, depending on how long your average transaction is.

To resolve the transaction, we need to decide whether we want that change or not. The best way is to check what happened externally to PostgreSQL. That should help you to decide.

If you need further help, look at the *There's more...* section for this recipe.

If you wish to commit these changes, then use the following command:

```
COMMIT PREPARED 'prep1';
```

If you want to roll back the changes, then use the following command:

```
ROLLBACK PREPARED 'prep1';
```

How it works...

Prepared transactions are persistent across crashes, so you can't just do a fast restart to get rid of them. They have both an internal transaction identifier and an external global identifier. Either of these can be used to locate locked resources and decide how to resolve the transactions.

There's more...

If you're not sure what the prepared transaction actually did, you can go and look, but this is time-consuming. The `pg_locks` view shows locks that are held by prepared transactions. You can get a full report of what is being locked by using the following query:

```
postgres=# SELECT l.locktype, x.database, l.relation, l.page,
l.tuple,l.classid, l.objid, l.objsubid, l.mode, x.transaction, x.gid,
x.prepared, x.owner
FROM pg_locks l JOIN pg_prepared_xacts x ON l.virtualtransaction = '-1/' ||
x.transaction::text;
```

The documents mention that you can join `pg_locks` to `pg_prepared_xacts`, but they don't mention that, if you join directly on the transaction ID, all it tells you is that there is a transaction lock unless there are some row-level locks. The table locks are listed as being held by a virtual transaction. A simpler query is the following:

```
postgres=# SELECT DISTINCT x.database, l.relation FROM pg_locks l JOIN
pg_prepared_xacts x ON l.virtualtransaction = '-1/' || x.transaction::text
WHERE l.locktype != 'transactionid';
database | relation
---------+----------
postgres |    16390
postgres |    16401
 (2 rows)
```

This tells you which relations in which databases have been touched by the remaining prepared transactions. We don't know their names because we'd need to connect to those databases to check.

Finally, we can inspect which rows have been changed by the transaction. We will use `xmin`, which is a hidden column in each table. For more details on that, refer to the *Identifying and fixing bloated tables and indexes* recipe in this chapter.

You can then fully scan each of those tables and look for changes like the following:

```
SELECT * FROM table WHERE xmax = 121083;
```

This query will show you all of the rows in that table that will be deleted or updated by transaction `121083`, which has been taken from the transaction column of `pg_prepared_xacts`.

Not all rows touched by the transaction can be displayed, however. Newly inserted rows and new versions of updated rows will not be accessible in this way, for the very good reason that they must be invisible before the transaction is committed.

As you might expect, the PostgreSQL developers did their homework properly. Say that you have some prepared transactions and you change `max_prepared_transactions` to zero, which requires a restart to come into effect. No prepared transaction will sneak into your database unnoticed. When starting, PostgreSQL will try to recover every prepared transaction and refuse to start unless `max_prepared_transactions` is large enough.

Actions for heavy users of temporary tables

If you are a heavy user of temporary tables in your applications, then there are some additional actions that you may need to perform.

How to do it...

There are four main things to check, which are as follows:

- Make sure you run VACUUM on system tables or enable autovacuum to do this for you.
- Monitor running queries to see how many temporary files are active and how large they are.
- Tune the memory parameters. Think about increasing the `temp_buffers` parameter, but be careful not to over-allocate memory by doing so.
- Separate the `temp` table's I/O. In a query-intensive system, you may find that reads/writes to temporary files exceed reads/writes on permanent data tables and indexes. In this case, you should create new tablespace(s) on separate disks, and ensure that the `temp_tablespaces` parameter is configured to use the additional tablespace(s).

How it works...

When we create a temporary table, we insert entries into the `pg_class`, `pg_type`, and `pg_attribute` catalog tables. These catalog tables and their indexes begin to grow and bloat—an issue that will be covered in further recipes. To control that growth, you can either vacuum those tables manually or let `autovacuum` do its work. You cannot run `ALTER TABLE` against system tables, so it is not possible to set specific `autovacuum` settings for any of these tables.

If you vacuum the system catalog tables manually, make sure that you get all of the system tables. You can get the full list of tables to vacuum and a list of their indexes by using the following query:

```
postgres=# SELECT relname, pg_relation_size(oid) FROM pg_class
WHERE relkind in ('i','r') AND relnamespace = 'pg_catalog'::regnamespace
ORDER BY 2 DESC;
```

This results in the following output:

relname	pg_relation_size
pg_proc	450560
pg_depend	344064
pg_attribute	286720
pg_depend_depender_index	204800
pg_depend_reference_index	204800
pg_proc_proname_args_nsp_index	180224
pg_description	172032
pg_attribute_relid_attnam_index	114688
pg_operator	106496
pg_statistic	106496
pg_description_o_c_o_index	98304
pg_attribute_relid_attnum_index	81920
pg_proc_oid_index	73728
pg_rewrite	73728
pg_class	57344
pg_type	57344
pg_class_relname_nsp_index	40960
...(partial listing)	

The preceding values are for a newly created database. These tables can get very large if they're not properly maintained, with values of 11 GB for one index being witnessed in one unlucky installation.

Identifying and fixing bloated tables and indexes

PostgreSQL implements **Multiversion Concurrency Control** (**MVCC**), which allows users to read data at the same time as writers make changes. This is an important feature for concurrency in database applications, as it can allow the following:

- Better performance because of fewer locks
- Greatly reduced deadlocking
- Simplified application design and management

Bloated tables and indexes are a natural consequence of MVCC design in PostgreSQL. It is caused mainly by updates, as we must retain both the old and new updates for a certain period of time.

Bloating results in increased disk consumption, as well as performance loss—if a table is twice as big as it should be, scanning it takes twice as long. VACUUM is one of the best ways of removing bloat.

Many users execute VACUUM far too frequently, while at the same time complaining about the cost of doing so. This recipe is all about understanding when you need to run VACUUM by estimating the amount of bloat in tables and indexes.

Getting ready

MVCC is a core part of PostgreSQL and cannot be turned off, nor would you really want it to be. The internals of MVCC have some implications for the DBA that need to be understood: each row represents a row version, and therefore it has two system columns, xmin and xmax, indicating the identifiers of the two transactions when the version was created and deleted, respectively. The value of xmax is NULL if that version has not been deleted yet.

The general idea is that, instead of actually removing row versions, we alter their visibility by changing their xmin and/or xmax values. To be more precise, when a row is inserted, its xmin value is set to the number of the creating transaction, while xmax is emptied; when a row is deleted, xmax is set to the number of the deleting transaction, without actually removing the row. An UPDATE operation is treated exactly like a DELETE operation, followed by INSERT; the deleted row represents the older version, and the row inserted is the newer version. Finally, when rolling back a transaction, all of its changes are made invisible by marking that transaction ID as aborted.

In this way, we get faster DELETE, UPDATE, and ROLLBACK statements, but the price of these benefits is that the SQL UPDATE command can cause tables and indexes to grow in size, because they leave behind dead row versions. The DELETE and aborted INSERT statements take up space, which must be reclaimed by garbage collection. VACUUM is the mechanism by which we reclaim space, though there is another internal feature named **Heap-Only Tuples** (**HOT**), which does much of this work for us automatically.

How to do it...

The best way to understand things is to look at things the same way that autovacuum does, by using a view that's been created with the following query:

```
CREATE OR REPLACE VIEW av_needed AS
SELECT N.nspname, C.relname
, pg_stat_get_tuples_inserted(C.oid) AS n_tup_ins
, pg_stat_get_tuples_updated(C.oid) AS n_tup_upd
, pg_stat_get_tuples_deleted(C.oid) AS n_tup_del
, CASE WHEN pg_stat_get_tuples_updated(C.oid) > 0
       THEN pg_stat_get_tuples_hot_updated(C.oid)::real
          / pg_stat_get_tuples_updated(C.oid)
       END
  AS HOT_update_ratio
, pg_stat_get_live_tuples(C.oid) AS n_live_tup
, pg_stat_get_dead_tuples(C.oid) AS n_dead_tup
, C.reltuples AS reltuples
, round(COALESCE(threshold.custom,
current_setting('autovacuum_vacuum_threshold'))::integer
       + COALESCE(scale_factor.custom,
current_setting('autovacuum_vacuum_scale_factor'))::numeric
       * C.reltuples)
  AS av_threshold
, date_trunc('minute',
    greatest(pg_stat_get_last_vacuum_time(C.oid),
             pg_stat_get_last_autovacuum_time(C.oid)))
  AS last_vacuum
, date_trunc('minute',
    greatest(pg_stat_get_last_analyze_time(C.oid),
             pg_stat_get_last_analyze_time(C.oid)))
  AS last_analyze
, pg_stat_get_dead_tuples(C.oid) >
  round( current_setting('autovacuum_vacuum_threshold')::integer
       + current_setting('autovacuum_vacuum_scale_factor')::numeric
       * C.reltuples)
  AS av_needed
, CASE WHEN reltuples > 0
```

```
        THEN round(100.0 * pg_stat_get_dead_tuples(C.oid) / reltuples)
        ELSE 0 END
  AS pct_dead
FROM pg_class C
LEFT JOIN pg_namespace N ON (N.oid = C.relnamespace)
NATURAL LEFT JOIN LATERAL (
    SELECT (regexp_match(unnest,'^[^=]+=(.+)$'))[1]
    FROM unnest(reloptions)
    WHERE unnest ~ '^autovacuum_vacuum_threshold='
) AS threshold(custom)
  NATURAL LEFT JOIN LATERAL (
    SELECT (regexp_match(unnest,'^[^=]+=(.+)$'))[1]
    FROM unnest(reloptions)
    WHERE unnest ~ '^autovacuum_vacuum_scale_factor='
) AS scale_factor(custom)
WHERE C.relkind IN ('r', 't', 'm')
  AND N.nspname NOT IN ('pg_catalog', 'information_schema')
  AND N.nspname NOT LIKE 'pg_toast%'
ORDER BY av_needed DESC, n_dead_tup DESC;
```

We can then use this to look at individual tables, as follows:

```
postgres=# \x
postgres=# SELECT * FROM av_needed WHERE nspname = 'public' AND relname =
'pgbench_accounts';
```

We get the following output:

```
-[ RECORD 1 ]----+------------------------
nspname          | public
relname          | pgbench_accounts
n_tup_ins        | 100001
n_tup_upd        | 117201
n_tup_del        | 1
hot_update_ratio | 0.123454578032611
n_live_tup       | 100000
n_dead_tup       | 0
reltuples        | 100000
av_threshold     | 20050
last_vacuum      | 2010-04-29 01:33:00+01
last_analyze     | 2010-04-28 15:21:00+01
av_needed        | f
pct_dead         | 0
```

How it works...

We can compare the number of dead row versions, shown as `n_dead_tup`, against the required threshold, `av_threshold`.

The preceding query doesn't take into account table-specific autovacuum thresholds. It could do so if you really need it, but the main purpose of the query is to give us information to understand what is happening, and then set the parameters accordingly—not the other way around.

Notice that the table query shows insertions, updates, and deletions so that you can understand your workload better. There is also something named the `hot_update_ratio`. This shows the fraction of updates that take advantage of the HOT feature, which allows a table to self-vacuum as the table changes. If that ratio is high, then you may avoid VACUUM activities altogether or at least for long periods. If the ratio is low, then you will need to execute VACUUM commands or autovacuums more frequently. Note that the ratio never reaches 1.0, so if you have it above 0.95, then that is very good and you need not think about it further.

HOT updates take place when the UPDATE statement does not change any of the column values that are indexed by any index, and there is enough free space in the disk page where the updated row is located. If you change even one column that is indexed by just one index, then it will be a non-HOT update, and there will be a performance hit. So, careful selection of indexes can improve update performance and reduce the need for maintenance. Also, if HOT updates do occur, though not often enough for your liking, you might want to try to decrease the `fillfactor` storage parameter for the table to make more space for them. Remember that this will be important only on your most active tables. Seldom touched tables don't need much tuning.

To recap, non-HOT updates cause indexes to bloat. The following query is useful in investigating the index size and how it changes over time. It runs fairly quickly, and can be used to monitor whether your indexes are changing in size over time:

```
SELECT
nspname,relname,
round(100 * pg_relation_size(indexrelid) /
                pg_relation_size(indrelid)) / 100
            AS index_ratio,
  pg_size_pretty(pg_relation_size(indexrelid))
            AS index_size,
  pg_size_pretty(pg_relation_size(indrelid))
            AS table_size
FROM pg_index I
LEFT JOIN pg_class C ON (C.oid = I.indexrelid)
```

```
LEFT JOIN pg_namespace N ON (N.oid = C.relnamespace)
WHERE
    nspname NOT IN ('pg_catalog', 'information_schema', 'pg_toast') AND
    C.relkind='i' AND
    pg_relation_size(indrelid) > 0;
```

Another route is to use the `pgstattuple` contrib module, which provides very detailed statistics. You can scan tables using `pgstattuple()`, as follows:

```
test=> SELECT * FROM pgstattuple('pg_catalog.pg_proc');
```

The output will look like as follows:

```
-[ RECORD 1 ]------+--------
table_len          | 458752
tuple_count        | 1470
tuple_len          | 438896
tuple_percent      | 95.67
dead_tuple_count   | 11
dead_tuple_len     | 3157
dead_tuple_percent | 0.69
free_space         | 8932
free_percent       | 1.95
```

The downside of `pgstattuple` is that it derives exact statistics by scanning the whole table and literally counting everything. If you have time to scan the table, you may as well vacuum the whole table anyway. So, a better idea is to use `pgstattuple_approx()`, which is much, much faster, and yet is still fairly accurate. It works by accessing the table's visibility map first and then only scanning the pages that need VACUUM, so I recommend that you use it in all cases for checking tables (there is no equivalent for indexes):

```
postgres=# select * from pgstattuple_approx('pgbench_accounts');
-[ RECORD 1 ]--------+------------------
table_len            | 268591104
scanned_percent      | 0
approx_tuple_count   | 1001738
approx_tuple_len     | 137442656
approx_tuple_percent | 51.1717082037088
dead_tuple_count     | 0
dead_tuple_len       | 0
dead_tuple_percent   | 0
approx_free_space    | 131148448
approx_free_percent  | 48.8282917962912
```

You can also scan indexes using `pgstatindex()`, as follows:

```
postgres=> SELECT * FROM pgstatindex('pg_cast_oid_index');
-[ RECORD 1 ]-------+------
version             | 2
tree_level          | 0
index_size          | 8192
root_block_no       | 1
internal_pages      | 0
leaf_pages          | 1
empty_pages         | 0
deleted_pages       | 0
avg_leaf_density    | 50.27
leaf_fragmentation  | 0
```

There's more...

You may want to set up monitoring for the bloated tables and indexes. Look at the Nagios plugin called `check_postgres_bloat`, which is a part of the `check_postgres` plugins.

It provides some flexible options to assess bloat. Unfortunately, it's not that well-documented, but if you've read this, it should make sense. You'll need to play with it to get the thresholding correct anyway, so that shouldn't be a problem.

Also, note that the only way to know for certain the exact bloat of a table or index is to scan the whole relation. Anything else is just an estimate and might lead to you running maintenance either too early or too late.

Monitoring and tuning a vacuum

If you're currently waiting for a long-running vacuum (or autovacuum) to finish, go straight to the *How to do it...* section.

If you've just had a long-running vacuum complete, then you may want to think about setting a few parameters.

Getting ready

`autovacuum_max_workers` should always be set to more than 2. Setting it too high may not be very useful, and so you need to be careful.

Setting `vacuum_cost_delay` too high is counterproductive. VACUUM is your friend, not your enemy, so delaying it until it doesn't happen at all just makes things worse.

`maintenance_work_mem` should be set to anything up to 1 GB, according to how much memory you can allocate to this task at this time.

Let's watch what happens when we run a large VACUUM. Don't run VACUUM FULL, because it runs for a long time while holding an `AccessExclusiveLock` on the table.

First, locate which process is running the VACUUM by using the `pg_stat_activity` view to identify the specific `pid` (`34399` is just an example).

How to do it...

Repeatedly execute the following query to see the progress of the VACUUM command:

```
postgres=# SELECT * FROM pg_stat_progress_vacuum WHERE pid = 34399;
```

How it works...

VACUUM works in three phases:

- The first main phase is *scanning heap*. The `heap_blks_scanned` columns will increase from 0 up to the value of `heap_blks_total`. The number of blocks vacuumed is shown as `heap_blks_vacuumed`, and the resulting rows to be removed are shown as `num_dead_tuples`:

```
Pid                 | 34399
datid               | 12515
datname             | postgres
relid               | 16422
phase               | scanning heap
heap_blks_total     | 32787
heap_blks_scanned   | 25207
heap_blks_vacuumed  | 0
index_vacuum_count  | 0
max_dead_tuples     | 9541017
num_dead_tuples     | 537600
```

- After this, we switch to the second phase, where we start *vacuuming indexes*. In PostgreSQL 11, it's possible that we can skip scanning the indexes altogether, so you may find that VACUUM is faster in this release. You can control whether indexes are vacuumed by setting the `vacuum_cleanup_index_scale_factor` parameter, which can also be set at table-level if needed. The default value seems good in this instance.

While this phase is happening, the progress data doesn't change until it has vacuumed all of the indexes. This phase can take a long time; more indexes increase the time that is required. PostgreSQL 11 will skip index vacuum in some cases, so expect some vacuums to run quickly and others to run for longer:

```
Pid                 | 34399
datid               | 12515
datname             | postgres
relid               | 16422
phase               | vacuuming indexes
heap_blks_total     | 32787
heap_blks_scanned   | 32787
heap_blks_vacuumed  | 0
index_vacuum_count  | 0
max_dead_tuples     | 9541017
num_dead_tuples     | 999966
```

- Once the indexes have been vacuumed, we move onto the third phase, where we return to the *vacuuming heap*. The value of `max_dead_tuples` is defined by the setting of `maintenance_work_mem`. PostgreSQL makes space for the largest meaningful number of entries allowed by that setting. If `num_dead_tuples` reaches the limit of `max_dead_tuples`, then we repeat phases two and three until complete. Each iteration will increment `index_vacuum_count`. It's a good idea to set `maintenance_work_mem` high enough to avoid multiple iterations:

```
Pid                 | 34399
datid               | 12515
datname             | postgres
relid               | 16422
phase               | vacuuming heap
heap_blks_total     | 32787
heap_blks_scanned   | 32787
heap_blks_vacuumed  | 25051
index_vacuum_count  | 1
max_dead_tuples     | 9541017
num_dead_tuples     | 999966
```

VACUUM moves through various other fairly short phases. If there are many empty blocks at the end of the table, VACUUM will attempt to get AccessExclusiveLock on the table, and once acquired, it will truncate the end of the table, showing a phase of truncating heap. Truncation does not occur every time, because PostgreSQL will attempt it only if the gain is significant and if there's no conflicting lock; if it does, it can often last a long time.

All phases of VACUUM will be slowed down by vacuum_cost_delay, but there's nothing you can do there to speed it up.

If you need to change the settings to speed up a running process, then autovacuum will pick up any new default settings when you reload the postgresql.conf file.

There's more...

VACUUM doesn't run in parallel on a single table.

If you want to run multiple VACUUMs at once, you can do it like so, for example, by running four vacuums at once to scan all databases:

```
$ vacuumdb --jobs=4 --all
```

If you run multiple VACUUM at once, you'll use more memory and I/O, so be careful. The exact calculation is complex, especially if you have tables with custom VACUUM settings, but the general idea is that I/O can be slowed down by raising vacuum_cost_delay or lowering vacuum_cost_limit.

Maintaining indexes

Indexes can become a problem in many database applications that involve a high proportion of INSERT/DELETE commands. Just as tables can become bloated, so can indexes.

In the *Identifying and fixing bloated tables and indexes* recipe, you saw that non-HOT updates can cause bloated indexes.
Non-primary key indexes are also prone to some bloat from normal INSERT commands, as is common in most relational databases.

Autovacuum does not detect bloated indexes, nor does it do anything to rebuild indexes. Therefore, we need to look at other ways to maintain indexes.

Getting ready

PostgreSQL supports commands that will rebuild indexes for you. The client utility, reindexdb, allows you to execute the REINDEX command in a convenient way from the operating system:

```
$ reindexdb
```

This executes the SQL REINDEX command on every table in the default database. If you want to reindex all databases, then use the following command:

```
$ reindexdb -a
```

That's what the manual says, anyway. My experience is that most indexes don't need rebuilding, and even if they do, REINDEX puts a full-table lock (AccessExclusiveLock) on the table while it runs. That locks your database for possibly hours, and I advise that you think about not doing that.

Try these steps instead:

1. First, let's create a test table with two indexes—a primary key and an additional index—as follows:

   ```
   DROP  TABLE  IF  EXISTS  test; CREATE  TABLE  test
   (id  INTEGER  PRIMARY  KEY
   ,category  TEXT
   ,  value  TEXT);
   CREATE  INDEX  ON  test  (category);
   ```

2. Now, let's look at the internal identifier of the tables, oid, and the current file number (relfilenodes), as follows:

   ```
   SELECT oid, relname, relfilenode
   FROM pg_class
   WHERE oid in (SELECT indexrelid
                 FROM pg_index
                 WHERE indrelid = 'test'::regclass);
     oid  |      relname       | relfilenode
   -------+--------------------+-------------
    16639 | test_pkey          |       16639
    16641 | test_category_idx  |       16641
   (2 rows)
   ```

How to do it...

PostgreSQL supports a command known as CREATE INDEX CONCURRENTLY, which builds an index without taking a full table lock. PostgreSQL also supports the ability to have two indexes, with different names, that have exactly the same definition. So, the trick is to build another index identical to the one you wish to rebuild, drop the old index, and then rename the new index to the same name as the old index. Et voilà, fresh index, and no locking! Let's see that in slow motion:

```
CREATE INDEX CONCURRENTLY new_index
  ON test (category);
BEGIN;
DROP INDEX test_category_idx;
ALTER INDEX new_index RENAME TO test_category_idx;
COMMIT;
```

When we check our internal identifiers again, we get the following:

```
SELECT oid, relname, relfilenode
FROM pg_class
WHERE oid in (SELECT indexrelid
               FROM pg_index
               WHERE indrelid = 'test'::regclass);
  oid  |       relname       | relfilenode
-------+---------------------+-------------
 16639 | test_pkey           |       16639
 16642 | test_category_idx   |       16642
(2 rows)
```

We can see that test_category_idx is now a completely new index.

This seems pretty good, and it works on primary keys too, but in a slightly complex way—you need to create a new index using UNIQUE and CONCURRENTLY, and then issue this to make it a primary key:

```
ALTER TABLE ... ADD PRIMARY KEY USING INDEX ...
```

This is not optimal yet, because a primary key could be the target of one or more foreign keys. In that case, we need to drop and recreate the foreign keys, which unfortunately has no CONCURRENTLY variant. The next recipe, *Adding a constraint without checking existing rows*, is a recommended read.

How it works...

The CREATE INDEX CONCURRENTLY statement allows INSERT, UPDATE, and DELETE commands while the index is being created. It cannot be executed inside another transaction, and only one index per table can be created concurrently at any time.

Swapping the indexes is easy and doesn't use any trickery.

There's more...

CREATE INDEX for B-tree indexes can be run in parallel for PostgreSQL 11. The amount of parallelism will be directly controlled by the setting of a table's parallel_workers parameter. Be careful, since setting this at the table level affects all queries, not just the index build/rebuild. If the table-level parameter is not set, then the maintenance_work_mem and max_parallel_maintenance_workers parameters will determine how many workers will be used; the default is 64 MB for maintenance_work_mem and 2 MB for max_parallel_maintenance_workers—increase both to get further gains in performance and/or concurrency. Note that these workers are shared across all users, so be careful not to over-allocate jobs, otherwise there won't be enough workers to let everybody run in parallel.

If you are fairly new to database systems, you might think rebuilding indexes for performance is something that only PostgreSQL needs to do. Other DBMSs require this as well —they just don't say so.

Indexes are designed for performance, and in all databases, deleting index entries causes contention and loss of performance. PostgreSQL does not remove index entries for a row when that row is deleted, so an index can be filled with dead entries. PostgreSQL attempts to remove dead entries when a block becomes full, but that doesn't stop a small number of dead entries from accumulating in many data blocks.

At the time of writing, no REINDEX CONCURRENTLY command has been added to PostgreSQL yet.

Adding a constraint without checking existing rows

A table constraint is a guarantee that must be satisfied by all of the rows in the table. Therefore, adding a constraint to a table is a two-phase procedure—first, the constraint is created, and then all of the existing rows are checked. Both happen in the same transaction, and the table cannot be accessed in the meantime. The constraint becomes visible after the check, yielding perfect consistency, which is usually the desired behavior, but it's at the expense of availability, which is not that great.

This recipe demonstrates another case—how to enforce a constraint on future transactions *only*, without checking existing rows. This may be desirable in some specific cases, such as the following:

- Enabling the constraint on newer rows of a large table that cannot remain unavailable for a long time
- Enforcing the constraint on newer rows, while keeping older rows that are known to violate the constraint

The constraint is marked as NOT VALID to make it clear that it does not exclude violations, unlike ordinary constraints.

As we will see, it is possible to validate the constraint at a later time, for example, when allowed by the workload or business continuity requirements. All existing rows will be checked, and then the NOT VALID mark will be removed from the constraint. Conversely, the constraint will never be validated, and its only purpose will be to prevent further violations by rejecting incompatible transactions.

Getting ready

We'll start this recipe by creating two tables with a few test rows:

```
postgres=# CREATE TABLE ft(fk int PRIMARY KEY, fs text);
CREATE TABLE
postgres=# CREATE TABLE pt(pk int, ps text);
CREATE TABLE
postgres=# INSERT INTO ft(fk,fs) VALUES (1,'one'), (2,'two');
INSERT 0 2
postgres=# INSERT INTO pt(pk,ps) VALUES (1,'I'), (2,'II'), (3,'III');
INSERT 0 3
```

How to do it...

We have inserted inconsistent data on purpose so that any attempt to check existing rows will be revealed by an error message.

If we attempt to create an ordinary foreign key, we get an error, since the number 3 does not appear in the ft table:

```
postgres=# ALTER TABLE pt ADD CONSTRAINT pc FOREIGN KEY (pk) REFERENCES
ft(fk);
ERROR: insert or update on table "pt" violates foreign key constraint
pc"
DETAIL: Key (pk)=(3) is not present in table "ft".
```

However, the same constraint can be successfully created as NOT VALID:

```
postgres=# ALTER TABLE pt ADD CONSTRAINT pc FOREIGN KEY (pk) REFERENCES
ft(fk) NOT VALID;
ALTER TABLE

postgres=# \d pt
      Table "public.pt"
 Column |  Type   | Modifiers
--------+---------+------------
 pk     | integer |
 ps     | text    |
Foreign-key constraints:
    "pc" FOREIGN KEY (pk) REFERENCES ft(fk) NOT VALID
```

 Note that the invalid state of the foreign key is mentioned by psql.

The violation is detected when we try to transform the NOT VALID constraint into a valid one:

```
postgres=# ALTER TABLE pt VALIDATE CONSTRAINT pc;
ERROR: insert or update on table "pt" violates foreign key constraint
pc"
DETAIL: Key (pk)=(3) is not present in table "ft".
```

Validation becomes possible after removing the inconsistency, and the foreign key is upgraded to an ordinary one:

```
postgres=# DELETE FROM pt WHERE pk = 3;
DELETE 1
postgres=#
ALTER TABLE
postgres=# \d pt
        Table "public.pt"
 Column |  Type   | Modifiers
--------+---------+------------
 pk     | integer |
 ps     | text    |
Foreign-key constraints:
    "pc" FOREIGN KEY (pk) REFERENCES ft(fk)
```

How it works...

ALTER TABLE ... ADD CONSTRAINT.. NOT VALID uses ShareRowExclusiveLock, which blocks writes, and VACUUM, yet allows reads on the table to continue. The ALTER TABLE ... VALIDATE CONSTRAINT command executes using ShareUpdateExclusiveLock, which allows both reads and writes on the table, yet blocks DDL and VACUUM while it scans the table.

PostgreSQL takes SQL locks according to the ISO standard, that is, locks are taken during the transaction and then released at its end. This means that algorithms like this one, where there is a short activity requiring stronger locks, followed by a longer activity that needs only lighter locks, cannot be implemented as a single command.

Finding unused indexes

Selecting the correct set of indexes for a workload is known to be a hard problem. It usually involves trial and error by developers and DBAs to get a good mix of indexes.

Tools for identifying slow queries exist and many SELECT statements can be improved by the addition of an index.

What many people forget is to check whether the mix of indexes remains valuable over time, which is something for the DBA to investigate and optimize.

How to do it...

PostgreSQL keeps track of each access against an index. We can view that information and use it to see whether an index is unused, as follows:

```
postgres=# SELECT schemaname, relname, indexrelname, idx_scan FROM
pg_stat_user_indexes ORDER BY idx_scan;
 schemaname |          indexrelname          | idx_scan
------------+--------------------------------+----------
 public     | pgbench_accounts_bid_idx       |        0
 public     | pgbench_branches_pkey          |    14575
 public     | pgbench_tellers_pkey           |    15350
 public     | pgbench_accounts_pkey          |   114400
(4 rows)
```

As we can see in the preceding code, there is one index that is totally unused, alongside others that have some usage. You now need to decide whether unused means that you should remove the index. That is a more complex question, and we first need to explain how it works.

How it works...

The PostgreSQL statistics accumulate various pieces of useful information. These statistics can be reset to zero using an administrator function. Also, as the data accumulates over time, we usually find that objects that have been there for longer periods of time have higher apparent usage. So, if we see a low number for idx_scan, then it might be that the index was newly created (as was the case in my preceding demonstration), or that the index is only used by a part of the application that runs only at certain times of the day, week, month, and so on.

Another important consideration is that the index may be a unique constraint index that exists specifically to safeguard against duplicate INSERT commands. An INSERT operation does not show up as idx_scan, even if the index was actually used while checking the uniqueness of the newly inserted values, whereas UPDATE or DELETE might show up because they have to locate the row first. So, a table that only has INSERT commands against it will appear to have unused indexes.

Here is an updated version of the preceding query, which excludes unique constraint indexes:

```
SELECT schemaname
  , relname
  , indexrelname
  , idx_scan
  FROM pg_stat_user_indexes i
  LEFT JOIN pg_constraint c
    ON i.indrelid = c.conindid
  WHERE c.contype IS NULL;
```

Also, some indexes that show usage might be showing usage that was historical, and there is no further usage. Or it might be the case that some queries use an index where they could just as easily and almost as cheaply use an alternative index. Those things are for you to explore and understand before you take action. A very common approach is to regularly monitor such numbers in order to gain knowledge by examining their evolution over time on both the master database and on any replicated hot standby nodes.

In the end, you may decide from this that you want to remove an index. If only there was a way to try removing an index and then put it back again quickly, in case you cause problems! Rebuilding an index might take hours on a big table, so these decisions can be a little scary. No worries! Just follow the next recipe, *Carefully removing unwanted indexes*.

Carefully removing unwanted indexes

Carefully removing? You mean press *Enter* gently after typing DROP INDEX? Err, no!

The reasoning is that it takes a long time to build an index and a short time to drop it.

What we want is a way of removing an index so that if we discover that removing it was a mistake, we can put the index back again quickly.

Getting ready

The following query will list all invalid indexes, if any:

```
SELECT ir.relname AS indexname
  , it.relname AS tablename
  , n.nspname AS schemaname
  FROM pg_index i
  JOIN pg_class ir ON ir.oid = i.indexrelid
  JOIN pg_class it ON it.oid = i.indrelid
```

```
JOIN pg_namespace n ON n.oid = it.relnamespace
WHERE NOT i.indisvalid;
```

Take note of these indexes, so that later you can tell whether a given index is invalid because we marked it as invalid during this recipe, in which case it can safely be marked as valid, or because it was already invalid for other reasons.

How to do it...

Here, we will describe a procedure that allows us to deactivate an index without actually dropping it so that we can appreciate what its contribution was and possibly reactivate it:

1. First, create the following function:

   ```
   CREATE  OR  REPLACE  FUNCTION  trial_drop_index(iname  TEXT)
   RETURNS  VOID
   LANGUAGE  SQL  AS  $$ UPDATE  pg_index
   SET  indisvalid  =  false
   WHERE  indexrelid  =  $1::regclass;
   $$;
   ```

2. Then, run it to do a trial of dropping the index.
3. If you experience performance issues after dropping the index, then use the following function to undrop the index:

   ```
   CREATE  OR  REPLACE  FUNCTION  trial_undrop_index(iname  TEXT)
   RETURNS  VOID
   LANGUAGE  SQL  AS
   $$ UPDATE  pg_index
   SET  indisvalid  =  true
   WHERE  indexrelid  =  $1::regclass;
   $$;
   ```

 Be careful to avoid undropping any index that was detected by the query in the *Getting Ready* section; if it wasn't marked as invalid when applying this recipe, then it may be unusable because it really isn't valid.

How it works...

This recipe also uses some inside knowledge. When we create an index using CREATE INDEX CONCURRENTLY, it is a two-stage process. The first phase builds the index and then marks it invalid. INSERT, UPDATE, and DELETE statements now begin maintaining the index, but we perform a further pass over the table to see if we missed anything, before declaring the index valid. User queries don't use the index until it says that it is valid.

Once the index is built and the valid flag is set, if we set the flag to invalid, the index will still be maintained. It's just that it will not be used by queries. This allows us to turn the index off quickly, though with the option to turn it on again if we realize that we actually do need the index after all. This makes it practical to test whether dropping the index will alter the performance of any of your most important queries.

Planning maintenance

Monitoring systems are not a substitute for good planning. They alert you to unplanned situations that need attention. The more unplanned things you respond to, the greater the chance that you will need to respond to multiple emergencies at once. And when that happens, something will break. Ultimately, that is your fault. If you wish to take your responsibilities seriously, you should plan ahead.

How to do it...

This recipe is about planning, so we'll provide discussion points rather than portions of code. We'll cover the main points that should be addressed and provide a list of points as food for thought, around which the actual implementation should be built:

- **Let's break a rule**: If you don't have a backup, take one now. I mean now—go on, off you go! Then, let's talk some more about planning maintenance. If you already do, well done! It's hard to keep your job as a DBA if you lose data because of missing backups, especially today, when everybody's grandmother knows to keep their photos backed up.
- **First, plan your time**: Decide a regular date on which to perform certain actions. Don't allow yourself to be a puppet of your monitoring system, running up and down every time the lights change. If you keep getting dragged off on other assignments, then you must understand that you need to get a good handle on the database maintenance to make sure that it doesn't bite you.

- **Don't be scared**: It's easy to worry about what you don't know, and either overreact or underreact. Your database probably doesn't need to be inspected daily, but it's never bad practice.

How it works...

Build a regular cycle of activity around the following tasks:

- **Capacity planning**: Observe long-term trends in system performance and keep track of the growth of database volumes. Plan to schedule any new data feeds and new projects that increase the rates of change. This is best done monthly so that you can monitor what has happened and what will happen.
- **Backups, recovery testing, and emergency planning**: Organize regular reviews of written plans and test scripts. Check the tape rotation, confirm that you still have the password to the off-site backups, and so on. Some sysadmins run a test recovery every night so that they always know that successful recovery is possible.
- **Vacuum and index maintenance**: Do this to reduce bloat, as well as collecting optimizer statistics through the ANALYZE command. Also, regularly check index usage and drop unused indexes. Consider VACUUM again, with the need to manage the less frequent **freezing** process. This is listed as a separate task so that you don't ignore this and let it bite you later!
- **Server log file analysis**: How many times has the server restarted? Are you sure you know about each incident?
- **Security and intrusion detection**: Has your database already been hacked? What did they do?
- **Understanding usage patterns**: If you don't know much about what your database is used for, then I'll wager it is not very well-tuned or maintained.
- **Long-term performance analysis**: It's a common occurrence for me to get asked to come and tune a system that is slow. Often, what happens is that a database server gets slower over a very long period. Nobody ever noticed any particular day when it got slow—it just got slower over time. Keeping records of response times over time can help to confirm whether everything is as good now as it was months or years earlier. This activity is where you might reconsider current index choices.

Many of these activities are mentioned in this chapter or throughout the rest of this cookbook. Some are not because they aren't very technical, but more about planning and understanding your environment.

There's more...

You might also find time to consider the following:

- **Data quality**: Are the contents of the database accurate and meaningful? Could the data be enhanced?
- **Business intelligence**: Is the data being used for everything that can bring value to the organization?

10
Performance and Concurrency

Performance and concurrency are two problems that are often tightly coupled—when concurrency problems are encountered, performance usually degrades, and in some cases, a lot. If you take care of concurrency problems, you will achieve better performance.

In this chapter, we will show you how to find slow queries and how to find queries that make other queries slow.

Performance tuning, unfortunately, is still not an exact science, so you may also encounter a performance problem that's not covered by any of the given methods.

We will also show you how to get help in the final recipe, *Reporting performance problems*, in case none of the other recipes that are covered here work.

In this chapter, we will cover the following recipes:

- Finding slow SQL statements
- Finding out what makes SQL slow
- Collecting regular statistics from pg_stat* views
- Reducing the number of rows returned
- Simplifying complex SQL queries
- Speeding up queries without rewriting them
- Discovering why a query is not using an index
- Forcing a query to use an index
- Using parallel query
- Creating time series tables
- Using optimistic locking
- Reporting performance problems

Finding slow SQL statements

There are two main kinds of slowness that can manifest themselves in a database.

The first kind is a single query that can be too slow to be really usable, such as a customer information query in a CRM running for minutes, a password check query running in tens of seconds, or a daily data aggregation query running for more than a day. These can be found by logging queries that take over a certain amount of time, either at the client end or in the database.

The second kind is a query that is run frequently (say a few thousand times a second) and used to run in single-digit milliseconds, but is now running in several tens or even hundreds of milliseconds, hence slowing the system down. This kind of slowness is much harder to find.

Here, we will show you several ways to find the statements that are either slow or cause the database as a whole to slow down (although they are not slow by themselves).

Getting ready

Connect to the database as the user whose statements you want to investigate or as a superuser to investigate all users' queries.

Check that you have the `pg_stat_statements` extension installed:

```
postgres=# \x
postgres=# \dx pg_stat_statements
```

The following is a list of our installed extensions:

```
-[ RECORD 1 ]-----------------------------------------------------------
Name        | pg_stat_statements
Version     | 1.4
Schema      | public
Description | track execution statistics of all SQL statements executed
```

If you can't see them, then issue the following command:

```
postgres=# CREATE EXTENSION pg_stat_statements;
postgres=# ALTER SYSTEM
          SET shared_preload_libraries = 'pg_stat_statements';
```

Then, restart the server, or refer to the *Using an installed module* and *Managing installed extensions* recipes from Chapter 3, *Configuration*, for more details.

How to do it...

Run this query to look at the top ten highest workloads on your server side:

```
postgres=# SELECT calls, total_time, query FROM pg_stat_statements
        ORDER BY total_time DESC LIMIT 10;
```

The output is ordered by `total_time`, so it doesn't matter whether it was a single query or thousands of smaller queries.

There are many additional columns that are useful in tracking down further information about particular entries:

```
postgres=# \d pg_stat_statements
          View "public.pg_stat_statements"
       Column          |        Type        | Modifiers
-----------------------+--------------------+-----------
 userid                | oid                |
 dbid                  | oid                |
 queryid               | bigint             |
 query                 | text               |
 calls                 | bigint             |
 total_time            | double precision   |
 min_time              | double precision   |
 max_time              | double precision   |
 mean_time             | double precision   |
 stddev_time           | double precision   |
 rows                  | bigint             |
 shared_blks_hit       | bigint             |
 shared_blks_read      | bigint             |
 shared_blks_dirtied   | bigint             |
 shared_blks_written   | bigint             |
 local_blks_hit        | bigint             |
 local_blks_read       | bigint             |
 local_blks_dirtied    | bigint             |
 local_blks_written    | bigint             |
 temp_blks_read        | bigint             |
 temp_blks_written     | bigint             |
 blk_read_time         | double precision   |
 blk_write_time        | double precision   |
```

How it works...

`pg_stat_statements` collects data on all running queries by accumulating data in memory, producing minimal overheads.

Similar SQL statements are normalized so that the constants and parameters that are used for execution are removed. This allows you to see all similar SQL statements in one line of the report, rather than seeing thousands of lines, which would be fairly useless. While useful, it can sometimes mean that it's hard to work out which parameter values are actually causing the problem.

There's more...

Another way to find slow queries is to set up PostgreSQL to log them all. So, if you decide to monitor a query that takes over 10 seconds, then set up logging queries over 10 seconds by executing the following command:

```
postgres=# ALTER SYSTEM
        SET log_min_duration_statement = 10000;
```

Remember that the duration is in milliseconds. After doing this, reload PostgreSQL. All queries that are slow enough to exceed the threshold will be logged.

The PostgreSQL log files are usually located together with other log files; for example, on Debian/Ubuntu Linux, they are in the `/var/log/postgresql/` directory.

You can also log every query, though that can often swamp the log files and cause performance problems itself and so is hardly ever recommend.

Query logging will show the parameters that are being used for the slow query, even when `pg_stat_statements` does not.

Finding out what makes SQL slow

A SQL statement can be slow for a lot of reasons. Here, we will give a short list of these reasons, with at least one way of recognizing each.

Getting ready

If the SQL statement is still running, look at `Chapter 8`, *Monitoring and Diagnosis*.

How to do it...

The core issues are likely to be the following:

- You're asking it to do too much work
- Something is stopping it from doing the work

This might not sound that helpful at first, but it's good to know that there's nothing really magical going on that you can't understand if you look.

In more detail, the main reasons are as follows:

- Returning too much data
- Processing too much data index needed
- Wrong plan for other reasons
- Cache or I/O problems
- Locking problems

The first reason can be handled as described in the *Reducing the number of rows returned* recipe. The rest of the preceding reasons can be investigated from two perspectives: the SQL itself and the objects that the SQL touches. Let's start by looking at the SQL itself by running the query with `EXPLAIN ANALYZE`. We're going to use the optional form, as follows:

```
postgres=# EXPLAIN (ANALYZE, BUFFERS) ...SQL...
```

The `EXPLAIN` command provides output to describe the execution plan of the SQL, showing access paths and costs (in abstract units). The `ANALYZE` option causes the statement to be executed (be careful), with instrumentation to show the number of rows accessed and the timings for that part of the plan. The `BUFFERS` option provides information about the number of database buffers read and the number of buffers that were hit in the cache. Taken together, we have everything we need to diagnose whether the SQL performance is slow in the preceding last three reasons:

```
postgres=# EXPLAIN (ANALYZE, BUFFERS) SELECT count(*) FROM t;
                          QUERY PLAN
-----------------------------------------------------------------
   Aggregate   (cost=4427.27..4427.28 rows=1 width=0) \
```

```
                    (actual time=32.953..32.954 rows=1 loops=1)
         Buffers: shared hit=X read=Y
      ->  Seq Scan on t   (cost=0.00..4425.01 rows=901 width=0) \
                  (actual time=30.350..31.646 rows=901 loops=1)
              Buffers: shared hit=X read=Y
    Planning time: 0.045 ms
     Execution time: 33.128 ms
    (6 rows)
```

Let's use this technique to look at an SQL statement that would benefit from an index.

For example, if you want to get the three latest rows in a one million row table, run the following query:

```
SELECT * FROM events ORDER BY id DESC LIMIT 3;
```

You can either read through just three rows using an index on the id SERIAL column, or you can perform a sequential scan of all rows followed by a sort, as shown in the following snippet. Your choice depends on whether you have a usable index on the field from which you want to get the top three rows:

```
postgres=# CREATE TABLE events(id SERIAL);
CREATE TABLE
postgres=# INSERT INTO events SELECT generate_series(1,1000000);
INSERT 0 1000000
postgres=# EXPLAIN (ANALYZE)
           SELECT * FROM events ORDER BY id DESC LIMIT 3;
                         QUERY PLAN
-----------------------------------------------------------------
   Limit   (cost=25500.67..25500.68 rows=3 width=4) \
           (actual time=3143.493..3143.502 rows=3 loops=1)
     ->  Sort   (cost=25500.67..27853.87 rows=941280 width=4)
             (actual time=3143.488..3143.490 rows=3 loops=1)
           Sort Key: id DESC
           Sort Method: top-N heapsort Memory: 25kB
     ->  Seq Scan on events
             (cost=0.00..13334.80 rows=941280 width=4)
             (actual time=0.105..1534.418 rows=1000000 loops=1)
   Planning time: 0.331 ms
    Execution time: 3143.584 ms
   (10 rows)
postgres=# CREATE INDEX events_id_ndx ON events(id);
CREATE INDEX
postgres=# EXPLAIN (ANALYZE)
           SELECT * FROM events ORDER BY id DESC LIMIT 3;
                         QUERY PLAN
-----------------------------------------------------------------
   Limit   (cost=0.00..0.08 rows=3 width=4) (actual
```

```
        time=0.295..0.311 rows=3 loops=1)
    ->   Index Scan Backward using events_id_ndx on events
         (cost=0.00..27717.34 rows=1000000 width=4) (actual
         time=0.289..0.295 rows=3 loops=1)
  Total runtime: 0.364 ms
(3 rows)
```

This produces a huge difference in query runtime, even when all of the data is in the cache.

If you run the same analysis using EXPLAIN (ANALYZE, BUFFERS) on your production system, you'll be able to see the cache effects as well. Remember that each new index you add increases the pressure on the cache, so it is possible to have too many indexes.

You can also look at the statistics for the objects touched by queries, as mentioned in the *Knowing whether anybody is using a specific table* recipe from Chapter 8, *Monitoring and Diagnosis*. In pg_stat_user_tables, fast growth of seq_tup_read means that there are lots of sequential scans occurring. The ratio of seq_tup_read to seq_scan shows how many tuples each seqscan reads. Similarly, the idx_scan and idx_tup_fetch columns show whether indexes are being used and how effective they are.

There's more...

If not enough of the data fits in the shared buffers, lots of rereading of the same data happens, causing performance issues. In pg_statio_user_tables, watch the heap_blks_hit and heap_blks_read fields, or the equivalent ones for index and toast relations. They give you a fairly good idea of how much of your data is found in PostgreSQL's shared buffers (heap_blks_hit) and how much had to be fetched from the disk (heap_blks_read). If you see large numbers of blocks being read from the disk continuously, you may want to tune those queries; if you determine that the disk reads were justified, you can make the configured shared_buffers value bigger.

If your shared_buffers parameter is tuned properly and you can't rewrite the query to perform less block I/O, you might need a beefier computer.

You can find a lot of resources on the web that explain how shared buffers work and how to set them based on your available hardware and your expected data access patterns. Our professional advice is to always test your database servers and perform benchmarks before you deploy them in production. Information on the shared_buffers configuration parameter can be found at http://www.postgresql.org/docs/11/static/runtime-config-resource.html.

Not enough CPU power or disk I/O capacity for the current load

These issues are usually caused by suboptimal query plans, but sometimes, your computer is just not powerful enough.

In this case, `top` is your friend. For quick checks, run the following from the command line:

```
user@host:~$ top
```

First, watch the percentage of idle CPU from `top`. If this is in low single digits most of the time, you probably have problems with the CPU's power.

If you have a high load average with a lot of CPU idle left, you are probably out of disk bandwidth. In this case, you should also have lots of Postgres processes in the `D` status, meaning that the process is in an uninterruptible state (usually waiting for I/O).

Locking problems

Thanks to its MVCC design, PostgreSQL does not suffer from most locking problems, such as writers locking out readers or readers locking out writers, but it still has to take locks˙ when more than one process wants to update the same row. Also, it has to hold the write lock until the current writer's transaction finishes.

So, if you have a database design where many queries update the same record, you can have a locking problem.

Refer to the *Knowing who is blocking a query* recipe of `Chapter 8`, *Monitoring and Diagnosis*, for more detailed information.

To diagnose locking problems retrospectively, use the `log_lock_waits` parameter to generate log output for locks that are held for a long time.

EXPLAIN options

Use the `FORMAT` option to retrieve the output of `EXPLAIN` in a different format, such as `JSON`, `XML`, and `YAML`. This could allow us to write programs to manipulate the outputs.

The following command is an example of this:

```
EXPLAIN (ANALYZE, BUFFERS, FORMAT JSON) SELECT count(*) FROM t;
```

See also

For further information on the syntax of the EXPLAIN SQL command, refer to the PostgreSQL documentation at http://www.postgresql.org/docs/11/static/sql-explain.html.

Collect regular statistics from pg_stat* views

This recipe describes how to collect the statistics that are needed to understand what is going on in the database system on a regular basis so that they can be used to further optimize the queries that are slow or are becoming slow as the database changes.

We have included an example extension, called pgstatslog. It can be used to track these changes. The extension works on PostgreSQL 9.1+.

Look at the *Using an installed module* and *managing installed extensions* recipes from Chapter 3, *Configuration,* for an overview of the extensions infrastructure in PostgreSQL.

Getting ready

Find the pgstatslog directory in the set of files that were distributed with this book.

Find out the directory to place shared files using pg_config --sharedir and then copy the files to the extension subdirectory of that directory.

Now that the extension has been installed in your PostgreSQL server, it is time to install it in each database that you want to monitor:

```
postgres=# CREATE EXTENSION pgstatslog;
CREATE EXTENSION
```

You can verify that the extension is installed by typing \dx in psql.

How to do it...

You can collect information by executing the following query for each database that you intend to monitor:

```
SELECT collect_deltas();
```

This will collect the changes in the pg_stat_user_* and pg_statio_user_* tables that have occurred since the last invocation.

You should probably set up a cron job to run on a regular basis so that you have good coverage of what happens at what time of the day and week. Running it at an interval of 5 to 15 minutes should usually give you enough temporal resolution to understand what is going on with your tables.

For example, you can add the following (or a similar variation) to the postgres user's cron table:

```
*/5 * * * * /usr/bin/psql -c 'SELECT collect_deltas()' mydbname
```

How it works...

The collect_deltas() function makes static copies of the pg_stat_user_tables, pg_statio_user_tables, pg_stat_user_indexes, and pg_statio_user_indexes tables at each run. It then compares the current copies with the copies saved at the last run, and saves the timestamped deltas in the stat_user_tables_delta_log and stat_user_indexes_delta_log log tables. These tables can then be analyzed later to get insight into access and I/O patterns.

The latest set of deltas is also kept in the stat_user_tables_delta and stat_user_indexes_delta tables, which can be used for external monitoring systems, such as Cacti, to get a graphical representation of it.

There's more...

The collect_deltas() function simply appends data to the same tables. This should not cause performance problems, as the large log tables are without indexes. Thus, insertions in them are fast, but if you are low on disk space and have many tables, you may want to introduce a rotation scheme for these tables that throws away older data.

In case you experience performance issues with the proposed approach, you might want to either purge the old data from the `*_delta_log` tables (and keep a window of the last four weeks) or use horizontal partitioning.

In the first approach, you can set a weekly cron job that deletes all records that are older than four weeks from the tables. For this purpose, we have created the `rotate_deltas()` function in the `pgstatslog` extension.

Take some time and investigate the content of the extension—in particular, the `pgstatslog--1.0.sql` file. It contains definitions for tables, views, and functions, as well as usage instructions.

In regards to the second approach, refer to the *Creating Time Series tables* recipe.

Another statistics collection package

If you are interested in a more powerful way of tracking database statistics over time, I suggest that you look at `pg_statsinfo`, an open source package available at `http://pgstatsinfo.sourceforge.net/` and developed by our friends from NTT.

Reducing the number of rows returned

Although the problem is often producing many rows in the first place, it is made worse by returning all of the unnecessary rows to the client. This is especially true if the client and server are not on the same host.

Here are some ways to reduce the traffic between the client and server.

How to do it...

Consider the following scenario: a full-text search returns 10,000 documents, but only the first 20 are displayed to users. In this case, order the documents by rank on the server, and return only the top 20 that actually need to be displayed:

```
SELECT title, ts_rank_cd(body_tsv, query, 20) AS text_rank
FROM articles, plainto_tsquery('spicy potatoes') AS query
WHERE body_tsv @@ query
ORDER BY rank DESC
LIMIT 20
;
```

If you need the next 20 documents, don't just query with a limit of 40 and throw away the first 20. Instead, use `OFFSET 20 LIMIT 20` to return the next 20 documents.

To gain some stability so that documents with the same rank still come out in the same order when using `OFFSET 20`, add a unique field (such as the `id` column of the `articles` table) to `ORDER BY` in both queries:

```
SELECT title, ts_rank_cd(body_tsv, query, 20) AS text_rank
FROM articles, plainto_tsquery('spicy potatoes') AS query
WHERE body_tsv @@ query
ORDER BY rank DESC, articles.id
OFFSET 20 LIMIT 20;
```

Another use case is an application that requests all products of a branch office so that it can run a complex calculation over them. In such a case, try to do as much data analysis as possible inside the database.

There is no need to run the following:

```
SELECT * FROM accounts WHERE branch_id = 7;
```

Also, instead of counting and summing the rows on the client side, you can run this:

```
SELECT count(*), sum(balance) FROM accounts WHERE branch_id = 7;
```

With some research on the SQL language, which is supported by PostgreSQL, you can carry out an amazingly large portion of your computation using plain SQL (for example, do not underestimate the power of window functions).

If SQL is not enough, you can use PL/pgSQL or any other embedded procedural languages supported by PostgreSQL for even more flexibility.

There's more...

Consider one more scenario: an application runs a huge number of small lookup queries. This can easily happen with modern **Object Relational Mappers** (**ORMs**) and other toolkits that do a lot of work for the programmer, but at the same time, hide a lot of what is happening.

For example, if you define an HTML report over a query in a templating language, and then define a lookup function to resolve an ID inside the template, you may end up with a form that performs a separate, small lookup for each row displayed, even when most of the values looked up are the same. This doesn't usually pose a big problem for the database, as queries of the SELECT name FROM departments WHERE id = 7 form are really fast when the row for id = 7 is in shared buffers. However, repeating this query thousands of times still takes seconds, due to network latency, process scheduling for each request, and other factors.

The two proposed solutions are as follows:

- Make sure that the value is cached by your ORM
- Perform the lookup inside the query that gets the main data so that it can be displayed directly

Exactly how to carry out these solutions depends on the toolkit, but they are both worth investigating, as they really can make a difference in speed and resource usage.

PostgreSQL 9.5 introduced the TABLESAMPLE clause into SQL. This allows you to run commands much faster by using a sample of a table's rows, giving an approximate answer. In certain cases, this can be just as useful as the most accurate answer:

```
postgres=# SELECT avg(id) FROM events;
        avg
--------------------
 500000.500
(1 row)
postgres=# SELECT avg(id) FROM events TABLESAMPLE system(1);
        avg
--------------------
 507434.635
(1 row)
postgres=# EXPLAIN (ANALYZE, BUFFERS) SELECT avg(id) FROM events;
                                        QUERY PLAN
---------------------------------------------------------------------------
-----------------------------------------------------
 Aggregate (cost=16925.00..16925.01 rows=1 width=32) (actual
time=204.841..204.841 rows=1 loops=1)
    Buffers: shared hit=96 read=4329
    -> Seq Scan on events (cost=0.00..14425.00 rows=1000000 width=4) (actual
time=1.272..105.452 rows=1000000 loops=1)
          Buffers: shared hit=96 read=4329
 Planning time: 0.059 ms
 Execution time: 204.912 ms
(6 rows)
postgres=# EXPLAIN (ANALYZE, BUFFERS)
```

```
SELECT avg(id) FROM events TABLESAMPLE system(1);
                                          QUERY PLAN
--------------------------------------------------------------------
-----------------------------------------------
 Aggregate (cost=301.00..301.01 rows=1 width=32) (actual time=4.627..4.627
rows=1 loops=1)
   Buffers: shared hit=1 read=46
   -> Sample Scan on events (cost=0.00..276.00 rows=10000 width=4) (actual
time=0.074..2.833 rows=10622 loops=1)
         Sampling: system ('1'::real)
         Buffers: shared hit=1 read=46

 Planning time: 0.066 ms
  Execution time: 4.702 ms
 (7 rows)
```

Simplifying complex SQL queries

There are two types of complexity that you can encounter in SQL queries.

First, the complexity can be directly visible in the query if it has hundreds or even thousands of rows of SQL code in a single query. This can cause both maintenance headaches and slow execution.

This complexity can also be hidden in subviews, so the SQL code of the query may seem simple, but it uses other views and/or functions to do part of the work, which can, in turn, use others. This is much better for maintenance, but it can still cause performance problems.

Both types of queries can either be written manually by programmers or data analysts, or emerge as a result of a query generator.

Getting ready

First, verify that you really have a complex query.

A query that simply returns lots of database fields is not complex by itself. In order to be complex, the query has to join lots of tables in complex ways.

The easiest way to find out whether the query is complex is to look at the output of EXPLAIN. If it has lots of rows, the query is complex, and it's not just that there is a lot of text.

All of the examples in this recipe have been written with a very typical use case in mind: sales.

What follows is a description of the fictitious model that's used in this recipe. The most important fact is the `sale` event, stored in the `sale` table (I specifically used the word fact, as this is the right term to use in a *data warehousing* context). Every sale takes place at a point of sale (the `salespoint` table) at a specific time, and involves an item. That item is stored in a warehouse (see the `item` and `warehouse` tables, as well as the `item_in_wh` link table).

Both `warehouse` and `salespoint` are located in a geographical area (the `location` table). This is important, for example, to study the provenance of a transaction.

Here is a simplified entity-relationship model, which is useful for understanding all of the joins that occur in the following queries:

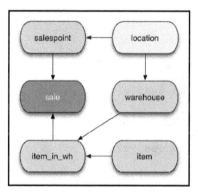

How to do it...

Simplifying a query usually means restructuring it so that parts of it can be defined separately and then used by other parts.

We'll illustrate these possibilities by rewriting the following query in several ways.

The complex query in our example case is a so-called **pivot** or **cross-tab** query. This query retrieves the quarterly profit for non-local sales from all shops, as shown in the following code:

```
SELECT shop.sp_name AS shop_name,
       q1_nloc_profit.profit AS q1_profit,
       q2_nloc_profit.profit AS q2_profit,
```

```
                q3_nloc_profit.profit AS q3_profit,
                q4_nloc_profit.profit AS q4_profit,
                year_nloc_profit.profit AS year_profit
        FROM (SELECT * FROM salespoint ORDER BY sp_name) AS shop
        LEFT JOIN (
            SELECT
                spoint_id,
                sum(sale_price) - sum(cost) AS profit,
                count(*) AS nr_of_sales
            FROM sale s
            JOIN item_in_wh iw ON s.item_in_wh_id=iw.id
            JOIN item i ON iw.item_id = i.id
            JOIN salespoint sp ON s.spoint_id = sp.id
            JOIN location sploc ON sp.loc_id = sploc.id
            JOIN warehouse wh ON iw.whouse_id = wh.id
            JOIN location whloc ON wh.loc_id = whloc.id
            WHERE sale_time >= '2013-01-01'
              AND sale_time < '2013-04-01'
              AND sploc.id != whloc.id
            GROUP BY 1
            ) AS q1_nloc_profit
            ON shop.id = Q1_NLOC_PROFIT.spoint_id
        LEFT JOIN (
    < similar subquery for 2nd quarter >
            ) AS q2_nloc_profit
            ON shop.id = q2_nloc_profit.spoint_id
        LEFT JOIN (
    < similar subquery for 3rd quarter >
            ) AS q3_nloc_profit
            ON shop.id = q3_nloc_profit.spoint_id
        LEFT JOIN (
    < similar subquery for 4th quarter >
            ) AS q4_nloc_profit
            ON shop.id = q4_nloc_profit.spoint_id
        LEFT JOIN (
    < similar subquery for full year >
            ) AS year_nloc_profit
            ON shop.id = year_nloc_profit.spoint_id
        ORDER BY 1
        ;
```

Since the preceding query has an almost identical repeating part for finding the sales for a period (the four quarters of 2013, in this case), it makes sense to move it to a separate view (for the whole year) and then use that view in the main reporting query, as follows:

```
CREATE VIEW non_local_quarterly_profit_2013 AS
        SELECT
            spoint_id,
```

```
        extract('quarter' from sale_time) as sale_quarter,
        sum(sale_price) - sum(cost) AS profit,
        count(*) AS nr_of_sales
      FROM sale s
      JOIN item_in_wh iw ON s.item_in_wh_id=iw.id
      JOIN item i ON iw.item_id = i.id
      JOIN salespoint sp ON s.spoint_id = sp.id
      JOIN location sploc ON sp.loc_id = sploc.id
      JOIN warehouse wh ON iw.whouse_id = wh.id
      JOIN location whloc ON wh.loc_id = whloc.id
    WHERE sale_time >= '2013-01-01'
      AND sale_time < '2014-01-01'
      AND sploc.id != whloc.id
    GROUP BY 1,2;
SELECT shop.sp_name AS shop_name,
       q1_nloc_profit.profit as q1_profit,
       q2_nloc_profit.profit as q2_profit,
       q3_nloc_profit.profit as q3_profit,
       q4_nloc_profit.profit as q4_profit,
       year_nloc_profit.profit as year_profit
  FROM (SELECT * FROM salespoint ORDER BY sp_name) AS shop
  LEFT JOIN non_local_quarterly_profit_2013 AS q1_nloc_profit
      ON shop.id = Q1_NLOC_PROFIT.spoint_id
   AND q1_nloc_profit.sale_quarter = 1
  LEFT JOIN non_local_quarterly_profit_2013 AS q2_nloc_profit
      ON shop.id = Q2_NLOC_PROFIT.spoint_id
  AND q2_nloc_profit.sale_quarter = 2
  LEFT JOIN non_local_quarterly_profit_2013 AS q3_nloc_profit
      ON shop.id = Q3_NLOC_PROFIT.spoint_id
  AND q3_nloc_profit.sale_quarter = 3
  LEFT JOIN non_local_quarterly_profit_2013 AS q4_nloc_profit
      ON shop.id = Q4_NLOC_PROFIT.spoint_id
  AND q4_nloc_profit.sale_quarter = 4
  LEFT JOIN (
      SELECT spoint_id, sum(profit) AS profit
        FROM non_local_quarterly_profit_2013 GROUP BY 1
    ) AS year_nloc_profit
    ON shop.id = year_nloc_profit.spoint_id
ORDER BY 1;
```

Moving the subquery to a view has not only made the query shorter but also easier to understand and maintain.

You might want to consider **materialized views**. Even though their support does not yet allow for differential updates, you can still benefit from on-demand refreshing of the view results and, most importantly, indexes. Materialized views are described later in this recipe.

Before that, we will be using common table expressions (also known as WITH queries) instead of a separate view. Starting with PostgreSQL version 8.4, you can use the WITH statement to define the view in line, as follows:

```
WITH nlqp AS (
      SELECT
          spoint_id,
          extract('quarter' from sale_time) as sale_quarter,
          sum(sale_price) - sum(cost) AS profit,
          count(*) AS nr_of_sales
        FROM sale s
        JOIN item_in_wh iw ON s.item_in_wh_id=iw.id
        JOIN item i ON iw.item_id = i.id
        JOIN salespoint sp ON s.spoint_id = sp.id
        JOIN location sploc ON sp.loc_id = sploc.id
        JOIN warehouse wh ON iw.whouse_id = wh.id
        JOIN location whloc ON wh.loc_id = whloc.id
        WHERE sale_time >= '2013-01-01'
         AND sale_time < '2014-01-01'
         AND sploc.id != whloc.id
        GROUP BY 1,2
)
SELECT shop.sp_name AS shop_name,
        q1_nloc_profit.profit as q1_profit,
        q2_nloc_profit.profit as q2_profit,
        q3_nloc_profit.profit as q3_profit,
        q4_nloc_profit.profit as q4_profit,
        year_nloc_profit.profit as year_profit
   FROM (SELECT * FROM salespoint ORDER BY sp_name) AS shop
   LEFT JOIN nlqp AS q1_nloc_profit
        ON shop.id = Q1_NLOC_PROFIT.spoint_id
    AND q1_nloc_profit.sale_quarter = 1
   LEFT JOIN nlqp AS q2_nloc_profit
        ON shop.id = Q2_NLOC_PROFIT.spoint_id
    AND q2_nloc_profit.sale_quarter = 2
   LEFT JOIN nlqp AS q3_nloc_profit
        ON shop.id = Q3_NLOC_PROFIT.spoint_id
    AND q3_nloc_profit.sale_quarter = 3
   LEFT JOIN nlqp AS q4_nloc_profit
        ON shop.id = Q4_NLOC_PROFIT.spoint_id
    AND q4_nloc_profit.sale_quarter = 4
   LEFT JOIN (
          SELECT spoint_id, sum(profit) AS profit
```

```
        FROM nlqp GROUP BY 1
    ) AS year_nloc_profit
    ON shop.id = year_nloc_profit.spoint_id
ORDER BY 1;
```

For more information on WITH queries (also known as **Common Table Expressions (CTEs)**), read the official documentation at `http://www.postgresql.org/docs/11/static/queries-with.html`.

There's more...

Another ace in the hole is represented by temporary tables, which are used for parts of the query. By default, a temporary table is dropped at the end of a Postgres session, but the behavior can be changed at the time of creation.

PostgreSQL itself can choose to materialize parts of the query during the query optimization phase, but sometimes, it fails to make the best choice for the query plan, either due to insufficient statistics, or because—as it can happen for large query plans, where **Genetic Query Optimization (GEQO)** is used—it may have just overlooked some possible query plans.

If you think that materializing (separately preparing) some parts of the query is a good idea, you can do this by using a temporary table, simply by running CREATE TEMPORARY TABLE my_temptable01 AS <the part of the query you want to materialize> and then using my_temptable01 in the main query, instead of the materialized part.

You can even create indexes on the temporary table for PostgreSQL to use in the main query:

```
BEGIN;
CREATE TEMPORARY TABLE nlqp_temp ON COMMIT DROP
  AS
      SELECT
          spoint_id,
          extract('quarter' from sale_time) as sale_quarter,
          sum(sale_price) - sum(cost) AS profit,
          count(*) AS nr_of_sales
      FROM sale s
      JOIN item_in_wh iw ON s.item_in_wh_id=iw.id
      JOIN item i ON iw.item_id = i.id
      JOIN salespoint sp ON s.spoint_id = sp.id
      JOIN location sploc ON sp.loc_id = sploc.id
      JOIN warehouse wh ON iw.whouse_id = wh.id
```

```
        JOIN location whloc ON wh.loc_id = whloc.id
    WHERE sale_time >= '2013-01-01'
      AND sale_time < '2014-01-01'
      AND sploc.id != whloc.id
    GROUP BY 1,2
;
```

You can create indexes on the table and analyze the temporary table here:

```
SELECT shop.sp_name AS shop_name,
       q1_NLP.profit as q1_profit,
       q2_NLP.profit as q2_profit,
       q3_NLP.profit as q3_profit,
       q4_NLP.profit as q4_profit,
       year_NLP.profit as year_profit
  FROM (SELECT * FROM salespoint ORDER BY sp_name) AS shop
  LEFT JOIN nlqp_temp AS q1_NLP
      ON shop.id = Q1_NLP.spoint_id AND q1_NLP.sale_quarter = 1
  LEFT JOIN nlqp_temp AS q2_NLP
      ON shop.id = Q2_NLP.spoint_id AND q2_NLP.sale_quarter = 2
  LEFT JOIN nlqp_temp AS q3_NLP
      ON shop.id = Q3_NLP.spoint_id AND q3_NLP.sale_quarter = 3
  LEFT JOIN nlqp_temp AS q4_NLP
      ON shop.id = Q4_NLP.spoint_id AND q4_NLP.sale_quarter = 4
  LEFT JOIN (
        select spoint_id, sum(profit) AS profit FROM nlqp_temp GROUP BY 1
      ) AS year_NLP
      ON shop.id = year_NLP.spoint_id
  ORDER BY 1
;
COMMIT; -- here the temp table goes away
```

Using materialized views (long-living temporary tables)

If the part you put in the temporary table is large, does not change very often, and/or is hard to compute, then you may be able to do it less often for each query by using a technique named **materialized views**.

Materialized views are views that are prepared before they are used (similar to a cached table). They are either fully regenerated as underlying data changes, or in some cases, can update only those rows that depend on the changed data.

PostgreSQL natively supports materialized views through the CREATE MATERIALIZED VIEW, ALTER MATERIALIZED VIEW, REFRESH MATERIALIZED VIEW, and DROP MATERIALIZED VIEW commands. At the time of writing, PostgreSQL only supports full regeneration of the cached tables and does so by using a concurrent REFRESH of MATERIALIZED VIEW.

A fundamental aspect of materialized views is that they can have their own indexes, like any other table. See http://www.postgresql.org/docs/11/static/sql-creatematerializedview.html for more information on creating materialized views.

For instance, you can rewrite the example in the previous recipe using a materialized view instead of a temporary table:

```
CREATE MATERIALIZED VIEW nlqp_temp AS
        SELECT spoint_id,
               extract('quarter' from sale_time) as sale_quarter,
               sum(sale_price) - sum(cost) AS profit,
               count(*) AS nr_of_sales
        FROM sale s
        JOIN item_in_wh iw ON s.item_in_wh_id=iw.id
        JOIN item i ON iw.item_id = i.id
        JOIN salespoint sp ON s.spoint_id = sp.id
        JOIN location sploc ON sp.loc_id = sploc.id
        JOIN warehouse wh ON iw.whouse_id = wh.id
        JOIN location whloc ON wh.loc_id = whloc.id
               WHERE sale_time >= '2013-01-01'
               AND sale_time < '2014-01-01'
               AND sploc.id != whloc.id
               GROUP BY 1,2
```

Using set-returning functions for some parts of queries

Another possibility for achieving similar results to temporary tables and/or materialized views is by using a **set-returning function** for some parts of the query.

It is easy to have a materialized view freshness check inside a function. However, a detailed analysis and an overview of these techniques go beyond the goals of this book, as they require a deep understanding of the PL/pgSQL procedural language.

Speeding up queries without rewriting them

Often, you either can't or don't want to rewrite the query. However, you can still try and speed it up through any of the techniques we will discuss here.

How to do it...

By now, we assume that you've looked at various problems already, so the following are more advanced ideas for you to try.

Increasing work_mem

For queries involving large sorts or for join queries, it may be useful to increase the amount of working memory that can be used for query execution. Try setting the following:

```
SET work_mem = '1TB';
```

Then, run EXPLAIN (not EXPLAIN ANALYZE). If EXPLAIN changes for the query, then it may benefit from more memory. I'm guessing that you don't have access to 1 terabyte of RAM; the previous setting was only used to prove that the query plan is dependent on available memory. Now, issue the following:

```
RESET work_mem;
```

Now, choose a more appropriate value for production use, such as the following:

```
SET work_mem = '128MB';
```

Remember to increase maintenace_work_mem when creating indexes or adding foreign keys, rather than work_mem.

More ideas with indexes

Try and add a multicolumn index that is specifically tuned for that query.

If you have a query that, for example, selects rows from the t1 table on the a column and sorts on the b column, then creating the following index enables PostgreSQL to do it all in one index scan:

```
CREATE INDEX t1_a_b_idx ON t1(a, b);
```

PostgreSQL 9.2 introduced a new plan type: **index-only scans.** This allows you to utilize a technique known as **covering indexes.** If all of the columns requested by the SELECT list of a query are available in an index, that particular index is a covering index for that query. This technique allows PostgreSQL to fetch valid rows directly from the index, without accessing the table (**heap**), so performance improves significantly. If the index is non-unique, you can just add columns onto the end of the index, like so. However, please be aware that this only works for non-unique indexes:

```
CREATE INDEX t1_a_b_c_idx ON t1(a, b, c);
```

PostgreSQL 11 provides syntax to identify covering index columns in a way that works for both unique and non-unique indexes, like this:

```
CREATE INDEX t1_a_b_cov_idx ON t1(a, b) INCLUDE (c);
```

Another often underestimated (or unknown) feature of PostgreSQL is **partial indexes.** If you use SELECT on a condition, especially if this condition only selects a small number of rows, you can use a conditional index on that expression, like this:

```
CREATE INDEX t1_proc_ndx ON t1(i1)
WHERE needs_processing = TRUE;
```

The index will be used by queries that have a WHERE clause that includes the index clause, like so:

```
SELECT id, ... WHERE needs_processing AND i1 = 5;
```

There are many types of indexes in Postgres, so you may find that there are multiple types of indexes that can be used for a particular task and many options to choose from:

- **Identifier data**: BTREE and HASH
- **Text data**: GIST and GIN
- **JSONB or XML data**: GIN
- **Time-range data**: BRIN
- **Geographical data**: BRIN, GIST, and SP-GIST

Performance gains in Postgres can also be obtained with another technique: **clustering tables on specific indexes.** However, index access may still not be very efficient if the values that are accessed by the index are distributed randomly, all over the table. If you know that some fields are likely to be accessed together, then cluster the table on an index defined on those fields. For a multicolumn index, you can use the following command:

```
CLUSTER t1_a_b_ndx ON t1;
```

Clustering a table on an index rewrites the whole table in index order. This can lock the table for a long time, so don't do it on a busy system. Also, CLUSTER is a one-time command. New rows do not get inserted in cluster order, and to keep the performance gains, you may need to cluster the table every now and then.

Once a table has been clustered on an index, you don't need to specify the index name in any cluster commands that follow. It is enough to type this:

```
CLUSTER t1;
```

It still takes time to rewrite the entire table, though it is probably a little faster once most of the table is in index order.

There's more...

We will complete this recipe by listing four examples of query performance issues that can be addressed with a specific solution.

Time series partitioning

Refer to the *Creating time series tables* recipe for more information on this.

Using a TABLESAMPLE view

Where some queries access a table, replace that with a view that retrieves fewer rows using a TABLESAMPLE clause. In this example, we are using a sampling method that produces a sample of the table using a scan lasting no longer than 5 seconds; if the table is small enough, the answer is exact, otherwise progressive sampling is used to ensure that we meet our time objective:

```
CREATE EXTENSION tsm_system_time;
CREATE SCHEMA fast_access_schema;
CREATE VIEW tablename AS
  SELECT * FROM data_schema TABLESAMPLE system_time(5000); --5 secs
SET search_path = 'fast_access_schema, data_schema';
```

So, the application can use the new table without changing the SQL. Be careful, as some answers can change when you're accessing fewer rows (for example, sum()), making this particular idea somewhat restricted; the overall idea of using views is still useful.

In case of many updates, set fillfactor on the table

If you often update only some tables and can arrange your query/queries so that you don't change any indexed fields, then setting `fillfactor` to a lower value than the default of `100` for those tables enables PostgreSQL to use **Heap-Only Tuples** (**HOT**) updates, which can be an order of magnitude faster than ordinary updates. HOT updates not only avoid creating new index entries, but can also perform a fast mini-vacuum inside the page to make room for new rows:

```
ALTER TABLE t1 SET (fillfactor = 70);
```

This tells PostgreSQL to fill only `70` percent of each page in the `t1` table when performing insertions so that 30 percent is left for use by in-page (HOT) updates.

Rewriting the schema – a more radical approach

In some cases, it may make sense to rewrite the database schema and provide an old view for unchanged queries using views, triggers, rules, and functions.

One such case occurs when refactoring the database, and you would want old queries to keep running while changes are made.

Another case is an external application that is unusable with the provided schema, but can be made to perform OK with a different distribution of data between tables.

Discovering why a query is not using an index

This recipe explains what to do if you think your query should use an index, but it isn't.

There could be several reasons for this, but most often, the reason is that the optimizer believes that, based on the available distribution statistics, it is cheaper and faster to use a query plan that does not use that specific index.

Getting ready

First, check that your index exists, and ensure that the table has been analyzed. If there is any doubt, rerun it to be sure:

```
postgres=# ANALYZE;
ANALYZE
```

How to do it...

Force index usage and compare plan costs with an index and without, as follows:

```
postgres=# EXPLAIN ANALYZE SELECT count(*) FROM itable WHERE id > 500;
                        QUERY PLAN
-------------------------------------------------------------------
  Aggregate  (cost=188.75..188.76 rows=1 width=0)
             (actual time=37.958..37.959 rows=1 loops=1)
    ->  Seq Scan on itable (cost=0.00..165.00 rows=9500 width=0)
             (actual time=0.290..18.792 rows=9500 loops=1)
          Filter: (id > 500)
 Total runtime: 38.027 ms
(4 rows)
postgres=# SET enable_seqscan TO false;
SET
postgres=# EXPLAIN ANALYZE SELECT count(*) FROM itable WHERE id > 500;
                        QUERY PLAN
-------------------------------------------------------------------
  Aggregate  (cost=323.25..323.26 rows=1 width=0)
             (actual time=44.467..44.469 rows=1 loops=1)
    ->  Index Scan using itable_pkey on itable
             (cost=0.00..299.50 rows=9500 width=0)
             (actual time=0.100..23.240 rows=9500 loops=1)
          Index Cond: (id > 500)
 Total runtime: 44.556 ms
(4 rows)
```

Note that you must use EXPLAIN ANALYZE, rather than just EXPLAIN. EXPLAIN ANALYZE shows you how much data is being requested and measures the actual execution time, while EXPLAIN only shows what the optimizer thinks will happen. EXPLAIN ANALYZE is slower, but it gives an accurate picture of what is happening.

How it works...

By setting the `enable_seqscan` parameter to `off`, we greatly increase the cost of sequential scans for the query. This setting is never recommended for production use, only for testing.

This allows us to generate two different plans, one with `SeqScan` and one without. The optimizer works by selecting the lowest cost option available. In this case, the cost of `SeqScan` is `188.75` and the cost of `IndexScan` is `323.25`, so for this specific case, `IndexScan` will not be used.

Remember that each case is different, and always relates to the exact data distribution.

There's more...

Be sure that the `WHERE` clause you are using can be used with the type of index you have. For example, the `WHERE` clause, `abs(val) < 2`, won't use an index, because you're performing a function on the column, while `val BETWEEN -2 AND 2` could use the index. With more advanced operators and data types, it's easy to get confused as to the type of clause that will work, so check the documentation for the data type carefully.

In PostgreSQL 10, join statistics were also improved by the use of foreign keys, since they can be used in some queries to prove that joins on those keys return exactly one row.

Forcing a query to use an index

Often, we think we know better than the database optimizer. Most of the time, your expectations are wrong, and if you look carefully, you'll see that. So, recheck everything and come back later.

It is a classic error to try to get the database optimizer to use indexes when the database has very little data in it. Put some genuine data in the database first, then worry about it. Better yet, load some data on a test server first, rather than doing this in production.

Sometimes, the optimizer gets it wrong. You feel elated, and possibly angry, that the database optimizer doesn't see what you see. Please bear in mind that the data distributions within your database change over time, and this causes the optimizer to change its plans over time as well.

If you have found a case where the optimizer is wrong, it might have been correct last week, and will be correct again next week: it correctly calculated that a change of plan was required, but it made that change slightly ahead of time, or slightly too late. Again, trying to force the optimizer to do the right thing *now* might prevent it from doing the right thing *later*, when the plan changes again.

Some optimizer estimation errors can be corrected using CREATE STATISTICS, a new command added in PostgreSQL 10, which is described in this recipe's *There's more...* section.

In the long run, it is not recommended to try to force the use of a particular index.

Getting ready

Still here? Oh well.

In fact, it is not possible to tell PostgreSQL to use an index by submitting an access path hint, like other DBMS products do. However, you can trick it into using an index by telling the optimizer that all other options are prohibitively expensive.

First, you have to make sure that it is worth it to use the index. This is best done on a development or testing system, but if you are careful, it can also be done on the production server. Sometimes, it is very hard to generate a load similar to a live system in a test environment, and then your best option may be to carefully test it on the production server.

Since the PostgreSQL optimizer does not take into account the parallel load caused by other backends, it may make sense to lie to PostgreSQL about some statistics in order to make it use indexes.

How to do it...

The most common problem is selecting too much data.

A typical point of confusion comes from data that has a few very common values among a larger group. Requesting data for the very common values costs more because we need to bring back more rows. As we bring back more rows, the cost of using the index increases. Therefore, it is possible that we won't use the index for the very common values, whereas we would use the index for the less common values. To use an index effectively, make sure you're reducing the number of rows that are returned.

Another technique for making indexes more usable is **partial indexes**. Instead of indexing all of the values in a column, you might choose to index only the set of rows that are frequently accessed, for example, by excluding NULL or other unwanted data. By making the index smaller, it will be cheaper to access and fit within the cache better, avoiding pointless work by targeting the index at only the important data. Data statistics are kept for such indexes, so it can also improve the accuracy of query planning. Let's look at an example:

```
CREATE INDEX ON customer(id)
  WHERE blocked = false AND subscription_status = 'paid';
```

Another nudge toward using indexes is to set random_page_cost to a lower value—maybe even equal to seq_page_cost. This makes PostgreSQL prefer index scans on more occasions, but it still does not produce entirely unreasonable plans, at least for cases where data is mostly cached in shared buffers, or system disk caches or underlying disks are solid-state drives.

The default values for these parameters are as follows:

```
random_page_cost = 4;
seq_page_cost = 1;
```

Try setting this:

```
set random_page_cost = 2;
```

See if it helps; if not, you can try setting it to 1.

Changing random_page_cost allows you to react to whether data is on disk or in memory. Letting the optimizer know that more of an index is in the cache will help it to understand that using the index is actually cheaper.

Index scan performance for larger scans can also be improved by allowing multiple asynchronous I/O operations by increasing effective_io_concurrency. Both random_page_cost and effective_io_concurrency can be set for specific tablespaces, or for individual queries.

Rather than trying to force the use of an index, you might want to consider using a parallel query to speed up scans. Refer to the *Using parallel query* recipe for more information.

There's more...

If you have multi-column indexes (or joins), the optimizer will assume that the column values are independent of each other, which can lead to misestimation in cases where there is a correlation between the values.

If you have two dependent columns, such as `state` and `area_code`, then you can define additional statistics that will be collected when you next `ANALYZE` the table:

```
CREATE STATISTICS cust_s1 (ndistinct, dependencies) ON state, area_code
FROM cust;
```

The execution time of `ANALYZE` will increase to collect the additional stats information, plus there is a small increase in query planning time, so use this sparingly when you can confirm this will make a difference. You don't need to have both distinct and dependencies in all cases, only when it matters.

Include the table name in the statistics you create since the name cannot be repeated on different tables. In future releases, we will also add cross-table statistics.

Unfortunately, you cannot collect statistics on individual fields within JSON documents at the moment, nor collect dependency information between them; this command only applies to whole column values at this time.

There's more

If you absolutely, positively have to use the index, then you'll want to know about an extension called `pg_hint_plan`. It is available for PostgreSQL 9.1 and later versions. For more information and to download it, go to `http://pghintplan.sourceforge.jp/`.

It works, but as I said previously, try to avoid fixing things now and causing yourself pain later.

Using parallel query

PostgreSQL now has an increasingly effective parallel query feature.

Response times from long-running queries can be improved by the use of parallel processing. The concept is that we divide a large task up into multiple smaller pieces. We get the answer faster, but we use more resources to do that.

Very short queries won't get faster by using parallel query, so if you have lots of those you'll gain more by thinking about better indexing strategies. Parallel query is aimed at making very large tasks faster, so it is useful for reporting and business intelligence queries.

How to do it...

Take a query that needs to do a big chunk of work, such as the following:

```
\timing
SELECT count(*) FROM accounts;
count
----------
1000000
(1 row)
Time: 261.652 ms
SET max_parallel_workers_per_gather = 8;
SELECT count(*) FROM accounts;
count
----------
1000000
(1 row)
Time: 180.513 ms
```

By setting the `max_parallel_workers_per_gather` parameter, we've improved performance using parallel query. Note that we didn't need to change the query at all.

In PostgreSQL 9.6 and 10, parallel query only works for read-only queries, so only SELECT statements that do not contain the FOR clause (for example, SELECT ... FOR UPDATE). In addition, a parallel query can only use functions or aggregates that are marked as PARALLEL SAFE. No user-defined functions are marked PARALLEL SAFE by default, so read the docs carefully to see whether your functions can be enabled for parallelism for the current release.

How it works...

By default, a query will use only one process. Parallel query is enabled by setting `max_parallel_workers_per_gather` to a value higher than zero. This parameter specifies the maximum number of **additional** processes that are available, if needed. So, a setting of 1 will mean you have the leader process plus one additional worker process, so two processes in total.

The query optimizer will decide whether parallel query is a useful plan based upon cost, just like other aspects of the optimizer. Importantly, it will decide how many parallel workers to use in its plan, up to the maximum you specify.

Across the whole server, the maximum number of worker processes available is specified by the `max_worker_processes` parameter and is set at server start only. PostgreSQL 10 introduced the `max_parallel_workers` parameter to further control the number of worker processes that are available.

At execution time, the query will use its planned number of worker processes if that many are available. The plan for our earlier example of parallel query looks like this:

```
postgres=# EXPLAIN ANALYZE
  SELECT count(*) FROM demo;
                  QUERY PLAN
---------------------------------------------------------------------
Finalize Aggregate (cost=78117.63..78117.64 rows=1 width=8) (actual
time=203.426..203.426 rows=1 loops=1)
   -> Gather (cost=78117.21..78117.62 rows=4 width=8) (actual
time=203.286..203.421 rows=5 loops=1)
         Workers Planned: 4
         Workers Launched: 4
         -> Partial Aggregate (cost=77117.21..77117.22 rows=1 width=8)
(actual time=194.315..194.315 rows=1 loops=5)
               -> Parallel Seq Scan on demo (cost=0.00..76863.57
 rows=101457 width=0) (actual time=115.632..164.688 rows=200200 loops=5)
 Planning time: 0.076 ms
 Execution time: 206.197 ms
(8 rows)
```

If worker processes aren't available, the query will run with fewer worker processes. As a result, it pays to not be too greedy, since if all concurrent users specify more workers than are available, you'll end up with variable performance as the number of concurrent parallel queries changes.

Also note that the performance increase from adding more workers isn't linear for anything other than simple plans, so there are diminishing returns from using too many workers. The biggest gains are from adding the first few extra processes.

As a result of those factors, I recommend a setting of just 1-3 extra worker processes for general use, meaning that two processes will be used for queries, when needed. For specific long-running queries, there may be as many as 8-16 workers, though that will vary considerably, depending on the kind of servers you're running on.

There's more...

PostgreSQL 9.6 includes the basic parallel query feature. In this release, it works with Seq Scans, aggregation, and to a certain extent, with joins. For many cases, this is a very useful addition. PostgreSQL 10 added plan improvements that allow parallel query to work with B-tree index scans, bitmap heap scans, merge joins, and non-correlated subqueries. Also, starting PostgreSQL 10, you can now get parallel query plans from SQL inside procedural language functions.

If you have an immediate requirement for higher levels of scalability or very large databases, then you'll want to look at the Postgres-XL project. Postgres-XL is an open source project that uses the PostgreSQL License and has a modified PostgreSQL to provide multi-node parallel query, or **Massively Parallel Processing** (**MPP**) as it's commonly known. MPP parallel queries are much faster than single node parallel queries. The project has been running for many years now and provides a fully functional version of Postgres that's aimed at larger and/or more scalable workloads. Almost all of the operations are fully parallelized, including many types of queries, as well as maintenance commands and DDL operations. Postgres-XL features are expected to be integrated into PostgreSQL core within the next two to three years.

Creating time series tables

In many applications, we need to store data in time series.

There are various mechanisms in PostgreSQL that are designed to support this, and it is an area that has changed dramatically in PostgreSQL 11.

How to do it...

If you have a huge table and a query to select only a subset of that table, then you may wish to use a BRIN index (block range index). These indexes give performance improvements when the data is naturally ordered as it is added to the table, such as `logtime` columns or a naturally ascending `OrderId` column. Adding a BRIN index is fast and very easy, and works well for the use case of time series data logging, though it works less well under intensive updates. INSERTs into BRIN indexes are specifically designed to not slow down as the table gets bigger, so they perform much better than B-tree indexes.

You may also think that you need to manually partition a table. This can involve significant effort to set up an effective partitioning scheme using multiple DDL statements, so try BRIN first, like so:

```
CREATE TABLE measurement (
    logtime     TIMESTAMP WITH TIME ZONE NOT NULL,
    measures    JSONB NOT NULL);

CREATE INDEX ON measurement USING BRIN (logtime);
```

Partitioning syntax was introduced in PostgreSQL 10. In this release, it is effective for INSERTs and large/slow SELECT queries, which makes it suitable for time series logging and business intelligence. It is not yet fully optimized for fast OLTP SELECT, UPDATE, or DELETE commands, unless you explicitly request those commands against the specific partition you wish to target. Some of those restrictions were substantially lifted in the PostgreSQL 11 release, allowing partitioning to be effective for more use cases, but there are still many cases where you will need to wait for PostgreSQL 12 or use enhanced versions of PostgreSQL.

For example, to create a table for time series data, you may want something like this:

```
CREATE TABLE measurement (
    logtime     TIMESTAMP WITH TIME ZONE NOT NULL,
    measures    JSONB NOT NULL
    ) PARTITION BY RANGE (logtime);

CREATE TABLE measurement_week1 PARTITION OF measurement
    FOR VALUES FROM ('2019-03-01') TO ('2019-04-01');

CREATE INDEX ON measurement_week1 USING BRIN (logtime);

CREATE TABLE measurement_week2 PARTITION OF measurement
    FOR VALUES FROM ('2019-04-01') TO ('2019-05-01');

CREATE INDEX ON measurement_week2 USING BRIN (logtime);
```

Notice that you can use both BRIN indexes and partitioning at the same time, so there is less need to have a huge numbers of partitions. A typical partition size should allow the whole current partition to sit within shared buffers. For more details on partitioning, check out https://www.postgresql.org/docs/11/ddl-partitioning.html.

How it works...

Each partition is actually a normal table, so you can refer to it in queries. A partitioned table is similar in many ways to a view, since it links all of the partitions under it together. The partition key defines which data goes into which partition, so that each row lives in exactly one partition. Partitioning can also be defined with multiple levels, so a single top-level partitioned table, then with each sub-table also having sub-sub-partitions.

Using a single partition indexed with a B-tree will give poor performance. B-tree performance degrades slowly as tables get bigger, so limiting the size of your partitions will prevent any bad news. Using a B-tree on columns such as `logtime` can be done – this has been optimized recently for INSERTs.

The best reason to use partitioning is to allow you to drop old data quickly. For example, if you are only allowed to keep data for 30 days, it might make sense to store data in 30 partitions. Each day, you would add one new empty partition and detach the last partition in the time series.

Often, people want to have a very structured approach, such as hourly partitions, which can lead to thousands of partitions. This can have considerable overhead without any useful benefit. Drop partitions less frequently, say once a week at most, to avoid issues with DDL locking.

There's more...

PostgreSQL 11 adds the ability to have primary keys defined over a partitioned table, enforcing uniqueness across partitions. This requires that the partition key is the same, or a subset of the columns of the primary key.

You can define references from a partitioned table to normal tables to enforce foreign key constraints. References to a partitioned table should be possible in PostgreSQL 12.

Partition tables can now have row triggers.

Partitioned tables also support default partitions, but I recommend against using them because of the way table locking works with that feature.

Using optimistic locking

If you perform work in one long transaction, the database will lock rows for long periods of time. Long lock times often result in application performance issues because of long lock waits:

```
BEGIN;
SELECT * FROM accounts WHERE holder_name ='BOB' FOR UPDATE;
<do some calculations here>
UPDATE accounts SET balance = 42.00 WHERE holder_name ='BOB';
COMMIT;
```

If that is happening, then you may gain some performance by moving from explicit locking (`SELECT ... FOR UPDATE`) to optimistic locking.

Optimistic locking assumes that others don't update the same record, and checks this at update time, instead of locking the record for the time it takes to process the information on the client side.

How to do it...

Rewrite your application so that the SQL is transformed into two separate transactions, with a double-check to ensure that the rows haven't changed (pay attention to the placeholders):

```
SELECT A.*, (A.*::text) AS old_acc_info
FROM accounts a WHERE holder_name ='BOB';
<do some calculations here>
UPDATE accounts SET balance = 42.00
WHERE holder_name ='BOB'
AND (A.*::text) = <old_acc_info from select above>;
```

Then, check whether the `UPDATE` operation really did update one row in your application code. If it did not, then the account for `BOB` was modified between `SELECT` and `UPDATE`, and you probably need to rerun your entire operation (both transactions).

How it works...

Instead of locking Bob's row for the time the data from the first `SELECT` command is processed in the client, PostgreSQL queries the old state of Bob's account record in the `old_acc_info` variable and then uses this value to check that the record has not changed when we eventually update.

You can also save all fields individually and then check them all in the UPDATE query; if you have an automatic last_change field, then you can use that instead. Alternatively, if you only care about a few fields changing, such as balance, and are fine ignoring others, such as email, then you only need to check the relevant fields in the UPDATE statement.

There's more...

You can also use the serializable transaction isolation level when you need to be absolutely sure that the data you are looking at is not affected by other user changes.

The default transaction isolation level in PostgreSQL is read committed, but you can choose from two more levels, repeatable read and serializable, if you require stricter control over visibility of data within a transaction; see http://www.postgresql.org/docs/11/static/transaction-iso.html for more information.

Another design pattern that's available in some cases is to use a single statement for the UPDATE and return data to the user via the RETURNING clause, as in the following example:

```
UPDATE accounts
  SET balance = balance - i_amount
WHERE username = i_username
AND balance - i_amount > - max_credit
RETURNING balance;
```

In some cases, moving the entire computation to the database function is a very good idea. If you can pass all of the necessary information to the database for processing as a database function, it will run even faster, as you save several round-trips to the database. If you use a PL/pgSQL function, you also benefit from automatically saving query plans on the first call in a session and using saved plans in subsequent calls.

Therefore, the preceding transaction is replaced by a function in the database, like so:

```
CREATE OR REPLACE FUNCTION consume_balance
( i_username text
, i_amount numeric(10,2)
, max_credit numeric(10,2)
, OUT success boolean
, OUT remaining_balance numeric(10,2)
) AS
$$
BEGIN
  UPDATE accounts SET balance = balance - i_amount
  WHERE username = i_username
```

```
        AND balance - i_amount > - max_credit
        RETURNING balance
        INTO remaining_balance;
        IF NOT FOUND THEN
            success := FALSE;
            SELECT balance
            FROM accounts
            WHERE username = i_username
            INTO remaining_balance;
        ELSE
            success := TRUE;
        END IF;
    END;
    $$ LANGUAGE plpgsql;
```

You can call it by simply running the following line from your client:

```
SELECT * FROM consume_balance ('bob', 7, 0);
```

The output will return the success variable. It tells you whether there was a sufficient balance in Bob's account. The output will also return a number telling the balance bob has left after this operation.

Reporting performance problems

Sometimes, you face performance issues and feel lost, but you should never feel alone when working with one of the most successful open source projects ever.

How to do it...

If you need to get some advice on your performance problems, then the right place to do so is the performance mailing list at http://archives.postgresql.org/pgsql-performance/.

First, you may want to ensure that it is not a well-known problem by searching the mailing list archives.

A very good description of what to include in your performance problem report is available at http://wiki.postgresql.org/wiki/Guide_to_reporting_problems.

There's more...

More performance-related information can be found at
`http://wiki.postgresql.org/wiki/Performance_Optimization`.

11
Backup and Recovery

Most people admit that backups are essential, though they also devote a very small amount of time to thinking about the topic.

The first recipe is about understanding and controlling crash recovery. You need to understand what happens if the database server crashes so that you can understand whether you need to perform a recovery operation.

The next recipe is all about planning. That's really the best place to start before you perform backups.

The physical backup mechanisms here were initially written by Simon Riggs (one of the authors of this book) for PostgreSQL 8.0 in 2004 and have been supported by him ever since, now with increasing help from the community as its popularity grows. 2ndQuadrant has also been providing database recovery services since 2004, and regrettably, many people have needed them as a result of missing or damaged backups.

It is important to note that, in the last few years, the native streaming replication protocol has become more and more relevant in PostgreSQL. It can be used for backup purposes too; not only to take a base backup with `pg_basebackup`, but also to stream WAL files using `pg_receivewal`.

As authors, we had a dilemma when planning this book. Should we introduce streaming replication before backups or leave it to the replication section? For now, we decided to leave it out of this chapter and postpone it to the next. We would like your feedback on this subject for future editions of this book.

As a final note, all of the examples regarding physical backup and recovery in this chapter are thoroughly explained so that you understand what is happening behind the scenes. However, unless you have very specific requirements dictating otherwise, we highly recommend that, when in production, you use Barman (our open source backup and recovery tool) or a similar product that is specialized in this area. The last two recipes in this chapter will introduce Barman.

In this chapter, we will cover the following recipes:

- Understanding and controlling crash recovery
- Planning backups
- Hot logical backup of one database
- Hot logical backup of all databases
- Backup of database object definitions
- Standalone hot physical database backup
- Hot physical backup and continuous archiving
- Recovery of all databases
- Recovery to a point in time
- Recovery of a dropped/damaged table
- Recovery of a dropped/damaged database
- Improving performance of backup/recovery
- Incremental/differential backup and restore
- Hot physical backups with Barman
- Recovery with Barman
- Validating backups

Understanding and controlling crash recovery

Crash recovery is the PostgreSQL subsystem that saves us, should the server crash or fail as part of a system crash.

It's good to understand a little about it and to do what we can to control it in our favor.

How to do it...

If PostgreSQL crashes, there will be a message in the server log with the severity level set to PANIC. PostgreSQL will immediately restart and attempt to recover using the transaction log or **Write-Ahead Log (WAL)**.

The WAL consists of a series of files written to the pg_wal subdirectory of the PostgreSQL data directory. Each change made to the database is recorded first in WAL, hence the name write-ahead log, as a synonym of *transaction log*. Note that the former is probably more accurate since, in the WAL, there are also changes not related to transactions. When a transaction commits, the default (and safe) behavior is to force the WAL records to disk. Should PostgreSQL crash, the WAL will be replayed, which returns the database to the point of the last committed transaction, and hence ensures the durability of any database changes.

 Database changes themselves aren't written to disk at transaction commit. Those changes are written to disk some time later by the background writer on a well-tuned server.

Crash recovery replays the WAL, but from what point does it start to recover? Recovery starts from points in the WAL known as **checkpoints**. The duration of a crash recovery depends on the number of changes in the transaction log since the last checkpoint. A checkpoint is a known safe starting point for recovery, since it guarantees that all of the previous changes to the database have already been written to disk.

A checkpoint can become a performance bottleneck on busy database servers because of the number of writes required. We will look at a number of ways to fine-tune that, but you must also understand the effect that those tuning options may have on crash recovery.

A checkpoint can be either immediate or scheduled. Immediate checkpoints are triggered by some action of a superuser, such as the CHECKPOINT command. Scheduled checkpoints are decided automatically by PostgreSQL.

Two parameters control the occurrence of scheduled checkpoints. The first is checkpoint_timeout, which is the number of seconds until the next checkpoint. While this parameter is time-based, the second parameter, max_wal_size, influences the amount of WAL data that will be written before a checkpoint is triggered; the actual limit is computed from that parameter, taking into account the fact that WAL files can only be deleted after one checkpoint (two in older releases). A checkpoint is called whenever either of these two limits is reached.

It's tempting to banish checkpoints as much as possible by setting the following parameters:

```
max_wal_size = 20GB
checkpoint_timeout = 3600
```

However, if you do this, you should give some thought to how long crash recovery will take, and whether you want that; you must also consider how many changes will accumulate before the next checkpoint, and more importantly how much I/O the checkpoint will generate due to those changes.

Also, you should make sure that the `pg_wal` directory is mounted on disks with enough disk space. By default, `max_wal_size` is set to 1 GB. The amount of disk space required by `pg_wal` might also be influenced by the following:

- Unexpected spikes in workload
- Failures in continuous archiving (see `archive_command` in the *Hot physical backup and continuous archiving* recipe)
- The `wal_keep_segments` setting (you will need 16 MB `wal_keep_segments` of space)

In contrast to `max_wal_size`, with `min_wal_size`, you can control the minimum size allotted to WAL storage, and allow PostgreSQL to recycle existing WAL files instead of removing them.

How it works...

Recovery continues until the end of the transaction log. WAL data is being written continually, so there is no defined endpoint; it is literally the last correct record. Each WAL record is individually CRC-checked so that we know whether a record is complete and valid before trying to process it. Each record contains a pointer to the previous record, so we can tell that the record forms a valid link in the chain of actions recorded in the WAL. As a result of that, recovery always ends with some kind of error in reading the next WAL record. That is normal and means *the next record does not exist (yet)*.

Recovery performance can be very fast, though its speed does depend on the actions being recovered. The best way to test recovery performance is to set up a standby replication server, as described in `Chapter 12`, *Replication and Upgrades*, which is actually implemented as a variant of crash recovery.

There's more...

It's possible for a problem to be caused by replaying the transaction log so that the database server will fail to start.

Some people's response to this is to use a utility named `pg_resetwal`, which removes the current transaction log files and tidies up after that operation has taken place.

The `pg_resetwal` utility destroys data changes and that means data loss. If you do decide to run that utility, make sure that you take a backup of the `pg_wal` directory first. Our advice is to seek immediate assistance rather than do this. You don't know for certain that doing this will fix a problem though, once you've done it, you will have difficulty going back.

When discussing `min_wal_size`, we mentioned that WAL files are recycled; what this actually means is that older WAL files are renamed so that they are ready to be reused as future WAL files. This reduces commit latency in case of heavy write workloads, because creating a new file is slower than writing into an existing one.

Planning backups

This recipe is all about thinking ahead and planning. If you're reading this recipe before you've decided to take a backup, well done!

The key thing to understand is that you should plan your recovery, not your backup. The type of backup you take influences the type of recovery that is possible, so you must give some thought to what you are trying to achieve beforehand.

If you want to plan your recovery, then you need to consider the different types of failure that can occur. What type of recovery do you wish to perform?

You need to consider the following main aspects:

- Full or partial database?
- Everything or just object definitions?
- **Point-In-Time Recovery (PITR)**
- Restore performance

We need to look at the characteristics of the utilities to understand what our backup and recovery options are. It's often beneficial to have multiple types of backup to cover the different types of failure possible.

Your main backup options are the following:

- Logical backup, using pg_dump
- Physical backup, which is a filesystem backup

The pg_dump utility comes in two main flavors—pg_dump and pg_dumpall.
The pg_dump utility has a -F option for producing backups in various file formats. The file format is very important when it comes to restoring from backup, so you need to pay close attention to it.

As far as physical backup is concerned, in this chapter, we will focus on filesystem backup using pg_start_backup() and pg_stop_backup(). However, it is important to note that PostgreSQL has its own built-in application for physical base backups, pg_basebackup, which relies on the native streaming replication protocol. As authors, in order to distribute the content more evenly, we have decided to cover pg_basebackup and streaming replication in the next chapter, that is, Chapter 12, *Replication and Upgrades*.

How to do it...

The following table shows the features that are available, depending on the backup technique selected. The details of these techniques are covered in the remaining recipes in this chapter:

	SQL dump to an archive file: pg_dump -F c	SQL dump to a script file: pg_dump -F p or pg_dumpall	Filesystem backup using pg_start_backup and pg_stop_backup
Backup type	Logical	Logical	Physical
Recover to point in time	No	No	Yes
Zero data loss	No	No	Yes (see note 6)
Back up all databases	One at a time	Yes (pg_dumpall)	Yes
All databases backed up at the same time	No	No	Yes
Selective backup	Yes	Yes	No (see note 2)
Incremental backup	No	No	Possible (see note 3)
Selective restore	Yes	Possible (see note 1)	No (see note 4)
DROP TABLE recovery	Yes	Yes	Possible (see note 4)
Compressed backup files	Yes	Yes	Yes
Backup in multiple files	No	No	Yes

	SQL dump to an archive file: `pg_dump -F c`	SQL dump to a script file: `pg_dump -F p` or `pg_dumpall`	Filesystem backup using `pg_start_backup`
Parallel backup possible	No	No	Yes
Parallel restore possible	Yes	No	Yes
Restore to later release	Yes	Yes	No (but see note 7)
Standalone backup	Yes	Yes	Yes (see note 6)
Allows DDL during backup	No	No	Yes

The following notes were referenced in the preceding table:

1. If you've generated a script with `pg_dump` or `pg_dumpall` and need to restore just a single object, then you will need to go deeper. You will need to write a Perl script (or similar) to read the file and extract the parts you want. This is messy and time-consuming, but probably faster than restoring the whole thing to a second server and then extracting just the parts you need with another `pg_dump`.

2. Selective backup with a physical backup is possible, but will cause problems later when you try to restore.

3. See the *Incremental/differential backup and restore* recipe.

4. Selective restore with a physical backup isn't possible with the currently supplied utilities. See the *Recovery of a dropped/damaged table* recipe for partial recovery.

5. See the *Standalone hot physical database backup* recipe.

6. See the *Hot physical backups with Barman* recipe. Barman 2 fully supports synchronous WAL streaming, allowing you to achieve **Recovery Point Objective (RPO)** equal to 0, meaning *zero data loss*.

7. A physical backup cannot be directly restored to a different PostgreSQL major version. However, it is possible to restore it to the same PostgreSQL major version, and then follow the procedure described in the *Major upgrades in-place* recipe, in `Chapter 12`, *Replication and Upgrades*, to upgrade restored files to a newer major version.

Hot logical backups of one database

Logical backup makes a copy of the data in the database by dumping the content of each table, as well as object definitions for that same database (such as schemas, tables, indexes, views, privileges, triggers, and constraints).

How to do it...

The command to do this is simple. The following is an example of doing this when using a database called `pgbench`:

```
pg_dump -F c pgbench > dumpfile
```

Alternatively, you can use the following command:

```
pg_dump -F c -f dumpfile pgbench
```

Finally, we note that you can also run `pg_dump` via the **pgAdmin 4** GUI, as shown in the following screenshot:

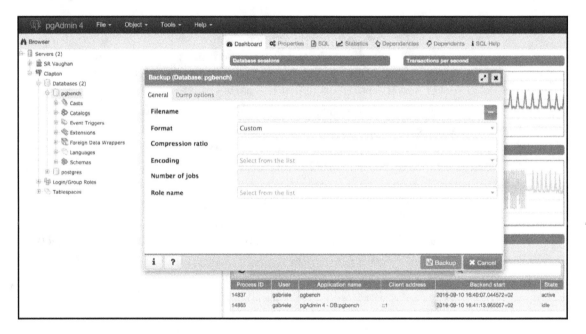

How it works...

The `pg_dump` utility produces a single output file. This output file can use the `split` command to separate the file into multiple pieces, if required.

The `pg_dump` archive file, also known as the **custom format**, is lightly compressed by default. Compression can be removed or made more aggressive.

Even though, by default, `pg_dump` writes an SQL script directly to standard output, it is recommended to use the archive file instead by enabling the custom format through the `-F c` option. As we will cover later in this chapter, backing up in the form of archive files gives you more flexibility and versatility when restoring. Archive files must be used with a tool called `pg_restore`.

The `pg_dump` utility runs by executing SQL statements against the database to unload data. When PostgreSQL runs a SQL statement, we take a *snapshot* of transactions that are currently running, which freezes our viewpoint of the database. The `pg_dump` utility can take a parallel dump of a single database using the **snapshot export** feature.

We can't (yet) share that snapshot across sessions connected to more than one database, so we cannot run an exactly consistent `pg_dump` in parallel across multiple databases.

The time of the snapshot is the only moment we can recover to—we can't recover to a time either before or after. Note that the snapshot time is the start of the backup, not the end.

When `pg_dump` runs, it holds the very lowest kind of lock on the tables being dumped. Those are designed to prevent DDL from running against the tables while the dump takes place. If a dump is run at the point at which other DDLs are already running, then the dump will sit and wait. If you want to limit the waiting time, you can do so by setting the `--lock-wait-timeout` option.

Since `pg_dump` runs SQL queries to extract data, it will have some performance impact. This must be taken into account when executing on a live server.

The `pg_dump` utility allows you to take a selective backup of tables. The `-t` option also allows you to specify views and sequences. There's no way to dump other object types individually using `pg_dump`. You can use some supplied functions to extract individual snippets of information from the catalog.

More details on these functions are available at
https://www.postgresql.org/docs/11/static/functions-info.html#FU
NCTIONS-INFO-CATALOG-TABLE.

The `pg_dump` utility works against earlier releases of PostgreSQL, so it can be used to migrate data between releases.

When migrating your database from an earlier version, it is generally recommended to use pg_dump of the same version of the target PostgreSQL. For example, if you are migrating a PostgreSQL 10.7 database to PostgreSQL 11, you should use pg_dump v11 to remotely connect to the 10.7 server and back up the database.

As far as extensions are concerned, pg_dump is aware of any objects (namely tables and functions) that have been installed as part of an additional package, such as PostGIS or Slony. Thanks to that, they can be recreated by issuing appropriate CREATE EXTENSION commands instead of dumping and restoring them together with the other database objects. Extension support removes such difficulties when restoring from a logical backup, maintaining the list of additional tables that have been created as part of the software installation process. Look at the *Managing installed extensions* recipe in Chapter 3, *Configuration*, for more details.

There's more...

What time was pg_dump taken? The snapshot for pg_dump is taken at the beginning of a backup. The file modification time will tell you when the dump finished. The dump is consistent at the time of the snapshot, so you may need to know that time.

If you are making a script dump, you can do a verbose dump, as follows:

```
pg_dump -v
```

This adds the time to the top of the script. Custom dumps store the start time as well, and that can be accessed using the following command:

```
pg_restore --schema-only -v dumpfile 2>/dev/null | head | grep Started
-- Started on 2018-06-03 09:05:46 BST
```

See also

Note that pg_dump does not dump roles (such as users and groups) and tablespaces. Those two are only dumped by pg_dumpall; see the following recipes for more detailed descriptions.

Hot logical backups of all databases

If you have more than one database in your PostgreSQL server, you may want to take a logical backup of all of the databases at the same time.

How to do it...

Our recommendation is that you do exactly what you do for one database to each database in your cluster.

You can run individual dumps in parallel if you want to speed things up.

Once this is complete, dump the global information using the following command:

```
pg_dumpall -g
```

How it works...

To back up all databases, you may be told that you need to use the pg_dumpall utility. The following are four good reasons why you shouldn't do that:

- If you use pg_dumpall, the only output produced will be in a script file. Script files can't benefit from all the features of archive files, such as parallel and selective restore of pg_restore. By making your backup in this way, you will immediately deprive yourself of flexibility and versatility at restore time.
- The pg_dumpall utility produces dumps of each database, one after another. This means that pg_dumpall is slower than running multiple pg_dump tasks in parallel, one against each database.
  - The dumps of individual databases are not consistent to a particular point in time. As we pointed out in the *Hot logical backups of one database* recipe, if you start the dump at 04:00 and it ends at 07:00, then you cannot be sure exactly what time the dump relates to; it could be any time between 04:00 and 07:00.
- Options for pg_dumpall and pg_dump are similar in many ways. pg_dump has more options and therefore gives you more flexibility.

See also

If you are taking a logical backup of all of your databases for disaster recovery purposes, you should look at *hot physical backup* options instead.

Backups of database object definitions

Sometimes, it's useful to get a dump of the object definitions that make up a database. This is useful for comparing what's in the database against the definitions in a data- or object-modeling tool. It's also useful to make sure you can recreate objects in the correct schema, tablespace, and database with the correct ownership and permissions.

How to do it...

The basic command to dump the definitions for every database of your PostgreSQL instance is as follows:

```
pg_dumpall --schema-only > myscriptdump.sql
```

This includes all objects, including roles, tablespaces, databases, schemas, tables, indexes, triggers, constraints, views, functions, ownerships, and privileges.

If you want to dump PostgreSQL role definitions, use the following command:

```
pg_dumpall --roles-only > myroles.sql
```

If you want to dump PostgreSQL tablespace definitions, use the following command:

```
pg_dumpall --tablespaces-only > mytablespaces.sql
```

If you want to dump both roles and tablespaces, use the following command:

```
pg_dumpall --globals-only > myglobals.sql
```

The output is a human-readable script file that can be re-executed to recreate each of the databases.

The short form for the `--globals-only` option is `-g`, which we have already seen in a previous recipe, *Hot logical backups of all databases*. Similar abbreviations exist for `--schema-only` (`-s`), `--tablespaces-only` (`-t`), and `--roles-only` (`-r`).

There's more...

In PostgreSQL, the word **schema** is also used to organize a set of related objects of a database in a logical container, similar to a directory. It is also known as a **namespace**. Be careful that you don't confuse what is happening here. The `--schema-only` option makes a backup of the database schema, that is, the definitions of all objects in the database (and in all namespaces). To make a backup of the data and definitions in just one namespace and one database, use `pg_dump` with the `-n` option. To make a backup of only the definitions, in just one namespace and one database, use `pg_dump` with both `-n` and `--schema-only` together.

You can also take advantage of a previously generated archive file (see the *Hot logical backups of one database* recipe) and generate a script file using `pg_restore`, as follows:

```
pg_restore --schema-only mydumpfile > myscriptdump.sql
```

Standalone hot physical database backup

Hot physical backup is an important capability for databases.

Physical backup allows us to get a completely consistent view of the changes to all databases at once. Physical backup also allows us to back up even while DDL changes are being executed on the database. Apart from resource constraints, there is no additional overhead or locking with this approach.

Physical backup procedures used to be slightly more complex than logical backup procedures, but in version 10, some defaults have been changed, making them easier; after these changes, making a backup with `pg_basebackup` has become very easy, even with default settings.

As specified in the introduction to this chapter, making a backup with `pg_basebackup` is covered in `Chapter 12`, *Replication and Upgrades*, and in this chapter, we will focus on the variant of the filesystem backup that uses `pg_start_backup()` and `pg_stop_backup()`, which is the only way to overcome some of the limitations of `pg_basebackup`, for instance, if you want an incremental backup or a parallel backup. For similar reasons, this method is also supported by many advanced backup solutions, such as Barman.

So, let's start with a simple procedure to produce a standalone backup.

Getting ready

The following steps assume that a number of environment variables have been set, which are as follows:

- $PGDATA is the path to the PostgreSQL data directory, ending with /
- All required PostgreSQL connection parameters have been set

These assumptions are not strictly required, but they make the whole procedure simpler and more readable because we can avoid adding lots of command-line options to specify the data directory or any connection detail every time we connect to the database.

The initial procedure is *step 1* onward. If you are running subsequent backups, start from step 3.

How to do it...

The steps are as follows:

1. Create a new backup directory as a sibling of $PGDATA, if it is not already present, as follows:

   ```
   cd $PGDATA
   mkdir ../standalone
   ```

2. Create the archive directory, as follows:

   ```
   mkdir ../standalone/archive
   ```

3. Start archiving with the following command:

   ```
   pg_receivewal -D ../standalone/archive/
   ```

   This command will not return, because pg_receivewal will run until interrupted. Therefore, you must open a new Terminal session to perform the next steps, starting with step 4.

First, we described how to configure streaming archiving (steps 2 and 3). For file-based archiving, follow the alternate steps, *2a* and *3a*, instead, which are as follows:

- **2a**: Set `archive_command`. In `postgresql.conf`, you will need to add the following lines and restart the server, or just confirm that they are present:

  ```
  archive_mode  =  on
  archive_command  =  'test  !  -f
  ../standalone/archiving_active  ||
  cp  -i  %p  ../standalone/archive/%f'
  ```

  The last setting is only split into two lines for typesetting reasons; in `postgresql.conf`, you must keep it in a single line.

  You must also check that `wal_level` is set to either `replica` or `logical`, which is normally true as `replica` is the default setting.

- **3a**: Start archiving, as follows:

  ```
  cd $PGDATA
  mkdir ../standalone/archive
  touch ../standalone/archiving_active
  ```

  Irrespective of whether you have chosen streaming archiving or file-based archiving, you can now proceed with step 4.

4. Define the name of the backup file. The following example includes time information in the filename:

   ```
   BACKUP_FILENAME=$(date '+%Y%m%d%H%M').tar
   ```

5. Start the backup, as follows:

   ```
   psql -c "select pg_start_backup('standalone')"
   ```

   This step could take a while because PostgreSQL performs a checkpoint before returning to ensure that the data files copied in the next step include all of the latest data changes. See the *Understanding and controlling crash recovery* recipe from earlier in this chapter for more details about checkpoints.

Depending on system configuration and workload, a checkpoint could take a long time, even several minutes. This time is part of the backup duration, which in turn affects the amount of WAL files needed for the backup; so it could be a good idea to reduce the duration of this checkpoint by issuing a CHECKPOINT command just before archiving is activated in step 3, and then by starting the backup in fast mode, as follows:

```
psql -c "select pg_start_backup('standalone', fast := true)"
```

fast mode means that the checkpoint included in pg_start_backup runs as quickly as possible, irrespective of its impact on the system; this should not be a problem because most of the shared buffers will have been written already by the CHECKPOINT command that was issued previously.

6. Make a base backup—copy the data files (excluding the content of the pg_wal and pg_wal directories) using the following command:

```
tar -cv \
--exclude="pg_wal/*" --exclude="pg_replslot/*" \
-f ../standalone/$BACKUP_FILENAME *
```

7. Stop the backup, as follows:

```
psql -c "select pg_stop_backup(), current_timestamp"
```

8. If you have followed *steps 2* and *step 3* (for example, if you are using streaming archiving), stop archiving by hitting *Ctrl + C* in the Terminal session where pg_receivewal is running:

- **8a**: Alternatively, if you have chosen steps *2a* and *3a* (for example, file-based archiving), enter the standalone directory and stop archiving, as follows:

```
rm ../standalone/archiving_active
```

9. Add the archived files to the standalone backup, as follows:

```
cd ../standalone
tar -rf $BACKUP_FILENAME archive
```

10. Write a recovery.conf file to recover with:

```
echo "restore_command = 'cp archive/%f %p'" > recovery.conf
echo "recovery_end_command = 'rm -R archive' " >> recovery.conf
```

11. Add `recovery.conf` to the `tar` archive, as follows:

    tar -rf $BACKUP_FILENAME recovery.conf

12. Clean up:

    rm -rf archive recovery.conf

13. Store `$BACKUP_FILENAME` somewhere safe. A safe place is definitely not on the same server.

This procedure ends with a file named `$BACKUP_FILENAME` in the standalone directory. It is imperative to remember to copy it somewhere safe. This file contains everything that you need to recover, including a recovery parameter file.

How it works...

The backup produced by the preceding procedure only allows you to restore to a single point in time. That point is the time of the `pg_stop_backup()` function.

A physical backup takes a copy of all files in the database (step *6*—the *base backup*). That alone is not sufficient as a backup, and you need the other steps as well. A simple copy of the database produces a time-inconsistent copy of the database files. To make the backup time consistent, we need to add all of the changes that took place from the start to the end of the backup. That's why we have steps *5* and *7* to bracket our backup step.

In technical terms, steps *5* and *7* take advantage of the API that controls exclusive backups, meaning that there can only be one physical backup at a time, and it has to be performed on a master server.

PostgreSQL supports non-exclusive backups as well, allowing users to perform `pg_start_backup()` and `pg_stop_backup()` functions on a read-only standby server. To make a backup non-exclusive, just add the `exclusive := false` parameter to those functions. However, programming backup scripts for the non-exclusive backup method is more complex and it is not covered in this recipe.

The changes that are made are put in the standalone/archive directory as a set of archived transaction log or WAL files. Steps *2* and *3* start streaming archiving, while the alternate steps, *2a* and *3a*, set the parameters that copy the files to the archive and start file-based archiving. Note that changing `archive_mode` requires us to restart the database server, so we use a well-known trick to avoid restarting while switching archiving on and off; `archive_command` is conditional upon the existence of a file named `archiving_active`, whose presence enables or disables the archiving process.

Note that these are just two of the possible ways to configure archiving, so PostgreSQL doesn't always need to work this way. Steps *3* and *8* enable and disable archiving, respectively, so we only store copies of the WAL files created during the period of the backup. Hence, steps *1* and *2* are setup and steps *3* to *9* are where the backup happens. Step *10* onward is gift wrapping, so that the backup script ends with everything in one neat file and proper cleanup operations take place.

Step *9* appends the WAL files to the backup file so that it is just one file.

Steps *10* and *11* add a `recovery.conf` file with its parameters set up so that there are no manual steps when we recover from this backup. This is explained in detail in the *Recovery of all databases* recipe.

In case your `PGDATA` does not contain configuration files, such as `postgresql.conf` and `pg_hba.conf`, you might have to manually copy them before performing a recovery. Remember that standard Debian and Ubuntu installations keep configuration files outside `PGDATA`, specifically under `/etc/postgresql`.

The important thing to understand in this recipe is that we need both the base backup and the appropriate archived WAL files to allow us to recover. Without both of these, we have nothing. Most of these steps are designed to ensure that we really will have the appropriate WAL files in all cases.

There's more...

One advantage of file-based WAL archiving is that it works in a *push* mode, without requiring inbound access to the database server. On the other hand, streaming WAL archiving has the advantage of transferring WAL as soon as it is produced, without waiting for the 16 MB WAL segment to be completed, which usually results in little or no data loss, even in the event of a disaster.

In summary, neither choice is superior to the other one, so we opted for documenting both. PostgreSQL ships a command-line utility called `pg_basebackup`, which uses the streaming replication infrastructure to carry out steps 4 to 6, as reported previously.

As an alternative, it is simpler than using `rsync` and issuing `pg_start_backup()` and `pg_stop_backup()` manually, but it's not a complete replacement because it has some limitations and restrictions.

If you want to make your life easier, you can rely on software that is specialized in backup and recovery. In this book, we will cover software that we at 2ndQuadrant have written and that has become very popular among PostgreSQL users: Barman. This open source tool is covered in two recipes—*Hot physical backups with Barman* and *Recovery with Barman*.

See also

It's common to use continuous archiving when using the physical backup technique because this allows you to recover to any point in time, should you need that.

Hot physical backup and continuous archiving

This recipe describes how to set up a hot physical backup with a continuous archiving mechanism. The purpose of continuous archiving is to allow us to recover to any point in time after the completion of the backup.

Manually performing each step of this procedure is a great way to gain a clear understanding of PostgreSQL's backup and restore infrastructure. However, to reduce the chances of human errors, it is good practice to avoid reliance on complex activities that must be performed by a human operator.

Procedures such as taking a hot physical backup or restoring it up to a given point in time can be performed using specialized third-party tools such as the following:

- **Barman**: `http://www.pgbarman.org/`
- **OmniPITR**: `https://github.com/omniti-labs/omnipitr`
- **PgBackRest**: `http://www.pgbackrest.org/`
- **PgHoard**: `https://github.com/ohmu/pghoard`
- **WAL-E**: `https://github.com/wal-e/wal-e`

Being the creators and developers of Barman, our preference goes with this tool. However, we strongly advise that you to look at each of the aforementioned tools and make your own decision based on your needs. If you are interested in Barman, you can read two recipes later in this chapter—*Hot physical backups with Barman* and *Recovery with Barman*.

Getting ready

This recipe builds upon the previous recipe, *Standalone hot physical database backup*. You should read that before following this recipe.

Before starting, you need to decide on a few things:

- Where will you store the WAL files (known as the **archive**)?
- How will you send WAL files to the archive?
- Where will you store your base backups?
- How will you take base backups?
- How many backups (also known as **retention policies**) will you keep?
- What is your policy for maintaining the archive?

These are hard questions to answer immediately. So, we will give a practical example as a way of explaining how this works, and then let you decide how you would like it to operate.

How to do it...

The rest of this recipe assumes the following answers to the key questions:

- The archive is a directory, such as /backups/archive, on a remote server for disaster recovery named $DRNODE
- We send WAL files to the archive using rsync; however, WAL streaming can also be used by changing the recipe in a way similar to the previous one
- Base backups are also stored on $DRNODE, in the /backups/base directory
- Base backups are made using rsync

The following steps assume that a number of environment variables have been set, which are as follows:

- $PGDATA is the path to the PostgreSQL data directory, ending with /
- $DRNODE is the name of the remote server

- $BACKUP_NAME is an identifier for the backup
- All the required PostgreSQL connection parameters have been set

We also assume that the PostgreSQL user can connect via SSH to the backup server from the server where PostgreSQL is running, without having to type a passphrase. This standard procedure is described in detail in several places, including Barman's documentation at http://docs.pgbarman.org/.

The procedure is as follows:

1. Create the archive and backup directories on a backup server.
2. Set archive_command. In postgresql.conf, you will need to add the following lines and restart the server or just confirm that they are present:

   ```
   archive_mode = on
   archive_command = 'rsync -a %p $DRNODE:/archive/%f'
   ```

3. Define the name of the backup, as follows:

   ```
   BACKUP_NAME=$(date '+%Y%m%d%H%M')
   ```

4. Start the backup, as follows:

   ```
   psql -c "select pg_start_backup('$BACKUP_NAME')"
   ```

5. Copy the data files (excluding the content of the pg_wal directory), like this:

   ```
   rsync -cva --inplace -exclude='pg_wal/*' \
   ${PGDATA}/     $DRNODE:/backups/base/$BACKUP_NAME/
   ```

6. Stop the backup, as follows:

   ```
   psql -c "select pg_stop_backup(), current_timestamp"
   ```

It's also good practice to put a README.backup file in the data directory prior to the backup so that it forms part of the set of files that make up the base backup. This should say something intelligent about the location of the archive, including any identification numbers, names, and so on.

Notice that we didn't put recovery.conf in the backup this time. That's because we're assuming we want flexibility at the time of recovery, rather than a gift-wrapped solution. The reason for that is that we don't know when, where, or how we will be recovering, nor do we need to make that decision yet.

How it works...

The key point here is that we must have both the base backup and the archive in order to recover. Where you put them is entirely up to you. You can use any filesystem backup technology and/or filesystem backup management system to do this.

Many backup management systems have claimed that they have a PostgreSQL interface or plugin, but most of the time they only support logical backups. However, there's no need for them to officially support PostgreSQL; no *Runs on PostgreSQL* badge or certification is required. If you can copy files, then you can run the preceding processes to keep your database safe.

In the event that the network or backup server goes down, then the command will begin to fail. When the `archive_command` fails, it will repeatedly retry until it succeeds.

You can monitor the status of `archive_command` and get current statistics through the `pg_stat_archiver` view in the catalog.

PostgreSQL does not remove WAL files from `pg_wal` directory until they have been successfully archived, so the end result is that your `pg_wal` directory fills up. It's a good idea to have an `archive_command` that reacts better to that condition, though this is left as an improvement for the sys admin. A typical action is to make it an emergency callout so that we can resolve the problem manually. Automatic resolution is difficult to get right, as this condition is one for which it is hard to test.

While continuously archiving, we will generate a considerable number of WAL files. If `archive_timeout` is set to 30 seconds, we will generate a minimum of *2*60*24 = 2,880* files per day, with each being 16 MB in size. This amounts to a total volume of 46 GB per day (minimum).

With a reasonable transaction rate, a database server might generate 100 GB of archive data per day. Use this as a rough figure for calculations until you get actual measurements. Of course, the rate could be much higher, with rates of 1 TB per day or higher being possible.

Clearly, we would only want to store WAL files that are useful for backup, so when we decide that we no longer wish to keep a backup, we will also want to remove files from the archive. In each base backup, you will find a file called `backup_label`. The earliest WAL file that's required by a physical backup is the filename we mentioned in the first line of the `backup_label` file. We can use a `contrib` module called `pg_archive_cleanup` to remove any WAL files that were created earlier than the earliest file.

Recovery of all databases

Recovery of a complete database server, including all of its databases, is an important feature. This recipe covers how to execute a recovery in the simplest way possible.

Some complexities are discussed here, though most are covered in later recipes.

Getting ready

Find a suitable server on which to perform the restore.

Before you recover onto a live server, always make another backup. Whatever problem you thought you had could get worse if you aren't prepared.

How to do it...

Here, we'll provide four distinct examples, depending on what type of backup was taken.

Logical – from custom dump taken with pg_dump -F c

The procedure is as follows:

1. Restoring of all databases means simply restoring each individual database from each dump you took. Confirm that you have the correct backup before you restore:

   ```
   pg_restore --schema-only -v dumpfile | head | grep Started
   ```

2. Reload the global objects from the script file, as follows:

   ```
   psql -f myglobals.sql
   ```

3. Reload all databases. Create the databases using parallel tasks to speed things up. This can be executed remotely without the need to transfer dump files between systems. Note that there is a separate dumpfile for each database:

   ```
   pg_restore -C -d postgres -j 4 dumpfile
   ```

Logical – from the script dump created by pg_dump -F p

As in the previous method, this can be executed remotely without needing to transfer `dumpfile` between systems:

1. Confirm that you have the correct backup before you restore. If the following command returns nothing, then it means that the file is not timestamped, and you'll have to identify it in a different way:

   head myscriptdump.sql | grep Started

2. Reload the globals from the script file, as follows:

   psql -f myglobals.sql

3. Reload all scripts, as follows:

   psql -f myscriptdump.sql

Logical – from the script dump created by pg_dumpall

In order to recover a full backup generated by pg_dumpall, you need to execute the following steps on a PostgreSQL server that has just been initialized:

1. Confirm that you have the correct backup before you restore. If the following command returns nothing, then it means that the file is not timestamped, and you'll have to identify it in a different way:

   head myscriptdump.sql | grep Started

2. Reload the script in full:

   psql -f myscriptdump.sql

Physical

The steps for this method are as follows:

1. If you've following the *Standalone hot physical database backup* recipe, then recovery is very easy. Restore the backup file in the target server.
2. Extract the backup file to the new data directory.

3. Confirm that you have the correct backup before you restore:

```
$ cat backup_label
START WAL LOCATION: 0/12000020 (file 000000010000000000000012)
CHECKPOINT LOCATION: 0/12000058
START TIME: 2018-06-03 19:53:23 BST
LABEL: standalone
```

4. Verify that all file permissions and ownerships are correct and that the links are valid. This should already be the case if you are using the `Postgres` user ID everywhere, which is recommended.
5. Start the server.

This procedure is so simple because, in the *Standalone hot physical database backup* recipe, we gift-wrapped everything for you. That also helped you to understand that you need both a base backup and the appropriate WAL files.

If you've used other techniques, then you need to step through the tasks to make sure you cover everything required, as follows:

1. Shut down any server running in the data directory.
2. Restore the backup so that any files in the data directory that have matching names are replaced with the version from the backup. (The manual says, *delete all files and then restore the backup*. You could speed up the recovery operation reusing the existing data directory, but unless you are familiar with `rsync` we recommend going by the book. You can look at the source code of Barman for an example, or otherwise simply use it.) Remember that this step can be performed in parallel to speed things up, though it is up to you to script that.
3. Ensure that all file permissions and ownerships are correct and that the links are valid. This should already be the case if you are using the Postgres user ID everywhere, which is recommended.
4. Remove any files that are in `pg_wal/`. If you've been following our recipes, you'll be able to skip this step because they were never backed up in the first place.
5. Add a `recovery.conf` file and set its file permissions correctly.
6. Start the server.

The only part that requires some thought and checking is selecting which parameters to use for the `recovery.conf` file. There's only one that matters here, and that is `restore_command`.

`restore_command` tells us how to restore archived WAL files. It needs to be the command that will be executed to bring back WAL files from the archive.

If you have been thinking ahead, there'll be a README.backup file for you to read to find out how to set restore_command. If it is not there, then presumably you've got the location of the WAL files you've been saving written down somewhere. Say, for example, that your files are being saved to a directory named /backups/pg/servername/archive, owned by the Postgres user.

On a remote server named backup1, we would then write all of this on one line of the recovery.conf file, as follows:

```
restore_command = 'scp backup1:/backups/pg/servername/archive/%f
    %p'
```

How it works...

PostgreSQL is designed to require very minimal information to perform a recovery. We'll try to wrap all of the details up for you:

- **Logical recovery**: This recreates database objects by executing SQL statements. If performance is an issue, look at the *Improving performance of backup/recovery* recipe.
- **Physical recovery**: This reapplies data changes at the block level, and so tends to be much faster than logical recovery. It requires both a base backup and a set of archived WAL files.

There is a file named backup_label in the data directory of the base backup. If you want to know the start and stop WAL locations of the base backup, look for a .backup file in the archive.

Recovery then starts to apply changes from the starting WAL location, and it must proceed as far as the stop address for the backup to be valid.

After the recovery is complete, the recovery.conf file is renamed to recovery.done to prevent the server from re-entering recovery in case of a restart.

The server log records each WAL file restored from the archive, so you can check their progress and rate of recovery. You can query the archive to find the name of the latest restored WAL file so that you can calculate how many files are left to recover.

`restore_command` should return 0 if a file has been restored and non-zero for cases of failure. Recovery will proceed until there are no more WAL files remaining, so eventually there will be an error recorded in the logs.

If you have lost some of the WAL files, or they are damaged, then recovery will stop at that point. No further changes after that will be applied, and you will likely lose those changes. This would be the time to call your support vendor.

There's more...

You can start and stop the server once recovery has started without any problems. It will not interfere with the recovery.

You can connect to the database server while it is recovering and run queries, if that is useful. This is known as **hot standby** mode and is discussed in `Chapter 12`, *Replication and Upgrades*.

See also

- Once the recovery reaches the stop address, you can stop it at any point, as discussed in the *Recovery to a point in time* recipe
- The procedure described in this recipe is covered by the command-line utility, Barman, which is mentioned in the *Hot physical backup and continuous archiving* recipe

Recovery to a point in time

If your database suffers a problem at 3:22 p.m and your backup was taken at 4:00 a.m, you're probably hoping there is a way to recover the changes made between those two times. What you need is known as **Point-in-Time Recovery** (**PITR**).

Regrettably, if you've made a backup with the `pg_dump` utility at 4:00 a.m, then you won't be able to recover to any other time. As a result, the term PITR has become synonymous with the physical backup and restore technique in PostgreSQL.

Getting ready

If you have a backup made with `pg_dump` utility, then give up all hope of using that as a starting point for a PITR. It's a frequently asked question, but the answer is still *no*. The reason it gets asked is exactly why we are pleading with you to plan your backups ahead of time.

First, you need to decide from what point in time you would like to recover. If the answer is *as late as possible*, then you don't need to do a PITR at all—just recover until the end of the logs.

How to do it...

How do you decide at what point to recover to? The point where we stop recovery is known as the recovery target. The most straightforward way is to do this based on a timestamp.

In the `recovery.conf` file, you can add (or uncomment) a line that says the following or something similar:

```
recovery_target_time = '2018-06-01 16:59:14.27452+01'
```

Note that you need to be careful to specify the time zone of the target so that it matches the time zone of the server that wrote the log. That might differ from the time zone of the current server, so be sure to double-check them.

After that, you can check the progress during a recovery by running queries in hot standby mode. By default, when hot standby mode is enabled, the recovered server is paused once the target is reached. You can change this behavior with the `recovery_target_action` option in the `recovery.conf` file, as discussed in the *Delaying, pausing, and synchronizing replication* recipe in `Chapter 12`, *Replication and Upgrades*.

How it works...

Recovery works by applying individual WAL records. These correspond to individual block changes, so there are many WAL records for each transaction. The final part of any successful transaction is a commit WAL record, though there are abort records as well. Each transaction completion record has a timestamp that allows us to decide whether or not to stop at that point.

You can also define a recovery target using a transaction ID (xid), though finding out which xid to use is somewhat difficult, and you may need to refer to external records, if they exist. Using a **Log Sequence Number** (LSN) is also possible, and equally tricky; in both cases, you can get an idea of what transaction IDs, or LSN, to use, by inspecting the contents of a given WAL file with the pg_waldump utility, which is part of PostgreSQL.

Another practical way, which rarely applies after an unexpected disaster, is to define a recovery target with a label, formally known as a named restore point. A restore point is created with the pg_create_restore_point() function, and requires superuser privileges. For example, let's you have to perform a critical update of part of the data in your database. As a precaution, before you start the update, you can execute the following query as a superuser:

```
SELECT pg_create_restore_point('before_critical_update');
```

Then, you can use the before_critical_update label in the recovery_target_name option.

Finally, you can simply stop as soon as the recovery process becomes consistent by specifying recovery_target = 'immediate' in place of any other recovery target parameter.

The recovery target is specified in the recovery.conf file and cannot change while the server is running. If you want to change the recovery target, you can shut down the server, edit recovery.conf, and then restart the server. Be careful, however; if you change the recovery target and recovery is already past the new point, it can lead to errors. If you define a recovery_target_timestamp that has already been passed, then the recovery will stop almost immediately, though this will be after the correct stopping point. If you define a recovery_target_xid or recovery_target_name that has already been passed, then the recovery will just continue until the end of the logs. Restarting a recovery from the beginning using a fresh restore of the base backup is always the safest option.

Once a server completes the recovery, it will assign a new timeline. Once a server is fully available, we can write new changes to the database. Those changes might differ from the changes we made in a previous future history of the database. So, we differentiate between alternate futures using different timelines. If we need to go back and run the recovery again, we can create a new server history using the original or subsequent timelines. The best way to think about this is that it is exactly like a Sci-Fi novel – you can't change the past, but you can return to an earlier time and take a different action instead. However, you'll need to be careful not to get confused.

There's more...

The `pg_dump` utility cannot be used as a base backup for a PITR. The reason for this is that a log replay contains the physical changes to data blocks, not the logical changes based on primary keys. If you reload the `pg_dump` utility, the data will likely go back into different data blocks, so the changes won't correctly reference the data.

WAL files don't contain enough information to fully reconstruct all of the SQL that produced those changes. Later feature additions to PostgreSQL may add the required information to WAL files. It will be very interesting and exciting to follow how logical replication evolves in the future.

The timeline is a 32-bit integer which constitutes the first eight characters in the name of a WAL file; changing timeline therefore means using a new series of file names. There are cases where this is important; for instance, if you restore a backup and start that server while the original server is still running, then it's convenient that both servers archive the WAL they produce without disturbing each other. In other words, if you made a backup, then you want to be able to restore it as many times as you want, and you don't want that the restored instances overwriting some files in the original backup.

See also

PostgreSQL can pause, resume, and stop recovery while the server is up dynamically. This allows you to use the hot standby facility to locate the correct stopping point more easily. You can trick hot standby into stopping recovery, which may help. See the *Delaying, pausing, and synchronizing replication* recipe in Chapter 12, *Replication and Upgrades*, on managing hot standby. This procedure is also covered by the command-line utility Barman, as mentioned in the *Hot physical backup and continuous archiving* recipe.

You can use the `pg_waldump` utility to print the content of WAL files in a human-readable way. This can be very valuable to locate the exact transaction ID, or timestamp, or when a certain change was committed, for instance, if we want to stop recovery exactly before that. `pg_waldump` is part of PostgreSQL and is described here: `https://www.postgresql.org/docs/11/static/pgwaldump.html`.

Recovery of a dropped/damaged table

You may drop or even damage a table in some way. Tables could be damaged for physical reasons, such as disk corruption, or they could also be damaged by running poorly specified UPDATE or DELETE commands, which update too many rows or overwrite critical data.

Recovering from this backup situation is a common request.

How to do it...

The methods to this approach differ, depending on the type of backup you have available. If you have multiple types of backup, you have a choice.

Logical – from custom dump taken with pg_dump -F c

If you've taken a logical backup using the pg_dump utility in a custom file, then you can simply extract the table you want from the dumpfile, like so:

```
pg_restore -t mydroppedtable dumpfile | psql
```

Alternatively, you can directly connect to the database using -d. If you use this option, then you can allow multiple jobs in parallel with the -j option.

When working with just one table, as in this case, this is useful only if there are things that can be done at the same time, that is, if the table has more than one index and/or constraint. More details about parallel restore are available in the *Improving performance of backup/recovery* recipe, later in this chapter.

Note that PostgreSQL can also use multiple jobs when creating single B-Tree indexes. This is controlled by an entirely different set of parameters; see the *Maintaining indexes* recipe in Chapter 9, *Regular Maintenance*, for more details.

The preceding command tries to recreate the table and then load data into it. Note that the pg_restore -t option does not dump any of the indexes on the selected table. This means that we need a slightly more complex procedure than would first appear, and the procedure needs to vary depending on whether we are repairing a damaged table or putting back a dropped table.

To repair a damaged table, we want to replace the data in the table in a single transaction. There isn't a specific option to do this, so we need to do the following:

1. Dump the data of the table (the −a option) to a script file, as follows:

```
pg_restore -a -t mydamagedtable dumpfile > mydamagedtable.sql
```

2. Edit a script named repair_mydamagedtable.sql with the following code:

```
BEGIN;
TRUNCATE mydamagedtable;
\i mydamagedtable.sql
COMMIT;
```

3. Then, run it using the following command:

```
psql -f repair_mydamagedtable.sql
```

If you've already dropped a table, then you need to perform these steps:

1. Create a new database in which to work and name it restorework, as follows:

```
CREATE DATABASE restorework;
```

2. Restore the complete schema (−s option) to the new database, like this:

```
pg_restore -s -d restorework dumpfile
```

3. Now, dump only the definitions of the dropped table in a new file. It will contain CREATE TABLE, indexes, and other constraints and grants. Note that this database has no data in it, so specifying −s is optional, as follows:

```
pg_dump -t mydroppedtable -s restorework > mydroppedtable.sql
```

4. Now, recreate the table on the main database:

```
psql -f mydroppedtable.sql
```

5. Now, reload only the data into the maindb database:

```
pg_restore -t mydroppedtable -a -d maindb dumpfile
```

If you've got a very large table, then the fourth step can be a problem because it builds indexes as well. If you want, you can manually edit the script in two pieces—one before the load (preload) and one after the load (postload). There are some ideas for that at the end of this recipe.

Logical – from the script dump

Once you have located the PostgreSQL server on which you will prepare and verify the data to restore (the staging server), you can proceed like so:

1. Reload the script in full on the staging server, as follows:

   ```
   psql -f myscriptdump.sql
   ```

2. From the recovered database server, dump the table, its data, and all of the definitions of the dropped table into a new file:

   ```
   pg_dump -t mydroppedtable -F c mydatabase > dumpfile
   ```

3. Now, recreate the table in the original server and database, using parallel tasks to speed things up (here, we will pick two parallel jobs as an example):

   ```
   pg_restore -d mydatabase -j 2 dumpfile
   ```

 The last step can be executed remotely without having to transfer `dumpfile` between systems. Just add connection parameters to `pg_restore`, as in the following example:
`pg_restore -h remotehost -U remoteuser ...`

The only way to extract a single table from a script dump without doing all of the preceding steps is to write a custom script to read and extract only those parts of the file that you want. This can be complicated because you may need certain SET commands at the top of the file, the table, and data in the middle of the file, and the indexes and constraints on the table are near the end of the file. Writing a custom script can be very complex. The safer route is to follow the recipe we just described.

Physical

To recover a single table from a physical backup, you first need to recreate a PostgreSQL server from scratch, usually in a confined environment. Typically, this server is called the **recovery server**, if dedicated to recovery drills and procedures, or the **staging server**, if used for a broader set of cases including testing. Then, you need to proceed as follows:

1. Recover the database server in full, as described in the previous recipes on physical recovery, including all databases and all tables. You may wish to stop at a useful point in time, in which case you can look at the *Recovery to a point in time* recipe later in this chapter.

2. From the recovered database server, dump the table, its data, and all the definitions of the dropped table into a new file, as follows:

```
pg_dump -t mydroppedtable -F c mydatabase > dumpfile
```

3. Now, recreate the table in the original server and database using parallel tasks to speed things up. This can be executed remotely without needing to transfer dumpfile between systems:

```
pg_restore -d mydatabase -j 2 dumpfile
```

How it works...

Restoring a single table from a logical backup is relatively easy, as each logical object is backed up separately from the others, and its data and metadata can be filtered out.

However, a physical backup is composed of a set of binary data files, in a complex storage format that can be interpreted by a PostgreSQL engine.

This means that the only way to extract individual objects from it, at present, is to restore the backup on a new instance, and then make a logical dump, as explained in the previous recipe: there's no way to restore a single table from a physical backup in just a single step.

See also

The pg_dump and pg_restore utilities are able to split the dump into three parts: pre-data, data, and post-data. Both commands support a section option that's used to specify which section(s) should be dumped or reloaded.\

Recovery of a dropped/damaged database

Recovering a complete database is also required sometimes. It's actually a lot easier than recovering a single table. Many users choose to place all of their tables in a single database; in that case, this recipe isn't relevant.

How to do it...

The methods differ, depending on the type of backup you have available. If you have multiple types of backup, you have a choice.

Logical – from the custom dump -F c

Recreate the database in the original server using parallel tasks to speed things along. This can be executed remotely without needing to transfer `dumpfile` between systems, as shown in the following example, where we use the `-j` option to specify four parallel processes:

```
pg_restore -h myhost -d postgres --create -j 4 dumpfile
```

Logical – from the script dump created by pg_dump

Recreate the database in the original server. This can be executed remotely without needing to transfer dump files between systems, as shown here, where we must create the empty database first:

```
createdb -h myhost myfreshdb
psql -h myhost -f myscriptdump.sql myfreshdb
```

Logical – from the script dump created by pg_dumpall

There's no easy way to extract the required tables from a script dump. You need to operate on a separate PostgreSQL server for recovery or staging purposes, and then follow these steps:

1. Reload the script in full, as follows:

   ```
   psql -f myscriptdump.sql
   ```

2. Once the restore is complete, you can dump the tables in the database by following the *Hot logical backups of one database* recipe.
3. Now, recreate the database on the original server, as described for logical dumps earlier in this recipe.

Physical

To recover a single database from a physical backup, you need to work on a separate PostgreSQL server (for recovery or staging purposes), and then you must follow these steps:

1. Recover the database server in full, as described in the previous recipes on physical recovery, including all databases and all tables. You may wish to stop at a useful point in time, in which case you can look at the *Recovery to a point in time* recipe, earlier in this chapter.
2. Once the restore is complete, you can dump the tables in the database by following the *Hot logical backups of one database* recipe.
3. Now, recreate the database on the original server, as described for logical dumps earlier in this recipe.

Improving performance of backup/recovery

Performance is often a concern in any medium-sized or large database.

Backup performance is often a delicate issue, because resource usage may need to be limited to remain within certain boundaries. There may also be a restriction on the maximum runtime for the backup, for example, a backup that runs every Sunday.

Again, restore performance may be more important than backup performance, even if backup is the more obvious concern.

Getting ready

If performance is a concern or is likely to be, then you should read the *Planning backups* recipe first.

How to do it...

Backup and restore performance can be improved in different ways, depending on the backup type:

- **Physical backup**: Improving the performance of a physical backup can be done by performing the backup in parallel and copying the files using more than one task. The more tasks you use, the more it will impact the current system. When backing up, you can skip certain files. You won't need the following:
    - Any files placed in the data directory by DBA that shouldn't actually be there
    - Any files in pg_wal
    - Any old server log files in pg_log (even the current one)

  Remember, it's safer not to try to exclude files at all because, if you miss something critical, you may end up with data loss. Also, remember that your backup speed may be bottlenecked by your disks or your network. Some larger systems have dedicated networks in place, solely for backups.

- **Logical backup**: As explained in a *Recovery of a dropped/damaged database* recipe, if you want to back up all databases in a database server, then you should use multiple pg_dump tasks running in parallel. You may want to increase the dump speed of a pg_dump task, but there really isn't an easy way of doing that right now. If you're using compression, look at the *There's more...* section at the end of this recipe.

- **Physical restore**: Just like the physical backup, it's possible for us to put everything back quicker if we use parallel copy, which is able to speed things up by automatically reusing existing files.

- **Logical restore**: Whether you use psql or pg_restore, you can speed up the program by assigning maintenance_work_mem = 128MB or more, either in postgresql.conf or on the user that will run the restore. If neither of those ways is easily possible, you can specify the option using the PGOPTIONS environment variable, as follows:

  ```
  export PGOPTIONS ="-c work_mem = 128000"
  ```

This will then be used to set that option value for subsequent connections.

If you are running archiving or streaming replication then transaction log writes may become a problem. This can be mitigated by increasing the size of the WAL buffer and making checkpoints less frequent for the duration of the recovery operation. Set `wal_buffers` between 16 MB and 64 MB, and set `max_wal_size` to a large value such as 20 GB so that it has room to breathe.

If you aren't running archiving or streaming replication, or you've turned it off during the restore, then you'll be able to minimize the amount of transaction log writes. In that case, you may wish to use the single transaction option, as that will also help to improve performance.

If `pg_dump` was made using `-F c` (custom format), then we can restore in parallel, as follows:

```
pg_restore -j NumJobs
```

You'll have to be careful about how you select the degree of parallelism to use. A good starting point is the number of CPUs of the server. Be very careful that you don't overflow the available memory when using parallel restore. Each job will use memory up to the value of `maintenance_work_mem`, so the whole restore could begin swapping when it hits larger indexes later in the restore. Plan the size of `shared_buffers` and `maintenance_work_mem` according to the number of jobs specified.

Whatever you do, make sure that you run ANALYZE afterwards on every object that was created. This will happen automatically if `autovacuum` is enabled. It often helps to disable `autovacuum` completely while running a large restore, so double-check that you have it switched on again after the restore. The consequence of skipping this step will be extremely poor performance when you start your application again, which can easily make everybody panic.

How it works...

A physical backup and restore is completely up to you. Copy those files as fast as you like and in any way you like. Put them back in the same way or a different way.

Logical backup and restore involves moving data out of and into the database. That's typically going to be slower than physical backup and restore. Particularly with a restore, rebuilding indexes and constraints takes time, even when run in parallel. Plan ahead and measure the performance of your backup and restore techniques so that you have a chance when you need your database back in a hurry.

There's more...

Compressing backups is often considered as a way to reduce the size of the backup for storage. Even mild compression can use large amounts of CPU. In some cases, this might offset network transfer costs, so there isn't any hard rule as to whether compression is always good.

Compression for WAL files from physical backups is a common practice. Physical backups can be compressed in various ways, depending on the exact backup mechanism used. By default, the custom dump format for logical backups will be compressed. Even when compressed, the objects can be accessed individually if required.

Using `--compress` with script dumps will result in a compressed text file, just as if you had dumped the file and then compressed it. Access to individual tables is not possible.

Using multiple processes is known as pipeline parallelism. If you're using a physical backup, then you can copy the data in multiple streams, which also allows you to take advantage of parallel compression/decompression.

See also

If taking a backup is an expensive operation, then a way around this is to take the backup from a replica instead, which offloads the cost of the backup operation away from the master. Look at the recipes in `Chapter 12`, *Replication and Upgrades*, to see how to set up a replica.

Incremental/differential backup and restore

If you have performance problems with a backup of a large PostgreSQL database, then you may consider incremental or differential backups.

An incremental backup is a backup of all files that have changed since the last backup, either incremental or full. In order to restore a given incremental backup, you must restore the full backup and then all of the incremental backups in-between.

A differential backup is a backup of all individual changes since the last full backup. In order to restore a differential backup, you only need that backup and the full backup it refers to.

How to do it...

To perform a differential physical backup, you can use `rsync` to compare the existing files against the previous full backup and then overwrite only the changed data blocks. It's a bad plan to overwrite your last backup because, if the new backup fails, you are left without backups. Therefore, keep two or more copies. An example backup schedule is as follows:

Day of the week	Backup set 1	Backup set 2
Sunday	New full backup to set 1	New full backup to set 2
Monday	Differential to set 1	Differential to set 2
Tuesday	Differential to set 1	Differential to set 2
Wednesday	Differential to set 1	Differential to set 2
Thursday	Differential to set 1	Differential to set 2
Friday	Differential to set 1	Differential to set 2
Saturday	Differential to set 1	Differential to set 2

You should keep at least two full backup sets.

Many large databases have tables that are insert-only. In that case, it's easy to store parts of those tables. If the tables are partitioned by insertion date, creation date, or a similar field, it makes our task much simpler. Either way, you're still going to need a good way of recording which data is where in your backup.

In general, there's no easy way to run a differential backup using `pg_dump`.

How it works...

PostgreSQL doesn't explicitly keep track of the last changed date or similar information for a file or table. PostgreSQL tables are held as files, so you should be able to rely on the modification time (`mtime`) of the files on the filesystem.

Another problem with this approach is that filesystem timestamps might not have a resolution that is sufficiently granular to separate all changes. This means that some additional verification, such as computing a checksum, is required to confirm that two files with the same `mtime` are indeed identical. If, for this or some other reason, you don't trust `mtime`, or it has been disabled, then incremental and differential backups are not for you.

The `pg_dump` utility doesn't allow `WHERE` clauses to be specified, so even if you add your own columns to track `last_changed_date`, you'll still need to manually perform that somehow.

There's more...

The article at `http://en.wikipedia.org/wiki/Backup_rotation_scheme` gives further useful information on this.

When thinking about incremental backups, you should note that replication techniques work by continually applying changes to a full backup. This could be considered a technique for an incremental updated backup, also known as an *incremental forever* backup strategy. The changes are applied ahead of time so that you can restore easily and quickly. You should still take a backup, but you can take it from the replication standby instead.

It's possible to write a utility that takes a differential backup of data blocks. You can read each data block and check the block's LSN to see whether it has changed in comparison to a previous copy. This is similar to the approach followed by `pgBackRest`.

In the *Hot physical backup and continuous archiving* recipe, we discussed using third-party backup and recovery software. All of the tools we mentioned support compression of WAL files by invoking popular general-purpose compression utilities such as `bzip2`, `gzip`, and `lzh` directly on WAL files. This is safe and does not increase the actual risk of data loss. Such utilities have been extensively used for many years, and all serious bugs have been ironed out.

The `pg_rman` and `pgBackRest` utilities can also read changed data pages and interpret their contents, for instance, to compress them using detailed knowledge of the internals of PostgreSQL's data page format, or for deciding whether to include the page in an incremental/differential backup. Any bugs that exist there could cause data loss in your backups, and issues with third-party tools aren't resolved by the main PostgreSQL project. This is why we personally advise against using third-party software that operates on individual data pages without a formal support contract. Various companies support this; ask them.

In order to avoid taking those risks, the Barman utility follows the opposite approach of not handling the contents of each PostgreSQL data page directly, choosing instead to delegate the file transfer logic to other well-known tools such as `rsync` or `pg_basebackup`.

Hot physical backups with Barman

The main reason we came up with the idea of starting a new open source project for disaster recovery of PostgreSQL databases was the lack (back in 2011) of a simple and standard procedure for managing backups and, most importantly, recovery. Disasters and failures in ICT will happen.

As a database administrator, your duty is to plan for backups and the recovery of PostgreSQL databases and perform regular tests in order to sweep away stress and fear, which typically follow those unexpected events. Barman, which stands for Backup and Recovery Manager, is definitely a tool that you can use for these purposes.

Before you dive into this recipe and the next one, which will introduce you to Barman, I recommend that you read the following recipes from earlier in this chapter—*Understanding and controlling crash recovery, Planning backups, Hot physical backup and continuous archiving*, and *Recovery to a point in time*. Although Barman hides the complexity of the underlying concepts, it is important that you be aware of them, as it will make you more resilient to installation, configuration, and recovery issues with Barman.

Barman is currently available only for Linux systems and is written in Python. It supports PostgreSQL versions from 8.3 onward. Among its main features worth citing are remote backup, remote recovery, multiple server management, backup catalogs, incremental backups, retention policies, WAL streaming, compression of WAL files, parallel copy (backup and restore), backup from a standby server, and georedundancy.

For the sake of simplicity, in this recipe, we will assume the following architecture:

- One Linux server named `angus`, running your PostgreSQL production database server
- One Linux server named `malcolm`, running Barman for disaster recovery of your PostgreSQL database server
- Both the servers are in the same LAN and, for better business continuity objectives, the only resource they share is the network

Later on, we will see how easy it is to add more PostgreSQL servers (such as `bon`) to our disaster recovery solution on `malcolm` with Barman.

Getting ready

Although Barman can be installed via sources or through pip—Python's main package manager—the easiest way to install Barman is by using the software package manager of your Linux distribution.

Currently, 2ndQuadrant maintains packages for RHEL, CentOS 6/7, Debian, and Ubuntu systems. If you are using a different distribution or another Unix system, you can follow the instructions written in the official documentation of Barman, available at `http://docs.pgbarman.org/`.

In this book, we will cover the installation of Barman 2.6 (currently the latest stable release) on CentOS 7 and Ubuntu 16.04 LTS Linux servers.

If you are using RHEL or CentOS 7 on the `malcolm` server, you need to install the following repositories:

- Fedora **Extra Packages Enterprise Linux** (**EPEL**), available at `http://fedoraproject.org/wiki/EPEL`
- The PostgreSQL Global Development Group RPM repository, available at `http://yum.postgresql.org/`

Then, as root, type in the following:

```
yum install barman
```

If you are using Ubuntu on `malcolm`, you need to install the APT PostgreSQL repository, following the instructions available at `http://apt.postgresql.org/`. Then, as root, type in the following:

```
apt-get install barman
```

From now on, we will assume the following:

- A freshly installed PostgreSQL is running on `angus` as the `postgres` system user and listening to the default port (`5432`). Its configuration allows the `barman` system user on `malcolm` to connect as the `postgres` database user without having to type in a password.
- Barman is installed on `malcolm` and runs as the `barman` system user.
- TCP connections for SSH and PostgreSQL are allowed between the two servers (check your firewall settings).
- Two-way automated communication via SSH is properly set up between these users.

- You have created a superuser called **Barman** in your PostgreSQL server on angus and it can only connect from the malcolm server. See Chapter 1, *First Steps*, the *Enabling access for network/remote users* recipe, and Chapter 6, *Security*, the *PostgreSQL Superuser* recipe, for more information.

The last operation requires exchanging a public SSH key without a passphrase between the postgres user on angus and the barman user on malcolm. If you are not familiar with this topic, which goes beyond the scope of this book, you are advised to follow Barman's documentation or surf the net for more information.

Alternatively, if your system administrator complains about opening SSH access to your PostgreSQL server, you can always take your backups via streaming replication. Indeed, Barman transparently integrates with pg_basebackup, meaning that base backups can be taken through the 5432 port and permissions can be granted at PostgreSQL level.

However, in this book, we will concentrate on the rsync method, which uses rsync via SSH. If you are interested in setting up backups via streaming replication, look at Barman's documentation, in particular the backup_method and streaming_conninfo options, as well as the *Setting up streaming replication* recipe in Chapter 12, *Replication and Upgrades*.

How to do it...

We will start by looking at Barman's main configuration file:

1. As root on malcolm, open the /etc/barman.conf file for editing. This file contains global options for Barman. Once you are familiar with the main configuration options, I recommend that you set the default compression method by uncommenting the following line:

   ```
   compression = gzip
   ```

2. Add the configuration file for the angus server. Drop the angus.conf file, containing the following lines, into the /etc/barman.d directory:

   ```
   [angus]
   description = "PostgreSQL Database on angus"
   active = off
   archiver = on
   backup_method = rsync
   ssh_command = ssh postgres@angus
   conninfo = host=angus user=barman dbname=postgres
   ```

3. You have just added the `angus` server to the list of Postgres servers managed by Barman. The server is temporarily inactive until configuration is completed. You can verify this by typing `barman list-server`, as follows:

```
[root@malcolm]# barman list-server
angus - PostgreSQL Database on angus (inactive)
```

4. In this recipe, you will be executing commands as the root user. Be aware, however, that every command will be executed by the `barman` system user (or, more generally, as specified in the configuration file by the `barman_user` option).

Anyway, it is now time to set up continuous archiving of WAL files between Postgres and Barman. Execute the `barman show-server angus` command and write down the directory for incoming WALs (`incoming_wals_directory`):

```
[root@malcolm]# barman show-server angus

Server angus (inactive):
active: False
archive_command: None
archive_mode: None
        incoming_wals_directory:
        /var/lib/barman/angus/incoming
```

5. The next task is to initialize the directory layout for the `angus` server through the `check` command. You are advised to add this command to your monitoring infrastructure as, among other things, it ensures that the connection to the Postgres server via `SSH` and `libpq` is working properly, as well as continuous archiving. It returns `0` if everything is fine:

```
[root@malcolm]#

barman check angus
Server angus (inactive):
 WAL archive: FAILED (please make sure WAL shipping is setup)
  PostgreSQL: OK
  superuser: OK
  wal_level: FAILED (please set it to a higher level than
'minimal')
  directories: OK
  retention policy settings: OK
  backup maximum age: OK (no last_backup_maximum_age provided)
  compression settings: OK
  failed backups: OK (there are 0 failed backups)
  minimum redundancy requirements: OK (have 0 backups, expected
```

```
at least 0)
  ssh: OK (PostgreSQL server)
  not in recovery: OK
  archive_mode: FAILED (please set it to 'on' or 'always')
  archive_command: FAILED (please set it accordingly to
documentation)
  archiver errors: OK

[root@malcolm]# echo $?
1
```

6. As you can see, the returned value is 1, meaning that the angus server is not yet ready for backup. The output suggests that archive_mode and archive_command in Postgres are not set for continuous archiving. Connect to angus and modify the postgresql.conf file by adding this:

```
archive_mode = on
archive_command = 'rsync -a %p
barman@malcolm:/var/lib/barman/angus/incoming/%f'

wal_level = replica
```

7. Restart the PostgreSQL server.
8. Activate the server in Barman by removing the line that starts with active.
9. Run the check command on malcolm (suppressing the output with -q) again, and compare the results with what you got earlier:

```
[root@malcolm]# barman -q check angus
[root@malcolm]# echo $?
0
```

It returned 0. Everything is good! PostgreSQL on angus should now be regularly shipping WAL files to Barman on malcolm, depending on the write workload of your database.

Don't worry if the check command complains with the following error:

```
WAL archive: FAILED (please make sure WAL shipping is setup)
```

It is a precautionary measure we had to take in order to prevent users from going live without a working archiving process. This means that your server (like angus, in this case) has a very low workload and no WAL files have been produced, shipped, and archived yet. If you want to speed up the installation, you can execute the following commands:

```
[root@malcolm]# barman switch-wal --force --archive angus
[root@malcolm]# barman archive-wal angus
```

I recommend that you check both the PostgreSQL and Barman log files and verify that the WALs have been correctly shipped. Continuous archiving is indeed the main requirement for physical backups in Postgres.

10. Once you have set up continuous archiving, in order to add the disaster recovery capability to your Postgres server, you need to have at least one full base backup. Taking a full base backup in Barman is as easy as typing one single command. It should not be hard for you to guess that the command to execute is barman backup angus.

   Barman initiates the physical backup procedure and waits for the checkpoint to happen, before copying the data files from angus to malcom using rsync:

```
[root@malcolm]# barman backup angus
Starting backup using rsync-exclusive method for server angus
in /var/lib/barman/angus/base/20181003T194717
Backup start at xlog location: 0/3000028
(000000010000000000000003, 00000028)
This is the first backup for server angus
WAL segments preceding the current backup have been found:
    000000010000000000000001 from server angus has been removed
Copying files.
Copy done.
This is the first backup for server angus
Asking PostgreSQL server to finalize the backup.
Backup size: 21.1 MiB
Backup end at xlog location: 0/3000130
(000000010000000000000003, 00000130)
Backup completed
Processing xlog segments from file archival for angus
    000000010000000000000002
    000000010000000000000003
    000000010000000000000003.00000028.backup
```

It is worth noting that, during the backup procedure, your PostgreSQL server is available for both read and write operations. This is because PostgreSQL natively implements hot backup, a feature that other DBMS vendors might make you pay for.

From now on, your `angus` PostgreSQL server is continuously backed up on `malcolm`. You can now schedule weekly backups (using the `barman` user's cron) and manage retention policies so that you can build a catalog of backups covering you for weeks, months, or years of data, allowing you to perform recovery operations at any point in time between the first available backup and the last successfully archived WAL file.

How it works...

Barman is a Python application that wraps PostgreSQL core technology for continuous backup and PITR. It also adds some practical functionality focused on helping the database administrator to manage the disaster recovery of one or more PostgreSQL servers.

When devising Barman, we decided to keep the design simple and not to use any daemon or client/server architecture. Maintenance operations are simply delegated to the `barman cron` command, which is mainly responsible for archiving WAL files (moving them from the incoming directory to the WAL file and compressing them) and managing retention policies.

If you have installed Barman through RPM or APT packages, you will notice that maintenance is run every minute through cron:

```
[root@malcolm ~]# cat /etc/cron.d/barman
# m h  dom mon dow    user       command
  * *    *   *   *     barman    [ -x /usr/bin/barman ] && /usr/bin/barman -q
cron
```

Barman follows the *convention over configuration* paradigm and uses an INI format configuration file with options operating at two different levels:

- **Global options**: These are options specified in the [barman] section, and are used by any Barman command and for every server. Several global options can be overridden at the server level.
- **Server options**: These are options specified in the [SERVER_ID] section, used by server commands. These options can be customized at the server level (including overriding general settings).

The SERVER_ID placeholder (such as `angus`) is fundamental, as it identifies the server in the catalog (therefore, it must be unique).

Similarly, commands in Barman are of two types:

- **Global commands**: These are general commands, not tied with any server in particular, such as a list of the servers managed by the Barman installation (`list-server`) and maintenance (`cron`)
- **Server commands**: These are commands executed on a specific server, such as diagnostics (`check` and `status`), backup control (`backup`, `list-backup`, `delete` and `show-backup`), and recovery control (recover, which is discussed in the next recipe, *Recovery with Barman*)

The previous sections of this recipe showed you how to add a server (`angus`) to a Barman installation on the `malcolm` server. You can easily add a second server (`bon`) to the Barman server on malcolm. All you have to do is create the `bon.conf` file in the `/etc/barman.d` directory and repeat the steps outlined in the *How it works...* section, as you have done for `angus`.

There's more...

Every time you execute the `barman backup` command for a given server, you take a full base backup (a more generic term for this is periodical full backup). Once completed, this backup can be used as a base for any recovery operation from the start time of the backup to the last available WAL file for that server (provided there is continuity among all of the WAL segments).

As we mentioned earlier, by scheduling daily or weekly automated backups, you end up having several periodic backups for a server. In Barman's jargon, this is known as the backup catalog, and it is one of our favorite features of this tool.

At any time, you can get a list of available backups for a given server through the `list-backup` command:

```
[root@malcolm ~]# barman list-backup angus
7angus 20181003T194717 - Mon Oct 3 19:47:20 2018 - Size: 21.1 MiB - WAL
Size: 26.6 KiB
```

The last informative command you might want to get familiar with is `show-backup`, which gives you detailed information on a specific backup regarding the server, base backup time, WAL archive, and context within the catalog (for example, the last available backup):

```
[root@malcolm ~]# barman show-backup angus 20181003T194717
```

Rather than the full backup ID (`20181003T194717`), you can use a few synonyms, such as these:

- **Last or latest**: This refers to the latest available backup (the last in the catalog)
- **First or oldest**: This refers to the oldest available backup (the first in the catalog)

For the `show-backup` command, however, we will use a real and concrete example, taken directly from one of our customer's installations of Barman on a 16.4 TB Postgres 9.4 database:

```
Backup 20180930T130002:
    Server Name          : skynyrd
    Status               : DONE
    PostgreSQL Version   : 90409
    PGDATA directory     : /srv/pgdata

    Base backup information:
        Disk usage           : 16.4 TiB (16.4 TiB with WALs)
        Incremental size     : 5.7 TiB (-65.08%)
        Timeline             : 1
        Begin WAL            : 0000000100003588000000063
        End WAL              : 00000001000035A0000000A2
        WAL number           : 6208
        WAL compression ratio: 79.15%
        Begin time           : 2018-09-30  13:00:04.245110+00:00

    End time             : 2018-10-01  13:24:47.322288+00:00
        Begin Offset         : 24272
        End Offset           : 11100576
        Begin XLOG           : 3588/63005ED0
        End XLOG             : 35A0/A2A961A0

    WAL information:
        No of files          : 3240
        Disk usage           : 11.9 GiB
        WAL rate             : 104.33/hour
        Compression ratio    : 76.43%
        Last available       : 00000001000035AD0000004A

    Catalog information:
        Retention Policy     : not enforced
        Previous Backup      : 20180923T130001
        Next Backup          : - (this is the latest base backup)
```

As you can see, Barman is a production-ready tool that can be used in large, business-critical contexts, as well as in basic Postgres installations. It provides good **Recovery Point Objective** (**RPO**) outcomes, allowing you to limit potential data loss to a single WAL file.

Finally, Barman also supports WAL streaming, which dramatically reduces the amount of data you can lose. With synchronous replication and replication slot support, you can achieve *zero data loss* backups. For further information, please refer to Barman's documentation, in particular: `streaming_archiver`, `streaming_archiver_name`, `streaming_conninfo`, and `slot_name`.

Barman is distributed under GNU GPL 3 terms and is available for download at `http://www.pgbarman.org/`.

There is also a module for Puppet, which is available at `https://github.com/2ndquadrant-it/puppet-barman`.

For further and more detailed information, refer to the following:

- The `man barman` command, which gives the man page for the Barman application
- The `man 5 barman` command, which gives the man page for the configuration file
- The `barman help` command, which gives a list of the available commands
- The official documentation for Barman, which is publicly available at `http://docs.pgbarman.org/`
- The mailing list for community support at `http://www.pgbarman.org/support/`

Recovery with Barman

This recipe assumes that you have read the previous recipe, *Hot physical backups with Barman*, and successfully installed Barman on the `malcolm` server, hence backing up the Postgres databases running on `angus` and `bon`. We will use the same nomenclature in the examples in this recipe.

A recovery procedure is a reaction to a failure. In database terms, this could be related to an unintentional human error (for example, a `DROP` operation on a table), an attack (think of Little Bobby Tables), a hardware failure (for example, a broken hard drive), or (less likely) a natural disaster.

Even though you might be tempted to think that you are immune to disasters or failures (we wish you were), you are advised to perform regular tests and simulations of recovery procedures. If you have a team of engineers, we suggest that you schedule a simulation every six months (at least) and regularly test your backups through the safest way of checking their content—performing a recovery.

You don't want to take backups for years and, in your moment of need, suddenly discover that they have not been working for the last three months.

Barman allows you to perform two types of recovery:

- **Local recovery**: This involves restoring a PostgreSQL instance on the same server where Barman resides
- **Remote recovery**: This involves restoring a PostgreSQL instance directly from the Barman server to another server, through the network

It is important to note that the terms *local* and *remote* are defined from Barman's standpoint, as every recovery command is executed where Barman is installed.

In this recipe, we will cover a single use case—total failure of one of the servers where PostgreSQL is running (fortunately, it is backed up by Barman) and a full remote recovery on a third server.

Getting ready

Even though Barman can centrally manage backups of several servers that have different versions of PostgreSQL, when it comes to recovery, the same requirements for PostgreSQL's PITR technology apply—in particular, the following:

- You must recover on a server with the same hardware architecture and PostgreSQL version
- Recovery is full, meaning that the entire Postgres cluster will be restored (and not a single database)

The use case of this recipe is as follows:

- The bon server has been lost forever, due to a permanent hardware failure
- The brian server, which has similar characteristics to bon, has been selected for recovery
- The same Linux distribution and PostgreSQL packages have been installed on brian
- Barman will be used to perform remote recovery of the latest backup available for bon on the brian server

In order to proceed, you need to add the public SSH key of the `barman` user on `malcolm` in the `~/.ssh/authorized_keys` file of the `Postgres` user on `brian`. If you are not familiar with the process of exchanging a public SSH key, which goes beyond the scope of this book, you are advised to follow Barman's documentation or surf the net for more information.

The first step is to make sure that the `PGDATA directory`, as specified in the `bon` backup, exists on `brian` and can be written by the `postgres` user.

Ask `barman` for the location of `PGDATA` by querying the latest available `backup` metadata:

```
barman show-backup bon last
```

Write down the content of the `PGDATA directory` entry:

```
PGDATA directory : /var/lib/pgsql/11/data
```

You might have noticed that we are using the default `PGDATA directory` for a RHEL/CentOS cluster based on packages maintained by the PostgreSQL community. On Ubuntu, you will probably have `/var/lib/postgresql/11/main`.

As the second step, also make sure that PostgreSQL is not running on `brian`, using either the `service` or `pg_ctl` command.

Executing a recovery operation on a target directory that's being used by a running PostgreSQL instance will permanently damage that instance. Be extremely careful when you perform such an operation.

How to do it...

Connect as the `barman` user on `malcolm` and type the following:

```
barman recover --remote-ssh-command 'ssh postgres@brian' bon last
/var/lib/pgsql/11/data
```

The preceding command will use the latest available backup for the `bon` server and prepare everything you need to restore your server in the PostgreSQL destination directory (`/var/lib/pgsql/11/data`), as shown in the following output:

```
Starting remote restore for server bon using backup 20181003T194717
Destination directory: /var/lib/pgsql/11/data
Copying the base backup.
Copying required WAL segments.
Generating archive status files
Identify dangerous settings in destination directory.
```

```
IMPORTANT
These settings have been modified to prevent data losses

postgresql.conf line 645: archive_command = false

Your PostgreSQL server has been successfully prepared for recovery!
```

Once again, Ubuntu users will have to use a different destination directory, such as `/var/lib/postgresql/11/main`.

Before you start the server, you are advised to connect to Brian as Postgres and inspect the content of the Postgres destination directory. You should notice that its content should be very similar to what was in the `bon` server before the crash.

You are also strongly encouraged to review the content of the `postgresql.conf` file before starting the server, even though Barman takes care of disabling or removing some potentially dangerous options. The most critical option is `archive_command`, which is preemptively set to `false`, forcing you to deliberately analyze and consider new continuous archiving strategies (for example, you might want to add the new Brian server to Barman by repeating the steps outlined in the previous recipe).

When you are ready, you can start Postgres as a standard service. On CentOS 7, for example, you can execute as root, as follows:

```
systemctl start postgresql-11
```

On Ubuntu, use the following command:

```
systemctl start postgresql
```

Look at the logs to verify that you do not have any problems and then at `ps -axf`.

Your PostgreSQL databases that were hosted on `bon` have been successfully restored on `brian`, using all of the WAL files that were shipped to the backup server.

How it works...

When executed with the `--remote-ssh-command` option, the `recover` command will activate remote recovery and will use those credentials to connect to the remote server (similar to what the `ssh-command` configuration option does in the backup phase but in reverse—see the *Hot physical backups with Barman* recipe for more information). Internally, Barman relies on `rsync` for this operation.

When performing a full recovery (up to the latest available archived WAL file), Barman recreates the structure of the PGDATA according to the backup. It will then deposit all of the necessary WAL files in the pg_wal directory.

A careful analysis of the content of the restored PGDATA directory shows that no recovery.conf file is generated by Barman in the case of a full recovery.

It will just simulate a standard crash recovery of PostgreSQL and start replaying the WAL files from the REDO point, contrary to the *Recovery of all databases* recipe, where recovery.conf was used.

We decided to adopt this strategy in Barman so that we could maintain the same timeline (as a recovery.conf file would start a new era in the cluster's existence) and avoid setting restore_command.

There's more...

If you are using tablespaces, you may be wondering if and how Barman manages them. Barman fully supports tablespaces, including their relocation at recovery time, through the --tablespace runtime option. For information on the syntax of the relocation rules, type any of the following commands:

- barman help recover
- man barman

In this recipe, we have seen only one use case, which covers remote recovery. As we mentioned previously, however, Barman also allows DBAs to recover instances of PostgreSQL on the same server as Barman.

This is called **local recovery**. For local recovery, you will need to have installed the binaries and libraries of the same version of PostgreSQL on the Barman server as the backup file you want to restore.

You can dedicate a directory in Barman for local recovery, which will be used as the destination directory for your recover commands.

A typical use case for local recovery is to restore the situation of a PostgreSQL server at a specific point in time, usually before an unintentional action such as the DROP of a table.

Barman supports PITR, as explained in the *Recovery to a point in time* recipe, through three options that define the recovery target:

- `--target-time TARGET_TIME`: The target is a timestamp
- `--target-xid TARGET_XID`: The target is a transaction ID
- `--target-name TARGET_NAME`: The target is a named restore point, which was created previously with the `pg_create_restore_point(name)` function

When executed with one of these options, Barman will generate the `recovery.conf` file for you. Advanced users might want to activate the hot standby facility and take advantage of the `recovery_target_action` option (by default, this is set to `pause` and is effective only if `hot_standby` is enabled in the `postgresql.conf` file).

This will allow you to check whether the database is in the desired state or not. If not, you can stop the server, change the recovery target time, and start it again. Repeat this operation until you reach your goal, keeping in mind that PostgreSQL can only roll forward WAL files (they are called **REDO operations** for a reason).

You can then follow the instructions outlined in the *Recovery of a dropped/damaged table* recipe to restore the objects in the primary database.

At the end of any recovery operation, remember to stop the running of local servers and remove recovered instances (even though this is not mandatory, as Barman uses `rsync` and will be able to perform an incremental copy of the files where applicable).

The `-j` command-line switch can be used to specify the number of parallel jobs that Barman can use while copying files between itself and PostgreSQL. This feature is generically referred to as **parallel copy**, which includes both taking a backup and restoring it.

Another interesting feature of Barman is the `get-wal` command, which transforms Barman into an infinite basin of WAL files. Instead of copying WAL files before the actual start of the server, you can let PostgreSQL pull the required WAL files on demand at recovery time, via `restore_command`. For further information, look at the `barman-cli` package—more specifically the `barman-wal-restore` script—at `https://github.com/2ndquadrant-it/barman-cli`.

As a final note for this recipe, another important use case for Barman is to regularly create copies of the server to be used for business intelligence purposes or even staging/development. These environments do not normally require a strict up-to-date situation and are very often happy to work on a snapshot of the previous day.

A typical workflow for this use case can be as follows:

1. Stop the PostgreSQL server on the BI/staging server
2. Issue a full remote recovery operation of the desired backup from Barman to the BI server (`rsync` will use the existing data directory for incremental copy)
3. Start the PostgreSQL server on the BI/staging server

This recipe has covered only a few aspects of the recovery process in Barman. For further and more detailed information, refer to the following links:

- The official documentation for Barman, which is publicly available at `http://docs.pgbarman.org/`
- The mailing list for community support at `http://www.pgbarman.org/support/`
- The Barman section of our blog at `https://blog.2ndquadrant.com/tag/barman`

Validating backups

In this recipe, we will use the Data Checksum feature to detect data corruption caused by I/O malfunctioning in advance.

It is important to discover such problems as soon as possible. For instance, we want a chance to recover lost data from one of our older backups, or we may want to stop data errors before they spread to the rest of the database, when newer data depends on existing data.

Getting ready

This feature is disabled by default, since it results in some overhead; it must be enabled when the cluster is initialized by using the `--data-checksums` option of the `initdb` utility.

Also, before trying this recipe, you should be familiar with how to take backups and how to restore them afterward, which are the subjects of most of this chapter.

How to do it...

First, check whether data checksums are enabled:

```
postgres=# SHOW data_checksums ;
 data_checksums

-----------------
 on

(1 row)
```

If not, then we must regrettably stop here. We mentioned previously that this feature needs to be enabled *before* you need it; you shouldn't be surprised because the same is true for most business continuity capabilities, such as high availability or disaster recovery.

If data checksums are enabled, and you are taking a backup with pg_basebackup, then checksums are verified while pages are read from data files. Let's look at an example:

```
$ pg_basebackup -D backup2
```

If nothing goes wrong, then the backup finishes with no output—we know already that pg_basebackup operates by default in no news good news mode. Conversely, if a checksum fails, then the return code is non-zero and we get a warning like the following:

```
WARNING:   checksum verification failed in file "./base/16385/16388", block
0: calculated 246D but expected C938

pg_basebackup: checksum error occurred
```

In the (unlikely) case that you have a good reason for skipping this check, you can use the no-verify-checksums option.

When a physical backup is taken without pg_basebackup, there is no PostgreSQL utility that can verify checksums while the backup is being taken; the check must be carried out afterwards by running the pg_verify_checksums utility against the actual files in the data directory.

Unfortunately, this utility requires the data directory to be in a clean shutdown state, which is not the case when hot physical backups are taken. Therefore, we need to restore the backup to a temporary directory, and then carry out a recovery process, as described in the *Recovery to a point in time* recipe previously, for instance, by using the following settings in recovery.conf:

```
recovery_target = 'immediate'
recovery_target_action = shutdown
```

The `immediate` target means that the recovery will stop as soon as the `data` directory becomes consistent, and then PostgreSQL will shut down, which is the specified target action.

Once we have a clean `data` directory, we just run `pg_verify_checksums` against the temporary directory, as follows:

```
$ pg_verify_checksums -D tempdir1
```

Should any checksum fail, you will see an output like the following:

```
pg_verify_checksums: checksum verification failed in file
"tempdir1/base/16385/16388", block 0: calculated checksum 246D but block
contains C938

Checksum scan completed
Data checksum version: 1
Files scanned:   1226
Blocks scanned: 3852
Bad checksums:   1
```

How it works...

When the data checksum feature is enabled, each page header includes a 16-bit checksum of its contents and block number, which is updated when the page is flushed to disk.

If enabled, data checksums are verified every time a block is read from disk to shared buffers as well as when `pg_basebackup` is used to perform a backup.

Since the checksum is computed and added to the block when flushing to disk, a failure must be caused by a change inside the block that occurred while the block was not cached in the shared buffers; conversely, a change occurring while the block was buffered would be overwritten at the next flush.

There's more...

In our example, we have showed a case where the checksum fails. The checksum mismatch will also be detected when a query causes PostgreSQL to attempt reading that block into the shared buffers.

In that case, the query will fail with an error, which is good because it protects the user from inadvertently using corrupt data:

```
postgres=# SELECT * FROM t;

WARNING:  page verification failed, calculated checksum 42501 but expected
37058
ERROR:  invalid page in block 0 of relation base/16385/16388
```

If we want to intentionally load corrupt data, for example, to attempt some repair activities, we can temporarily disable the checksum, as in the following example:

```
postgres=# SET ignore_checksum_failure = on;
postgres=# SELECT * FROM t;
WARNING:  page verification failed, calculated checksum 42501 but expected
37058
  x


----
 88
(1 row)
```

We can see that the warning is still displayed, but we can proceed to read the data.

> In the case that the data corruption results in an invalid page format, the user will get the same error, irrespective of the value of `ignore_checksum_failure`. This is intentional: this parameter eliminates the risk of undetected failures. In other words, a page with an invalid format does not need checksums to be detected, nor it can be read, or amended, within SQL queries.

As you would expect, only a superuser can change the `ignore_checksum_failure` parameter.

12
Replication and Upgrades

Replication isn't magic, though it can be pretty cool! It's even cooler when it works, and that's what this chapter is all about.

Replication requires understanding, effort, and patience. There are a significant number of points to get right. My emphasis here is on providing simple approaches to get you started, and some clear best practices on operational robustness.

PostgreSQL has included some form of native or in-core replication since Version 8.2, though that support has steadily improved over time. External projects and tools have always been a significant part of the PostgreSQL landscape, with most of them being written and supported by very skilled PostgreSQL technical developers. Some people with a negative viewpoint have observed that this weakens PostgreSQL or emphasizes shortcomings. My view would be that PostgreSQL has been lucky enough to be supported by a huge range of replication tools, together offering a wide set of supported use cases from which to build practical solutions. This view extends throughout this chapter on replication, with many recipes using tools that are not part of the core PostgreSQL project yet.

All the tools mentioned in this chapter are actively enhanced by current core PostgreSQL developers. The pace of change in this area is high, and it is likely that some of the restrictions mentioned here could well be removed by the time you read this book. Double-check the documentation for each tool or project.

Which technique is the best? is a question that gets asked many times. The answer varies depending on the exact circumstances. In many cases, people use one technique on one server and a different technique on other servers. Even the developers of particular tools use other tools when it is appropriate. Use the right tools for the job. All the tools and techniques listed in this chapter have been recommended by me at some point, in relevant circumstances. If something isn't mentioned here by me, that probably does imply that it is less favorable for various reasons, and there are some tools and techniques that I would personally avoid altogether in their present form or level of maturity.

I (*Simon Riggs*) must also confess to being the developer or designer of many parts of the basic technology presented here. That gives me some advantages and disadvantages over other authors. It means I understand some things better than others, which hopefully translates into better descriptions and comparisons. It may also hamper me by providing too narrow a focus, though the world is big and this book is already long enough!

This book, and especially this chapter, covers technology in depth. As a result, we face the risk of minor errors. We've gone to a lot of trouble to test all of our recommendations, but just like software, I have learned that books can be buggy too. I hope our efforts to present actual commands, rather than just words, will be appreciated by you.

In this chapter, we will cover the following recipes:

- Replication best practices
- Setting up file-based replication—deprecated
- Setting up streaming replication
- Setting up streaming replication security
- Hot standby and read scalability
- Managing streaming replication
- Using repmgr
- Using replication slots
- Monitoring replication
- Performance and synchronous replication
- Delaying, pausing, and synchronizing replication
- Logical replication
- Bidirectional replication
- Archiving transaction log data
- Upgrading—minor releases
- Major upgrades in-place
- Major upgrades online

Replication concepts

Replication technology can be confusing. You might be forgiven for thinking that people have a reason to keep it that way. My observation is that there are many techniques, each with their own advocates, and their strengths and weaknesses are often hotly debated.

There are some simple, underlying concepts that can help you understand the various options that are available. The terms used here are designed to avoid favoring any particular technique, and we've used standard industry terms whenever available.

Topics

Database replication is the term we use to describe the technology that's used to maintain a copy of a set of data on a remote system.

There are usually two main reasons for you wanting to do this, and those reasons are often combined:

- **High availability**: Reducing the chances of data unavailability by having multiple systems, each holding a full copy of the data.
- **Data movement**: Allowing data to be used by additional applications or workload on additional hardware. Examples of this are **reference data management** (**RDM**), where a single central server might provide information to many other applications, and **business intelligence/reporting systems**.

Of course, both of those topics are complex areas, and there are many architectures and possibilities for implementing each of them.

What we will talk about here is high availability, where there is *no transformation* of the data. We simply copy the data from one PostgreSQL database server to another. So, we are specifically avoiding all discussion on ETL tools, EAI tools, inter-database migration, data-warehousing strategies, and so on. Those are valid topics in IT architecture; it's just that we don't cover them in this book.

Basic concepts

Let's look at the basic architecture. Typically, individual database servers are referred to as nodes. The whole group of database servers involved in replication is known as a cluster. That is the common usage of the term, but be careful; the term **cluster** is also used for two other quite separate meanings elsewhere in PostgreSQL. Firstly, "cluster" is sometimes used to refer to the database instance, though I prefer the term **database server**. Secondly, there is a command named cluster. It is designed to sort data in a specific order within a table.

A database server that allows a user to make changes is known as a **master** or **primary**, or may be described as a source of changes.

A database server that only allows read-only access is known as a **hot standby**, or sometimes, a slave server, or read replica.

The key aspect of replication is that data changes are captured on a master, and then transferred to other nodes. In some cases, a node may send data changes to other nodes, which is a process known as **cascading** or **relay**. Thus, the master is a sending node, but a sending node does not need to be a master.

Replication is often categorized by whether more than one master node is allowed, in which case it will be known as multimaster replication. There is a significant difference between how single-master and multimaster systems work, so we'll discuss that aspect in more detail later. Each has its advantages and disadvantages.

History and scope

PostgreSQL didn't always have in-core replication. For many years, PostgreSQL users needed to use one of many external packages to provide this important feature.

Slony was the first package to provide useful replication features. **Londiste** was a variant system that was somewhat easier to use. Both of those systems provided single-master replication based around triggers. Another variant of this idea was the **bucardo** package, which offered multimaster replication using triggers.

Trigger-based replication has now been superseded by transaction-log-based replication, which provides considerable performance improvements. There is some discussion on exactly how much difference that makes, but log-based replication is approximately twice as fast, though many users have reported much higher gains. Trigger-based systems also have considerably higher replication lag. Lastly, triggers need to be added to each table involved in replication, making these systems more time-consuming to manage and more sensitive to production problems. These factors taken together mean that trigger-based systems will likely be avoided for new developments, and I'm taking the decision not to cover them at all in the latest edition of this book.

Outside the world of PostgreSQL, there are many competing concepts and there is a lot of research being done on them. This is a practical book, so we've mostly avoided comments on research or topics concerning computer science.

The focus of this chapter is replication technologies that are part of the core software of PostgreSQL, or will be in the reasonably near future. The first of these is known as **streaming replication**, introduced in PostgreSQL 9.0, but based on earlier file-based mechanisms for physical transaction log replication. In this book, we refer to this as **physical streaming replication** (**PSR**) because we take the transaction log (often known as the **write-ahead log** (**WAL**)) and ship that data to the remote node. The WAL contains an exact physical copy of the changes made to a data block, so the remote node is an exact copy of the master. Therefore, the remote node cannot execute transactions that write to the database; this type of node is known as a standby.

Starting with PostgreSQL 9.4, we introduced an efficient mechanism for reading the transaction log (WAL) and transforming it into a stream of changes; that is, a process known as **logical decoding**. This is then the basis for the later, even more useful mechanism, known as **logical streaming replication** (**LSR**). This allows a receiver to replicate data without needing to keep an exact copy of the data blocks, as we do with PSR. This has significant advantages, which we will discuss later.

PSR requires us to have only a single master node, though it allows multiple standbys. LSR can be used for all the same purposes as PSR. It just has fewer restrictions and allows a great range of additional use cases. Crucially, LSR can be used as the basis of multimaster clusters.

PSR and LSR are sometimes known as **physical log streaming replication** (**PLSR**) and **logical log streaming replication** (**LLSR**). Those terms are sometimes used to explain differences between transaction-log-based and trigger-based replication.

Practical aspects

Since we refer to the transfer of replicated data as streaming, it becomes natural to talk about the flow of data between nodes as if it were a river or stream. Cascaded data can flow through a series of nodes to create complex architectures. From the perspective of any node, it may have downstream nodes that receive replicated data from it and/or upstream nodes that send data to it. Practical limits need to be understood to allow us to understand and design replication architectures.

After a transaction commits on the master, the time taken to transfer data changes to a remote node is usually referred to as the **latency** or **replication delay**. Once the remote node has received the data, changes must then be applied to the remote node, which takes an amount of time known as the **apply delay**. The total time a record takes from the master to a downstream node is the replication delay plus the apply delay. Be careful to note that some authors describe those terms differently, and sometimes confuse the two, which is easy to do. Also, note that these delays will be different for any two nodes.

Replication delay is best expressed as an interval (in seconds), but that is much harder to measure than it first appears. In PostgreSQL 11, the delays of particular phases of replication are given with the lag columns on `pg_stat_replication`. These are derived from sampling the message stream and interpolating the current delay from recent samples.

All forms of replication are initialized in roughly the same way. First, you enable change capture, and then make a full replica of the dataset on the remote node, which we refer to as the **base backup**. After that, we begin applying the changes, starting from the point immediately before the base backup started and continuing with any changes that occurred while the base backup was taking place. As a result, the replication delay immediately following the initial copy task will be equal to the duration of the initial copy task. The remote node will then begin to catch up with the master, and the replication delay will begin to reduce. The time taken to get the lowest replication delay possible is known as the catch-up interval. If the master is busy generating new changes, which can increase the time it takes for the new node to catch up, you should try to generate new nodes during quieter periods, if any exist. Note that in some cases, the catch-up period will be too long to be acceptable. Be sure to include this understanding in your planning and monitoring. The faster and more efficient your replication system is, the easier it will be to operate in the real world. *Performance matters!*

Either replication will copy all tables, or in some cases, we can copy a subset of tables, in which case we call it **selective replication**. If you choose selective replication, you should note that the management overhead increases roughly as the number of objects managed increases. Replicated objects are often manipulated in groups known as **replication sets** to help minimize the administrative overhead.

Data loss

By default, PostgreSQL provides **asynchronous replication**, where data is streamed out whenever convenient for the server. If replicated data is acknowledged back to the user prior to committing, we refer to that as **synchronous replication**.

With synchronous replication, the replication delay *directly* affects the elapsed time of transactions on the master. With asynchronous replication, the master may continue at full speed, though this opens up a possible risk that the standby may not be able to keep pace with the master. All replication must be monitored to ensure that a significant lag does not develop, which is why we must be careful to monitor the replication delay.

Synchronous replication guarantees that data is written to at least two nodes before the user or application is told that a transaction has committed. You can specify the number of nodes and other details that you wish to use in your configuration.

Single-master replication

In single-master replication, if the master dies, one of the standbys must take its place. Otherwise, we will not be able to accept new write transactions. Thus, the designations master and standby are just roles that any node can take at some point. To move the master role to another node, we perform a procedure named **switchover**. If the master dies and does not recover, then the more severe role change is known as a **failover**. In many ways, these can be similar, but it helps to use different terms for each event.

We use the term **clusterware** for software that manages the cluster. Clusterware may provide features such as automatic failover, and in some cases, load balancing.

The complexity of failover makes single-master replication harder to configure correctly than many people would like it to be. The good news is that from an application perspective, it is safe and easy to retrofit this style of replication to an existing system. Or, put another way, since application developers don't really worry about high availability and replication until the very end of a project, single-master replication is frequently the best solution, be it PSR or LSR.

Multinode architectures

Multinode architectures allow users to write data to multiple nodes concurrently. There are two main categories—tightly coupled and loosely coupled:

- **Tightly coupled database clusters**: These allow a single image of the database, so there is less perception that you're even connected to a cluster at all. This consistency comes at a price—the nodes of the cluster cannot be separated geographically, which means if you need to protect against site disasters, then you'll need additional technology to allow disaster recovery. Clustering requires replication as well.

- **Loosely coupled database clusters**: These have greater independence for each node, allowing us to spread out nodes across wide areas, such as across multiple continents. You can connect to each node individually. There are two benefits of this. The first is that all data access can be performed quickly against local copies of the data. The second benefit is that we don't need to work out how to route read-only transactions to (a) standby node(s) and read/write transactions to the master node.

Clustered or massively parallel databases

An example of a tightly coupled system is the open source Postgres-XL. This supersedes the earlier Postgres-XC clustering software. These systems introduced the concept of a **global transaction manager** (**GTM**), which allows nodes in a tightly coupled system to work together while guaranteeing consistency across reads and writes.

Postgres-XL spreads data across multiple nodes. Larger tables can be distributed evenly using a hash-based distribution scheme. This feature allows Postgres-XL to scale well for both high-transaction-rate (OLTP) and business intelligence (OLAP) systems.

On Postgres-XL, smaller tables can be duplicated on all nodes. Changes to smaller tables are coordinated, so there is no possibility of the multiple copies diverging from one another. The synchronization cost is high, and XL is not suitable for geographically distributed databases, though it does support high availability.

Postgres-XL is not covered in more detail in this book, simply because of the lack of time and space. Postgres-XL is released with the PostgreSQL license.

Multimaster replication

An example of a loosely coupled system would be **bidirectional replication** (**BDR**). Postgres-BDR does not utilize a GTM, so the nodes contain data that is eventually consistent between nodes. This is a performance optimization since tests have showed that trying to use tightly coupled approaches catastrophically limits performance when servers are geographically separated.

In its simplest multimaster configuration, each node has a copy of similar data. You can update data on any node and the changes will flow to other nodes. This makes it ideal for databases that have users in many different locations, which is probably the case with most websites. Each location can have its own copy of the application code and database, giving fast response times for all your users, wherever they are located.

It is *possible* to make changes to the same data at the same time on different nodes, causing update conflicts. These could become a problem, but the reality is that it is also *easily possible* to design applications that do not generate conflicts in normal running, especially if each user is modifying their own data (for example, in social media, retail, and so on).

We need to understand where conflicts might arise so that we can resolve them. On a single node, any application that allows concurrent updates to the same data will experience poor performance because of contention. The negative effect of contention will get much worse on multimaster clusters. In addition, multiple nodes require us to allow for the possibility that the updated data differs, so we must implement conflict-handling logic to resolve data differences between nodes. With some thought and planning, we can use multimaster technologies very effectively in the real world. Visit `https://en.wikipedia.org/wiki/Replication_(computing)` for more information on this.

Scalability tools

Many PostgreSQL users have designed applications that scale naturally by routing database requests based on the client number or a similar natural sharding key. This is what we call manual sharding at the application level.

For PostgreSQL 11 and earlier versions, PostgreSQL does not directly support features for automatic write scalability, such as sharding. This is an active area of work, and much will change in this area, though it may take some time.

Postgres-XL provides automatic hash sharding and is currently the most complete open source implementation that allows automatic write scalability at the database level.

PL/Proxy provides a mature mechanism for database scalability. It was originally designed for Skype, but it is also in use at a number of high-volume sites. It provides most of the things that you'll need to create a scalable cluster. PL/Proxy requires that you define your main database accesses as functions, which requires early decisions about your application architecture.

Other approaches to replication

This book covers in-database replication only. Replication is also possible in the application layer (that is, above the database) or in the **operating system (OS)** layers (that is, below the database):

- **Application-level replication**: For example, HA-JDBC, and rubyrep
- **OS-level replication**: For example, DRBD

None of these approaches are very satisfying, since core database features cannot easily integrate with them in ways that truly work. From a sysadmin's perspective, they work, but not very well from the perspective of a database architect.

Replication best practices

Some general best practices for running replication systems are described in this recipe.

Getting ready

Reading the list of best practices should be the very first thing you do when designing your database architecture. So, the best way to get ready for it is to avoid doing anything and start with the next section, *How to do it....*

How to do it...

- Use the latest release of PostgreSQL. Replication features are changing fast, with each new release improving on the previous in major ways based on our real-world experience. The idea that earlier releases are somehow more stable, and thus more easily usable, is definitely not the case for replication.
- Use similar hardware and OSes on all systems. Replication allows nodes to switch roles. If we switch over or failover to different hardware, we may get performance issues and it will be hard to maintain a smoothly running application.
- Configure all systems identically as far as possible. Use the same mount points, directory names, and users; keep everything the same, where possible. Don't be tempted to make one system more important than others in some way. It's just a single point of failure and gets confusing.

- Give systems/servers good names to reduce confusion. Never, ever call one of your systems "master" and the other "slave." When you do a switchover, you will get very confused! Try to pick system names that have nothing to do whatsoever with their role. Replication roles will inevitably change; system names should not. If one system fails, and you add a new system, never reuse the name of the old system; pick another name, or it will be too confusing. Don't pick names that relate to something in the business. Colors are also a bad choice, because if you have two servers named "Yellow" and "Red," you then end up saying things like, *There is a red alert on Server Yellow*, which can easily be confusing. Don't pick place names, either. Otherwise, you'll be confused trying to remember that "London" is in Edinburgh and "Paris" is in Rome. Make sure that you use names, rather than IP addresses.

- Set the `application_name` parameter to be the server name in the replication connection string. Set the `cluster_name` parameter to be the server name in the `postgresql.conf`.

- Make sure that all tables are marked as `LOGGED` (the default). `UNLOGGED` and `TEMPORARY` tables will not be replicated by either **PSR** or **LSR**.

- Keep the system clocks synchronized. This helps you keep sane when looking at log files that are produced by multiple servers. You should automate this, rather than doing it manually, but however you do it, make sure it works.

- Use a single, unambiguous time zone. Use **Coordinated Universal Time** (**UTC**) or something similar. Don't pick a time zone that has **daylight saving time** (**DST**), especially in regions that have complex DST rules. This just leads to (human) confusion with replication, as servers are often in different countries, and time zone differences vary throughout the year. Do this even if you start with all your servers in one country, because over the lifetime of the application, you may need to add new servers in different locations. Think ahead.

- Monitor each of the database servers. If you want high availability, then you'll need to check regularly that your servers are operational. I speak to many people who would like to regard replication as a one-shot deal. Think of it more as a marriage and plan for it to be a happy one!

- Monitor the replication delay between servers. All forms of replication are only useful if the data is flowing correctly between the servers. Monitoring the time it takes for the data to go from one server to another is essential for understanding whether replication is working for you or not. Replication can be bursty, so you'll need to watch to make sure it stays within sensible limits. You may be able to set tuning parameters to keep things low, or you may need to look at other factors.

The important point is that your replication delay is directly related to the amount of data you're likely to lose when running asynchronous replication. Be careful here, because it is the replication delay, not the apply delay, that affects data loss. A long apply delay may be more acceptable as a result.

As described previously, your initial replication delay will be high, and it should reduce to a lower and more stable value over a period of time. For large databases, this could take days, so be careful to monitor it during the catch-up period.

There's more...

The preceding list doesn't actually say this explicitly, but you should use the same major version of PostgreSQL for all systems. With PSR, you are required to do that, so it doesn't even need to be said.

I've heard people argue that it's OK to have dissimilar systems and even that it's a good idea because if you get a bug, it only affects one node. I'd say that the massive increase in complexity is much more likely to cause problems.

Setting up file-based replication – deprecated

This technique is mostly superseded by streaming replication (PSR), so if you are a novice, you probably don't want to read this recipe yet. Nonetheless, this is relevant and useful as part of a comprehensive backup strategy. It is also worth understanding how this works, as this technique can also be used as the starting phase for a large streaming replication setup. Look at the following recipes for some further details on that.

Log shipping is a replication technique used by many database management systems. The master records database changes in its transaction log, and then the log files are shipped from the master to the standby, where the log is replayed.

File-based log shipping has been available for PostgreSQL for many years now. It is simple, has very low overhead, and is a trustworthy form of replication.

Getting ready

If you haven't read the *Replication concepts* section and the *Replication best practices* recipe at the start of this chapter, go and read them now. Replication is complex, and even if you think, *No problem, I know that*, it's worth just checking out the basic concepts and names that I'll be using here. Note that log-shipping replication refers to the master node as the primary node, and these two terms are used interchangeably.

How to do it...

Follow these steps for the initial configuration of file-based log shipping:

1. Identify your archive location and ensure that it has sufficient space. This recipe assumes that the archive is a directory on the standby node, identified by the $PGARCHIVE environment variable. This is set on both the master and standby nodes, as the master must write to the archive and the standby must read from it. The standby node is identified on the master using $STANDBYNODE.

2. Configure replication security. Perform a key exchange to allow the master and the standby to run the rsync command in either direction.

3. Adjust the master's parameters in postgresql.conf, as follows:

```
wal_level = 'archive'
archive_mode = on
archive_command = 'scp %p $STANDBYNODE:$PGARCHIVE/%f'
archive_timeout = 30
```

4. Adjust the hot standby parameters, if required (see the *Hot standby and read scalability* recipe).

5. Take a base backup, which is very similar to the process for taking a physical that we backup described in Chapter 11, *Backup and Recovery*.

6. Start the backup by running the following command:

```
psql -c "select pg_start_backup('base backup for log
shipping')"
```

7. Copy the data files (excluding the `pg_wal` directory). Note that this requires some security configuration to ensure that `rsync` can be executed without needing to provide a password when it executes. If you skipped Step 2, do this now, as follows:

```
rsync -cva --inplace --exclude=*pg_wal* \
${PGDATA}/ $STANDBYNODE:$PGDATA
```

8. Stop the backup by running the following command:

```
psql -c "select pg_stop_backup(), current_timestamp"
```

9. Set the `recovery.conf` parameters in the `data` directory on the `standby` server, as follows:

```
standby_mode  =  'on'
restore_command  =  'cp  $PGARCHIVE/%f  %p'
archive_cleanup_command  =  'pg_archivecleanup  $PGARCHIVE  %r'
trigger_file  =  '/tmp/postgresql.trigger.5432'
```

10. Start the `standby` server.

11. Carefully monitor the replication delay until the catch-up period is over. During the initial catch-up period, the replication delay will be much higher than we would normally expect it to be. You are advised to set `hot_standby` to `off` for the initial period only.

Use a script; don't do this by hand, even when testing or just exploring the capabilities. If you make a mistake, you'd want to rerun things from the start again, and doing things manually is both laborious and an extra source of error.

How it works...

Transaction log (WAL) files will be written on the master. Setting `wal_level` to `archive` ensures that we collect all of the changed data and that WAL is never optimized away. WAL is sent from the master to the archive using `archive_command` and, from there, the standby reads WAL files using `restore_command`. Then, it replays the changes.

The `archive_command` is executed when a file becomes full or an `archive_timeout` number of seconds has passed since any user inserted change data into the transaction log. If the server does not write any new transaction log data for an extended period, then files will switch every `checkpoint_timeout` seconds. This is normal and not a problem.

The preceding configuration assumes that the archive is on the standby, so the restore_command that's shown is a simple copy command (cp). If the archive were on a third system, then we would need to either mount the filesystem remotely or use a network copy command.

The archive_cleanup_command ensures that the archive only holds the files that the standby needs for restarting, in case it stops for any reason. Files older than the last file required are deleted regularly to ensure that the archive does not overflow. Note that if the standby is down for an extended period, then the number of files in the archive will continue to accumulate, and eventually they will overflow. The number of files in the archive should also be monitored.

In the configuration shown in this recipe, a command named pg_archivecleanup is used to remove files from the archive. (This used to be a contrib module but is now part of the main server.) The pg_archivecleanup module is designed to work with one standby node at a time. Note that pg_archivecleanup requires two parameters: the archive directory and %r, with a space between them. PostgreSQL transforms %r into the cut-off filename.

If you wish to have multiple standby nodes, then a shared archive would be a single point of failure and should be avoided, so each standby should maintain its own archive. We must modify the archive_command to be a script, rather than execute the command directly.

This allows us to handle archiving to multiple destinations:

```
archive_command = 'myarchivescript %p %f'
```

Then, we can write myarchivescript so that it looks something like the following, though you'll need to add some suitable error checking for your environment:

```
scp $1 $STANDBYNODE1:$PGARCHIVE/$2
scp $1 $STANDBYNODE2:$PGARCHIVE/$2
scp $1 $STANDBYNODE3:$PGARCHIVE/$2
```

The initial copy, or base backup, is performed using the rsync utility, which may require you to have direct security authorization, for example, using SSH and key exchange. You may also choose to perform the base backup in a different way. If so, feel free to substitute your preferred method.

There's more...

Monitoring file-based log shipping can be performed in a number of ways. You can look at the current files on both the `master` and `standby`, as follows:

```
ps -ef | grep archiver        on master
postgres: archiver process  last was   000000010000000000000040
ps -ef | grep startup         on standby
postgres: startup process   waiting for  000000010000000000000041
```

This allows you to see the replication delay in terms of the number of WAL files, by which the `standby` is behind the `master`. Prior to PostgreSQL 9.0, it was difficult to measure the replication delay as a time interval with any accuracy, and some hackish methods were needed. Those aren't presented here. The latest ways of monitoring replication are covered in more detail in the *Monitoring replication* recipe.

See also

- If you have configuration instructions written for versions ranging from PostgreSQL 8.2 to 8.4, then they will work almost exactly the same from PostgreSQL 9.0 onwards. The only difference is that you will also need to specify `wal_level`, as we've just shown.
- Note that the procedures covered here are not the default configuration, and they do differ from earlier releases. In PostgreSQL 9.0, the `pg_standby` utility is no longer required, as many of its features are now performed directly by the server.
- If you prefer to continue using `pg_standby` with PostgreSQL 9.0, then you do not need to use the `archive_cleanup_command`, `standby_mode`, or `trigger_file` parameters at all.

Setting up streaming replication

Log shipping is a replication technique that's used by many database management systems. The master records change in a transaction log (WAL), and then the log data is shipped from the master to the standby, where the log is replayed.

In PostgreSQL, PSR transfers WAL data directly from the master to the standby, giving us integrated security and reduced replication delay.

There are two main ways to set up streaming replication: with or without an additional archive. Setting it up without an external archive is presented here, as it is the simpler and more efficient way. However, there is one downside that suggests that the simpler approach may not be appropriate for larger databases, which is explained later in this recipe.

Getting ready

If you haven't read the *Replication concepts* section and the *Replication best practices* recipes at the start of this chapter, go and read them now. Note that streaming replication refers to the master node as the primary node, and the two terms can be used interchangeably.

How to do it...

You can use the following procedure for base backups:

1. Identify your master and standby nodes and ensure that they have been configured according to the *Replication best practices* recipe.

2. Configure replication security. Create or confirm the existence of the replication user on the master node:

```
CREATE USER repuser
  REPLICATION
  LOGIN
  CONNECTION LIMIT 2
  ENCRYPTED PASSWORD 'changeme';
```

3. Allow the replication user to authenticate. The following example allows access from any IP address using MD5-encrypted password authentication; you may wish to consider other options. Add the following line to pg_hba.conf:

```
host    replication    repuser    0.0.0.1/0    md5
```

4. Set the logging options in postgresql.conf on both the master and the standby so that you can get more information regarding replication connection attempts and associated failures:

```
log_connections = on
```

5. Set `max_wal_senders` on the master in `postgresql.conf`, or increase it if the value is already nonzero. Check the server first, since the default is now `10`:

```
max_wal_senders = 10
wal_level = 'archive'
archive_mode = on
archive_command = 'cd .'
```

6. Adjust the hot standby parameters, if required (see a *Setting up streaming replication security* recipe).

7. Create a replication slot, if needed (see a later recipe). A new option in PostgreSQL 11 can do this for you, if you wish—add the `--create-slot` parameter in *Step 11*.

8. Take a base backup:

```
pg_basebackup -d 'connection string' -D /path/to_data_dir
```

9. You are advised to use the following additional option on the `pg_basebackup` command line. This option allows the required WAL files to be streamed alongside the base backup on a second session, greatly improving the startup time on larger databases, without the need to fuss over large settings of `wal_keep_segments` (as seen in *Step 6*):

```
--wal-method=stream
```

10. If the backup uses too many server resources (CPU, memory, disk, or bandwidth), you can throttle down the speed for the backup using the following additional option on the `pg_basebackup` command line. The RATE value is specified in kb/s by default:

```
--max-rate=RATE
```

11. If you are using replication slots, specify the slot name. If you want to create the slot as well, please use the `--create-slot` option as well:

```
--slot=myslotname --create-slot
```

12. Set the `recovery.conf` parameters on the standby. Note that `primary_conninfo` must not specify a database name, though it can contain any other PostgreSQL connection option. Also, note that all options in `recovery.conf` are enclosed in quotes, whereas the `postgresql.conf` parameters need not be. For PostgreSQL 9.4 and later versions, you can skip this step if you wish by specifying the `--write-recovery-conf` option on `pg_basebackup`:

```
standby_mode = 'on'
primary_conninfo = 'host=192.168.0.1 user=repuser'
# trigger_file = ''   # no need for trigger file 9.1+
```

13. Start the standby server.
14. Carefully monitor the replication delay until the catch-up period is over. During the initial catch-up period, the replication delay will be much higher than we would normally expect it to be. The `pg_basebackup` utility also allows you to produce a compressed TAR file using the following command:

```
pg_basebackup -F -z
```

An alternate procedure can be used if needed or desirable:

1. First, perform *Steps 1* to *Step 5* of the preceding procedure.
2. Use `wal_keep_segments`, or use replication slots (see a later recipe).
3. Adjust `wal_keep_segments` on the master in `postgresql.conf`. Set this to a value no higher than the amount of free space on the drive on which the `pg_wal` directory is mounted, divided by 16 MB (note: this value is configurable).
4. If `pg_wal` isn't mounted on a separate drive, then don't assume that all of the current free space is available for transaction log files: `wal_keep_segments = 10000 #   160 GB`.
5. Adjust the hot standby parameters, if required (see the *Hot standby and read scalability* recipe). Take a base backup, which is very similar to the process for taking a physical backup, as described in `Chapter 11`, *Backup and Recovery*.

6. Start the backup:

```
psql -c "select pg_start_backup('base backup for streaming
rep')"
```

7. Copy the data files (excluding the `pg_wal` directory):

```
rsync -cva --inplace --exclude=*pg_wal* \
${PGDATA}/ $STANDBYNODE:$PGDATA
```

8. Stop the backup:

```
psql -c "select pg_stop_backup(), current_timestamp"
```

9. Set the `recovery.conf` parameters on the standby. Note that `primary_conninfo` must not specify a database name, though it can contain any other PostgreSQL connection option. Also, note that all options in `recovery.conf` are enclosed in quotes, whereas the `postgresql.conf` parameters need not be:

```
standby_mode = 'on'
primary_conninfo = 'host=alpha user=repuser'
trigger_file = '/tmp/postgresql.trigger.5432'
```

10. Start the standby server.
11. Carefully monitor the replication delay until the catch-up period is over. During the initial catch-up period, the replication delay will be much higher than we would normally expect it to be.

How it works...

Multiple standby nodes can connect to a single master. Set `max_wal_senders` to the number of standby nodes, plus at least 1. If you are planning to use `pg_basebackup – wal-method=stream`, then allow for an additional connection per concurrent backup you plan for. You may wish to set up an individual user for each standby node, though it may be sufficient just to set the `application_name` parameter in `primary_conninfo`.

The architecture for streaming replication is this: on the master, one `WALSender` process is created for each standby that connects for the streaming replication. On the standby node, a `WALReceiver` process is created to work cooperatively with the master. Data transfer has been designed and measured to be very efficient, and data is typically sent in 8,192-byte chunks, without additional buffering at the network layer.

Both `WALSender` and `WALReceiver` will work continuously on any outstanding data, and will be replicated until the queue is empty. If there is a quiet period, then `WALReceiver` will sleep for a while.

The standby connects to the master using native PostgreSQL libpq connections. This means that all forms of authentication and security work for replication, just as they do for normal connections. Note that, for replication sessions, the standby is the client and the master is the server, if any parameters need to be configured. Using standard PostgreSQL libpq connections also means that normal network port numbers are used, so no additional firewall rules are required. You should also note that if the connections use SSL, then encryption costs will slightly increase the replication delay and the CPU resources required.

There's more...

If the connection between the master and standby drops, it will take some time for that to be noticed across an indirect network. To ensure that a dropped connection is noticed as soon as possible, you may wish to adjust the timeout settings.

The standby will notice that the connection to the master has dropped after `wal_receiver_timeout` milliseconds. Once the connection is dropped, the standby will retry the connection to the sending server every `wal_retrieve_retry_interval` milliseconds. Set these parameters in the `postgresql.conf` file on the standby.

A sending server will notice that the connection has dropped after `wal_sender_timeout` milliseconds, set in the `postgresql.conf` file on the sender. Once the connection is dropped, the standby is responsible for reestablishing the connection.

You may also wish to increase `max_wal_senders` to one or two more than the current number of nodes so that it will be possible to reconnect even before a dropped connection is noted. This allows a server restart to reestablish connections more easily. If you do this, then also increase the connection limit for the replication user. Check the existing value first, since defaults have been increased in PostgreSQL 11.

Data transfer may stop if the connection drops or the standby server or the standby system is shut down. If replication data transfer stops for any reason, it will attempt to restart from the point of the last transfer. Will that data still be available? There are a few options here, though the preferred option is now to use replication slots.

Replication slots reserve WAL files for use by disconnected nodes. Therefore, it is important to be careful that WAL files don't build up, causing *out of disk space* errors due to physical replication slots created with no currently connected standby. The amount of space taken by WAL should be monitored, and the slot should be dropped if space reaches a critical limit.

An alternate approach is to reserve WAL data, but only up to a limit. For streaming replication, the master keeps a number of files that is at least equal to `wal_keep_segments`. If the standby database server has been down for long enough, the master will have moved on and will no longer have the data for the last point of transfer. If that should occur, then the standby needs to be reconfigured using the same procedure with which we started.

You should plan to use `pg_basebackup --wal-method=stream`. If you choose not to, you should note that the standby database server will not be streaming during the initial base backup. So, if the base backup is long enough, we might end up with a situation where replication will never start because the desired starting point is no longer available on the master. This is the error that you'll get:

```
FATAL:   requested WAL segment 000000010000000000000002 has already been
removed
```

It's very annoying, and there's no way out of it—you need to start over. So, start with a very high value of `wal_keep_segments`. Don't guess this randomly; set it to the available disk space on `pg_wal` divided by 16 MB, or less if it is a shared disk. If you still get that error, then you need to increase `wal_keep_segments` and try again, possibly also using techniques to speed up the base backup, which were discussed in `Chapter 11`, *Backup and Recovery*.

If you can't set `wal_keep_segments` high enough, there is an alternative. You must configure a third server or storage pool with increased disk storage capacity, which you can use as an archive. The master will need to have an `archive_command` that places files on the archive server, rather than the dummy command shown in the preceding procedure, in addition to parameter settings to allow streaming to take place. The standby will need to retrieve files from the archive using `restore_command`, as well as streaming using `primary_conninfo`. Thus, both the master and standby have two modes for sending and receiving, and they can switch between them should failures occur. This is the typical configuration for large databases. Note that this means that the WAL data will be copied twice: once to the archive and once directly to the standby. Two copies are more expensive, but they are also more robust.

Setting up streaming replication security

Streaming replication is at least as secure as normal user connections to PostgreSQL.

Replication uses standard libpq connections, so we have all the normal mechanisms for authentication and SSL support, and all the firewall rules are similar.

Replication must be specifically enabled on both the sender and standby sides. Cascading replication does not require any additional security.

When performing a base backup, the `pg_basebackup`, `pg_receivewal`, and `pg_recvlogical` utilities will use the same type of libpq connections as a running, streaming standby. You can use other forms of base backup, such as `rsync`, though you'll need to set up the security configuration manually.

> Standbys are identical copies of the master, so all users exist on all nodes with identical passwords. All of the data is identical (eventually), and all the permissions are the same too. If you wish to control access more closely, then you'll need different `pg_hba.conf` rules on each server to control this. Obviously, if your config files differ between nodes, then failover will be slightly more dramatic, unless you've given that some prior thought.

Getting ready

Identify or create a user/role to be used solely for replication. Decide what form of authentication will be used. If you are going across data centers or the wider internet, take this very seriously.

How to do it...

On the master, perform these steps:

1. Enable replication by setting a specific host access rule in `pg_hba.conf`
2. Give the selected replication user/role the `REPLICATION` and `LOGIN` attributes:

   ```
   ALTER ROLE replogin REPLICATION;
   ```

3. Alternatively, create it using this command:

   ```
   CREATE ROLE replogin REPLICATION LOGIN;
   ```

On the standby, perform these steps:

1. Request replication by setting `primary_conninfo` in `recovery.conf`.
2. If you are using SSL connections, use `sslmode=verify-full`.
3. Enable per-server rules, if any, for this server in `pg_hba.conf`.

How it works...

Streaming replication connects to a virtual database called `replication`. We do this because the WAL data contains changes to objects in all databases, so in a way, we aren't just connecting to one database—we are connecting to all of them.

Streaming replication connects similarly to a normal user, except that instead of a normal user process, we are given a `WALSender` process.

You can set a connection limit on the number of replication connections in two ways:

- At the role level, you can do it by issuing the following command:

    ALTER ROLE replogin CONNECTION LIMIT 2;

- By limiting the overall number of `WALSender` processes via the `max_wal_senders` parameter

Always allow one more connection than you think is required to allow for disconnections and reconnections.

There's more...

You may notice that the `WALSender` process may hit 100% CPU if you use SSL with compression enabled and write lots of data, or generate a large WAL volume from things such as DDL or vacuuming. You can disable compression on fast networks when you aren't paying per-bandwidth charges by using `sslcompression=0` in the connection string specified for `primary_conninfo`. Note that security can be compromised if you use compression, since the data stream is easier to attack.

Hot standby and read scalability

Hot standby (or read replicas) is the name for the PostgreSQL feature that allows us to connect to a standby node and execute read-only queries. Most importantly, hot standby allows us to run queries while the standby is being continuously updated through either file-based or streaming replication.

Hot standby allows you to offload large or long-running queries or parts of your read-only workload to the standby nodes. Should you need to switch over or failover to the standby node, your queries will keep executing during the promotion process to avoid any interruption of service.

You can add additional hot standby nodes to scale the read-only workload. There is no hard limit on the number of standby nodes, as long as you ensure that enough server resources are available and parameters are set correctly—10, 20, or more nodes are easily possible.

There are two main capabilities provided by a hot standby node. The first is that the standby node provides a secondary node in case the primary node fails. The second capability is that we can run queries on that node. In some cases, these two aspects can come into conflict with each other and can result in queries being cancelled. We need to decide the importance we attach to each capability ahead of time so that we can prioritize between them.

In most cases, the role of standby will take priority. Queries are good, but it's OK to cancel them to ensure that we have a viable standby. If we have more than one hot standby node, it may be possible to have one node nominated as standby and others dedicated to serving queries, without any regard for their need to act as standbys.

Standby nodes are started and stopped using the same server commands as master servers, which were covered in earlier chapters.

Getting ready

Hot standby is usable with the following:

- File-based replication
- Streaming replication
- While performing a point-in-time recovery
- When using a permanently frozen standby

For the first two replication mechanisms, you will need to configure replication as described in earlier recipes. In addition, you will need to configure the following parameters:

On the master, set the following in `postgresql.conf`:

```
wal_level = 'replica'  # PostgreSQL 9.6 and above, else hot_standby
```

On the standby, set the following in `postgresql.conf`:

```
hot_standby = on
```

Both of those settings are now the defaults in PostgreSQL 11. In earlier versions, you will need to make these changes. You will need to do a clean restart of the database server on the master. Then, wait a few seconds and restart the standby for those changes to take effect. If you restart the standby too quickly, it will still keep reading the older transaction log data and fail to start. It will give a log message saying you need to enable hot standby, so be patient. You only need to configure this once, not every time you restart. See the *Delaying, pausing, and synchronizing replication* recipe to work out how to wait for actions on the master to arrive on the standby.

A permanently frozen standby can be created by specific settings in the `recovery.conf` file. Neither `restore_command` nor `primary_conninfo` should be set, in the case of `standby_mode = on`. In this mode, the server will start, but will always remain at the exact state of the database, as it was when the `pg_stop_backup()` function completed.

Another point to note is that during the initial catch-up period, the replication delay will be much higher than we would normally expect it to be. You are advised to set `hot_standby = off` for the initial period immediately following the creation of the standby only. User connections during that initial period may use system resources or cause conflicts that could extend the catch-up delay. When the standby is fully caught up with the primary, then we can set `hot_standby = on` and restart, or simply prevent user access via `pg_hba.conf` until the standby catches up.

How to do it...

On the standby node, changes from the master are read from the transaction log and applied to the standby database. Hot standby works by emulating running transactions from the master so that queries on the standby have the visibility information they need to respect MVCC. This makes the hot standby mode particularly suitable for serving a large workload of short or fast SELECT queries. If the workload is consistently short, then few conflicts will delay the standby and the server will run smoothly.

Queries that run on the standby node see a version of the database that is slightly behind the primary node. Eventually, we describe this as being consistent. *How long is eventually?* That time is exactly the replication delay plus the apply delay, as discussed in the *Replication concepts* section. You may also request that standby servers delay applying changes. See the *Delaying, pausing, and synchronizing replication* recipe later on in this chapter for more information.

Resource contention (CPU, I/O, and so on) may increase apply delay. If the server is busy applying changes from the master, then you will have fewer resources to use for queries. This means that if there are no changes arriving, then you'll get more query throughput. If there are predictable changes in the write workload on the master, then you may need to throttle back your query workload on the standby when they occur.

Replication apply may also generate conflicts with running queries. Conflicts may cause the replay to pause, and eventually queries on the standby may be canceled or disconnected. There are three main types of conflicts that can occur between the master and queries on the standby, which are as follows:

- Locks such as access exclusive locks
- Cleanup records
- Other special cases

If cancellations do occur, they will throw either error or fatal-level errors. These will be marked with SQLSTATE 40001 SERIALIZATION FAILURE. This could be trapped by an application, and then the SQL can be resubmitted.

You can monitor the number of conflicts that occur in two places. The total number of conflicts in each database can be seen using this query:

```
SELECT datname, conflicts FROM pg_stat_database;
```

You can drill down further to look at the types of conflict using the following query:

```
SELECT datname, confl_tablespace, confl_lock, confl_snapshot,
confl_bufferpin, confl_deadlock
FROM pg_stat_database_conflicts;
```

Tablespace conflicts are the easiest to understand. If you try to drop a tablespace that someone is still using, then you're going to get a conflict. Don't do that!

Lock conflicts are also easy to understand. If you wish to run a command on the master, such as ALTER TABLE ... DROP COLUMN, then you must lock the table first to prevent all types of access. The lock request is sent to the standby server as well, which will then cancel standby queries that are currently accessing that table after a configurable delay.

On high-availability systems, making DDL changes to tables that cause long periods of locking on the master can be difficult. You may want the tables on the standby to stay available for reads during the period in which the changes are being made on the master. To do that, temporarily set these parameters on the standby: max_standby_streaming delay = -1 and max_standby_archive_delay = -1. Then, reload the server. As soon as the first lock record is seen on the standby, all further changes will be held. Once the locks on the master are released, you can reset the original parameter values on the standby, which will then allow the changes to be made there.

Setting the max_standby_streaming_delay and max_standby_archive_delay parameters to -1 is very timid and may not be useful for normal running if the standby is intended to provide high availability. No user query will ever be canceled if it conflicts with applying changes. It will cause the apply process to wait indefinitely. As a result, the apply delay can increase significantly over time, depending on the frequency and duration of queries and the frequency of conflicts. To work out an appropriate setting for these parameters, you need to understand more about the other types of conflict, though there is also a simple way to avoid this problem entirely.

Snapshot conflicts require some understanding of the internal workings of MVCC, which many people find confusing. To avoid snapshot conflicts, you should set hot_standby_feedback = on in the standby's postgresql.conf file.

In some cases, this could cause table bloat on the master, so it is not set by default. If you don't wish to set hot_standby_feedback = on, then you have further options to consider. You can set an upper limit on the acceptable apply delay caused by conflicts by controlling two similar parameters: max_standby_streaming_delay and max_standby_archive_delay. As a last resort, you can also provide some protection against cancelled queries by setting vacuum_defer_cleanup_age to a value higher than 0. This parameter is fairly hard to set accurately, though I would suggest starting with a value of 1000 and then tune upwards. A vague and inaccurate assumption would be to say that each 1000 will be approximately 1 second of additional delay. This is probably helpful more often than it is wrong. Other conflict types (bufferpin, deadlocks, and so on) are possible, but they are rare.

If you want a completely static standby database with no further changes applied, then you can do this by stopping the server, modifying `recovery.conf` so that neither `restore_command` nor `primary_conninfo` are set but `standby_mode` is on, and then restarting the server. You can come back out of this mode, but only if the archive contains the required WAL files to catch up. Otherwise, you will need to reconfigure the standby from a base backup again.

If you attempt to run a non-read-only query, then you will receive an error marked with `SQLSTATE 25006 READ ONLY TRANSACTION`. This could be used to redirect SQL to the master, where it can execute successfully.

How it works...

Changes made by a transaction on the master will not be visible until the commit is applied onto the standby. So, for example, we have a master and a standby with a replication delay of 4 seconds between them. A long-running transaction may write changes to the master for 1 hour. How long does it take before those changes are visible on the standby? With hot standby, the answer is 4 seconds after the commit on the master. This is because the changes made during the transaction on the master are streamed while the transaction is still in progress, and in most cases, they are already applied on the standby when the commit record arrives.

You may also wish to use the `remote_apply` mode; see the *Delaying, pausing, and synchronizing replication* recipe later on in this chapter.

Hot standby can also be used when running a point-in-time recovery, so the WAL records that are applied to the database need not arrive immediately from a live database server. We can just use file-based recovery in that case, not streaming replication.

Finally, query performance has been dramatically improved in hot standby over time, so it's a good idea to upgrade for that reason alone.

Managing streaming replication

Replication is great, provided that it works. Replication works well if it's understood, and it works even better if it's tested.

Getting ready

You need to have a plan for the objectives for each individual server in the cluster. *Which standby server will be the failover target?*

How to do it...

Switchover is a controlled switch from the master to the standby. If performed correctly, there will be no data loss. To be safe, simply shut down the master node cleanly, using either the `smart` or `fast` shutdown modes. Do not use the `immediate` mode shutdown because you will almost certainly lose data that way.

Failover is a forced switch from the master node to a standby because of the loss of the master. So, in that case, there is no action to perform on the master; we presume it is not there anymore.

Next, we need to promote one of the standby nodes to be the new master. A standby node can be triggered into becoming a master node in one of two ways:

- `pg_ctl promote`
- Suppose you originally specified a `trigger_file` parameter like this:

```
trigger_file = '/tmp/postgresql.trigger.5432'
```

Then, you can create the `trigger` file by executing this:

```
touch /tmp/postgresql.trigger.5432
```

The `trigger_file` will be deleted when the transition is complete.

Note that the `trigger` file has nothing to do whatsoever with a trigger-based replication. The `trigger` filename can be anything you like. We use a suffix of `5432` to ensure that we trigger only one server if there are multiple PostgreSQL servers operating on the same system.

The standby will become the master only once it has fully caught up. If you haven't been monitoring replication, this could take some time.

In versions before PostgreSQL 9.3, switching from standby to master may take some time while the database performs an immediate checkpoint, at least with database servers with large caches and high rates of changes being replicated from the master. From PostgreSQL 9.3 onwards, we can switch from the standby to the master very quickly, and then perform a smooth background checkpoint. There may still be significant I/O as writes begin on the new master.

Once the ex-standby becomes a master, it will begin to operate all normal functions, including archiving files, if configured. Be careful and verify that you have all the correct settings for when this node begins to operate as a master.

It is likely that the settings will be different from those on the original master from which they were copied.

Note that I refer to this new server as **a master**, not **the master**. It is up to you to ensure that the previous master doesn't continue to operate a situation known as **split-brain**. You must be careful to ensure that the previous master stays down.

Management of complex failover situations is not provided with PostgreSQL, nor is automated failover. Situations can be quite complex with multiple nodes, and clusterware is used in many cases to manage this.

The role of the `recovery_end_command` is to clean up at the end of the switchover or failover process. You do not need to remove the `trigger` file explicitly, as was recommended in previous releases.

There's more...

When following a switchover from one node to another, it is common to think of performing a switchover back to the old master server, which is sometimes called failback or switchback.

Once a standby has become a master, it cannot go back to being a standby again. So, with log replication, there is no explicit switchback operation. This is a surprising situation for many people and there is a repeated question, but it is quick to work around. Once you have performed a switchover, all you need to do is the following:

- Reconfigure the old master node again, repeating the same process as before to set up a standby node
- Switchover from the current to the old master node

The important part here is that if we perform the first step without deleting the files on the old master, it allows `rsync` to go much faster. When no files are present on the destination, `rsync` just performs a copy. When similarly named files are present on the destination, then `rsync` will compare the files and send only the changes. So, the `rsync` we perform on a switchback operation performs much less data transfer than in the original copy. It is likely that this will be enhanced in later releases of PostgreSQL. There are also ways to avoid this, as shown in the `repmgr` utility, which will be discussed later.

The `pg_rewind` utility has been developed as a way to perform an automated switchback operation. It performs a much faster switchback when there is a large database with few changes to apply. To allow correct operation, this program can only run on a server that was previously configured with the `wal_log_hints = on` parameter.

Using that parameter can cause more I/O on large databases, so while it improves performance for switchback, it has a considerable overhead for normal running. If you think you would like to run `pg_rewind`, then make sure you work out how it behaves ahead of time. Trying to run it for the first time in a stress situation with a down server is a bad idea.

If all goes wrong, then please remember that `pg_resetwal` is not your friend. It is specifically designed to remove WAL files, destroying your data changes in the process. Always back up WAL files before using it.

See also

Clusterware may provide additional features, such as automated failover, monitoring, or ease of management of replication:

- The `repmgr` utility is designed to manage PostgreSQL replication and failover
- This is discussed in more detail in the *Using repmgr* recipe
- The `pgpool` library is designed to allow session pooling and routing of requests to standby nodes

Using repmgr

As we stated previously, replication is great, provided that it works. It works well if it's understood, and it works even better if it's tested. This is a great reason to use the `repmgr` utility.

`repmgr` 4.0 is an open source tool that was designed specifically for PostgreSQL replication. To get additional information about `repmgr`, visit `http://www.repmgr.org/`.

The `repmgr` utility provides a command-line interface and a management process (daemon) that's used to monitor and manage PostgreSQL servers involved in replication. The `repmgr` utility easily supports more than two nodes, with automatic failover detection.

Getting ready

Install the `repmgr` utility from binary packages on each PostgreSQL node.

Set up replication security and network access between nodes according to the *Setting up streaming replication security* recipe.

How to do it...

The `repmgr` utility provides a set of single command-line actions that perform all the required activities on one node:

1. To start a new cluster with `repmgr` with the current node as its primary, use the following command:

   ```
   repmgr primary register
   ```

2. To add an existing standby to the cluster with `repmgr`, use the following command:

   ```
   repmgr standby register
   ```

3. Use the following command to request `repmgr` to create a new standby for you by copying `node1`. This will fail if you specify an existing `data` directory:

   ```
   repmgr standby clone node1 -D /path/of_new_data_directory
   ```

4. To reuse an old master as a standby, use the `rejoin` command:

   ```
   repmgr node rejoin -d 'host=node2 user=repmgr'
   ```

5. To switch from one primary to another one, run this command on the `standby` that you want to make a primary:

   ```
   repmgr standby switchover
   ```

6. To promote a `standby` to be the new primary, use the following command:

   `repmgr standby promote`

7. To request a `standby` to follow a new primary, use the following command:

   `repmgr standby follow`

8. Check the status of each registered node in the cluster, like this:

   `repmgr cluster show`

9. Request a cleanup of monitoring data, as follows. This is relevant only if `--monitoring-history` is used:

   `repmgr cluster cleanup`

10. Create a `witness` server for use with auto-failover voting, like this:

    `repmgr witness create`

The preceding commands are presented in a simplified form. Each command also takes one of these options:

- `--verbose`: This is useful when exploring new features
- `-f`: This specifies the path to the `repmgr.conf` file

For each node, create a `repmgr.conf` file containing at least the following parameters. Note that the `node_id` and `node_name` parameters need to be different on each node:

```
node_id=2
node_name=beta
conninfo='host=beta user=repmgr'
data_directory=/var/lib/pgsql/11/data
```

Once all the nodes are registered, you can start the `repmgr` daemon on each node, like this:

```
repmgrd -d -f /var/lib/pgsql/repmgr/repmgr.conf &
```

If you would like the daemon to generate monitoring information for that node, you should set `monitoring_history=yes` in the `repmgr.conf` file.

Monitoring data can be accessed using this:

```
repmgr=# select * from repmgr.replication_status;
-[ RECORD 1 ]-------------+-----------------------------
primary_node_id           | 1
```

```
standby_node_id          | 2
standby_name             | node2
node_type                | standby
active                   | t
last_monitor_time        | 2017-08-24 16:28:41.260478+09
last_wal_primary_location | 0/6D57A00
last_wal_standby_location | 0/5000000
replication_lag          | 29 MB
replication_time_lag     | 00:00:11.736163
apply_lag                | 15 MB
communication_time_lag   | 00:00:01.365643
```

How it works...

Repmgr 4 works with PostgreSQL 9.3+ and PostgreSQL 10 and later versions. The repmgr supports the latest features of PostgreSQL, such as cascading, synchronous replication, and replication slots. It uses pg_basebackup, allowing you to clone from a standby. The use of pg_basebackup also removes the need for rsync and key exchange between servers. Also, cascaded standby nodes no longer need to re-follow.

There's more...

The default behavior for the repmgr utility is manual failover.

The repmgr utility also supports automatic failover capabilities. It can automatically detect failures of other nodes, and then decide which server should become the new master by voting among all of the still-available standby nodes. The repmgr utility supports a witness server to ensure that there are an odd number of voters in order to get a clear winner in any decision.

Using replication slots

Replication slots allow you to define your replication architecture explicitly. They also allow you to track details of nodes even when they are disconnected. Replication slots work with both PSR and LSR, though they operate slightly differently.

Replication slots ensure that data required by a downstream node persists until the node receives it. They are crash-safe, so if a connection is lost, the slot still continues to exist. By tracking data on downstream nodes, we avoid these problems:

- When a standby disconnects, the feedback data provided by `hot_standby_feedback` is lost. When the standby reconnects, it may be sent cleanup records that result in query conflicts. Replication slots remember the standby's `xmin` value even when disconnected, ensuring that cleanup conflicts can be avoided.
- When a standby disconnects, the knowledge of which WAL files were required is lost. When the standby reconnects, we may have discarded the required WAL files, requiring us to regenerate the downstream node completely (assuming that this is possible). Replication slots ensure that nodes retain the WAL files needed by all downstream nodes.

Replication slots are required by LSR and for any other use of logical decoding. Replication slots are optional with PSR.

Getting ready

This recipe assumes that you have already set up replication according to the earlier recipes so that `wal_level`, `max_wal_senders`, and the other parameters are set.

A replication slot represents one link between two nodes. At any time, each slot can support one connection. If you draw a diagram of your replication architecture, then each connecting line is one slot. Each slot must have a unique name. The slot name must contain only lowercase letters, numbers, and underscores.

As we discussed previously, each node should have a unique name. So, a suggestion would be to construct the slot name from the two node names that it links. For various reasons, there may be a need for multiple slots between two nodes, so additional information is also required for uniqueness. For two servers called `alpha` and `beta`, an example of a slot name would be `alpha_beta_1`.

For LSR, each slot refers to a single database rather than the whole server. In that case, slot names could also include database names.

How to do it...

1. Set `max_replication_slots > 0` on each sending node. This change requires a restart, though the default of `10` is usually enough. Set the value to at least one more than the number of planned slots:

   ```
   max_replication_slots = 2
   ```

2. For PSR slots, you first have to create the slot on the sending node, like this:

   ```
   SELECT (pg_create_physical_replication_slot
   ('alpha_beta_1', true)).wal_position;
   wal_position
   -----------------
    0/5000060
   ```

3. Monitor it in use by using the following code:

   ```
   SELECT * FROM pg_replication_slots;
   ```

4. In the `recovery.conf` file in the `data` directory on the standby, set the `primary_slot_name` parameter using the unique name that you assigned earlier:

   ```
   primary_slot_name = 'alpha_beta_1'
   ```

   Slots can be removed using the following query:

   ```
   SELECT pg_drop_physical_replication_slot('alpha_beta_1');
   ```

There's more...

If all of your replication connections use slots, then there is no need to set the `wal_keep_segments` parameter.

Replication slots can be used to support applications where downstream nodes are disconnected for extended periods of time. Replication slots prevent the removal of WAL files, which are needed by disconnected nodes. Therefore, it is important to be careful that WAL files don't build up, causing *out of disk space* errors due to physical replication slots being created with no currently connected standby.

See also

See the *Logical replication* recipe for more details on using slots with LSR.

Monitoring replication

Monitoring the status and progress of your replication is essential. We'll start by looking at the server status and then query the progress of replication.

Getting ready

You'll need to start by checking the state of your server(s).

Check whether a server is up using `pg_isready` or another program that uses the `PQping()` API call. You'll get one of the following responses:

- `PQPING_OK (return code 0)`: The server is running and appears to be accepting connections.
- `PQPING_REJECT (return code 1)`: The server is running, but is in a state that disallows connections (startup, shutdown, or crash recovery) or a standby that is not enabled with hot standby.
- `PQPING_NO_RESPONSE (return code 2)`: The server could not be contacted. This might indicate that the server is not running, there is something wrong with the given connection parameters (for example, wrong port number), or there is a network connectivity problem (for example, a firewall blocking the connection request).
- `PQPING_NO_ATTEMPT (return code 3)`: No attempt was made to contact the server, for example, invalid parameters.

 We don't differentiate between a master and a standby, though this may change in later releases. Neither do we say whether a server is accepting write transactions or only read-only transactions (a standby or a master connection in read-only mode).

You can find out whether a server is a master or a standby by connecting and executing this query:

```
SELECT pg_is_in_recovery();
```

There are also two other states that may be important for backup and replication: paused and in-exclusive-backup. The paused state doesn't affect user queries, but replication will not progress at all when paused. Only one exclusive backup may occur at any one time.

You can also check whether replay is paused by executing this query:

```
SELECT pg_is_wal_replay_paused();
```

If you want to check whether a server is in exclusive backup mode, execute the following query:

```
SELECT pg_is_in_backup();
```

There is no supported function that shows whether a nonexclusive backup is in progress, though there isn't as much to worry about if there is. If you care about that, make sure that you set the application_name of the backup program so that it shows up in the session status output of pg_stat_activity, as discussed in Chapter 8, *Monitoring and Diagnosis*.

How to do it...

The rest of this recipe assumes that you have enabled hot_standby. This is not an absolute requirement, but it makes things much, much easier.

Both repmgr and pgpool provide replication monitoring facilities. Munin plugins are available for graphing replication and apply delay.

Replication works by processing the WAL transaction log on other servers. You can think of WAL as a single, serialized stream of messages. Each message in the WAL is identified by an 8-byte integer known as a **log sequence number** (**LSN**). For historical reasons, we show this as two separate hex numbers; for example, the LSN value X is shown as XXXX/YYYY.

You can compare any two LSNs using pg_wal_lsn_diff(). In some places, prior to PostgreSQL 10, an LSN was referred to as a **location**, a term that's no longer in use.

To understand how to monitor progress, you need to understand a little more about replication as a transport mechanism. The stream of messages flows through the system like water through a pipe. You can work out how much progress has been made by measuring the LSN at different points in the pipe. You can also check for blockages in the pipe by measuring the relative progress between points.

New WAL records are inserted into the WAL files on the master. The current insert LSN can be found using this query:

```
SELECT pg_current_wal_insert_lsn();
```

However, WAL records are not replicated until they have been written and synced to the WAL files on the master. The LSN of the most recent WAL write is given by this query on the master:

```
SELECT pg_current_wal_lsn();
```

Once written, WAL records are then sent to the standby. The recent status can be found by running this query on the standby (this and the later functions return NULL on a master):

```
SELECT pg_last_wal_receive_lsn();
```

Once WAL records have been received, they are written to WAL files on the standby. When the standby has written those records, they can then be applied to it. The LSN of the most recent apply is found using this standby query:

```
SELECT pg_last_wal_replay_lsn();
```

Remember that there will always be timing differences if you run status queries on multiple nodes. What we really need is to see all of the information on one node. A view called pg_stat_replication provides the information that we need:

```
SELECT pid, application_name /* or other unique key */
,pg_current_wal_insert_lsn() /* WAL Insert lsn */
,sent_lsn /* WALSender lsn */
,write_lsn /* WALReceiver write lsn */
,flush_lsn /* WALReceiver flush lsn */
,replay_lsn /* Standby apply lsn */
,backend_start /* Backend start */
FROM pg_stat_replication;
-[ RECORD 1 ]-------------------+----------------------------- pid |
16496
application_name                | pg_basebackup pg_current_wal_insert_lsn    |
0/80000D0
sent_lsn                        |
write_lsn                       |
flush_lsn                       |
replay_lsn                      |
backend_start                   | 2017-01-27  15:25:42.988149+00
-[ RECORD 2 ]-------------------+--------------------pid
16497
application_name                | pg_basebackup pg_current_wal_insert_lsn    |
0/80000D0
```

```
sent_lsn             |  0/80000D0
write_lsn            |  0/8000000
flush_lsn            |  0/8000000
replay_lsn |
backend_start        |  2017-01-27   15:25:43.18958+00
```

Each row in this view represents one replication connection. The preceding snippet shows the output from a `pg_basebackup` that is using `--wal-method=stream`. The first connection that's shown is the base backup, while the second session is streaming WAL changes. Note that the `replay_lsn` is NULL, indicating that this is not a standby.

Standby nodes send regular status messages to let the sender know how far it has progressed. If you run this query on the master, you'll be able to see all the directly connected standbys. If you run this query on a standby, you'll see values representing any cascaded standbys, but nothing about the master or any of the other standbys connected to the master. Note that because the data has been sent from a remote node, it is very likely that processing will have progressed beyond the point being reported, but we don't know that for certain. That's just physics. Welcome to the world of distributed systems!

In PostgreSQL 11, replication delay times are provided directly using sampled message timings to provide the most accurate viewpoint of current delay times. Use this query:

```
SELECT pid, application_name /* or other unique key */
   ,write_lag, flush_lag, replay_lag
 FROM pg_stat_replication;
```

Another view called `pg_stat_wal_receiver` provides information about the standby that we may be interested in; this view returns zero rows on the master. `pg_stat_wal_receiver` contains connection information to allow you to connect to the master server.

There's more...

The `pg_stat_replication` view shows only the currently connected nodes. If a node is supposed to be connected but it isn't, then there is no record of it at all, anywhere. If you don't have a list of the nodes that are supposed to be connected, then you'll just miss it.

Replication slots give you a way to define which connections are supposed to be present. If you have defined a slot and it is currently connected, then you will get one row in `pg_stat_replication` for the connection and one row in `pg_replication_slots` for the corresponding slot. To find out which slots don't have current connections, you can run this query:

```
SELECT slot_name, database, age(xmin), age(catalog_xmin)
 FROM pg_replication_slots
 WHERE NOT active;
```

To find the details of the currently connected slots, run something like the following:

```
SELECT slot_name
 FROM pg_replication_slots
 JOIN pg_stat_replication ON pid = active_pid;
```

Performance and synchronous replication

We usually refer to synchronous replication as simply **sync rep**. Sync rep allows us to offer a confirmation to the user that a transaction has been committed and fully replicated on at least one standby server. To do that, we must wait for the transaction changes to be sent to at least one standby, and then have that feedback returned to the master.

The additional time taken for the message's round trip will add elapsed time for write transactions, which increases in proportion to the distance between servers. PostgreSQL offers a choice to the user as to what balance they would like between durability and response time.

Getting ready

The user application must be connected to a master to issue transactions that write data. The default level of durability is defined by the `synchronous_commit` parameter. That parameter is user-settable, so it can be set for different applications, sessions, or even individual transactions. For now, ensure that the user application is using this level:

```
SET synchronous_commit = on;
```

We must decide which standbys should take over from the master in the event of a failover. We do this by setting a parameter called `synchronous_standby_names`.

You will need to configure at least three nodes to use sync rep correctly.

How to do it...

Make sure that you have set the `application_name` on each standby node. Decide the order of servers to be listed in the `synchronous_standby_names` parameter. Note that the standbys named must be directly attached standby nodes or else their names will be ignored. Synchronous replication is not possible for cascaded nodes, though cascaded standbys may be connected downstream. An example for a simple four-node config of `nodeA` (master), `nodeB`, `nodeC`, and `nodeD` (standbys) would be set on `nodeA`, as follows:

```
synchronous_standby_names = 'nodeB, nodeC, nodeD'
```

If you want to receive replies from the first two of the nodes in a list, then we would specify this using the following special syntax:

```
synchronous_standby_names = '2 (nodeB, nodeC, nodeD)'
```

If you want to receive replies from any two nodes, known as **quorum commit**, then use the following:

```
synchronous_standby_names = 'any 2 (nodeB, nodeC, nodeD)'
```

Set `synchronous_standby_names` on all of the nodes, not just the master.

You can see the `sync_state` of connected standbys by using this query on the master:

```
    SELECT
application_name
,state                  /* startup, backup, catchup or streaming */
,sync_priority          /* 0, 1 or more */
,sync_state             /* async, sync or potential */
FROM pg_stat_replication
ORDER BY sync_priority;
```

There are a few columns here with similar names, so be careful not to confuse them.

The `sync_state` column is just a human-readable form of `sync_priority`. When `sync_state` is `async`, the `sync_priority` value will be zero (0). Standby nodes that are mentioned in the `synchronous_standby_names` parameter will have a nonzero priority that corresponds to the order in which they are listed. The standby node with a priority of one (1) will be listed as having a `sync_state` value of `sync`. We refer to this node as the **sync standby**. Other standby nodes configured to provide feedback are shown with a `sync_state` value of `potential` and a `sync_priority` value of more than 1.

If a server is listed in the `synchronous_standby_names` parameter, but is not currently connected, then it will not be shown at all by the preceding query, so it is possible that the node is shown with a lower actual priority value than the stated ordering in the parameter. Setting `wal_receiver_status_interval` to 0 on the standby will disable status messages completely, and the node will show as an `async` node, even if it is named in the `synchronous_standby_names` parameter. You may wish to do this when you are completely certain that a standby will never need to be a failover target, such as a test server.

The state for each server is shown as one of `startup`, `catchup`, or `streaming`. When another node connects, it will first show as `startup`, though only briefly before it moves to `catchup`. Once the node has caught up with the master, it will move to `streaming`, and only then will `sync_priority` be set to a nonzero value.

Catch-up typically occurs quickly after a disconnection or reconnection, such as when a standby node is restarted. When performing an initial base backup, the server will show as `backup`. After this, it will stay for an extended period at `catchup`. The delay at this point will vary according to the size of the database, so it could be a long period. Bear this in mind when configuring the sync rep.

When a new standby node moves to the `streaming` mode, you'll see a message like this in the master node log:

```
LOG standby $APPLICATION_NAME is now the synchronous
standby with priority N
```

How it works...

Standby servers send feedback messages that describe the LSN of the latest transaction they have processed. Transactions committing on the master will wait until they receive feedback saying that their transaction has been processed. If there are no standbys available for sending feedback, then the transactions on the master will wait for standbys, possibly for a very long time. That is why we say that you must have at least three servers to sensibly use sync rep. It probably occurs to you that you could run with just two servers. You can, but such a configuration does not offer any transaction guarantees; it just appears to. Many people are confused on that point, but please don't listen to them!

Sync rep increases the elapsed time of write transactions (on the master). This can reduce performance of applications from a user perspective. The server itself will spend more time waiting than before, which may increase the required number of concurrently active sessions.

Remember that when using sync rep, the overall system is still eventually consistent. Transactions committing on the master are visible first on the standby, and a brief moment later those changes will be visible on the master (yes, standby, and then master). This means that an application that issues a write transaction on the master followed by a read transaction on the sync standby will be guaranteed to see its own changes.

You can increase performance somewhat by setting the `synchronous_commit` parameter to `remote_write`, though you will lose data if both master and standby crashes. You can also set the `synchronous_commit` parameter to `remote_apply` when you want to ensure that all changes are committed to the synchronous standbys and the master before we confirm back to the user. However, this is not the same thing as synchronous visibility—the changes become visible on the different standbys at different times.

There's more...

There is a small window of uncertainty for any transaction that is in progress just at the point at which the master goes down. This can be handled within the application by checking the return code following a commit operation, rather than just assuming that it has completed successfully, as developers often do.

If the commit fails, it is possible that the server committed the transaction successfully, but was unable to communicate that to the client; however, we don't know for certain. Postgres-BDR resolves this problem, but unfortunately, PostgreSQL does not yet do that. A workaround to resolve that uncertainty is to recheck a unique aspect of the transaction, such as reconfirming the existence of a user identifier that was inserted.

If such an object identifier doesn't exist, we can create a table for this purpose:

```
CREATE TABLE TransactionCheck
  (TxnId     SERIAL PRIMARY KEY);
```

During the transaction, we insert a row into that table using this query:

```
INSERT INTO TransactionCheck DEFAULT VALUES RETURNING TxnId;
```

Then, if the commit appears to fail, we can later reread this value to confirm the transaction state as committed or aborted.

Delaying, pausing, and synchronizing replication

Some advanced features and thoughts for replication are covered here.

Getting ready

If you have multiple standby servers, you may want to have one or more servers operating in a delayed apply state, for example, 1 hour behind the master. This can be useful to help recover from user errors such as mistaken transactions or dropped tables.

How to do it...

Normally, a standby will apply changes as soon as possible. When you set the `recovery_min_apply_delay` parameter in `recovery.conf`, the application of commit records will be delayed by the specified duration. Note that only commit records are delayed, so you may receive hot standby cancellations when using this feature. You can prevent that by setting `hot_standby_feedback` to `on`, but use this with caution, since it can cause significant bloat on a busy master if `recovery_min_apply_delay` is large.

If something bad happens, then hit the **Pause** button.

Hot standby allows you to pause and resume a replay of change:

1. To pause the replay, issue this query:

    ```
    SELECT pg_wal_replay_pause();
    ```

Once paused, all queries will receive the same snapshot, allowing lengthy repeated analyses of the database, or retrieval of a dropped table.

2. To resume (un-pause) processing, use this query:

```
SELECT pg_wal_replay_resume();
```

Be careful not to promote a delayed standby. If your delayed standby is the last server available, you should reset `recovery_min_apply_delay`, then restart the server, and allow it to catch up before issuing a promote action.

There's more...

A standby is an exact copy of the master. But how do you synchronize things so that the query results you get from a standby are guaranteed to be the same as those you'd get from the master? Well, that in itself is not possible. It's just the physics of an eventually consistent system. We need it to be eventually consistent because otherwise, the synchronization would become a performance bottleneck.

What we can do is synchronize two requests on different servers, for example, if we wish to issue a write on the master and then later issue a read from a standby. Such a case is automatically handled by synchronous replication. If we aren't using sync rep, then we can wait for the standby to catch up with an action on the master, remembering that the master will have moved on by the time we've done this. To perform the wait, you need to do the following:

1. On the master, perform an action that writes WAL. Just for testing purposes—not for real usage—we can issue a request like this:

```
SELECT pg_create_restore_point('my action name')
```

2. On the master, commit the transaction using `commit`; with any setting other than `synchronous_commit = off`.
3. On the master, find the current write LSN using this query:

```
SELECT pg_current_wal_write_lsn();
```

4. On the standby, execute the following query repeatedly until the LSN value returned is equal to or higher than the LSN from the master:

```
SELECT pg_last_wal_replay_lsn();
```

The following function performs a wait:

```
CREATE OR REPLACE FUNCTION wait_for_lsn(lsn pg_lsn)
RETURNS VOID
LANGUAGE plpgsql
AS $$
BEGIN
    LOOP
        IF pg_last_wal_replay_lsn() IS NULL OR
           pg_last_wal_replay_lsn() >= lsn THEN
             RETURN;
        END IF;
        PERFORM pg_sleep(0.1);   /* 100ms */
    END LOOP;
END $$;
```

This isn't ideal, since it can be cancelled while waiting. Later releases may contain better solutions.

See also

- Logical replication allows us to control the flow of data in various ways. For `pglogical`, use these commands:

    ```
    SELECT alter_subscription_disable();
    SELECT alter_subscription_enable();
    ```

- We can also create a subscription with a parameter of `apply_delay`
- For PostgreSQL 11 subscriptions, use these commands:

    ```
    ALTER SUBSCRIPTION mysub DISABLE;
    ALTER SUBSCRIPTION mysub ENABLE;
    ```

Logical replication

Logical replication allows us to stream logical data changes between two nodes. By logical, we mean streaming changes to data without referring to specific physical attributes such as a block number and row ID.

The main benefits of logical replication are as follows:

- Performance is roughly two times better than that of the best trigger-based mechanisms
- Selective replication is supported, so we don't need to replicate the entire database (only available with pglogical at present)
- Replication can occur between different major releases, which can allow a zero-downtime upgrade

PostgreSQL 9.4 onwards provides a feature called logical decoding. This allows you to stream a set of changes out of a master server. This allows a master to become a sending node in logical replication. The receiving node requires a logical replication plugin to allow replication between two nodes.

Previously, we referred to physical replication as **streaming replication**. Now, we have to modify our descriptions so that we can refer to PSR and LSR. In terms of security, network data transfer, and general management, the two modes are very similar. Concepts that are used to monitor PSR can also be used to monitor LSR.

Since the target systems are fully writable masters in their own right, we can use the full power of PostgreSQL without restrictions. We can use temporary tables, triggers, different user accounts, and GRANT permissions differently. We can also define indexes differently, collect statistics differently, and run VACUUM on different schedules.

As a result, when calling nodes, since sending and receiving nodes isn't enough, LSR works on a publish/subscribe model, so we refer to the nodes as publishers and subscribers.

LSR works on a per-database level, not a whole-server level like PSR. One publishing node can feed multiple subscriber nodes without incurring additional disk write overhead.

PostgreSQL 10 contains native logical replication between servers for PostgreSQL 10 and above. Another option is the more flexible **pglogical** utility, which can send and receive data from PostgreSQL 9.4 and above (https://2ndquadrant.com/en/resources/pglogical/).

pglogical 2.2 allows you to perform the following actions:

- Full database replication
- Selective replication of subsets of tables using replication sets
- Selective replication of table rows at either the publisher or subscriber side
- Upgrades between major versions (see later recipe)
- Data forwarding to Postgres-XL or Postgres-BDR

Getting ready

To use `pglogical`, the publisher and subscriber must be running PostgreSQL 9.4 or higher, and you must install the `pglogical` extension on both nodes.

The procedure is as follows:

1. Identify all the nodes that will work together as parts of your replication architecture.
2. Each LSR link can replicate changes from a single database. If you have multiple databases in your PostgreSQL server, you will need one LSR link per database (not counting `template0` and `template1`).
3. Each LSR link will use one connection and one slot. Set the `max_replication_slots` and `max_connections` parameters to match those requirements.
4. Each LSR link requires one WAL sender on the publisher. Set `max_wal_senders` to match this requirement.
5. Each LSR link requires one apply process on the subscriber. Set `max_worker_processes` to match this requirement.
6. On each node, take all of the following steps:

   ```
   CREATE EXTENSION pglogical;
   ```

7. If using PostgreSQL 9.4, then also install the following:

   ```
   CREATE EXTENSION pglogical_origin;
   ```

8. Any user-installed data types must be installed on both nodes.
9. Add this to `postgresql.conf shared_preload_libraries = 'pglogical'` `--add` and to any existing list.
10. Set this parameter in `postgresql.conf`:

    ```
    wal_level = 'logical'
    ```

11. On each database, declare the node to `pglogical`:

    ```
    SELECT pglogical.create_node(
            node_name := 'nodeA',
            dsn := 'host=nodeA dbname=postgres');
    ```

An example of a `postgresql.conf` file on the source node for the preceding steps looks like this:

```
# Record data for Logical replication
wal_level = 'logical'
# Load the pglogical extension
shared_preload_libraries = 'pglogical'
# Allow replication slot creation (we need just one but it
does not hurt to have more)
max_replication_slots = 10
# Allow streaming replication (we need one for slot and
one for basebackup but again, it does not hurt to have more)
max_wal_senders = 10
max_worker_processes = 10
```

Logical replication supports selective replication, which means that you don't need to specify all the tables in the database. Identify the tables to be replicated. Define replication sets that correspond to groups of tables that should be replicated together. Ensure that all the transactions that touch any table in the set touch only a subset of the set, or the whole set.

Tables that will be replicated may need some preparatory steps as well. To allow logical replication to apply UPDATE and DELETE commands correctly on the target node, we need to define how we search for unique rows. This is known as replica identity. By default, the replica identity will be the primary key of a table, so you need not take any action if you have already defined primary keys on your tables. In some cases, you may need to define the replica identity explicitly by using a command like this:

```
ALTER TABLE mytable REPLICA IDENTITY USING INDEX myuniquecol_idx;
```

Tables about the publisher and subscriber must have the same names and be in the same schema. Tables must also have the same columns with the same data types in each column. Tables must have the same PRIMARY KEY on both nodes. CHECK, NOT NULL, and UNIQUE constraints must be the same or weaker (more permissive) on the subscriber.

Logical replication also supports filtered replication, which means that only certain actions are replicated on the target node; for example, we can specify that INSERT commands are replicated while DELETE commands are filtered away. We can also specify a subset of the rows to be sent from the publisher or applied on the subscriber. This allows logical replication to support a greater range of data movement applications than was previously possible with trigger replication.

Replication requires superuser access for the roles providing replication.

How to do it...

Let's look at a few different examples of how to use logical replication:

1. To publish changes from all tables on a `postgres` database on nodeA, use the following:

```
SELECT pglogical.replication_set_add_all_tables(
                set_name := 'default',
                schema_names := ARRAY['public'],
                true);
```

Then, issue the following command on nodeB:

```
SELECT pglogical.create_subscription(
                subscription_name := 'my_subscription_name',
                provide_dsn := 'host=nodeA dbname=postgres'
                );
```

2. Publish changes for TableX on the MyApp database on nodeA by using the following:

```
SELECT pglogical.create_replication_set(
                set_name := 'SmallSet');
SELECT pglogical.replication_set_add_table(
                set_name := 'SmallSet',
                relation := 'TableX');
```

Then, immediately copy all table data and subscribe to changes for TableX:

```
SELECT pglogical.create_subscription(
                subscription_name :=
'SmallSet_subscription',
                replication_sets := ARRAY['SmallSet'],
                provide_dsn := 'host=nodeA dbname=postgres'
                );
```

3. Publish changes for rows on TableY where status=7 on the MyApp database on nodeA, and add this into the existing replication set. Then, immediately synchronize the data to all subscribing nodes:

```
SELECT pglogical.replication_set_add_table(
                set_name := 'SmallSet',
                relation := 'TableY',
                row_filter := 'status = 7',
                synchronize_data = true);
```

How it works...

Logical decoding is very efficient because it reuses the transaction log data (WAL) that was already being written for crash safety. Triggers are not used at all for this form of replication. Physical WAL records are translated into logical changes, which are then sent to the receiving node. Only real data changes are sent; no records are generated from changes to indexes, cleanup records from VACUUM, and so on. So, bandwidth requirements are somewhat reduced, depending on the exact application.

Changes are discarded if the top-level transaction aborts (save points and other subtransactions are supported normally). Changes are applied in the order of the transactions that have been committed, so replication never breaks because it sees an inconsistent sequence of activities, which can also occur with other cruder replication techniques such as statement-based replication.

On the receiving side, changes are applied using direct database calls, leading to a very efficient mechanism. SQL is not re-executed, so volatile functions in the original SQL don't produce any surprises. For example, let's say you make an update like this:

```
UPDATE table
SET
  col1 = col1 + random()
,col2 = col2 + random()
WHERE key = value
```

Then, the final calculated values of `col1` and `col2` are sent, instead of repeating the execution of the functions when we apply the changes.

Triggers are fired on the subscribing node, so if you wish to filter the rows that are applied on the subscriber, you can define `BEFORE ROW` triggers that block or filter rows as you wish.

Logical replication will work even if you update one or more columns of the key (or any other replica identity), since it will detect that situation and send the old values of the columns with the changed row values. Statements that write many rows get turned into a stream of single row changes.

Locks taken at table-level (`LOCK`) or row-level (`SELECT ... FOR...`) are not replicated, nor are `SET` or `NOTIFY` commands.

Logical replication doesn't suffer from cancellations of queries on the apply node in the way hot standby does. There isn't any need for a feature such as `hot_standby_feedback`.

Both the publishing and subscribing nodes are masters, so technically it would be possible for writes (`INSERT`, `UPDATE`, and `DELETE`) and/or row-level locks (`SELECT ... FOR...`) to be made on the apply-side database. As a result, it is possible that local changes could lock out, slow down, or interfere with the application of changes from the source node. It is up to the user to enforce restrictions to ensure that this does not occur. You can do this by having a user role defined specifically for replication and then using `REVOKE` on all access apart from the `SELECT` privilege to replicated tables, rather than the user role applying the changes.

Data can be read on the apply side while changes are being made. That is just normal, and it's the beautiful power of PostgreSQL's MVCC feature.

The use of replication slots means that if the network drops, or if one of the nodes is offline, we can pick up the replication again from the precise point that we stopped.

There's more...

LSR can work alongside PSR. There are no conflicting parameters; just ensure that all requirements are met for both PSR and LSR.

With LSR and pglogical, neither DDL nor sequences are replicated; only the data changes (DML) are sent. Only the full version of Postgres-BDR provides these features at present. Support for the replication of `TRUNCATE` commands has been added in Postgres 11.

Logical replication is one-way only, so if you want multi-master replication, see the *Bidirectional Replication* recipe. Logical replication provides cascaded replication.

See also

In PostgreSQL 11, some aspects of LSR have been included with the core server. The same idea of publish and subscribe has been included among commands, allowing these to be dumped and restored between servers.

Let's look at the same examples we looked at earlier:

1. To publish changes from all tables on a `postgres` database on `nodeA`, use the following:

```
CREATE PUBLICATION pub_nodeA_postgres_all
    FOR ALL TABLES;
```

Then, immediately copy all table data and then subscribe to changes from the default replication set on the nodeA database postgres by issuing the following command on nodeB:

```
CREATE SUBSCRIPTION sub_nodeA_postgres_all
CONNECTION 'conninfo'
PUBLICATION pub_nodeA_postgres_all;
```

2. Publish changes for TableX on the MyApp database on nodeA by using the following:

```
CREATE PUBLICATION pub_nodeA_postgres_tablex
    FOR TABLE TableX;
```

Then, immediately copy all table data and then subscribe to changes for TableX:

```
CREATE SUBSCRIPTION sub_nodeA_postgres_tablex
CONNECTION 'conninfo'
PUBLICATION pub_nodeA_postgres_tablex;
```

Publishing a subset of DML operations is possible, though it isn't yet possible to filter rows.

Creating a PUBLICATION requires CREATE privilege on the current database. Creating a SUBSCRIPTION object will, by default, enable replication and have it start immediately, though it is often convenient to define these first with the option WITH (enabled = off) and then re-enable them later using ALTER SUBSCRIPTION. Subscriptions use normal user access security, so there is no need to enable *replication* via pg_hba.conf.

It is also possible to override the synchronous_commit parameter and demand that the server provides synchronous replication.

Bidirectional replication

Bidirectional replication (Postgres-BDR) is a project that's used to allow multi-master replication with PostgreSQL. There is a range of possible architectures. The first use case we support is all-nodes-to-all-nodes. Postgres-BDR will eventually support a range of complex architectures, which is discussed later.

Postgres-BDR aims for eventual inclusion within core PostgreSQL, though knowing that is a long and rigorous process. It also aims to provide working software solutions.

Postgres-BDR aims to allow the nodes of the cluster to be distributed physically, allowing worldwide access to data and allowing for disaster recovery. Each Postgres-BDR master node runs individual transactions; there is no globally distributed transaction manager. Postgres-BDR includes replication of data changes and **data definition language** (DDL) changes. New tables are added automatically, ensuring that managing BDR is a low-maintenance overhead for applications.

Postgres-BDR also provides global sequences, if you wish to have a sequence that works across a distributed system. Normal local sequences are not replicated.

The key advantage of Postgres-BDR is that you can segregate your write workload across multiple nodes by application, user group, or geographical proximity. Each node can be configured differently, yet all work together to provide access to the same data. Some examples of use cases for this are as follows:

- Social media applications, where users need fast access to their local server, yet the whole database needs a single database view to cater for links and interconnections.
- Distributed businesses, where orders are taken by phone in one location and by websites in another location. Then, they are fulfilled via several other locations.
- Multinational companies that need fast access to data from many locations, yet wish to see a single, common view of their data.

Postgres-BDR builds upon the basic technology of logical replication, enhancing it in various ways. We refer heavily to the previous recipe, *Logical replication*.

Getting ready

Currently, Postgres-BDR can be deployed in the all-to-all architecture, which has been tested on clusters of up to 99 master nodes. Each of those nodes is a normal, fully functioning PostgreSQL server that can perform both reads and writes.

Postgres-BDR connects directly between each node, forming a mesh of connections. Changes flow directly to other nodes in constant time, no matter how many nodes are in use. This is quite different from circular replication, which is used by other database management systems (DBMS).

All Postgres-BDR nodes should have `pg_hba.conf` definitions to allow paths between each node. It would be easier to have these settings the same on all nodes, but that is not required.

Each node requires an LSR link to all other nodes for each replicated database. So, an 8-node Postgres-BDR cluster will require seven LSR links per node. Ensure that the parameters are configured to allow for this and any possible future expansion. The parameters should be the same on all nodes to avoid confusion. Remember that these changes require a restart.

Postgres-BDR nodes also require the configuring of the mechanism for conflict detection:

```
track_commit_timestamps = on
```

Postgres-BDR 1 requires a modified version of PostgreSQL 9.4. Postgres-BDR 2 is available only as an interim measure as an extension for PostgreSQL 9.6. Postgres-BDR 3 is available as an extension for PostgreSQL 10 and 11. For the latest info, please consult `https://www.2ndquadrant.com/en/resources/bdr/`.

Future versions of PostgreSQL may contain multi-master replication, though this will not be until at least PostgreSQL 13 as we go to press.

How to do it...

To create a new node, we take a copy of one of the databases on the source nodes. This can be accomplished using either a physical base backup or a logical base backup. A physical copy includes all databases on the source node, so this mechanism is most suitable where there is only one active database on that node.

Command specifications are subject to change. Check out `https://www.2ndquadrant.com/en/resources/bdr/` for the latest details on them.

How it works...

Postgres-BDR optimistically assumes that changes on one node do not conflict with changes on other nodes. Any conflicts are detected and then resolved automatically using a predictable last update wins strategy, though custom conflict handlers are supported to allow more precise definition for particular applications.

Applications that regularly cause conflicts won't run very well on Postgres-BDR. Having said that, such applications would also suffer from lock waits and resource contention on a normal database; the effects will be slightly amplified by the distributed nature of Postgres-BDR, but only the existing problems are amplified. Applications that are properly designed to be scalable and contention-free will work well on Postgres-BDR.

Postgres-BDR replicates changes at the row level, though work is under way to apply changes at column-level and in a conflict-free manner. The current mechanism has some implications for applications:

- Suppose we perform two simultaneous updates on different nodes, like this:

  ```
  UPDATE foo SET col1 = col1 + 1 WHERE key = value;
  ```

- Then, in the event of a conflict, we will keep only one of the changes (the last change). What we might like in this case is to make the changes additive. This requires a custom conflict handler.
- Two updates that change different columns on different nodes will still cause replication conflicts.

Postgres-BDR1 and Postgres-BDR2 only support post-commit conflict resolution, though

Postgres-BDR3 also supports eager replication, meaning any issues are resolved before

commit.

Postgres-BDR provides tools to diagnose and correct contention problems. Conflicts are logged so that they can be identified and removed at the application level. You can log either the conflicting statement or the entire conflicting transaction. Optionally, they can be also saved in a table for easier analysis.

There's more...

If a master node fails, you can fail over to either logical or physical standby nodes. Other master nodes continue processing normally—there is no wait for failover, nor is there the need for complex voting algorithms to identify the best new master. Failed master nodes will need to rejoin the cluster.

Archiving transaction log data

PSR can send transaction log data to a remote node, even if the node is not a full PostgreSQL server. This can be useful for archiving copies of transaction log data for various purposes.

PostgreSQL includes two client tools to stream data from the server to the client. The tools are designed using a pull model; that is, you run the tools on the node you wish the data to be saved on:

- `pg_receivewal` archives physical transaction log data (WAL files). This utility produces a straight copy of the original WAL files. Replication slots are recommended when using this tool.
- `pg_recvlogical` archives the results of the logical decoding of transaction log data. This utility produces a copy of the transformed data rather than physical WAL. Replication slots are required for this tool. You will need to use that with a logical decoding plugin.

Getting ready

This recipe assumes that you have already set up replication according to the earlier recipes so that `wal_level`, `max_wal_senders`, and other parameters have been set. Remember that for
`pg_recvlogical`, you must set `wal_level` to `logical`.

This recipe is a different way of archiving WAL files than using `archive_command`, so you will likely want to unset that parameter if you use this recipe.

You will need to configure security just as you did for replication. So, you will need a PostgreSQL connection string, just as before.

Decide where you want to put the data on the client. Remember that WAL files look the same for each server, so you need to put them in a directory with a useful name so that you don't confuse files from different servers. You don't need to do this step for normal replication because streaming replication normally copies the files to the downstream node's `pg_wal` directory.

How to do it...

To archive a physical WAL from a server called `alpha`, follow these steps:

1. If you decide to use replication slots, then create a slot using *Steps 1* to *Step 3* of the *Using replication slots* recipe.
2. Execute the tool on the client:

```
pg_receivewal -D /pgarchive/alpha -d $MYCONNECTIONSTRING &
```

3. If you're using slots, also use the `--slot=slotname` parameter on the command line.

If the connection from the client tool to the server is lost, the default behavior is to loop indefinitely while trying to reestablish a connection. If you want the client tool to exit if the connection is lost, then specify the `-n` or `--no-loop` options.

The `pg_recvlogical` utility requires some form of logical decoding plugin, so look at the instructions for the plugin you are using to find out how to use that.

There's more...

While playing with this feature for the first time, try the `--verbose` option.

For more detail on logical decoding plugins, we refer to the *Logical replication* recipe, earlier in this chapter.

Replication monitoring will show `pg_receivewal` and `pg_recvlogical` in exactly the same way as it shows other connected nodes, so there is no additional monitoring required. The default `application_name` is the same as the name of the tool, so you may want to set that parameter to something more meaningful to you.

With `pg_receivewal` and `pg_recvlogical,` you can use the `--create-slot` and `--drop-slot` options to control replication slots.

You can archive WAL files using synchronous replication by specifying `pg_receivewal --synchronous`. This causes a disk flush (`fsync`) on the client so that WAL data is robustly saved to disk. It then passes status information back to the server to acknowledge that the data is safe (regardless of the setting of the `-s` parameter). The faster and more dangerous alternative is `pg_receivewal -no-sync`.

See also

- If you want to browse the content of the WAL files, you'll need the `pg_waldump` program, which is an additional server-side utility

Upgrading minor releases

Minor release upgrades are released regularly by all software developers, and PostgreSQL has had its share of corrections. When a minor release occurs, we bump the last number, usually by one. So, the first release of a major release such as 11 is 11.0. The first set of bug fixes is 11.1, then 11.2, and so on.

The PostgreSQL Community releases new bug fixes quarterly. If you want bug fixes more frequently than that, you will need to subscribe to a PostgreSQL support company. This recipe is about moving from a minor release to a minor release.

Getting ready

First, get hold of the new release, by downloading either the source or fresh binaries.

How to do it...

In most cases, PostgreSQL aims for minor releases to be simple upgrades. We put in great efforts to keep the on-disk format the same for both data/index files and transaction log (WAL) files, but this isn't always the case; some files can change.

The upgrade process is as follows:

1. Read the release notes to see whether there are any special actions that need to be taken for this particular release. Make sure that you consider the steps that are required by all extensions that you have installed.
2. If you have professional support, talk to your support vendor to see whether additional safety checks over and above the upgrade instructions are required or recommended. Also, verify that the target release is fully supported by your vendor on your hardware, OS, and OS release level; it may not be, yet.
3. Apply any special actions or checks; for example, if the WAL format has changed, then you may need to reconfigure log-based replication following the upgrade. You may need to scan tables, rebuild indexes, or perform some other actions. Not every release has such actions, but watch closely for them because if they exist, then they are important.
4. If you are using replication, test the upgrade by disconnecting one of your standby servers from the master.

5. Follow the instructions for your OS distribution and binary packager to complete the upgrade. These can vary considerably.

6. Start up the database server being used for this test, apply any post-upgrade special actions, and check that things are working for you.

7. Repeat Steps 4 to 6 for other standby servers.

8. Repeat Steps 4 to 6 for the primary server.

How it works...

Minor upgrades mostly affect the binary executable files, so it should be a simple matter of replacing those files and restarting, but please check.

There's more...

When you restart the database server, the contents of the buffer cache will be lost. The pg_prewarm module provides a convenient way to load relation data into the PostgreSQL buffer cache.

You can install the pg_prewarm extension that's provided by default as follows:

```
postgres=# CREATE EXTENSION pg_prewarm;
CREATE EXTENSION
```

You can perform pre-warming for any relation:

```
postgres=# select pg_prewarm('job_status');
 pg_prewarm
------------
 1
```

The return value is the number of blocks that have been pre-warmed.

Major upgrades in-place

PostgreSQL provides an additional supplied program, called `pg_upgrade`, which allows you to migrate between major releases, such as from 9.2 to 9.6; alternatively, you can upgrade straight to the latest server version. These upgrades are performed in-place, meaning that we upgrade our database without moving to a new system. That does sound good, but `pg_upgrade` has a few things that you may wish to consider as potential negatives, which are as follows:

- The database server must be shut down while the upgrade takes place.
- Your system must be large enough to hold two copies of the database server: old and new copies. If it's not, then you have to use the `link` option of `pg_upgrade`, or use the *Major upgrades online* recipe later. If you use the `link` option on `pg_upgrade`, then there is no `pg_downgrade` utility. The only option in that case is a restore from backup, and that means extended unavailability while you restore.
- If you copy the database, then the upgrade time will be proportional to the size of the database.
- The `pg_upgrade` utility does not validate all your additional add-in modules, so you will need to set up a test server and confirm that these work, ahead of performing the main upgrade.

The `pg_upgrade` utility supports versions from PostgreSQL 8.4 onwards and allows you to go straight from your current release to the latest release in one hop.

Getting ready

Find out the size of your database (using the *How much disk space does a database use?* recipe in `Chapter 2`, *Exploring the Database*). If the database is large or you have an important requirement for availability, you should consider making the major upgrade using replication tools as well. Then, check out the next recipe.

How to do it...

1. Read the release notes for the new server version to which you are migrating, including all of the intervening releases. Pay attention to the incompatibilities section carefully; PostgreSQL changes from release to release. Assume this will take some hours.

2. Set up a test server with the old software release on it. Restore one of your backups on it. Upgrade that system to the new release to verify that there are no conflicts from software dependencies. Test your application. Make sure that you identify and test each add-in PostgreSQL module you were using to confirm that it still works at the new release level.

3. Back up your production server. Prepare for the worst; hope for the best!

4. Most importantly, work out who you will call if things go badly, and exactly how to restore from that backup you just took.

5. Install new versions of all the required software on the production server and create a new database server.

6. Don't disable security during the upgrade. Your security team will do backflips if they hear about this. Keep your job!

7. Now, go and do that backup. Don't skip this step; it isn't optional. Check whether the backup is actually readable, accessible, and complete.

8. Shut down the database servers.

9. Run `pg_upgrade -v` and then run any required post-upgrade scripts. Make sure that you check whether any were required.

10. Start up the new database server and immediately run a server-wide `ANALYZE` operation using `vacuumdb -analyze-in-stages`.

11. Run through your tests to check whether it worked or you need to start performing the contingency plan.

12. If all is OK, re-enable wide access to the database server. Restart the applications.

13. Don't delete your old server directory if you used the link method. The old `data` directory still contains the data for the new database server. It's confusing! So don't get caught by this.

How it works...

The `pg_upgrade` utility works by creating a new set of database catalog tables, and then creating the old objects again in the new tables using the same identifiers as before.

The `pg_upgrade` utility works easily because the data block format hasn't changed between some releases. Since we can't (always) see the future, make sure you read the release notes.

Major upgrades online

Upgrading between major releases is hard, and it should be deferred until you have some good reasons and sufficient time to get it right.

You can use replication tools to minimize the downtime required for an upgrade, so we refer to this recipe as an **online upgrade**.

How to do it...

The following general steps should be followed, allowing at least a month for the complete process to ensure that everything is tested and everybody understands the implications:

1. Set up a new release of the software on a new test system.
2. Take a standalone backup from the main system and copy it to the test system.
3. Test the applications extensively against the new release on the test system.

When everything works and performs correctly, then do the following:

1. Set up a connection pooler to the main database (it may be there already).
2. Set up `pglogical` for all tables from the old to new database servers. Make sure that you wait until all the initial copy tasks have completed for all tables.

Retest the application extensively against the new release on live data. Then, when we're ready for the final cut-over, we can do the following:

1. Pause the connection pool.
2. Switch the config of the pool over to the new system, then reload
3. Resume the connection pool (so that it now accesses a new server).

Downtime for the application is the length of time to these last three steps.

How it works...

The preceding recipe allows online upgrades with zero data loss because of the use of the clean switchover process. There's no need for lengthy downtime during the upgrade, and there's much reduced risk in comparison with an in-place upgrade. It works best with new hardware, and is a good way to upgrade the hardware or change the disk layout at the same time.

This procedure is also very useful for those cases where binary compatibility is not possible, such as changing server encoding, or migrating the database to a different operating system or architecture, where the on-disk format will change as a result of low-level differences, such as endianness and alignment.

Other Books You May Enjoy

If you enjoyed this book, you may be interested in these other books by Packt:

Mastering PostgreSQL 11 - Second Edition
Hans-Jürgen Schönig

ISBN: 9781789537819

- Get to grips with advanced PostgreSQL 11 features and SQL functions
- Make use of the indexing features in PostgreSQL and fine-tune the performance of your queries
- Work with stored procedures and manage backup and recovery
- Master replication and failover techniques
- Troubleshoot your PostgreSQL instance for solutions to common and not-so-common problems
- Perform database migration from MySQL and Oracle to PostgreSQL with ease

Learning PostgreSQL 11 - Third Edition

Salahadin Juba, Andrey Volkov

ISBN: 9781789535464

- Understand the basics of relational databases, relational algebra, and data modeling
- Install a PostgreSQL server, create a database, and implement your data model
- Create tables and views, define indexes and stored procedures, and implement triggers
- Make use of advanced data types such as Arrays, hstore, and JSONB
- Connect your Python applications to PostgreSQL and work with data efficiently
- Identify bottlenecks to enhance reliability and performance of database applications

Leave a review - let other readers know what you think

Please share your thoughts on this book with others by leaving a review on the site that you bought it from. If you purchased the book from Amazon, please leave us an honest review on this book's Amazon page. This is vital so that other potential readers can see and use your unbiased opinion to make purchasing decisions, we can understand what our customers think about our products, and our authors can see your feedback on the title that they have worked with Packt to create. It will only take a few minutes of your time, but is valuable to other potential customers, our authors, and Packt. Thank you!

Index

A

access control list (ACL) 284
ACID properties 238
actions
    performing, on tables 261, 262, 263, 265, 266, 267
anonymous code block 265
application-level replication 502
apply delay 498
asymmetric cryptography 235
asynchronous replication 498
atomicity 238
auto-freezing
    avoiding 362, 364
automatic database maintenance
    controlling 356, 357, 359, 361, 362
autonomous transactions 290
average tuple density 73
AXLE project
    reference link 16

B

background worker processes
    reference link 336
backup performance
    improving 468, 471
backups
    planning 437, 439
    validating 489, 490, 491, 492
Barman
    about 476
    features 487, 488
    global commands 481
    global options 480
    local recovery 484
    remote recovery 484
    server commands 481
    server options 480
    URL 475
    used, for performing hot physical backups 474, 475, 476, 479, 480, 481, 483
    used, for performing recovery 483, 484, 486, 488
base backup 498
Berkeley Software Distribution (BSD) 16
Bi-Directional Replication (BDR)
    about 500, 547, 549, 550
    advantages 548
    working 549
biggest tables
    searching 69, 70
bloat
    causing, issues removing 364, 365, 366
bloated tables
    fixing 371, 373, 374, 375, 376
    identifying 371, 373, 374, 375, 376
bucardo package 496
bug
    investigating 345, 347
    reporting 345, 347
bulk data changes
    making, server-side procedures with transactions
        used 183, 184, 185
business intelligence 495

C

cascading 496
certificate authority (CA) 225
checkpoints 435
cluster 495
clustered parallel databases 500
columns uniqueness
    without indexes 163

columns
  adding, on table 268, 269, 270
  data type, changing 271, 272, 273, 275
  definition, enforcing 150, 152, 153
  name, enforcing 150, 152, 153
  removing, on table 268, 269, 270
Common Table Expressions (CTEs)
  reference link 411
complex SQL queries
  materialized views, using 412
  set-returning functions, using 413
  simplifying 406, 407, 411
computer connection
  checking 322, 323
conditional psql script
  writing 248
configuration settings
  searching 90
connection pool
  setting up 137, 138, 139, 140, 141
connection service file
  using 42
  working 43
connections
  preventing 123, 124, 125
constraint
  adding, without checking existing rows 383, 385
contrib
  about 319
  reference link 101
Coordinated Universal Time (UTC) 503
covering indexes 415
crash recovery
  about 434, 436, 437
  controlling 434, 436, 437
  working 436
cross_tab query 407
current configuration settings
  searching 89, 91
custom format 441

D

Data Definition Language (DDL) 238
data directory 52, 113
data loss 499

Data Manipulation Language (DML) 305
data type, column
  changing 271, 272, 273, 275
data type
  definition, changing 275, 276, 277, 278
data
  loading, from flat files 179, 180, 182, 183
  loading, from spreadsheet 176, 177, 178, 179
  sampling 173
  sampling, randomly 172, 174, 175
database access
  audit log, managing 216, 217
  auditing 213
  data changes, auditing 217, 218
  SQL, auditing 214, 215
  table access, auditing 215, 216
database cluster 20
Database File Layout
  reference link 338
database object definitions
  backups 444, 445
database objects
  name, selecting 145, 146, 147, 148
database physical storage
  reference link 346
database replication 495
database server files
  locating 52, 53, 54, 55
database server
  about 495
  message log, locating 56, 57, 58
  restarting 121, 122, 123
  starting 112, 113, 114, 115
  stopping 116, 117
  stopping, in emergency 118
  working 115, 116
database system identifier
  locating 59, 60
database
  disk space, measuring 66, 67
  extensions, listing 77, 78
  listing, on database server 60, 62, 63
  logical backup 439, 440, 441, 442, 443
  logical recovery 458
  logical recovery, from custom dump with

pg_dump -F c 455
logical recovery, from script dump created by
  pg_dump -F p 456
logical recovery, from script dump created by
  pg_dumpall 456
physical recovery 456, 458
planning 85, 86, 87
recovery, performing 455, 458, 459
tables, counting 64, 65, 66
Daylight Saving Time (DST) 503
debugging_info function
  writing, for developers 212
default privileges 194
differential backup
  about 471, 472, 473
  restoring 471, 472, 473
disk space
  usage, by temporary data 338, 340
dropped/damaged database
  logical recovery, from custom dump -F c 467
  logical recovery, from script dump created by
    pg_dump 467
  logical recovery, from script dump created by
    pg_dumpall 467
  physical recovery 468
  recovery, performing 466
dropped/damaged table
  logical recovery, from custom dump taken with
    pg_dump -F c 463
  logical recovery, from script dump 465
  physical recovery 465
  recovery, performing 463, 466
duplicate data
  identifying 154, 156, 158, 159
  removing 154, 156, 158, 159
duplicate indexes 163
duplicate rows
  preventing 159, 160, 161, 162
dynamic scripting 265

E

equal probability of selection (EPS) 175
equivalently extensions 77
EXPLAIN SQL command
  reference link 401

extensions 104
external module
  adding, to PostgreSQL 100, 101
external username
  mapping, to database roles 230, 231
Extra Packages Enterprise Linux (EPEL) 475
extrapolation 73

F

failback 523
failed connection
  troubleshooting 43, 44, 45
failover 499
features, PostgreSQL 10
  robustness 12
features, PostgreSQL 11
  commercial support 15
  concurrency 14
  extensions 13
  NoSQL data models 14
  performance 14
  popularity 15
  research and development funding 16
  robustness 12
  scalability 14
  security 12
  SQL data models 14
  user friendly 13
file-based replication
  setting up 504, 505, 506, 507
Filesystem Hierarchy Standard (FHS) 54
Foreign Data Wrapper infrastructure 290
foreign databases
  objects, accessing 300, 301, 302, 303
Free Space Map (FSM) 70
FreeBSD 115
freezing 362
frozen transaction ID 362
function side-effects 290

G

genetic query optimization (GEQO) 411
Geographical Information System (GIS) 13
Global Transaction Manager (GTM) 500
graphical administration tools

using 24, 25, 26
working 28
Graphite's Carbon 316

H

Heap-Only Tuples (HOT) 372, 417
heavy users, temporary tables
  actions for 369, 370
host 20
host-based authentication (HBA) 124
hot physical backup
  about 445, 446, 447, 449, 450
  performing, with Barman 474, 475, 476, 479,
    480, 481, 483
  setting up, with continuous archiving 451, 452,
    453, 454
  working 449
hot standby 14, 459, 496, 517, 518, 520, 521

I

Icinga tools 317
in-doubt prepared transaction
  detecting 333
incremental backup
  about 471, 472, 473
  restoring 471, 472, 473
index-only scan 71, 415
indexes
  fixing 371, 373, 374, 375, 376
  identifying 371, 373, 374, 375, 376
  maintaining 379, 380, 381, 382
information schema 65
Initialization Fork 70
installed extensions
  managing 105, 107, 109
installed module
  using 104, 105
Internet Assigned Numbers Authority (IANA)
  about 112
  reference link 20
IP address range allocation 164, 165

J

Java Transaction API (JTA) 366

L

latency 498
lesser attributes 192
Lightweight Directory Access Protocol (LDAP)
  about 42
  client, setting up 222
  integrating with 221
  replacement, for User Name Map feature 223
log file errors
  summary, producing 347, 349, 350
Log Sequence Number (LSN) 461, 473, 531
logical backup 469
logical decoding 497
logical log streaming replication (LLSR) 497
logical recovery 458
logical replication
  about 540, 543
  benefits 541
  using 545, 546
  working 545
logical restore 469
logical streaming replication (LSR) 497, 503

M

macOS 115
maintenance
  planning 389, 390
man-in-the-middle (MITM) 226
massively parallel databases 500
massively parallel processing (MPP) 425
master 496, 523
materialized views
  about 313, 410, 412
  reference link 413
  using 311, 312, 313
  working 313
minor releases
  upgrading 553
modules
  about 77
  installing, from PGXN 102
  installing, from source code 103
  installing, with software installer 101, 102
multimaster replication 500

multinode architecture
  about 499
  loosely coupled database clusters 500
  tightly coupled database clusters 499
multiple schema
  using 130, 131, 132, 133
multiple servers
  accessing, with host 142, 143
  accessing, with port 142, 143
  executing, on system 135, 136, 137
multitenancy
  about 129
  design, deciding 129, 130
Multiversion Concurrency Control (MVCC) 11, 71,
    117, 344, 371
Munin 316

N

Nagios 317
namespace 445
nested transaction style 240
network users
  access, enabling 21, 22, 23, 24
NOLOGIN users
  forcing, for disconnection 206

O

object dependencies 79, 80, 81
Object Relational Mappers (ORMs) 404
object-relational database management system
    (ORDBMS) 48
objects
  handling, with quoted names 148, 149, 150
old prepared transactions
  removing 366, 367, 368, 369
OmniDB
  about 29, 120
  URL 29
  used, for viewing real-time 319, 321
  using 29, 30, 31, 32, 33, 34
  using, for DBA tasks 256, 257, 258, 259, 260
ON_ERROR_STOP variable 244
Online Transaction Processing (OLTP) 325
online upgrade 557
OpenSSL library

reference link 236
Operating System (OS) 502
Optimal Flexible Architecture (OFA) 54
optimistic locking
  using 428, 429
OS-level replication 502
Out-Of-Memory (OOM) 98

P

page corruptions
  avoiding 362, 364
parallel copy 488
parallel query
  using 422, 423, 424, 425
parameter file
  updating 93, 94, 95, 96
parameter
  setting, for particular groups of users 96
parameters
  at non-default settings, checking 91, 92, 93
  setting, for particular groups of users 97
partial index 161, 415, 421
password authentication
  changing 39, 40
password
  hardcoding, avoiding 40, 41
performance issues
  reference link 430
  reporting 430
performance mailing list
  reference link 430
performance replication 534, 536, 537, 538
permission group 197
Personally Identifiable Information (PII) 216
pg_hint_plan
  reference link 422
pg_stat* views
  reference link 403
  regular statics, collecting 401, 402, 403
pg_stat_activity
  reference link 322
pg_stat_database
  reference link 340
pg_upgrade
  about 555

working 556
pgAdmin 4 24
pgAdmin
  used, for viewing real-time 319, 320
  using, for DBA tasks 251, 252, 253, 254, 255,
  256
  working 28
pgBadger 348
PgBouncer
  about 137
  reference link 223
pgcrypto
  reference link 236
pgfincore extension
  reference link 123
pgFouine 348
pglogical
  about 541
  reference link 541
  using 542, 543
PGXN
  references 101
physical backup 469
physical log streaming replication (PLSR) 497
physical recovery 458
physical restore 469
Physical Streaming Replication (PSR) 497, 503
pipeline parallelism 471
pivot query 407
PL/Proxy tool 299
Point-in-time recovery (PITR)
  about 12, 437, 459, 460, 461, 462
  working 460
PostGIS
  reference link 101
Postgres 11
PostgreSQL 10
  reference link 84
PostgreSQL 11
  about 10
  features 10, 11
  obtaining 16, 17
  URL, for downloading 17
  working 17
PostgreSQL databases

objects, accessing 290, 292, 293, 294, 296,
  297, 298, 299
PostgreSQL error codes
  URL 251
PostgreSQL Extension Network (PGXN) 300
PostgreSQL Flexible Architecture (PFA) 54
PostgreSQL Foreign Data Wrapper 290
PostgreSQL information
  generic monitoring tools, information finding 318
  providing, to monitoring tools 317, 318
PostgreSQL security
  references 13
PostgreSQL server
  connecting to 18, 19
  parameters, connecting 18
  working 20, 21
PostgreSQL software
  reference link 34
PostgreSQL superuser
  about 191, 192
  attributes, limitation 192
  privileges, adding 191
  privileges, removing 191
  super-like attributes 192
PostgreSQL, additional modules
  reference link 79
PostgreSQL, client authentication
  reference link 45
PostgreSQL, professional services
  reference link 15
PostgreSQL, run-time statistics
  reference link 327
PostgreSQL, versioning policy
  reference link 51
PostgreSQL
  about 48
  external module, adding 99, 100, 101
  libraries, loading 104
  version 49, 50
  working 50
postmaster 111
prefix ranges 165
primary 496
private database
  granting, to users 133, 134, 135

programs
  parameters, changing 87, 88, 89
Prometheus 316
psql error
  investigating 249, 250, 251
psql query tool
  about 34
  using 35
  working 37, 38
psql script
  writing, on first error 243, 244
psql scripting tool
  about 34
  using 35, 37
  working 38
psql utility
  reference link 324
psql variables
  query output, placing 246, 247, 248
  using 245, 246
public-key cryptography 235

Q

queries execution
  catching 325
  checking 324, 325
  watching 326
  watching, from ps 326
queries
  blocking 329, 330
  checking, as active 327, 328
  checking, as blocked 327, 328
  executing, in psql 323
  forcing, for index usage 419, 420, 421, 422
  index, avoiding 417, 419
  issues 343, 344, 345
  performance, slowing down 341, 342
  real-time performance, analyzing 351, 352
  speeding up 414
  speeding up, by increasing work_mem 414
  speeding up, by partitioning time series 416
  speeding up, by setting fillfactor on table 417
  speeding up, with indexes considerations 414, 416
  speeding up, with TABLESAMPLE view 416

  speeding, by rewriting schema 417
quick and dirty approach 265
quorum commit 535

R

range of time 165
read scalability 517, 518, 519, 520, 521
reading the fine manual (RTFM)
  about 84, 85
  using 84
  working 85
Recovery Point Objective (RPO) 439, 482
recovery server 465
REDO operations 488
reference data management 495
Referential Integrity 79
regular statistics
  collecting, from pg_stat* views 401, 402, 403
relay 496
remote users
  access, enabling 21, 22, 23, 24
Replication (computing)
  reference link 501
replication best practices 502, 504
replication concepts
  about 494
  basic architecture 495
  clustered parallel databases 500
  data loss 499
  database replication 495
  history 496
  massively parallel databases 500
  multimaster replication 500
  multinode architecture 499
  other approaches 502
  practical aspects 497, 498
  scalability tools 501
  scope 496
  single-master replication 499
replication delay 498
replication sets 498
replication slots
  using 527, 528, 529
replication
  delaying 538, 540

monitoring 530, 531, 533, 534
  pausing 538, 540
  synchronizing 538, 540
repmgr
  URL 525
  using 524, 526, 527
reporting systems 495
restore performance
  improving 468, 471
retention policies 452
returned number of rows
  reducing 403, 404, 405
Round Robin Database Tool (RRDtool) 316
Row Level Security (RLS) 190, 201

S

Salted Challenge Response Authentication
  Mechanism (SCRAM) 12
scalability tools 501
schema-level privileges
  using 280
schema
  about 445
  adding 278, 280
  objects, moving between 281
  removing 279, 280
script
  writing 238, 239, 240, 241, 242
selective replication 498
sensitive data
  encrypting 231, 232, 233, 235, 236
sequential scan 71
server configuration checklist 97, 98, 99
server configuration files
  reloading 119, 120
server uptime 51, 52
server version
  selecting 49, 50
service unit 113
session
  backend, killing from command line 333
  backend, termination 331
  killing 330
  query, cancelling 331
  statement_timeout, used to clean up queries 332

transaction queries, killing 332
set-returning function 413
shared_buffers configuration parameter
  reference link 399
Simple Network Management Protocol (SNMP)
  317
single-master replication 499
slow SQL statements
  finding 394, 396
snapshot export feature 441
Solaris 115
split-brain 523
SQL statements
  finding 396
SQL
  CPU power, lacking issue 400
  disk I/O capacity, lacking issue 400
  EXPLAIN options 400
  locking issues 400
  performance, testing 396, 398, 399
SSL certificates
  client certificate, using for database user
    selection 229
  duplicate SSL connection attempts, avoiding 228
  multiple client certificates, using 228
  used, for authentication 226, 227, 228
  working 227
SSL key and certificates
  reference link 229
SSL
  key and certificates, obtaining 225
  reference link 229
  server authenticity, verifying 226
  used, for database connection 223, 224
  using, with client setup 225
staging server 465
Standard Generalized Markup Language (SGML)
  85
static scripting 262
statistics collection package 403
streaming replication
  about 496
  managing 521, 522, 523, 524
  security, setting up 514, 515, 516
  setting up 508, 509, 510, 511, 514

working 512
switchover 499
sync standby 536
synchronous replication 498, 534, 536, 537, 538

T

table
  counting, in database 64, 65, 66
  disk space, measuring 67, 68, 69
  last usage, knowing 336, 338
  number of rows, estimating 72, 73, 74, 75
  quick-and-dirty way 335
  rows, counting 70, 71, 72
  size, computing without locks 75
tablespace
  adding 282, 283, 285
  objects, moving between 287, 288, 289
  pg_xlog, putting on separate device 286
  removing 282, 283, 285
  tablespace-level tuning 286
template databases 62
temporary file
  usage, finding 341
  usage, logging 341
test data generator
  reference link 172
test data
  generating 168, 170, 172
The Oversized-Attribute Storage Technique
    (TOAST) 69, 360
The PostgreSQL License (TPL) 16
time series tables
  creating 425, 426, 427
transaction isolation
  reference link 429
transaction log data
  archiving 550, 552
transaction manager (TM) 366
two-phase commit (2PC) 333

U

Uniform Resource Identifier (URI) 19
unique set of key columns
  searching 166, 167, 168
unused indexes

finding 385, 386
unwanted indexes
  removing 387, 388, 389
updatable views
  about 303, 304, 305, 307, 308
  example 310
  working 309, 310
upgrades
  major upgrades 555
  minor releases 553
  online upgrades 557
usage changes, table
  detecting 334, 335
  detecting, by collecting usage statistics 335
  detecting, with quick-and-dirty way 335
user access
  granting, to all objects in schema 198
  granting, to schema 197
  granting, to specific columns 198, 199, 200
  granting, to specific rows 200, 201, 202, 203
  granting, to table 197
  revoking, to table 192, 193, 194, 195
user and role management
  database creation scripts 195
  default search path 195
  views, securing 196
user connection
  checking 321, 322
user role
  administrators 190
  end users 190
user
  attributes, not inheriting 221
  creating 203, 204
  limited superuser powers, granting to specific
    user 209, 210, 211, 212
  logged in user, identifying 219, 220, 221
  number of concurrent connections, limiting 206
  preventing, from temporary connection 205, 206
  private database, granting 133, 134, 135
  pushing, off system 126, 127, 128
  removing, without dropping data 207, 208
  restricting, to one session each 125, 126
  restricting, to session 126
  secure password, verifying 208, 209

V

vacuum
  monitoring 376, 377, 378, 379
  tuning 376, 377, 378, 379
virtual private network (VPN) 223
Visibility Map (VM) 70

W

Write-Ahead Log (WAL) 56, 435, 497

Z

Zabbix 317

CPSIA information can be obtained
at www.ICGtesting.com
Printed in the USA
LVHW022205290820
664542LV00003B/24